One

Large Chandeliers showered golden light on the crowd as I surveyed the party in a gilded inlaid mirror over the mantel. Surprised to spot someone I barely recognized: myself. Brown tweed sports jacket, hair not quite under control, third or fourth drink, I started losing count, leaning against the wall like I was holding it up. I looked like someone hanging out at an airport, waiting for my life to take off.

Indefinitely delayed.

Every time I planted myself at one of these charity soirees, lost scenes from my married life, I wondered why I kept coming. What kind of redundant dribble would I hear?

Shawn McCarthy, great to see you!

Wish I could say the same.

Working on anything interesting these days?

My abs.

Still teaching that gun handling class over at the precinct?

They suggested I take a sabbatical. In other words, don't come back till you get your head out of your ass.

Didn't know you were still in the city.

I never knew what to say to that one. Did they think I had been exiled to Joliet, like Napoleon after Waterloo?

I came to this party thanks to one of my ex-wife Angela's friends. A woman named Christine. I found it both amusing and flattering that, long after my wife had divorced me, grazing off to greener pastures, a dense herd of her girlfriends hung around me as if I were a newly found acre of sweet alfalfa, looking for a huge clump to take back to the barn.

If I had known then Angela's cheese cake's would become world famous, I may have capitulated to her demands. Been a little more attentive to all those ridiculous, whimsical episodes when she entertained some of Chi-Towns elite.

Christine is a brunette, forties, and hadn't left my side for the better part of two hours. Every now and then, her hand squeezed my arm, a signal that her husband, some hedge-fund guy, *hedge fungi as I like to call it,* is out of town and her three children were Guantanamoed with a nanny. Only a summons from the hostess to show Christine her newly renovated kitchen pried the woman from my side.

I drained the rest of my scotch, about to head back to the bar, when I felt my phone buzzing.

I slipped through the door behind me onto the second-floor landing and glanced at the text. Mike O'Leary! I hadn't heard from my old partner since the incident six months ago.

<u>Esquivel's daughter found dead.</u>

Call me.

I closed the message, googled *Esquivel, and* scrolled through the information...

I found my name in quite a few articles. "Disgraced detective Shawn McCarthy ..."

I'd be a marked man, peppered with questions, as soon as the latest news circulated the party.

Suddenly I felt sober. I slipped through the crowd, down the spiraled marble stairs. No one said a word as I grabbed my coat, walked past the bronze bust of the hostess, out the front door, and down the townhouse steps onto north Clark Street. I headed to Fullerton breathing in the hot and humid August night. I hailed a taxi and climbed in.

"Erie and Michigan."

As we rode along I rolled the window down and felt a knot in my stomach as the reality settled in *Esquivel's daughter found dead.* My thoughts took me back to the statements I had blurted out on national TV.

Esquivel is human scum, same category as Charles Manson, Jim Jones, and John Wayne Gacy. I have an inside source that has worked in the family for years. Esquivel needs to be terminated with extreme prejudice.

That profound tidbit cost me my career, my reputation, not to mention all the lawsuits which in turn sent my wife looking for future security, but that didn't make it any less

I couldn't help but laugh at myself for feeling like a fugitive, or maybe the better comparison would be *the most wanted radical detective.* Yet I had to admit I felt something electrifying about seeing that name again.

<u>Esquivel</u>,

Maybe, just maybe, it's time to start running for my life again.

Two

I felt an incredible urge to get back into shape, save the human race from all predators, whether it wanted saving or not. After all, I have outlived Dr. Spock, beam that up! While jogging along the north shore of Lake Michigan watching the darkness release its hold on the earth. The sunlight breaking through on the horizon with an amazing medley of colors reflecting on the water, through scattered purple-gray clouds in the forefront. The breeze is warm and gentle in the cool air of an early August morning

I could see the lights at Navy Pier as I approached Grand Avenue heading towards Buckingham Fountain my turn around point. As I passed the famous Ferris wheel, I glanced over my shoulder and saw someone standing out on the rocks near the water. The back of her coat made a vivid red slice in the morning light.

A young woman out here alone? Really?

I kept on going faintly irritated by the girl's naïveté…or recklessness. The women of Chicago, although magnificent, sometimes forgot that they were not invincible They could throw themselves full force into a fun-filled Friday night, with no thought of where they would end up come Saturday morning.

I veered past a row of benches and made the turn around at Buckingham Fountain and started the last leg of my morning run. The woman disappeared. But then, far ahead, a flicker of red. It vanished as soon as I saw it, then seconds later, I could make out a thin silhouette walking slowly in front of me along the iron railing. She wore black boots, her platinum hair hung halfway down her back. I picked up my pace, deciding to pass her near a water fountain so when I stopped to take a drink I could get a closer look at her to make sure she was all right.

As I approached, however, I had this feeling she wasn't. Her footsteps sounded too heavy for such a slight person, the way she walked so stiffly as if waiting for me.

I suddenly had the feeling that as I passed she'd turn and I'd see the ravaged face of an old woman staring back at me with hollowed eyes, a mouth like an ax gash in a tree.

She's just a few feet ahead now.

She'd reach out and seize my arm, with a grip as strong as a vise, *ice cold...*

I ran and stopped at the water fountain. When I tried to get a look her head lowered, face hidden by her hair, I looked again but she had already passed me. *I'll stop and say something when I pass her again, tell her to go home.*

I waited a bit then quickened my pace to catch her.

But as I made the turn for home I looked over my shoulder.

Nothing!

THREE

I felt a need to contact my old college friend, Denise Cambridge, Editor, and Chief of the local occult periodical, *Fascinations*. If anyone would have the 411 on Esquivel's daughter, it would be her. The paper's headquarters located in the heart of Old Town, on Wells Street. I only visited the place once, long ago when she first got underway. She had some trouble with the neighboring tenants. They did not like the idea of witches and warlocks standing around discussing the finer points of casting spells.

As I interviewed the staff I got the impression that Denise could be a tyrannical micromanager, wielding her blue pencil like a Bowie knife, often scribbling barely legible comments that trailed along the margins and then off the page. After her usual wine drenched dinner at Truth Steak House, she would return to the office to drink pots of coffee and torment the staff until the paper was put to bed. The other editors dreaded her tirades, expecting her to demand that they rip up the entire layout and start over again.

Denise was a tall elegant woman, somewhere north of thirty-five, with a neatly styled fob of dark brown hair. Her blue-grey eyes seemed cold and imperious, yet they also carried glints of mischief. She wore impeccable French suits and dress shoes of supple Italian leather. To facilitate her long, if erratic, work hours, she kept a bed in her penthouse office, where she liked to snatch an early morning nap.

Denise, *the Duchess of Doom*, as her employee's referred to her, is quite flamboyant away from the office. She spent many hours in chic nightclubs around the city. On weekends she could usually be seen at the Columbia Yacht Club near Navy Pier. Often fueled with brandy, she would take out a sleek banana boat for a late night spin up and down the Chicago River. Alert bystanders tended to be both puzzled and shocked by these nocturnal escapades, for the duchess partied nearly always wild-eyed and nude.

Denise's most original contribution to modern journalism could be found in her notion that a newspaper should not merely report stories it should create them. Editors should not only cover the news, she felt; they should orchestrate large-scale public dramas that stir emotions and get people talking.

Critics often scoffed that these *"exclusives"* were mere stunts, and perhaps they were. But Denise had a conviction that a first-rate reporter if turned loose on the world to solve some mystery or unexplained puzzle of the human psyche, should come back with a story worth reading about. Her paper was many things, but it was rarely dull.

I always smile when I think of the time on an early September morning reading the latest copy of Fascinations. The junior editor must have been cringing as he sent the final copy to his mercurial boss. The Fascinations contained a lead story that, if executed properly, was guaranteed to cause the kind of stir that Denise delighted in. One of the most incredible and tragic news stories I had ever read. The story was headlined "Labor Day Carnival of Carnage."

The Duchess scanned the paper and began to take in the horrible details: late Sunday afternoon, around closing time at the Lincoln Park Zoo a rhinoceros had escaped from its cage. It had rampaged through to grounds killing one of its handlers, goring him beyond recognition. Other zookeepers ran to his aid and somehow in the confusion an entire cage of rare vampire bats were released. This specific species indigenous to a region of Romania known as Transylvania feeds exclusively on human blood. The vampire bats which numbered in the thousands instantly began feasting on the nearest food source. What happened next made for difficult reading. The bats, some attacking each other, the rest turned on nearby pedestrians who happened to be strolling through the park. One report had the bats gorging on a baby still in the stroller. Some reports stated that after feeding on human blood some bats transcended into humanlike creatures running away seeking sanctuary from the sunlight.

    The reporters had transcribed every detail in fine fashion. As Denise read she moaned in delight and never once pulled out her blue pencil. The reporters peppered it with intimate details and filled the roster of victims with the names of real, in some cases prominent, Chicagoans. But the story was entirely a hoax. With Denise's enthusiastic encouragement the editors had concocted the tale to show the city that the zoo did not have a valid evacuation plan in case of emergency.

That was her story and she stuck to it. Although most say she deceived readers to sell newspapers, the paper covered its butt by putting a disclaimer at the end of the story. We all know, just as Denise did, hardly anyone reads disclaimers. Now that is my kind of girl. I knew that my quest to know what happened to Gabriela Esquivel would dovetail perfectly with Denise's interests. She's the partner a person like me needs. If she was born male her testicles would be way bigger than mine.

FOUR

I called Denise and made arrangements to meet her at Snuffy's Monday morning at 9:00 AM. Snuffy's Grill is owned by a friend of mine named Tony. Actually, the restaurant started out to be a false front for Tony's booking business but it turned out to be the best breakfast in the city for under ten dollars. When I walked in I could see Denise was already there in my favorite booth. She wasn't just sitting in my booth it looked like she'd put down first and last month's rent, and security deposit, plus an exorbitant broker's fee, signed a lease and moved into to the booth.

On one side of her were two giant bags from Nordstrom, on the other side a large blue leather purse, unzipped and sagging open like a gutted Tiger shark, inside of which you could see all it had ingested that morning. On the table in front of her was a plate of half-finished French toast floating like a houseboat on an ocean of syrup.

Denise didn't notice me walking towards her because her eyes were closed as if trying to remember something, lips slightly moving up and down as if saying something under her breath. I scooted in my booth across from her.

"Of all the greasy spoons in the city you had to stop into mine."

She replied "Nothin shakin but the bacon good looking."

Denise eyed me up and down then asked: "How's your sex life?"

I said, "Are you kidding, I couldn't get laid in a women's prison with a fist full of pardons."

"Quid Pro Quo Duchess of Doom, how is your love life?"

"I make it a rule never to get involved with anyone I like, that way the distance between us is easier to maintain and the inevitable break-up less painful."

We smirked a bit then laughed out loud until tears ran down our faces. It felt good to let go with a hard laugh. It had been so long since I have had one of those.

"Good to see you, Denise."

"Good to see you too Shawn McCarthy."

I looked Denise in the eye.

"It's Esquivel's daughter, Gabriela. I want to know about her. What made her tick?"

Denise raised both hands looking down and shaking her head.

"Whoa, whoa, are you kidding? After all, you went through the last time you investigated **Mr. Carlos Esquivel**."

"This my shot at vindication, I can show everyone just what a scumbag Esquivel is."

Esquivel was not just the top drug lord in Central America, He also operated in human trafficking throughout all the cities along the Mexican border. Enslaving young girls into prostitution with the false promise of a green card. At one time it's estimated he took in over a million dollars a day.

I arrested Mr. Esquivel and charged him with everything I could. Even thought I was instructed to back off and let the feds handle it. The State of Illinois lawyers were no match for the high priced legal team of the infamous Mr. Esquivel. To make matters worse I came very close to getting charged with planting false evidence, intimidating witnesses, jury tampering, along with a host of bullshit charges that discredited me. The Chicago Police Department had no choice but to suspend me indefinitely without pay. I was also served with an order of protection to not come within three hundred feet of Esquivel or his family. If Esquivel needed protection, he surely didn't need the court to order it. He was protected better than Fort Knox.

"Well, are you going to help me or not?" I asked.

"If not let me know now before I pay for your breakfast."

I just stared at Denise, with a serious and prayerful expression. I noticed the corners of her lips turning up just a whisker, then she broke into a laugh. Probably at how ridiculous I looked, I didn't care it worked.

Denise said," I thought it peculiar that Gabriela would be in that part of town."

It was a seedy part of the southeast side of Chicago, abandoned buildings permeated the area. Gang members, drug addicts, bums are the normal people hanging around the area. A very dangerous place for anyone to be especially a young girl. Being Esquivel's daughter it is not a shield from the kind of evil that can happen in those neighborhoods.

Denise also told me "Esquivel was heavily involved in the dark occult world. The art of casting spells, bringing back spirits, and demon possession; that kind of stuff."

El Esplanade, Esquivel's estate his thirty-six-bedroom mansion sat extravagantly in the center of the 100-acre grounds.

She told me the chit chat going around the newsroom implied that séances aimed at bringing evil spirits back to life, seemed to be the common denominator. Midnight gatherings, strange chanting, all sorts of unfathomable things.

"What do you mean? Unfathomable!"

She looked directly into my soul. I felt anxious, almost a new sense of fear that I had never felt.

"Shawn there are things going on in the occult world that you evidently have no knowledge of. You had better make sure exactly how far you are willing to go before you take on this endeavor of yours."

She let her words sink in for a moment then I said, "I think it wise for you to just let it go and let the authorities look into it. The kind of depth these cults reach into society is extremely insidious." She went on to inform me very rich and powerful people often play a large part. They are extremely well protected. Getting close to their inner circle will be virtually impossible. They will go to any length to keep their anonymity. It's all very Machiavellian.

We just sat and looked at each other. Getting involved with Esquivel is equivalent to walking through hell with a gasoline soaked suit.

Well, I guess it was time to carry around a big fire extinguisher.

FIVE

A little over a week went by, at *3:00 A.M.*, I boarded a Cicero bound bus #1357, as Katie Horrigan had instructed, and took a secluded seat in the back.

If the city has one spot where murmured conversations and dubious glances are ignored, it is this bus at three in the morning. Whatever passengers are present, they will likely be dead tired, strung out, or involved in shady dealings themselves, so you could bet they wanted to remain in incognito as you did. I'd never understood how Katie arranged it, but now I swear it's the same driver from the last time we did this some five years ago.

I first met detective Katie Horrigan back in 1981 in my rookie year on the force. Patty also a rookie, helping out on a Lincoln Park jogger case. Even now, more than twenty years later, I still only knew snippets about her, but those bits went a long way. She is forty-six and lived alone in Bronzeville with a German shepherd named Nemo. For the past decade, she'd worked for the 8th Precinct Homicide Squad, a specialized unit that helped other precincts with homicides that occurred north of Sixty-Third Street, and she served her deceased victims with a devotion that's old-fashioned in its selflessness and dedication.

The bus turned west onto Twenty-Second Street, passing abandoned housing projects, empty lots, tattered churches, men loitering on corners. *Something must be wrong* I thought. *The last time we did this Katie had boarded by now.* I checked my phone, but there was no missed call, no text. The conversation we'd had the day before had not been promising, nor had she made any real commitment to helping me. "Shawn tomorrow night, same place and time," she said curtly and hung up.

The bus turned onto Ridgeland Avenue and I began to think she's blown me off, when we abruptly pulled over in front of a ramshackle townhouse, a lone figure stood by the curb. The doors opened Detective Katie Horrigan hurried toward me as if she'd known precisely where I sat all along.

She looked the same: still 5'5 and grim, lips thin and unsmiling, a button nose that curved up at the tip like a wood shaving. She wasn't unattractive. But she was *strange*.

Katie could pass for a pale nun staring out from a fifteenth-century portrait on the Flemish painting wing at the Chicago Art Museum. Only the artist hadn't *quite* mastered human proportions, so he'd given her an elongated neck, uneven shoulders, and too-small hands.

She slid next to me, eyeing the other passengers, letting the black shoulder bag fall to her feet.

"I don't have much time." She said as she unzipped the bag, pulled out a white 8 x 10 envelope, handed it to me. I slid out the thick stack of papers, the first page a photocopy of a file.

Case No. 22-24-5843.

"How's the investigation going?" I asked, slipped it back and tucking the envelope into my pocket.

"The Fifth precinct is handling it. They're getting a hundred calls a day. Anonymous tips, but they're bullshit. Last week Gabriela was spotted at Wrigley Field cheering on the lovable losers. Three people said they saw her in a Seattle coffee shop. Already they got two homicide confessions."

"Was it homicide?"

Katie shook her head. "No, she was a jumper."

"You're positive?"

She nodded. "No sign of a struggle. Finger nails clean. She took off her shoes and socks, placed them together at the edge. That kind of methodical preparation, very consistent with suicide. They haven't done a postmortem. Not sure they will."

"Why not?"

"The family attorney's all over it. No desecration of the body." She frowned. "I noticed some shots missing in the file. Front and back torso. My guess is they're being held in a separate file so some creep doesn't leak them to the tabloids, like *Fascinations*."

"The cause of death?"

"Standard for any jumper. Massive hemorrhaging. A broken neck, lacerated heart, multiple broken ribs, and a skull fracture. She was there a few days before they found her.

She'd been admitted last month to some swanky private hospital on the north shore, Mission Hills. They filed a missing person's report ten days before she jumped."

I stared at her in surprise. "Why? She ran away?"

She nodded "A nurse confirmed Gabriela was in her room, lights off, at eleven o'clock. At eight the next morning, she was gone. Somehow she appeared on just one security camera. Crazy because the place is outfitted like the Pentagon. You can't see her face. She's a figure in white pajamas running across the lawn. A man was with her.

"Who was he?"

"They don't know."

"Why was she in the hospital? A drug problem?"

"I don't think they knew what the hell was wrong with her. A few pages of her medical evaluation are in there."

When did the hospital report her missing?"

September fifteenth. It's in the report."

"And when did she jump?"

"Late night on the twenty-sixth. Eleven, twelve o'clock midnight."

"Where did she go during those ten, eleven days in between?"

"No one has any idea."

"Any activity on her credit cards?"

Katie shook her head. "Cell was off, too. She must have known not to turn it on. Seems like she didn't want to be found. There was just one confirmed sighting in those ten days. When they found the body, she was wearing Levi's and a T-shirt. They found a plastic ticket in her pocket, a panda bear insignia on the back. It was traced to the China Club Located on Wells and Lake.

I nodded. It was one of the most expensive restaurants in the city, although it played out like a rare wildlife reserve. One paid an exorbitant fee ($65 for crab cakes) to observe *but never disturb* the privileged and powerful as they fed and fought among themselves, displaying all the recognizable traits of their species: hardened expressions, thinning hair, gun-grey suits.

"A coat check girl identified her," Katie said. "Gabriela came in around ten but left minutes later, without her red leather coat, and never came back. A few hours later she jumped."

"She must have been meeting someone."

"They don't know."

"But someone will look into it."

"No. there's no crime here." She eyed me sharply. "To get to that elevator shaft the girl had to enter an abandoned building, which is a notorious squatter's hangout, the *Wells Gardens*. Then on the roof, she squeezed through a skylight about a foot wide. Few are small enough to get through such a narrow opening, much less if they were holding someone against their will. They combed the place for evidence. There's no sign anyone was there but her." Katie continued to watch me, or perhaps the right word is investigating because her brown eyes were slowly moving over my face.

"This is where I ask why you want this information." She said.

"Some unfinished business. Nothing for you to worry about."

She squinted at me. "You know what Confucius said?"

"Remind me."

"Before you embark on a journey of revenge, dig two graves."

Six

I got back to my place around 5:00 AM. The sun just starting to take away the night, birds beginning their morning medley. I could hardly wait to read the CPD file but I could barely keep my eyes open. I needed sleep. Waking up at the crack of 4:00 PM I dug into the police report while reheating some of the worst coffee in the world.

By five o'clock that evening I got in a taxi, cruising through Chinatown, past the shabby walk-ups and restaurants, dirty signs advertising back and foot rubs; awnings jumbled with English and Chinese. Men in dark jackets hurried past storefronts lit up in lethal colors, cough-syrup crimson, absinthe green, jaundiced yellow, all of it bleeding together in the crooked streets. The neighborhood looked as though it flourished, yet it remained void of any visible life.

We passed a church, **Transfiguration Church,** read the sign.

"Right here," I told the driver.

I paid him and climbed out, gazing up at the building. A seven-story derelict mess with peeling white paint, construction scaffolding, and every window boarded up. The warehouse where Gabriela Esquivel had been found dead. Flowers and handmade cards decorated the front entrance.

Bouquets of roses and carnations, lilies and candles, pictures of the Virgin Mary. *Rest in Peace Gabriela, God bless you. Your music will last forever.* It always surprised me how ferociously the public mourned a stranger. Into an empty form, they could unload the grief and regret of their own lives, and be rid of it. Comforted by the thought, *at least it wasn't me.*

Beyond the flowers lay a steel door. It's secured with two padlocks, **caution** and **danger** signs. The **Police Line Do Not Cross** tape remained intact.

Behind me, a beige coupe with a loud muffler cruised by, the dark silhouette of the driver hunched low. I leaned back staying hidden in the shadows of the scaffolding as it coasted to the end of Loomis street, it then made a left-hand turn and the night became silent again.

Yet I had the unmistakable feeling that someone else is present or had just been here.

I zipped up my jacket, and after surveying the sidewalk, *deserted,* with the exception of an Asian kid darting into a store called Wang Fungs.

I turned and went to the intersection of Loomis and Cermak. I rounded the turn, passing a red awning with faded and half missing letters that made it impossible to understand, a dented chain-link fence spanning an empty dark lot. When I reached the next building, a mangy walk up, and the next one after that, 1615 Cermak, I knew I went too far.

I backtracked, noticing that by Wang Fung's there's a hole in the fence. I made my way over, crouching down. A small red rag tied there, clearly to mark some kind of entrance. I could make out a narrow dirt path that twisted deep into the lot, leading toward an abandoned building.

That must be the place Katie talked about, *the hanging gardens* as she referred to it, *a known squatter's residence and local crack den,* according to the incident summary in Gabriela's file. The police concluded Gabriela entered the building on Loomis from here, the building at 1615 Cermak, then climbed up a flight of stairs all the way to the roof, entering the adjacent Loomis Street building from a skylight. Although the police canvass of the area turned up no witnesses and none of her personal belongings, this meant nothing. Detectives are notoriously lax when they conclude early in a case that the death must have been a suicide. Often overlooking crucial details that told an entirely different story.

I ducked through the opening, the overpowering rancid smell of garbage, unseen animals scurrying away as I made my way along the path. It's probably just another one of chi-towns south side mascots: *the cat-sized rat.* As my eyes adjusted to the dark, I could see the crumbling brick exterior of the building, and a door to my left. I stepped toward it, tripping on an old scooter, some plastic jugs, and pulled it open.

Entering the large warehouse, dim light trickled in from somewhere illuminating walls covered with indecipherable graffiti. The smell, putrid and filled with junk, newspapers and cans, scattered pieces of plasterboard, insulation, old clothes, and boxes, pots, and pans. Squatters had clearly been living here, though they appeared to have vacated most likely because of the police presence as of late. I stepped inside letting the heavy door screech closed behind me.

Looking around I realized how unwise this choice to come here without so much as the switchblade I used on my morning runs. I did not even think to bring a flashlight. I took a deep breath, ignoring the voice in my head reminding me, *didn't we establish you are not on your best game*? And headed to the back in search of some stairs.

They were rusted and corroded. I grabbed the railing to see if I could pry the handrail off the wall, but the bolts surprisingly sturdy.

I started up, the metallic echoes of my footsteps jolting. I paused every now and then to look around, make sure I'm alone, taking a few snapshots with my I-Phone. With my every step, the old building seemed to growl and cough, protesting my scaling its rusted spine. *This is where Gabriela climbed.* If her intention had been to commit suicide, a conclusion I didn't accept as gospel, no matter what Katie said, *why did she come here, to this derelict place?*

I passed the sixth floor and then climbed the final steepest flight into a claustrophobic attic space, with a stained futon lying on the floor. A sloping ceiling met the wall, where I spotted a square hatch. I heaved my shoulder against it, gasping as the hatch gave way, I hoisted myself outside.

A mangled sofa in the far corner adorned the deserted rooftop, landscaping the view past which I could see the beautiful Chicago skyline, looking down blunt stumps of low-income housing, wide municipal buildings, and black water towers sprouting up like a scene out of a Star Wars movie. All of it fighting for a piece of the night sky. The back of the Loomis building abutted this building, the space between them only a foot wide but cutting straight down to the street. I stepped onto the low wall's perimeter, and after making the mistake of looking down. I jumped to the adjacent roof if I fell I'd look like human parsley lodged between brick teeth.

I made my way around the massive water tower. I could see the skylight. Shaped like a rectangular pyramid, most of the glass missing. I walked over to it, crouching down looking through one of the shattered casements.

About twenty feet below me sat a dark floor. Further to my left, I could see directly into the empty shaft of a freight elevator, which extended seven stories below, the concrete brightly lit at the very bottom. It was like gazing down a throat, a corridor between two dimensions. The fall looked to be about a hundred feet. Even from this high angle, I could make out patches of rusty stains on the floor. *Gabriela's blood.* She allegedly climbed in through this skylight, removed her boots and socks and stepped to the elevator's ledge. It must have been so fast, the wind in her ears, her dark hair flying in her face, and then nothing.

Patty Horrigan's assessment is right on the button. The skylight's blown-out metal casements are so narrow; it would've been hard to force Gabriela down there against her will. Hard, but not impossible.

I stood up inspecting the ground. There's no evidence, no cigarette butts or scraps, no debris of any kind. I started to leave, heading back to the *Hanging Gardens*, when suddenly something moved, far below at the bottom of the elevator shaft. A shadow just swept across the floor.

I waited, wondering if I'd imagined it, staring at that empty, lit up space.

But then, again, a silhouette slowly slid into view.

Someone's standing in the mouth of the elevator, his shadow tossed in front of him. He remained there for a minute, immobile, and then stepped all the way inside.

I spotted dirty-blonde hair, a gray overcoat. *He must be a detective, back to inspect the scene.* He ducked down, ostensibly to study the blood patterns on the concrete. Then, to my surprise, he actually sat down in the corner, propping his elbows on his knees.

He did not move for what felt like a very long period of time.

I leaned forward to get a better view, dislodging shard of glass. It fell, smashing to the landing just below.

Startled, he looked up, then scrambled out of sight.

I lurched to my feet and took off across the roof.

He couldn't be a detective. No detective I know moved that fast.

Seven

I raced around the corner back to Cermak Street, fully expecting to find the entrance unsealed. But the police tape remained intact, the door still padlocked. How had he gotten in? *And who in the hell was he? Some death scene gawker? A transient?* I checked the windows, everyone nailed shut. The only other possibility, a narrow alleyway blocked with mountains of garbage. I pushed some of it aside, trying not to inhale, squeezing through. Sure enough, in the very back I spotted an open window casting light on the opposite wall.

I notice a crowbar lying on the ground, used to pry away the boards, leaving a space just wide enough to crawl through.

I stepped over, looking inside. It was a dimly lit construction site, bare light bulbs dangling from an unfinished ceiling, plastic barrels and tarps piled by the front entrance. Hundreds of studs for building walls lined the area. Toward the back, on the right-hand side, a band of yellow police line tape was strung across the elevator's entrance.

There wasn't any sign of the man.

"Hello?" I called out.

Silence. The only noise was the annoying sound of the buzzing lights. I grabbed the crowbar, just in case, and scrambled through, falling into bags of concrete.

Along the back wall, I noticed a stack of metal beams and a mixing barrel, a plastic tarp covering something.

I stepped cautiously toward it and yanked it aside.

It was a wheelbarrow. "Anyone here?" I called out, looking around.

There was no answer, no movement.

The guy probably got scared off.

I stepped toward the police tape, about to duck under it, when suddenly a hand seized my shoulder and something hard hit me on the side of the head. I wheeled around but and had gotten shoved to the ground, dropping the crowbar.

My eyes went white, blinded, though I managed to make out a man staring down at me. He shoved his foot onto my chest. "Who the hell are you?" he shouted. It was a young voice, slurred with rage. Bending over me again, he reached out as if to grab my throat, I wrestled free pushing him off balance, grabbing the crowbar I struck him in the shoulder.

It wouldn't have made Muhammad Ali proud, but it worked. He tried to grab onto a metal stud for support, missed, and stumbled backward.

I staggered over to him, to my surprise, he was too wasted to stand. He reeked of booze and cigarettes, and just a punk, mid-twenties, shaggy hair, dirty white Nike sneakers, a faded maroon T-shirt that read *Guns and Roses.* His bloodshot eyes, watery unable to focus, as they stared up at me.

"My turn, punk," I said. "Who the hell are you?"

He closed his eyes and appeared to pass out cold.

My first impulse was to strangle the kid. Touching the spot where he'd cracked me on the head, I could feel blood. He wasn't a cop, so that left random derelict or a friend of Gabriela's.

I pulled his black wool jacket out from under him. Checking his pockets, I found a pack of Camels, two smashed cigarettes left, a Bic lighter, a set of keys. I put them back, in the other pocket I pulled out an iPhone. The screen was cracked, the background a picture of a half-naked blonde.

I checked the inside pocket. It was empty. Yet I felt something else, then realized there was another pocket sewn into the ripped lining.

I reached in pulling out four tiny baggies. Every one of them containing a white substance. I knew it's either cocaine or china white heroin. So, he is a drug dealer and not a very good one considering he was sleeping through a body search. I returned the dope to his jacket and stood up.

"Can you hear me, Scarface?"

He didn't hear me.

"Hands on your head dirtbag, this is an F.B.I. raid!" I yelled.

As gentle as I could, although I didn't know why this kid could sleep through the apocalypse, I rolled him onto his side, removing the wallet from his back pocket. No driver's license, no credit cards, no pictures, only twenty bucks. This is a typical robbery wallet. If you get mugged, you give this to them and they get the twenty so they don't shoot you and leave. He must have his real cash down near his privates. He can keep it; I'm not searching there. I put the wallet back but kept the iPhone. Then I stepped around him and looked into the elevator.

There is nothing in there but some small pools of dried blood, and a few tendrils creeping into the cracks of the concrete.

I took some pictures, then moved back to the kid to check on his well-being. He was still breathing easily but I pushed him more over on his side so he would not suffocate. He appeared to be only drunk, not on anything else.

I assumed I'd learn nothing more about him until tomorrow morning when he discovered his phone missing. Yet during the cab ride home, and after a few hours later, after I'd taken a shower, downed four aspirin. I checked the kid's phone, it was bombarded with texts.

Hey, Where r u???

That was Sandra. Eight minutes later she wrote again

W8ting 3hrs 4 u whatttttts up???????

Then it was Elsa (I couldn't help but visualize her Nordic legs, like ice pics):

Johns out, come over.

One minute later:

I want you.

Ten minutes later

I'm so hot 4 u. R u downstairs yet?

Then it appears she sent him a sexy picture, which I couldn't open. Followed with:

Hello? Nothing??

F--- U

Then a text from Calvin

U out? Come by Artie's

Interspersed with all of this, a highly obsessive girl named Jessica called thirteen times. I let her go to voicemail.

Then Calvin again:

Cooper where the hell are U?

Well, I guess his name is Cooper.

Small time drug dealer in an old wool jacket, crouched in the corner of a freight elevator. He'd have something to tell me about Gabriela, whoever he was.

Eight

"Hello?" I answered. I heard plates clattering on the other end.

"Hey. You found my phone>"

"So I did." I took a drink of my coffee.

"Cool. Where?"

"Backseat of a taxi. I'm in the River North area. You want to come pick it up?"

An hour later, my buzzer rang. I let Cooper up. When he arrived at my front door I noticed the same coat from last night, the same faded jeans and sneakers. His shoulder hunched as if cold and smoking a cigarette. I realized in the stark light of day, even with greasy hair, the brown eyes hollowed out from booze, and who knew what else, he is a good looking kid. I don't know how I missed it. He stands about 6'0", just a tad shorter than me, slight, with a mangy scruff of a beard and the raw, good looking features of some brooding actor from the fifties, the ones who cry when drunk and die young.

"Hey." He smiled. "I'm here to pick up my phone."

He clearly had no recollection of the previous night; he was looking at me as if he'd never seen me before.

"Right." I stepped aside to let him enter, and after sizing me up and apparently deciding I wasn't going to jump him, he shoved his hands in his coat pockets and came in. I closed the door, heading into the living room, indicating his phone on the coffee table.

"Thanks, man."

"Don't mention it. Now, what were you doing at that warehouse?"

He looked startled.

"In Chinatown. Your name is Cooper, right?"

He opened his mouth to speak, but stopped himself, his eyes flitting past me to the door.

"I'm a suspended detective looking into Gabriela's death."

I gestured toward the dining room table. "My pictures are next to some newspaper articles about some old cases I work on. If you want to take a look."

With a doubtful glance, he stepped over to the table, reading the article about the Esquivel investigation. "A page-turning tour-de-force," He read about the drug Lord's billion-dollar business and the millions of mangled lives it sucks into its deadly machinery. He glanced at me. "Sounds epic, man"

He said with sarcasm.

"And now you want to know about Gabriela to get at the old man?"

"Depends on what I find. What do you know?"

"Nothing."

"What's your connection to her?"

"Don't have one."

"Then why'd you break into the warehouse where she died?"

He didn't answer, only returned the article to the table. After browsing a few more articles, he turned back, shoving his hands into his pockets.

"What department of the law are you with?"

"Chicago's finest," I smirked.

His face told the story I had seen many times. He wanted to talk but he felt skeptical. Not sure if he could trust me. He stared at me.

"Got some free time?" he asked softly, rubbing his nose.

Nine

I followed Cooper up the stairs of a dingy Eighteenth Street walk-up and into his apartment, #3f. Slinging his coat over a beach chair, he disappeared into a back bedroom, there didn't seem to be anything in there except a mattress on the floor, leaving me by the front door. The place definitely had a smell, like the woozy, stale air of a flop house.

The sagging army green couch along the far wall covered with an old turquoise comforter where someone had recently crashed, *maybe literally*.

In a plate, on a coffee table, there I saw an outbreak of cigarette butts; next to that, rolling papers, a pack of Newport's, an open package of Oreo cookies. A mangled copy of the Star Tribune, some emaciated starlet on the cover. His Guns & Roses T-shirt from the other night lay on the floor along with a blue sweatshirt and some other clothes. (As if to expressly avoid this pile, a women's pair of black pantyhose clung for dear life to the back of the other beach chair.) Some girl kissed one wall while wearing black lipstick, leaving a perfect imprint. An acoustic guitar propped up in the corner beside an old hiker's backpack, faded red nylon cover with some handwriting.

I stepped over to read some of it: If this gets lost return it with all contents to Cooper J. Davis, 150 Parks Street, Belcourt, N.D. 58316. Cooper Davis from Belcourt North Dakota. This kid Cooper is a long way from home.

Scribbled above that a hand-drawn Egyptian type symbol and the words: ***"Into every life falls a little rain, and with the rain comes a little pain. Through it all, I know I've got one thing to do. Ramble On!***

Cooper emerged from the bedroom with a UPS shipping envelope handing it to me while giving me a wary glance.

The address on the envelope read: **COOPER DAVIS, 424 W.18th Street, 3f.**

The address scribbled in black marker, all capital letters. The postmark dated Sept 10th. The last day Gabriela was seen alive. The return address simply read 1516 Cermak Street. The same address of the building that Gabriela Esquivel's body had been found.

Surprised, I looked at Cooper, but he said nothing. Watching me intently as if it were some kind of test. I pulled out the contents. An old small stuffed parrot, with green and yellow, matted down fur. The stitching coming out around the eyes, the whole thing encrusted with dry mud.

"What is it?" I asked.

"You've never seen it before?" he asked.

No. Whose is it?"

"No clue." He moved away, yanking aside the comforter and sitting on the couch.

"Who sent it?"

"She did."

"Gabriela."

He nodded and then hunching forward, grabbed the package of rolling papers off the table, and pulled one out.

"Why?" I asked.

"Some kind of sick joke."

"Then you were friends with her."

"Not exactly," he said, reaching across the table for his coat, fumbling in the pockets for one of the little baggies of pot. "Not friends. More like acquaintances. But even that's a stretch."

"Where'd you meet her?"

He sat down rolling a joint. "Camp."

"Camp?"

"Yeah."

"What camp?"

"Gateway Wilderness Therapy in Oregon." He looked at me, brushing hair out of his eyes as he began to dissect the reefer joint, pulling at the ends to get rid of loose stems and seeds. "You've heard of this first class organization?"

"No."

"Then you're missing out. If you have kids, I highly recommend it. Especially if you want your kid to grow up to be a great American maniac."

I didn't even bother to hide my surprise. "You met Gabriela there?"

He nodded.

"When?"

"I was sixteen. She must have been, like fifteen. Summer of 05."

That made Cooper twenty-three.

"It's one of those juvenile delinquent therapy camp scams," he went on, spreading a little bit of weed onto the rolling paper. "They advertise help for troubled teenagers by starring at the stars and singing *Kumbaya*. Instead, it's a bunch of bearded nutjobs, left in charge of some of the craziest kids I've ever seen in my life. Bulimics, nymphos, cutters trying to saw at their wrists with plastic sporks from lunch. You wouldn't believe the shit that went on." He shook his head. "Most of the kids had been so mentally screwed up by their parents they needed more than six weeks of *wilderness.* They needed reincarnation. Maybe die and come back as a grasshopper, or maybe a wild weed flower, that would be preferable to the agony they existed in just by being alive."

He said all this with such pissed off defiance. I gathered he wasn't talking about any of the other campers but about himself. I stepped over some of the clothes on the floor to one of the beach chairs, the one with the pantyhose climbing up the back, and sat down. Cooper went on, licking the edge of the rolling paper to tidy up is *doobie.*

"Who knows where they found the counselors." He lit up his precious joint and suck down the mellowing smoke. "Cook County Jail probably." This one kid, Mondo, an overweight Mexican they tortured him. He was some Holy Roller type, always talking about Jesus. They made him go without eating. That kid never went ten minutes without a Twinkie in his mouth. He couldn't keep up, got heat stroke. Still, they kept telling him to find inner strength, ask God for strength. God must have been busy because he never found that inner strength. The whole experience was *Lord of the Flies* on steroids. I still get nightmares.

"Why were you there?" I asked.

He sat back on the couch, amused. He stuck the fresh hand rolled joint in his mouth, lighting it. He inhaled, holding his breath and coughing then blowing out a long stream of smoke.

"My uncle," he said, stretching his arms over his head. "I'd been traveling with my mom in South America for this missionary cult shit she got into. Ran away as soon as I could. My uncle lives in Arizona. Hired some thug to track me down. I settled in with a friend of mine in Atlanta. One morning I'm eating Lucky Charms. This brown van pulls up. If the Grim Reaper had wheels it would be this thing. No windows, except the two in the back door. Behind which you just knew some innocent kid had been kidnapped. Next thing I know I'm in the back with a male nurse." He shook his head. "If that dude was a nurse, I'm a frigging congressman."

He paused to take another toke of his joint.

"They took me to base camp somewhere in the Great Smokey Mountains. You train there for three weeks with your fellow screwed up campers, making Native American dream catchers and learning how to scrub a toilet with your spit, *real vital life skills*, you know. Then the group sets off on a six-week trek through the wilderness. Camping at six different lakes. With every lake, you're supposed to be inching closer to God and self-worth, only the reality is you're inching closer to becoming a psychopath because of all the screwy mind game shit you have been exposed to."

"And Gabriela joined you as one of the campers?" I asked.

He nodded.

"Why was she there?"

"No clue. That became the big mystery. She didn't show up until the day we were setting out on the six-week hike. The night before, counselors announced there was a last minute arrival. Everyone became pissed because that meant whoever it was had been able to bypass basic training, which made *Full Metal Jacket* look like *Sesame Street.*" He paused, shaking his head then, eyeing me, he smiled faintly. "When we saw her, though, we were down."

"Why?"

He gazed at the table. "She was smoking hot!"

Ten

He seemed on the verge of adding something, but instead leaned forward, flicking the ash off the doobie. "Who dropped her off?" I asked.

He looked up at me. "Don't know. Next morning, she was just there. Sitting by herself at one of the picnic tables in the corner, eating a cookie. Everything packed up and ready to go with a blue bandana in her hair. The rest of us were totally disorganized, running around like deranged chickens to get ready. Finally, we left."

"And you introduced yourself," I suggested.

He shook his head, tapping the joint on a plate. "Nope. She kept to herself. Obviously, everyone knew who her father is and that she had been born with the proverbial silver spoon, so the people were all over her. But she iced everyone out, said nothing beyond yes, no." He shrugged. "It wasn't like she was stand-offish. She just wasn't into making friends. Soon came the feelings of resentment, especially from the other girls, about all the get out of jail free cards she got from the counselors. Every night around the campfire we had to wax poetic about all the shit we'd done to end up there. Burglary, suicide attempts, drugs. Hell, the rap sheets of some of the kids, longer than *War and Peace*. Gabriela never had to say anything. They'd skip over her, no explanation. The only clue was this ACE bandage on her hand, which she had when she first arrived. A couple of weeks into the hike she took it off, a bad burn mark became clearly visible. She never said what happened."

Surprised to learn about this. That very burn mark, along with a foot tattoo, mentioned in the police missing person's report as her only identifiable markings.

"Three days into the hike we made a bet." Cooper continued. "First one to sustain a conversation with Gabriela that lasted longer than fifteen minutes would get the two hits of ecstasy one of the kids from L.A., Justin had smuggled in taped into the hollow shoelace tip of his hiking boot." He tilted his head back, quickly exhaling smoke at the ceiling. "I decided to hold back, get my game together, let the others jihad themselves. And they did. Gabriela blew them off. One by one."

"Until you," I said.

It's easy to imagine; two good looking teenagers finding each other in the wilderness of adolescence, two wildflowers blooming in a desert.

"Just the opposite, actually," he said. "She blew me off, too."

I stared at him. "You're kidding."

He shook his head. "About a week after everyone else had crashed and burned, I made my move. Gabriela always walked in the back, so I did. I asked where she was from. She said Chicago. After that, it became just one-word replies, along with an occasional nod. I struck out."

He started rocking back and forth looking down on the floor.

Gabriela didn't say anything to anyone for six weeks?" I asked.

"Well, she did. But nothing more than the bare bones of conversation. Everyone broke down at some point, had their fifteen minute Shawshank Redemption where they howled at the sky. The hiking, the counselors, unbelievable shit-heads, they made you dredge up all this shit from your past. Everyone broke. Half of it real and half of it made up just to get them off your back. Everyone took their Oscar-nominated turn, howling about parents, how all they wanted was to be loved. Except for Gabriela. She never cried, never complained. Not once."

"Did she ever mention her family?"

"No."

"What about her father?"

"Nothing. She acted like a Sphinx. That's what we called her."

"So that's it?" I asked.

He shook his head, clearing his throat. "Three weeks into the hike, Mondo, the fat Mexican kid, was a mess. So sunburned he had blisters all over his face, which the counselors dealt with by handing him a bottle of calamine lotion. Crusty pink shit all over his face, crying all the time, he looked like a leper. So one night Justin slips him one of the pills of X, a gift, you know, to lift his spirits. He must have taken it when we started out the next morning, because at nine A.M. suddenly Mondo was out of his mind, hugging people, telling everyone they were beautiful, eyes dilated, shuffling his feet like he was Michael Jackson in a thriller video. We lost track of him at one point, had to back track and found him smiling up at the sky. Red Cloud, the head counselor went apeshit."

"Red Feather?" I repeated.

He smirked. "The counselors insisted we address ourselves with Native American tribal names even though most of us were white, out of shape, and about as much about the earth as a Big Mac and French fries. *Red Cloud*, one of the tightest wound assholes you will ever run into, hauled Mondo away demanding to know what he was on. Mondo was so ripped all he did was laugh and say, *it's only a little Tylenol*, over and over. *It's just a little Tylenol.*"

I couldn't help but laugh. Cooper smiled, too, though the amusement quickly left his face.

"That night everyone was scared shitless," he went on, brushing his hair out of his eyes.

"We didn't want to know what *Red Cloud* was going to do to Mondo or the rest of us, for that matter, on his mission to find out who'd smuggled in the X. that night Red Cloud announced that if someone doesn't come forward to explain who brought the ecstasy he was going to make our lives a living hell. Everyone felt scared. No one said a word. But I know it's just a matter of time before someone ratted out Justin. Suddenly this low voice announces, *it was me*. We all turned around. No one could believe it."

He fell silent, still amazed, even after all this time.

"It was Gabriela," I said when he didn't continue.

He glanced at me, his face solemn. "Yeah. At first, *Red Cloud* didn't believe her. She'd had all this preferential treatment. But then she produces the second pill of X, which somehow she stole from Justin's hiking boot. She says she'll accept whatever punishment he had in store for her." He shook his head. Red Cloud went ballistic. He grabbed her, hauled her away from the campsite. He ended up taking her to some far-off site in the middle of nowhere and made her sleep there by herself in just her sleeping bag, totally alone. She wasn't allowed to come back until morning when he went and got her."

"No one challenged this guy?" I asked. "What about the other counselors?"

He shrugged. "They were afraid of him. We were beyond civilization. It was like laws didn't exist out there." He sat back and reached for his lighter on the table, as he lit up another cigarette.

"The other part of her punishment was putting up all of our tents and collecting firewood. We weren't allowed to help.

When she got tired and slowed down, *Red Cloud* would scream at her. She'd just stare him down with this look on her face like she couldn't care less like she was so much stronger than him, which only made him more pissed. Finally, he let up. One of the other counselors warned him about going too far. So, after seven nights sleeping alone away from the campsite she rejoined the group."

He smiled, an unreadable look on his face. He then blew out a huge stream of smoke while watching it with that far-away look in his eye.

Eleven

"The first night back we all wake up at three in the morning because *Red Cloud* is screaming, like he just woke up next to the bride of Chuckie. He runs out of his tent in nothing but his underwear, this fat piece of shit stammering around like a little baby, crying that there's a rattlesnake in his sleeping bag. Everybody thought it had to be a joke, or maybe he just had a nightmare. But one of the other female counselors, *Still Waters*, she went in and got it, unzipped it right in front of us, shaking it out. Sure enough, a rattlesnake, six feet long fell out onto the ground and whipped right across the campsite, disappearing into the dark. *Red Cloud* white as a sheet, about to piss his pants, turned and stared directly at Gabriela. And she stared right back. He didn't say a frigging word, but I know he believed she put the snake in there. We all did."

He fell silent for a moment, gazing out into the room. "After that, he left us alone. And Mondo?" he paused swallowing. "He made it. His sunburn healed. He stopped crying. He became, like, this hero." He sniffled, wiping his nose. "When we finally made it back to base camp, we were supposed to have one night together where we all held hands and marveled at our accomplishments which became more like thanking God we hadn't died. Because the whole time death had been a possibility. Like death had been waiting for us at a moment's notice, right around the corner, beyond the rocks. And the person that prevented it was Gabriela."

I couldn't see his expression, his focus on the floor, hair hanging down hiding his eyes. "About an hour before dinner," he went on, I looked out the cabin window and saw her getting into a black SUV. She was leaving early. I felt disappointed. I'd wanted to talk to her, get to know her better. But it was too late. The driver gathered her stuff, put it in the back, and they drove off. It was the last time I saw her."

He lifted his head, staring at me as if looking for answers, yet saying nothing.

"You never heard from her again?"

He shook his head, pointing at the UPS packaging envelope in my hand.

"Not until that."

"How do you know she sent it?"

"It's her handwriting. And the return address is where she," he swallowed and took a deep breath. "Well you know. I thought she was messing with my head. I broke in a couple of nights ago, wondering if she left some kind of message or sign for me. But I haven't found anything."

I held up the stuffed parrot. "What's the significance?"

"I've never seen it before. I told you."

"You have no theory as to why she'd send it?"

He glared at me. "I hoped you could tell me, you're the cop."

The red mud that encrusted the stuffed animal looked like the kind found out west, certainly throughout the upper northwest. Which made me wonder if the animal didn't belong to one of those kids at the camp. Maybe Cooper himself. But he looked more likely to carry around a switchblade knife as a security blanket.

Cooper's account of the camping events became a helpful insight into Gabriela's character. It allowed her to come into focus, revealing he to be a kind of ferocious avenging angel, a persona entirely in keeping with the way she played music. I couldn't fathom why she sent Cooper the little stuffed parrot on the day she died if it had been her.

Cooper appeared to have fallen onto an irritated mood, slumped way down on the couch, arms crossed, his faded orange T-shirt that read *Garret's Famous Popcorn* on it. He reminded me of a teenage hitchhiker I'd once met in on my way to Texas. We were the only two at the diner counter at the crack of dawn. After we got to talking, swapping stories, he said goodbye, hitching a ride with the driver of an eighteen-wheeler. Later, I got up to pay my bill and realized he stole my wallet. Never trust a drifter that has the gift of gab.

"Maybe there's something inside," I said, turning the stuffed animal over. I took out my pocket knife, cutting an incision down the back of the parrot. I pulled out the stuffing, yellowed and crusty, feeling around inside. Nothing there.

I realized my cell started buzzing, the number a 312 area code.

"Hello?"

"May I speak to Shawn McCarthy?"

It sounded like a young woman, her voice crisp and musical.

"This is he."

"It's Elizabeth Michener, the coat check girl from the China Club. I 'm on west Madison, the Billy Goat, can you come by, we need to talk."

"The Billy Goat on Wells, give me twenty minutes."

"Okay." She hung up. Shaking my head, I stood up.

"Who was that?" Cooper asked me.

"Possibly the last person to see Gabriela alive, the coat check girl from China Club. She wants to talk.

I have to go. In the meantime, I'll hold on to the stuffed parrot."

"That's okay." He snatched it back, giving me a wary look, before putting it back into the envelope and disappearing into the bedroom, with the package.

"Thanks for your time," I called over my shoulder. "I'll be in touch if I hear anything." But suddenly Cooper slipped out into the hall right behind me, shrugging on his coat.

"Cool," he said. He locked the door and took off down the stairs. "Where are you going?"

"The Billy Goat on West Madison, I've got to meet a coat check girl."

As his footsteps echoed through the stairwell, I could have slapped myself for mentioning where I intended to go. I worked solo, I always had.

But then, I started down the stairs, maybe it wasn't such a terrible idea to team up with him, this one time. There's this quantum mechanics, string theory, and then there is also the most mind- bending frontier of the natural world, **women.** In my experience with that thorny subject, which includes decades of trial and error, throwing out the countless years' worth of shoddy results *(Angela)*, came the sad realization I'd never be a leader in the field, just another middling scientist, they really had only one identifiable constant: Around guys like Cooper, icebergs turned to puddles.

"**Fine**," I shouted. "But I'm doing all the talking."

Twelve

The Billy Goat became famous after the Saturday Night Live Show popularized it during the 70's in many of their skits. In reality, it's just a good place to get a burger and some chips without any wait time. It's a real old-time greasy spoon restaurant. Elizabeth Michener sat way in the back under a wall-size photo of the Rolling Stones in concert at Soldier Field. She had her fake Coach purse and a huge leather satchel next to her.

She didn't notice us walking toward her because her eyes were closed. Whispering to herself, apparently trying to memorize the block of highlighted text from the play in her hands. She glanced up at me, then Cooper. Instantly, probably from his stunning good looks, she jerked upright.

"This is Cooper," I said. "Hope it's okay he joins us."

Cooper remained tacit, only slid into the booth across from her.

She adorned a strange outfit: Zebra striped stretch pants, so tight it looked like they were sprayed on, a sweater so hot pink it scalded the eyes, lipstick a vivid shade of red. Her strawberry blonde hair hung down to her elbows, curly at the ends.

"So, you're an actress?" I asked sliding beside Cooper.

"What have you acted in?" Cooper asked.

This caused her eyes to narrow and glare confusedly at Cooper then look back at me. Even I know that is one of the rudest questions to ask an actor.

"Nothing yet. I've only been an actress four weeks. That's how long I've been in the city."

"So where'd you move from?" I asked.

"Minot, near Belcourt."

I could only nod, as I didn't know either place or where they were. I could imagine Minot have an Indian reservation gambling casino where you could play craps and watch a Crystal Gayle lookalike sing "Brown Eyes Blue." But Elizabeth smiled without shame, closing the play, touching the cover like it was a sacred Bible.

Yet it turned out to be David Mamet's *Glengarry Glen Ross*.

With a tiny frown, she swept her hands officiously over the surface of the table, brushing a few toast crumbs onto the floor. She then turned and opened up the Whole Foods bag, peering inside as if there were something alive in there. She reached in with both hands and gently pulled out a bulky red-and–black bundle, placing it on the table and sliding it toward me.

I recognized it immediately.

It was a woman's coat. And for the moment, the cafe and everything in it dissolved. There was only that article of clothing, so ferociously red, staring me down. It looked like a costume, ornate, faintly Russian, red leather, the cuffs black lamb, black cord embellishing the front.

The woman I'd encountered while jogging along Lake Shore Drive, weeks ago had been wearing it. Her platinum hair ambling in and out of her face, the coat like a flare, alerting me to *what, what, what?* Had she just been toying with me? How that woman managed to disappear like that defied all logic. The incident had been so odd that when I got home that night I couldn't sleep, infected by the strangeness of it all. I climbed out of bed more than a few times to take a peek out the window, half expecting her to be there. Her slender body like a red incision in the sidewalk, her face turned up to me with hard black eyes. I'd actually questioned my sanity, wondered if this was it: the substandard past few years had finally led to a mental break with reality. And now the floodgates open, there'd be no limit to the friends I'd encounter. They would simply crawl out of my head and into the world.

But the sidewalk had no red tear. The street, the night, remained flawless and still.

I'd actually started to forget the entire episode until now.

It had been Gabriela Esquivel.

The realization was startling, quickly followed by the paranoid feeling that something's wrong, including this coat-check girl. She had to be involved in some kind of set-up. But the girl only smiled innocently back at me. Cooper must have seen something on my face, total shock because he was squinting at me suspiciously.

"What is it?" he asked, nodding at the coat.

"Gabriela's coat," she said. "She wore it when she came into the restaurant." She picked up her coffee cup and took a loud sip. "She left it with me. When the police came later, asking about her I gave them a black coat from the lost and found. I told them that Gabriela wore that coat. If they found out I lied, I was going to say that I got the tickets mixed up. But they never came back."

Cooper slid the coat toward him, unfolded it, holding it up by the shoulders. For all its elaborate stitching, the coat looked worn, even seemed to smell of the city, the dirty wind, the sweat. The inside was lined with black silk, and I noticed, sewn into the back collar, a purple label, M.M.S. Maxine Michelle Seehafer used to be employed by Esquivel to keep the family wardrobe in vogue. Sort of like Mr. T's jeweler. I thought about mentioning this little tidbit when Cooper asked loudly, "Why'd you lie to the police?"

"I'll tell you guys why on one condition. I want to be part of the investigation." She looked at me. You said you were investigating Gabriela."

It's nothing that formal," I said, clearing my throat, managing to look away from the coat and at Elizabeth. "I'm really investigating her father. And Cooper's just here today. We're not partners."

"Yeah we are," he countered, shooting a look at me. *"Absolutely*. Welcome to *the team.* Be our *friggin' mascot.* Why'd you lie to the police?"

Elizabeth stared at him, taken aback by his intensity. Then she looked at me, awaiting my response.

I said nothing because I was adjusting to what it meant, this encounter with Gabriela. I took a deep breath, trying to at least pretend I was considering her request. For the record, it'd be over my dead body that I'd ever take on a sidekick, particularly one who'd just crawled out of the North Dakota boonies.

"This is not the adventure of a lifetime," I said. "I'm not Starsky and he's not Hutch."

"If I'm not involved from beginning to end when we find out who or what made Gabriela die before her time." She articulated all of this decisively as if she'd rehearsed it hundreds of times in front of the bathroom mirror. Then I am not telling you what she was like or what she did, and you can both get lost." She slid the coat back and began to mash it inside the bag.

Cooper looked at me expectantly.

"There's no need to be so black and white about it," I said.

She ignored me.

"Okay. You can work with us," I said.

"You swear?" she asked, smiling.

"I swear."

She extended her hand, and I shook it, mentally crossing my fingers.

It was a quiet night," she went on eagerly. "After ten, there wasn't anyone in the lobby. She walked right in wearing that, so, of course, I noticed her. She was beautiful. But really thin, with eyes almost clear. She looked right at me and my first thought was, *oh wow, she's gorgeous.* Her face more focused than everything else in the room. But as she turned and started walking towards me, I felt scared.

"Why? "I asked.

She bit her lip. "It was like when you looked into her eyes the human part was detached and there was something else looking out."

"Like what?" Cooper inquired.

"Don't know," she answered looking down at the table.

"She didn't seem to blink. Or breathe, even. Not when she pulled off that red coat, not when she handed it to me, not when I gave her the ticket. As I hung it up on the coat rack, I could feel her eyes on me. When I turned back, I thought she'd still be standing there, but she was already disappearing up the stairs."

I began to get that eerie feeling, like when I was jogging and had first seen that red jacket.

"At that point, other people came in. as I was checking their coats I noticed she was coming back down the stairs. Without looking at me she headed outside. I figured she went out for a smoke. I didn't see her come back, so I thought I'd been so busy I missed her, but at the end of the night her red coat was still hanging there. The only one left."

Elizabeth took a quick gulp of water.

"Three days went by," she went on. "Every night when I closed the coat-check booth I put her coat in the lost and found.

When I returned the next day. I'd take it out and hang it up. I felt sure she'd come back for it. I also dreaded the thought." She paused tucking her hair behind her ears. "On the fourth night after my shift it was cold out and I only had this light windbreaker. So after I closed up, instead of returning it back in the lost and found, I put it on and I walked out wearing it. I could have taken any of the coats from the lost and found. But I took hers."

Elizabeth stared down at her hands, her face flushed. "The next day when I arrived at the restaurant, the police were there canvassing the area around Gabriela's death. They saw me walk in with the coat. When they told me what happened, I was so upset at what I had done. I was afraid they'd think I had something to do with it. So I took the Yves Saint Laurent coat out of the lost and found and said that one was hers." She took a deep breath. I thought for sure they'd find out I lied, that they would show it to her family." She shook her head. But no one came around to ask me anything. Not yet, anyway." She looked at me. "Only you."

"What else did she have on?" I asked.

"Jeans, brown boots, a purple T-shirt with an angel on the front."

The Same clothing Gabriela was wearing when she died.

"Did she speak to you? Mention if she was meeting someone?"

Elizabeth shook her head. "I said my usual 'Good evening' and 'Will you be joining us for dinner tonight?' There's a little script they like you to memorize to be welcoming. But she didn't answer. Every night since I met her before I knew she'd passed away, I've had nightmares. You know the kind where you wake up fast and sounds are echoing through the room but you have no idea what it is, you'd just scream out loud.

She was waiting for an acknowledgment, so I nodded.

"That's what I've had. And my grandmother Bernice on my mother's side of the family said the Edges are in tune with stuff from the fourth and fifth dimensions."

I felt the urge to intervene here before we were treated to more wisdom from Grandmother Bernice.

I smiled. "Well, I'll look everything over and be in touch."

"Oh no you don't, first we need to exchange numbers," Elizabeth said.

She and Cooper gave each other their info. I was just starting to wonder how I was going to auto-eject myself out of this situation, when Elizabeth looked at her watch and let out a little squeal, scrambling out of the booth. "Shoot I'm late for work." She grabbed the check, digging through her purse. "No!" she looked at me, nibbling on a fingernail. "I left my wallet at home."

"Don't worry. I'll get it."

"Really? Thanks. I'll pay you back."

If this is any indication of her acting skills, not even a daytime soap would hire her. She zipped up her purse, heaved it onto her shoulder, and grabbed the satchel.

"I can take the coat. So you don't have to carry so much."

She glanced at me with a flash of mistrust, but then reconsidered, handing me the satchel.

"See ya later," she yelled out cheerfully as she jostled away, bags banging her shins. "And thanks for the grub."

I scooted out of the booth and, reading the check, saw that the little girl had actually consumed two meals. *So my little girl Friday had the appetite of a sumo wrestler.* I wondered if the reason she decided to talk so I would subsidize her next feeding. Not knowing I'm broker than a tooth fairy in a house full of meth addicts.

"What'd you think?" asked Cooper, sliding out behind me.

I shrugged. "Young and impressionable. Probably made most of it up."

"Yeah, right. That's why you looked so bored and nearly tripped over yourself to get your hands on that coat."

I said nothing, pulling a couple of double sawbucks from my wallet.

"For one thing," he said, "she's got no place to live." He stared out the window, where Elizabeth and her many bags were still visible. On the other side of the four-lane street, she was using the mirror reflection of a building to fix her hair into a ponytail. She then picked up her bags and vanished behind a delivery truck.

With a last hard look at me, clearly indicating he didn't trust me or particularly like me, Cooper put his phone to his ear.

"Keep those eyes open, Starsky," he said, heading out.

I stayed back, waiting for him to turn the corner. I doubted I'd ever see him again, or Hanna Montana, for that matter. When Chicago took over they would both fall by the wayside.

One of the magnificent things about the city: It was inherently Machiavellian. One rarely had to worry about follow-throughs, follow–ups or any kind of consistency in people due to machinations on one's own but the sheer force of living here. Chicago hit its residents daily, like a great debilitating deluge and only the strongest, the ones with a herculean type inner will, had the strength to stay the course. This pertained to work as well as personal lives. Most people ended up far, far away from where they intended to go, in only a couple of months, most stuck in some quagmire of the underbrush of the city life that no one ever sees. Others outright drowned in the backwash, become drug addicts, or become a part of the homeless society living on lower Wacker Drive.

Yet the two of them have been helpful.

All those nights ago, it had been Gabriela Esquivel. I thought I'd decided to on my own to look into her death, and yet incredibly she'd come to me first. Wedged herself like a splinter into my subconscious. I'd have to review the timing, but I recall the jogging encounter, had to be a little more than a week before her death. When I saw her it must have been just a few days after she'd escaped from Mission Hills.

How had she known I'd be jogging at that time and place? Not many people knew I jogged that early along the lake except Kim. One evening months ago, while tucking her into bed, she mentioned that I'm always too far away. I answered, not true since every morning I jogged right by her and I could look into her window and see that she was safe and sound. This, of course, was a stretch. I could no more see into Angela and Bruce's plush apartment on Michigan Avenue than see the Empire State Building. But the thought comforted her and she'd close her eyes and go right to sleep.

The only possible explanation, then is that Gabriela had been following me.

She would have known about me from her father's lawsuit. It's conceivable she tracked me down in order to tell me something about her father but lost her nerve.

But after what Cooper had told me, shyness didn't seem an underlying trait of Gabriela's personality. Quite the opposite.

I had to get back to my place: first, to make arraignments to drive upstate to Mission Hills so I could learn about Gabriela's stay there. I grabbed the satchel, exiting the diner. The sun was out, splattering brash light on the cars speeding down the Dan Ryan Expressway. It did nothing to lighten the unease I felt over the simple fact that the red coat, that blood red stitch in the night from the early morning lakeside jog had appeared one last time in front of me. It was in my own hands.

Thirteen

The following morning, an hour before I set out on my three-hour trip to Mission Hills. I had just started a fresh pot of coffee, standing in my kitchen, when I heard a knock on my front door

I walked into the foyer and checked the peephole.

I saw Elizabeth Michener standing outside my door.

I didn't know how in the hell she'd found out where I lived, but then I remembered. It was that damned business card I'd given her back at the restaurant. Someone must have buzzed her in. I considered pretending I wasn't at home, but she knocked again and I knew the old wood floors of my apartment squeaked with every step, so she could hear me standing there.

I unlocked the door. She was wearing a tight black wool jacket with a collar of ostrich feathers, black and white zebra striped tights, boots, and a black suede mini-skirt. Resembling a figure skater in the Lillehammer Olympics. She had no bags with her only that massive purse, she had enough piercings and gold in her ear's to start her own bling-bling shop on Maxwell Street. Her long strawberry blonde hair braided into two cords wrapped around her head.

"Hi," I said.

"Hi."

"What are you doing here?"

"I'm ready to work."

"It's six-thirty in the morning."

She picked at something on the strap of her purse. "Yeah, well, I thought you could use someone to bounce an idea off of."

I thought about telling her to come back tomorrow, then realizing if I did I would have to move or enter into the witness protection program. I remembered Cooper's observation that she may be homeless. She did look a little exhausted, and a little pale.

"You want some coffee?"

She perked up. "Sure."

"I'm about to leave for an appointment, so it won't be long."

"No problem."

"What exactly are you wearing?' I asked, leading her through the foyer into the kitchen. "Your mother doesn't let you go out dressed like that, does she?"

"Oh sure. She lets me do whatever. She's dead." She slung her purse beside the couch, I know it contained at least one sixteen pound bowling ball.

"How about your grandma, Bernice?"

"She's dead too."

Something told me to be smart and stop before I get in over my head. But what the hell, if they ever hung me for being smart they would be killing an innocent man.

"What about your father?"

She leaned forward studying a Dali painting over the fireplace.

"He's in Stateville Prison, in Joliet. They have Old Sparky there you know."

Old Sparky is the nickname given to the electric chair. I waited for her to clarify that her dad wasn't destined for a meeting with old sparky, but she moved to the bookcase inspecting the books leaving that strand of conversation to dangle like the end of a party streamer.

"How do you like your coffee?"

"Cream, four sugars, please. I hope it's not too much trouble.

"No trouble at all. Are you hungry?"

"Well if you have extra, I'll have a little something."

I set Liz up with some muffins, buttered with some jelly on the side, and a couple of granola bars. I went back to my office to get directions to Mission Hills.

"What are you doing?" Elizabeth yelled from the living room.

"I'm checking something on the computer, I'll be out in a minute."

"Have you ever heard of that website, *Rebel's Carnival*?"

"No, I haven't."

"You should check it out. It's a website where lots of young people go when they are on the run looking for help along the way."

"Thanks, I just might do that." Maybe Elizabeth would be helpful in tracking down Gabriela's last moves. She's about the Same age and the way young girls think when out there on their own.

When I returned to the living room Elizabeth had settled in. she'd taken off her boots, pulled a blanket over her legs, and drained some of the contents of that purse onto my coffee table. It looked like the remains from a survival kit.

"Who's in the picture?" she asked.

"My ex-wife and daughter. Angela and Kim, my daughter."

"You have an ex-wife?" She asked astonished.

"Doesn't everybody."

"Where is she?"

"Probably working out with her trainer."

"How about your daughter, Kim?"

"She's in school, first grade."

I figured it's as good as time as ever to bring up her mystery living arrangements.

"So where exactly do you live?"

"By Chinatown, on Princeton Avenue and like Twenty-third."

"Like Twenty-third?"

"Well I just moved in and I'm not sure about the cross street."

"Any roommates?"

She kept her head down. "Two."

"And what do they do?"

"What do you mean?"

"Are they pimps, drug addicts, or working in the porn industry?'

"Oh no. I mean; I don't know what they do during the day. They seem nice."

"What are their names?"

She hesitated. "Christine and Rachel."

I looked at my watch. No more time for babysitting.

"I have to leave for a doctor's appointment," I said. "So you'll have to go, we can talk tomorrow."

I collected her plate and coffee cup, Elizabeth watching with wide eyes, and carried then to the kitchen, loading the dishwasher.

"Thank you for the coffee and food," she called out.

"Don't mention it."

There was a stretch of rather dubious silence.

About to go check on her, but then I heard her unzipping and zipping her purse. She was packing up her things, *thank God!* But I knew this only bought me a little time; she'd be back tomorrow.

This girl is like one of those Remora, a little fish that swim relentlessly next to great white sharks for miles. I'd have to phone some old contact. Perhaps someone in one of the trade unions or in banking, twist his arm to get her a gainfully employed for twelve hours a day at some Bank of America out in Joliet.

"What's Galena?" she abruptly shouted.

"What?" I stepped out of the kitchen.

"You have directions to a place in Galena, Illinois."

She stood in the foyer, inspecting the folder containing the directions to Mission Hills and my e-mails with the director, which I'd put on the table next to the satchel containing Gabriela's coat.

"You're getting a tour of the facility?" she asked, glancing up in amazement. "What facility?"

I snatched the folder from her hand and checking my watch, I was supposed to be on the Eden's twenty minutes ago. I went to the closet and grabbed my black leather jacket, pulling it on.

"A mental hospital." I moved back into the hall, switching off the lights.

"Why do you want a tour of a mental hospital?"

"Because I just might admit myself. We'll catch up tomorrow."

I grabbed the directions and Elizabeth's skinny arm, escorting her to the front door and giving her a gentle push so she was launched outside, then stepped after her, locking the door.

"You lied in that e-mail," she said. "You said your name's George Schumer."

"A typo."

"You're going there to investigate Gabriela."

I took off down the hall, Elizabeth quickly following me. "No."

"But you're taking her coat. I should come."

"No."

"Consider this, I could be your daughter you're thinking of admitting. I could play, like, a dark and brooding teenager. I'm really good at improv."

"I'm going there to get information, not play charades."

I stepped outside holding the door for her while shading my eye's from the bright morning sun. Elizabeth had a fast, kind of side to side walk, I figured it was a result of carrying all those bags around the city.

"This place has the security of the Pentagon," I said, jogging down the steps. "Over the years I've developed a method of interviewing that allows people to trust me. It's because I work alone. Deep Throat would have never talked to Woodward if he'd been shadowed by a North Dakota teenager."

"What's Deep Throat?"

I stopped staring at her. She actually looked legitimately puzzled.

I kept going across the street. "You've at least seen the movie. *All the President's Men*. Robert Redford, Dustin Hoffman? You know who they are, don't you? Or aren't you aware of any movie stars older than Justin Timberlake?"

"I know who they are!" She shouted.

Well, they played Woodward and Bernstein. Legendary journalists who exposed Watergate. They forced a president of the United States to admit a cover-up and resign. One of the most powerful acts of patriotism by two journalists in the history of this country."

She looked at me then said, "Okay you'll be Woodward and I'll be Bernstein."

"That's not exactly what I am trying to tell you, yes they were a team, but they each brought something to the table."

"I can bring something to the table."

"Like what? Your personal in depth knowledge of Gabriela Esquivel?"

She stopped and announced, "I'm coming, or I'll call the hospital and tell them you're a phony, using a fake name."

I stopped in my tracks, turning to survey her. There it was, that Teflon personality I'd known so well from the survivors on the streets of Chicago. She began her morphing, into a streetwise woman from the city. One minute they were helpless, needing shelter and English muffins, the next they were ruthlessly bending you to their will like you were a soft pretzel, ready to be dipped in melted cheese and devoured.

"So it's blackmail."

With a fierce stare, she nodded.

I walked the remaining yards to my car, a dented black 1985 Cadillac Eldorado parked along the curb.

"Fine," I muttered over my shoulder. "But you're staying in the car."

Elizabeth, squeaking with excitement, hurried around to the passenger side.

"You'll do everything I say at all times." I unlocked the trunk, shoved the satchel inside. "You'll be a silent operative with no personality. You'll simply process and execute my orders like a machine."

"Oh, *sure.*"

I climbed in yanking on my seatbelt and starting the car.

"I don't want feedback or yammering. I don't chit and I sure as hell don't chat."

"Okay, but we can't leave yet." She leaned forward, turning up the radio.

"Why the hell not?"

"Coopers coming."

"No. He's not. This is not a third-grade field trip. And you not calling the shots here!"

"But he wanted to meet up with us. Wow, you really hate people, don't you?"

I ignored that comment, and inched out into the street, suddenly hearing the horn of a taxi barreling down the street. I slammed on the brakes and was forced meekly to retreat back to the curb. As a line of cars speed by and lined up at the light, trapping us at the curb.

"You remind me of this man back at Turtle Mountain."

"What the hell is Turtle Mountain?"

"It's a reservation back in North Dakota. I knew this man named Hank Storm. He used to come to the cafeteria where I worked. He would get his food and when he sat at his table he would put his walker right next to him so not one could sit next to him."

I didn't answer, silenced by the sudden realization that I had absolutely no idea if any of what came out of this girl's mouth was true. Maybe she really was good at improv. I couldn't be certain of anything she told me about herself, age, even her name. Maybe she was like one of those sweaters with an innocent thread hanging off of it. Once you pulled it the whole thing came unraveled.

"Do you drive?" I asked.

"You betcha."

"Let me see your license."

"Why?"

"I have to make sure that there is not an Amber Alert out for you. Or that you weren't profiled on America's Most Wanted as some kind of criminal."

Smirking, she leaned forward, dug around in that hulking bag she called her purse, removing a pink nylon LeSportsac wallet, so stained and worn it looked like it had been floating down the Chicago River for a couple of years. She flipped through a few snapshots encased in plastic, deliberately turning the wallet away so I couldn't see them, and slipped out the license, handing it to me.

In the picture, she looked about fifteen Elizabeth Lorena Michener, P.O. Box 1247, Belcourt, N.D. 58316. Her birthdate saying, she is twenty-one years old. I handed it back to her.

The light turned green. I put the car in drive, easing out.

"If you want to wait for Cooper, be my guest. I have work to do."

"But he's here," she yelled excitedly.

Sure enough, cooper was shuffling down the sidewalk in his best, *I am Mr. Cool walk*. Before I could stop her she reached over and repeatedly honked the horn. Seconds later, in a blast of cold air, cigarette smoke, and booze, Cooper collapsed in the back seat.

"What's up, amigos?"

Cooper, bombed again.

I accelerated through the yellow light on Eighteenth Street. Cooper muttered something incomprehensible. An hour later he asked me to pull over on the side of the Edens Expressway because he felt sick.

It didn't look like he'd been home all night. He still adorned the Same get up he wore yesterday. When he finished up-chucking he wanted to sit on the guard rail and watch the traffic whiz by my car like cannonballs. Elizabeth finally got out and helped him back into the car.

She did this with remarkable tenderness and care.

I couldn't help but sense that she had done this kind of thing many times before. *For whom? The dead mother? The convict father awaiting Old Sparky? Grandmother Bernice?*

Why in the hell did she give two shits about Gabriela Esquivel, or about any of this? And Cooper, was a stuffed parrot anonymously mailed to him really why he chose to be with me on a Wednesday morning, not in bed with Chloe or some other downtown girl reeking of cigarettes and booze?

These two kids clearly knew a hell of a lot more than they let on. But if they were hiding something, I'd learn what it was soon enough. Secrets, even in hardened criminals, were just air pockets lodged under some debris at the bottom of the ocean. It might take an earthquake, or you digging around down there, sifting through the sludge, but their natural proclivity is always to head straight to the surface, **to get out**.

Elizabeth loaded Cooper into the back seat. He mumbled something as she removed his sunglasses, and then stretching out across the seat with a boozy sigh. He conked out. Elizabeth resumed scanning the radio. She stopped on an old rock song "Everybody's got a Hungry Heart", by the Boss. Then she sat back and stared out the window.

The morning seemed to tiredly sponge off the sky, washing the road signs and windshields in dull, bathwater light as the rhythm of the highway thumped under the tires.

I didn't feel like talking. I am too stunned at where I found myself: with these two total strangers, an assortment of stories behind us and who the hell knows what's in front of us, but for the time being, our lives, three frail lives running side by side. We made our way toward Mission Hills.

Fourteen

"We don't think of our guests as patients," Christine Plath said to me as we strolled down the sidewalk. "They're part of the Mission Hills family for life. Now tell me more about your daughter, Kierstyn." She looked back at Elizabeth, known for the time being as Kierstyn, who'd fallen thirty paces behind us. "What year is she?"

"She recently became a college freshman," I said. "But she dropped out."

Christine waited for me to elaborate, but I just tried to look uncomfortable and glanced away. Christine Plath was a short plump woman, very good looking, In her late forties with a very sour expression. I initially assumed she had just finished sucking on a lemon. Only to realize as the minutes ticked by that expression showed no sign of subsiding. She wore high-waist mom jeans, her brown hair up in a tight bun.

Elizabeth and I had left Cooper passed out in my backseat and found Plath's office on the ground floor of Blaine House, a red brick building that housed Mission Hills administration, which didn't so much sit on the unspoiled pristine hill. It sat in a long stretch of boxy annexes and gray tendrils of sidewalks. I'd taken just one look at Plath as she jingled out from behind her desk, her snow-white, pink-barretted Maltese, Princess, who glided around her office like a tiny Thanksgiving Day parade float, and I immediately wanted to call off our ruse.

Making matters considerably worse, Elizabeth's acting ability, or the alarming lack thereof. As we sat down, I'd explained that my daughter, Kierstyn had disciplinary issues.

Elizabeth had grimaced and stared at the floor. I felt sure the many hard, knowing looks Plath shot me were not compassionate but coolly accusatory as if she knew my daughter was a sham. Just when I was certain she was going to order us off the premises, however, Plath, and the gasping, tingling Princess, had kick started the tour, leading us out of Blaine House and across Mission Hills sprawling grounds.

"What sort of security do you have in place?" I asked.

Plath slowed to consider Elizabeth again, who was glowering at the sidewalk.

"I'll go over the specifics with you in private," Plath said. "But in a nutshell, every patient is assigned a level of surveillance, which ranges from general observation, when the patient is checked by staff, to every thirty minutes all day and night.

At meal times a patient must stay within arm's length of a trained technician at all times. A spoon is the only tableware they are allowed. When she arrives, Kierstyn will be evaluated and assigned the appropriate level."

"Has there been any recent incidents of escape?" I asked.

The question caught her by surprise. "Escape?"

"Sorry. Don't mean it to sound like the Cook County Super Max. It's just if Kierstyn sees an opportunity, she'll make a run for it."

Plath nodded. If she was reminded of Gabriela Esquivel's breakout, she gave no indication.

"We have fifty-four acres," she said. "The perimeter is fenced in and secured with video surveillance. A twenty-four-hour detail at the gate house entrance monitors every vehicle entering and leaving." She smiled thinly. "Patient safety is our biggest priority."

So that was the official statement on Gabriela's escape: *It never happened.*

"The funny thing is, she continued, once people settle in it's harder to get them to leave than to stay. Mission Hills is a sanctuary. It's a refuge from the brutal world."

"I can see that. This is quite a beautiful place."

"Isn't it?"

I grinned in agreement. *As beautiful as an injection of morphine.*

A vast immaculate lawn spanned out on either side of us, smooth, flat, and endlessly green. Far off to the left stood a gigantic oak tree, an empty white bench beneath it. It resembled the front of a sympathy card. The grounds were eerily deserted, except for the occasional smiling nurse striding past us in pink pants with a matching flowery shirt. *To distract you as she fed you your daily meds.*

Plath had explained that at this hour everyone in the clinic, *clinic seemed to be the code word for psych ward,* was in a therapy session. This place has a creepy muzzled feel to it. Any second I expect to hear a man's gut-wrenching scream pierce through over the chirping birds and warm breeze.

Or to see the doors fly open from one of those buildings that Plath had expressly skipped on our tour; "Just another dormitory," she'd said when I inquired about it.

I half expected some client come out running for freedom being tackled be some male nurse with white pants and T-shirt and hauled off to an electro-convulsive therapy session.

"How many patients do you have?" I asked, glancing back at Elizabeth. She began to lag farther behind.

"One hundred and thirty-six adults between our mental health and substance abuse programs. That does not include outpatients."

"And the psychologists work closely with all the patients?"

"Oh, yes." She stated. "Upon admission, each resident is assigned a personal health care team. That includes a physician, a pharmacologist, and a psychologist."

"And how often do they meet?"

"It depends. Often daily, sometimes twice a day."

"Where?"

"In Membly Hall." She pointed to our right at a redbrick building half concealed by oak and pine trees. "We'll head over there in a minute. First, we'll take a look at Copley."

We veered off the path, heading toward a gray building, Princess trotting along right by my feet.

"This is where residents dine and meet for extracurricular activities." Plath moved up the steps, opening the heavy wooden doors ahead of me.

"Twice a week we have professors from the University of Chicago give talks in the auditorium on everything from global warming to endangered species to World War Two. Part of our philosophy for healing is giving our patients a global perspective and sense of history."

I nodded and smiled, looking over my shoulder to see where the hell Elizabeth was. She'd stopped following us, standing back at the center of the lawn. She was shading her eyes, surveying something behind her.

"I can see your trouble with her," Plath said, following my gaze. "Girls can have a tough time at her age. Where's Mrs. Dean in all of this, if you don't mind me asking?"

"Stacy, she is out of the picture. Although very beautiful, she was not cut out for the family life.

Plath nodded. Elizabeth looked like she was debating making a run for it. But then she shuffled toward us with a slumping posture, stopping to give Plath her best Dr. Evil look before skipping up the steps. Plath led us through the foyer, which smelled strongly like disinfectant, and into the dining hall. It was a large, sunlit room with round wooden tables, arched windows. A handful of female staff were busy arranging place settings.

"This is where residents eat all meals," said Plath. "Obviously, we promote physical health as well as mental, so the menu has a low-fat option, also vegetarian, vegan, and kosher. Out head chef used to work in the loop at a five-star restaurant."

"When do I get to meet the people that live here so I know they're not all psychotic?" asked Elizabeth.

Plath glanced at me with the wide-eyed shocked look, I stared back sheepishly, and then she recovered and smiled.

"You won't be meeting anyone today," she said diplomatically, holding out an arm to usher us down the hall, as Princess floated along beside her, nails clacking on the floor. "But if you come, you'll find the people here are as diverse as the people anywhere."

Plath stopped abruptly beside a dark alcove and after a pause switched on an overhead light. The walls were covered in bulletin boards decked with sign-up sheets and photos of activities at Mission Hills.

"As you can see," Plath said, gesturing inside, "people are really quite happy. We keep everyone busy, physically and mentally."

Scowling, Elizabeth stepped inside. "When were these pictures taken?" She asked.

"The last few months," said Plath.

Elizabeth glared skeptically, then inspected the pictures, her arms crossed over her stomach. I thought she'd lost it asking about the pictures when I realized what she was doing. She was looking for Gabriela. It wasn't a bad idea. I moved past Plath to take a look. The photos were of patients involved playing board games, nature hikes, enjoying picnic type activities. A few looked legitimately happy, though most appeared thin and fatigued.

Gabriela would be obvious. Beautiful girl, alone, with a challenging look about her. I scanned the photos of the recital, seated at the piano sat a man with dreadlocks. I had seen many pictures of patients crowded around picnic tables, eating hot dogs and hamburgers at a summer barbecue, but no sign of Gabriela anywhere.

I glanced back at the doorway and seen Plath looking at us, faintly alarmed. We must have been inspecting a little too intently.

"Everyone looks so happy," I said.

She coldly stared back. "Why don't we get moving along?"

I stepped out of the alcove, that little doily of a dog twirling in circles as it stared up at me, panting as if I had beef jerky in my pocket. Elizabeth had been flipping through the pages of a sign-up sheet for Mission Hills Book Club, noticeably reading all the names.

"Elizabeth," I said. "Let's go."

Plath led us back outside, across the lawn to Membly Hall, where we headed straight to the second floor. The level devoted to music, painting, and yoga. It was clear from Plath's clipped descriptions and tightened tone that she really didn't care for me or my huffy little daughter. I tried to fawn over the facilities, but she only smiled stiffly.

As we went by the reflection room, candles, photos of meadows and sky. A two-note chime sounded over a loudspeaker. It was a shrill and reverberating, the musical equivalent of a stubbed toe.

"I have to go to the bathroom," Elizabeth announced petulantly.

"Certainty," said Plath, stopping beside a water fountain, pointing at the door marked *women* in the middle of the corridor. "We'll wait for you here."

Elizabeth rolled her eyes and took off. The corridor walls were bright, painted half white, half kitten-nose pink, but the place felt clinical and claustrophobic, like an airplane bathroom. *Welcome to disoriented air-lines, ready for take-off to crazy town. All aboard.*

Patients crowded the hallways as classrooms let out. They wore jeans and baggy cotton shirts, no belts or shoelaces, I noticed. There was a surprising range of ages. One guy with spiky gray hair staggered out of an art room, he looked abut eighty. Most avoided eye contact as they walked past me. Various dunderheads and shrinks milled about, conferring, nodding, and trying to look constructive.

They were easy to spot because they were all dressed in L.L. Bean fleeces and Columbia nylon jackets, wool sweaters in earth tones, *most likely so the patients wouldn't mistake this place for Vail.*

Plath began fussing with the barrette in Princess's hair.

"I've heard very good things about Dr. Jana Mohan," I said.

She stood up, holding the dog in her arms.

Jana Mohan was a psychologist who had completed Gabriela's new patient assessment, which had been included in the CPD file.

"A friend of mine recommended her," I went on. "She's apparently very good with young women who have depressive disorders. Is there any way I could speak to her?"

"Her office is on the third floor. That area isn't open to visitors. And discussion of Dr. Mohan or any physician at this stage is premature. If Kierstyn comes, she'll be assigned a team of health professionals that suits her needs. Which reminds me. I'm going to go check on her."

She put Princess down, smiling at me, with the implication that said, *don't you dare move,* and marched down the hall, her white orthopedic shoes squishing on the floor.

When she came back a minute later, her face fire-engine red.

"She's not in there," she announced loudly.

I blankly stared back.

"Kierstyn is missing. Did you see her?"

"No."

Plath spun around on her heel and stomped down the hallway.

"She must have gone out the other end."

Princess and I, mutually stunned by this recent development, took off after her, as I passed by the lady's room I couldn't help but open the door and call out: "Kierstyn? Honey?"

Plath shot a look over her shoulder. "She's not in there. *Really.*"

She barged past patients, thrusting the door open at the end of the hall, storming into the stairwell. I followed close behind. She paused, squinted up at the next flight sectioned off by a metal gate and a sign that read, **authorized personnel only**, then turned, stomping down the stairs. We blasted out onto the ground floor, jostling a man carrying a stack of file folders, Princess's paws skidding on the slick wood floors as she rounded the sharp turn. We followed Plath into an office marked, **drug and alcohol extension program.**

"Beth, did you see a three-forty-two wandering around? Skinny blonde? Micro-mini? Hair in Heidi braids?" She eyed me scornfully. *"Feathers?"*

"No Miss Plath."

Plath muttering to herself, marched back down the hall.

"What's a three-forty-two?" I asked.

"A perspective. I'll have to review the security monitors. She likes to run away, does she? Any idea where she might go?"

"If she makes it to the main road she might try to hitchhike."

"Unless she has wings and can fly over a thirty-foot electrified fence, that girl's not going anywhere."

"I'm terribly sorry about this."

We exited through the glass doors. Outside, across the lawn where patients, most escorted by nurses, streamed down the sidewalks heading to lunch. There was no sign of Elizabeth anywhere. With the getup she was wearing, she'd be easy to spot. I had no idea where she was; this wasn't part of the orders I'd given her. She'd gone rogue.

A minute later, Plath deposited me on the floral couch in her office, "You wait here," she said. "I'll be right back with your daughter."

"Thank you." She only glared at me and slammed the door behind her.

Fifteen

I sat alone with Princess. The dog had gone over to her pillow bed by the potted plants and returned with a squeaking rubber ball.

The chime dinged over the loudspeakers for the second time. I studied the ceiling, No visible camera. I stood up and moved over to Plath's desk.

The screensaver on her computer unsurprisingly featured floating bubbles with pictures of Princess inside the bubbles. I tapped the keyboard and the prompt for the password came up. I tried Princess. It didn't work.

On the corner of the desk were stacks of papers amongst the, In and Out trays. I flipped through them: thank-you notes, admission applications, a signed confidentiality statement, an e-mail from Dr. Robert Griffin announcing his retirement. Surely there had to be some kind of internal administrative memo about Gabriela Esquivel. It'd be written by some hospital head, filled with phrases like *this is a very delicate matter* and *it's critical to the reputation of the hospital*, and so on.

I opened the desk drawers.

They were filled with office supplies, a Pottery Barn catalog, and strewn with wrapped hard mint candies. I moved to the row of filing cabinets along the back wall. They were all locked and no sign anywhere of the keys.

I moved back over to the door, opened it, and looked out. The hallway looked empty, with the exception of two nurses standing about halfway down in front of the main entrance.

Elizabeth is getting me thrown out. I may as well go down like a storm trooper. Suddenly Princess started gnawing the hotdog toy on my foot. A nurse stopped talking to glance curiously in our direction. I reached down, launched the toy across the room. It lodged in the leaves of a giant potted yucca plant by the window. Princess would have to scale the three-foot-tall base the plant was in to even have a chance to get the toy.

I checked and the nurses resumed talking to one another. I slipped out, walking straight through the side door. Once outside I headed towards Membly Hall.

The grounds were quiet again, a few stragglers making their way toward the dining hall. I hurried across the lawn, heading up to front steps, where patients were chatting and smoking cigarettes. They only glanced at me idly as I entered the building and headed straight for the elevator banks.

Stepping inside, I pressed 3. But the number did not light up. I needed some type of passcode. I had begun to exit when a silver-haired woman stepped in, her eyes glued to her iPhone. Without acknowledging me, she pressed a four-digit code into the panel. It didn't work, clearly, because I'd pressed a button. Frowning, she pressed reset, typed the code in again, and the doors closed. She pressed 6 and we began to move. I stepped forward and pressed 3, this time, it lit up.

She turned towards me, curiously looking me over.

The doors opened at 3, as I exited I could sense the woman looking at me and wondering who in the hell I was. But before she could react the doors closed.

I was alone on the third floor of Membly Hall, which looked identical to the second, except for the overhead neon lights. The lighting was softer, the floors waxed shinier, and the walls were a light spearmint green. Brown doors lined the hallways in both directions. They were doctor's offices. As I moved down the hall I notice a brass plaque with the names of each doctor on them. I could hear low voices and soft music; the kind you hear at a spa while getting a massage. Midway down the hall, there was a small windowed sitting area where two young men sat stretched out on couches, writing in notebooks.

They didn't notice me as I walked by. I spotted the plaque, Jana Mohan PH.D. I knocked lightly and hearing nothing tried the knob. *Locked.* I walked back to the young men.

"Excuse me?" I asked.

They looked up at me, startled. One was blond with a soft, uncertain face. The other had brown curly hair, his skin red and pockmarked.

"Maybe you can help me," I said. "Did either of you know a former resident who was here recently named Gabriela Esquivel?"

The blond kid looked hesitantly at the other boy. "No. But I just got here."

I turned to him. "What about you?"

He nodded slowly. "Yeah I heard about her."

"What did you hear?"

"Just that Esquivel's daughter was here."

"Did you ever get to meet her or see her?"

He shook his head. "She was Code Blue."

"What's Code Blue?"

"The acute care unit." They all lived in Ardsley."

"Excuse me," a male voice called out behind me. "Can I help you?"

I turned. A short heavy set man with a dense brown beard was in the hallway staring at me.

"Hopefully," I said. "I'm looking for my daughter, Kierstyn."

"Come with me." He held out his arm, beaconing me to step away from the boys with a rigidly pissed off smile. I nodded my thanks to them and followed the man around the corner.

"This floor is prohibited to everyone but residents and physicians. How did you get up here?"

I explained as confoundedly as I could that I'd been on a campus tour with Plath and had lost my daughter. Looking me over with great distaste, though seemingly buying into my stupidity, he stepped toward the office, fumbling with his keys. He shoved the door open, switching on the lights.

"Please wait with me in here until I speak with Kierstyn."

"Actually, I know the way. I'll just head back myself."

"Sir, get in here now or I'll call security."

He's was William McKeon, M.D., according to his plaque. I entered, sitting on his leather couch as he, with increasing frustration, dialed phone numbers from a contact sheet taped to the wall beside his medical diploma from the University of

Virginia. After leaving two messages for Plath, he finally reached her, and swiftly his face, or what was left of it; his beard had overrun his cheeks, flushed with outrage.

"He's in front of me," he said, staring me down. "He approached two one-seventeens. They were free writing in their journals. Yes. *Yes*." He paused listening. "No problem."

He hung up the phone and sat back in his swivel chair, interlacing his fingers.

"Am I dismissed?" I asked.

"You're not going anywhere."

He continued to frown at me until there was a knock on the door.

In walked two large uniformed security guards.

"Shawn McCarthy," said one of the guards, "you'll have to come with us."

The fact that he announced my first and last name did not bode well.

Sixteen

They escorted me across the grounds to the security center, a square cinder block bunker away from the other buildings, near the edge of the woods. We entered the dim lit building where a pocked marked guard sat behind a glass window. I was led down a hall past rooms buzzing with monitors, each displaying jumpy black and white shots of corridors and classrooms.

"Is this the part where I get water-boarded?" I asked.

They ignored me, stopping beside the open doorway at the end of the hall.

Elizabeth was there, hunched over a metal folding chair at the center of a green-carpeted room with plywood walls. Thankfully she appeared to be out of character, biting her nails, staring wide-eyed up at Plath. Now so red faced she seemed to be radiating thermo-nuclear heat. Beside her, perched on the edge of a desk, was a small man with salt-and-pepper hair. He was wearing ironed khaki slacks and a bright honey-boy-yellow sweater.

"Shawn," he said, rising and extending his hand. "I'm William Allen Piper. President of Mission Hills. Very nice to meet you."

"Pleasure is all mine."

He smiled. He was one of those beaming men not merely clean-cut but spic-and-span, with the unblemished complexion you usually find on babies or nuns.

"So Elizabeth," he said, looking down at her and smiling, she actually smiled back, "whose pseudonym today I understand has been Kierstyn. She's been explaining that you guys aren't potential guests, as you claimed, but here to dig illegally for information on a former patient."

"That's right," I said. "Gabriela Esquivel. She escaped from your care and died ten days later. We're trying to determine if there was misconduct on the part of the hospital, which directly resulted in her death."

"There was no misconduct here at the hospital."

"You admit, then, Gabriela Esquivel was a patient here."

"Absolutely not." It was taking considerable effort for Piper to keep that broad grin on his face. "But I will say there have been no breaches in patient safety."

"If Gabriela was authorized to leave with an unidentified male in the middle of the night, why did the hospital file a missing-persons report the next day?"

He looked incensed but didn't answer.

"She was Code blue. The acute-care unit. They're not authorized to leave without a guardian. So someone at the hospital must have been asleep at the wheel."

He took a deep breath. "Mr. McCarthy, this not a public hospital. You're subject to trespass laws. I could have you both taken straight to jail."

"Actually, you can't." I unzipped my pocket, handing him a folded brochure. "You'll find that in addition to our concerns about Gabriela Esquivel, Elizabeth and I are here to distribute religious materials about our faith, as we are legally allowed to do under Marsh versus Alabama, the Supreme Court ruling that upholds, under constitutional Amendments One and Fourteen, state trespass statutes do not apply to those involved in the distribution of religious literature, even if it takes place on private grounds."

Piper surveyed my old Jehovah's Witness brochure.

"Cute. Very cute," he said. "You'll be escorted off the premises. I'll file a complaint with the police. If I hear you or your friends, including the person sleeping in your car, try to enter our grounds again, you'll be arrested."

He crumpled up my brochure and shot like Mikael Jordon right in the garbage can. I was about to thank him for his time when suddenly something caught my eye in the window behind him. It was a woman racing through the woods along the dirt path encircling a deserted construction site. Her red hair flashing in the sun. She wore pink nurse's scrubs with a white cardigan and appeared to be in a serious hurry, heading straight for our building.

Piper glanced over his shoulder out the window but then turned back, nonchalant.

"Do I make myself clear, Mr. McCarthy?"

"Crystal."

Piper nodded at the guards, and they escorted us outside.

We filed down the sidewalk around the construction site. Elizabeth for all her bad-girl scowling certainly looked docile now. As we walked between the two guards she shot me countless freaked out, what are we going to do now, looks. All of which suggested she was relishing this clash with authority. If you could even call these security officers, *authority*. They looked more like La-Z-Boys.

Further down the line, I spotted that nurse again. The Same one, the red head I had seen out the window. She'd just stepped out of nowhere and was rushing toward us, staring emphatically at the ground. But when we were just a few yards away, she jerked her head up, staring agitatedly right at me.

I stopped in surprise.

She only picked up her pace, veering onto another route leading around the back of a dormitory.

"Mr. McCarthy. Let's go."

When we reached the parking lot, news of a security breach appeared to have traveled around the hospital, because we had a handful of onlookers, nurses, administrators, shrinks, all standing on the front steps of Membly Hall watching our procession.

"A going away party?" I said. "You shouldn't have."

"Kindly make your way to your vehicle," the guard ordered.

I unlocked the car, and the two of us climbed in. Cooper was still passed out in the back. He looked like he hadn't moved.

"Why don't you make sure he has a pulse?" I muttered, start the car.

I eased out of the parking space, edging the car toward the exit. There were people still milling around Membly hall, watching us, but no sign anywhere of that red-haired nurse. *Had she wanted me to follow her?* She had to have known with the security guards there it was impossible.

"He has a pulse," chirped Elizabeth happily turning back. "That was a close call, huh?"

"Close? No, I'd call that a bull's-eye."

I made a right, speeding up to merge onto the main road that would take us out of here, a dizzying four-minute ride through the woods.

"You mad or something?" Elizabeth asked.

"Yes. I'm mad."

"How come?"

"Your little Houdini act back there? You didn't just draw attention to us. You drew a red circle around us and added a *They* are *here* arrow. Next time bring a mariachi band."

She huffed, rolling her eye's fiddling with the radio.

"Right now Piper's on the phone with Gabriela's family, Esquivel himself, probably. Telling him a detective named McCarthy accompanied by a white cracker from North Dakota were there snooping around asking about his daughter. Any hope I had at keeping this investigation quiet is gone now, thanks to you, *Bernstein.* Which brings me to your acting. I don't know if anyone's told you this, but you may want to change your career choice."

I checked the rearview mirror. A black Lincoln had just appeared behind us. In the front seats, the unmistakable boxy forms of the security officer's.

"And now we've got Mumbo and Jumbo tailing us," I muttered.

Elizabeth excitedly whipped around in the seat to look. The girl was about as stealthy as a concrete mixer going down a dirt road.

We sped down the hill, rounding a grove of trees. I counted about fifteen seconds between the time our car rounded a curve and the black sedan appeared behind us. I pressed harder on the gas, racing around another bend.

"I'll bet I got more on Gabriela than you," Elizabeth announced.

"Oh yeah, I'm sure? Well, what have you got?"

She only shrugged, smiling.

"Diddly-squat, nada, nothing. Exactly what I thought."

We sped around another turn, the3 road straightening and intersecting with a dirt road. I paused at the stop sign and was just starting off take off when Elizabeth screamed.

That woman the redheaded nurse came crashing out of the steep wooded bank just to our right, running directly in front of our car.

I slammed on the brakes. She fell forward against the hood, red hair spilling everywhere. For a horrified moment I thought she was hurt, but then she lifted her head racing around the car to my side, leaning in an inch from the window.

She stared in at me, her brown eyes bloodshot, and her freckled face desperate.

"Stanley Dewitt," she shouted. "Find him. He'll tell you what you want to know."

"What?"

"Stanley Dewitt"

She lurched back in front of the car and ran to the shoulder, scrambling up the steep embankment just as the black sedan appeared behind us.

Frantically she was crawling on her hands and knees up the hill, sliding in the leaves and dirt. She reached the summit and wrapped her cardigan around herself, pausing to stare down at our car.

The guards had pulled up behind us and beeped.

They hadn't seen her.

I took my foot off the brake still intoxicated with shock, we continued down the drive. Through the rear view mirror, just before we rounded the next bend, I saw the woman still standing on the hill, a gust of wind whipping that red hair into her face, blotting it out.

Seventeen

A stone-faced guard opened the electronic gate and we accelerated through, the Lincoln behind us doing a U-turn, heading back to the hospital.

"Oh my god," said Elizabeth, pressing her hand to her chest.

"What name did she say?" I asked.

"Stanley Dewitt?"

"Write it down. D-E-W-I-T-T."

Elizabeth hurriedly dug through her purse for a pen and bit off the cap scribbling the name on the top of her hand.

"I saw her before when we were in the security center," she said. "And then she passed us on our way out. She wanted to talk to us."

"Apparently so."

"What's going on?" mumbled a hoarse voice from the backseat. Cooper was up, yawning. He rubbed his eyes, staring out at the rural landscape speeding by, unsurprised. I handed Elizabeth my phone. "Google *Stanley Dewitt* and *Chicago*. Tell me what you get."

It took a few minutes, due to the patchy cell service.

"There's nothing much," she said. "Just one of those genealogy websites. A man named Stanley Dewitt lived in Norway in 1836. He had a son named Erik."

"Nothing else?"

"The name turns up on a site called Whale Hunters."

We accelerated past another road sign. Tall Trail 3.

"Where the hell are we?" asked Cooper, rolling down the window. Elizabeth turned around, eagerly filling him in on what had transpired in the last four hours.

"We were about to be arrested," she went on. "But Shawn was a total rock star. He whipped out this brochure that read across the front, The Greatest Man Who Ever Lived." Questions about Jesus Christ for Young People." She giggled. "It was classic."

As she explained what had just happened with the nurse, I spotted a Qwik Mart approaching on the left. I turned in.

"Go inside," I said to Elizabeth, pulling up beside a gas tank and shutting off the engine. "Ask if we can borrow a phone book. And pick up some snacks." I gave her twenty bucks and started to fill the tank.

Cooper emerged from the backseat, stretching.

"What did you find out about Gabriela?" He asked hoarsely.

"Not much. Apparently, she was a Code Blue patient, which is the cost critical lever of care."

"But you didn't find out what was wrong with her."

"No."

He seemed about to ask me something else, but instead turned, strolling across the parking lot, pulling out his cigarettes.

It was after five o'clock. The sun had loosened its grip on the world, letting the shadows get sloppy, the light, thawed and soft. Directly across the street, a white farmhouse stood in the middle of a wild lawn, the grass, strewn with garbage. On a drooping telephone wire sat two black birds, too tiny and fat to be crows. The Qwik Mart door dinged behind me and I turned to see an old man in a green flannel shirt, heading to a pickup, a brown hound dog in the bed. The man climbed behind the wheel and they pulled out, swerving to make a right extremely close to Cooper.

Cooper didn't react. He was staring in a sort of melancholic trance out at the middle of the road, oblivious to the cars speeding by.

Maybe that was the point, he was contemplating stepping in front of one.

He looked like he was at a river's edge, about to throw himself in. It was a melodramatic thought, probably residual paranoia from the appearance of that nurse. I could still see her anxious, freckled face staring at me, her lips chapped, the window clouding over from her breath, erasing her mouth.

Cooper took a drag of his cigarette, brushing his hair from his eyes, and looked up at the sky, squinting at those birds on the telephone wires. More had appeared out of nowhere. Like tiny black notes on an otherwise empty piece of sheet music.

Another ding from the doorbell and Elizabeth appeared, her arms laden with coffee cups, jelly beans, Fritos, and a phone book. She spread it all out on the hood.

"I got Cooper some coffee," she said, holding up the jumbo sized cup and squinting worriedly across the parking lot at him. "He looks like he needs caffeine."

"He looks like he needs a hug."

She set the cups down, flipping through the phone book.

"It's here," she whispered in amazement.

I walked over, staring down at the page that read;

Stanley Dewitt-150 Spring Water Dr.- 815-424-6309.

Eighteen

"It's the next driveway," said Elizabeth, squinting at the phone book.

The drive to Benton Hollow Road took an hour and a half, through snaking backcountry roads. It was already getting dark, the sky fading to a bruising blue. There were no street signs along Sleepy Hollow Road, no house numbers, no streetlights, not even and lines. Just my car's faded headlights, which didn't so much push back the advancing dark as nervously rummage through it. To our left was a wall of solid shrubbery, barbed and impenetrable; to our right, vast black land stretched out, rumpled pastures and faded farmhouses, a single porch light punctuating the night.

"This is it," whispered Elizabeth excitedly, pointing at an opening in the shrubs.

There stood a metal mailbox, but no number and no name.

I made the turn. It was a narrow gravel drive straight uphill through dense foliage, an opening barely wide enough for a man, much less a car. The incline grew steeper, so I had to floor it, the entire car shimmying uncontrollably like the space shuttle trying to break the sound barrier. Skinny branches slapped the windshield.

After a minute or so we inched over the crest of the hill. Instantly I hit the brakes.

Far in front of us, across a scruffy lawn, wedged back between tall trees, sat a tiny wooden house so decrepit it rendered us mute.

The white paint was cracked and flaking. Shingles were missing from the roof, exposing a raw black hole, windows along the attic floor punched out and charred black. Strewn across the yard among the dead leaves and a large fallen tree, a child's wagon, and a tricycle. Further off along the edge of the yard where it was dark, an old plastic swimming pool all crinkled up like a popped blister.

There was something so inherently menacing about the house as it loomed, poised in the shadows, I automatically turned off the engine and headlights. A lone lit bulb by the front door illuminated a porch swing half on the ground and an old air conditioner. Another light was on in one of the back rooms. A tiny rectangular window lit with mint-green curtains pulled tightly closed.

It occurred to me that we had no contact whatsoever with this man, Stanley Dewitt. We were following the tip of a total stranger, a Mission Hills nurse, who recalling the way she'd thrown herself in front of the car hadn't appeared exactly rational. Parked beside the house in front of a wooden shed sat a pick-up truck and an old gray Chevy, a plastic tarp hanging out of the trunk.

"Now what?" Elizabeth said nervously, biting her nails.

"Let's go over the plan," I said.

"Plan?" Cooper said with a laugh, leaning forward between us. "It's simple. We talk to Stanley Dewitt and find out what he knows. Let's go."

Before I could say a word he jumped out, slammed the door, and was making his way across the yard. His dark wool coat caught the wind, flapping out behind him, and with his deliberate walk, head down as he headed straight for the house. It reminded me of some comic book character about to unleash brutal vengeance on the inhabitants.

"He's certainly come back from the dead," I said. "What'd you put in his coffee?"

Elizabeth didn't answer, she was too busy fumbling for the door handle like an eager kid sister who didn't want to be left behind. Within seconds she scrambled right up next to him.

I held back, waiting. Let them be the scouts, the lowly grunts who go in first to check for land mines before the officers arrive.

Their footsteps were the only sounds, soft crunches through the leaves and grass strewn with sticks. Maybe it was the peeling paint, giving the house scaly skin, but the place looked reptilian and alive, poised beyond the trees, waiting, that lone lit window like an eye watching us.

Somewhere far away, a dog barked.

Cooper was already on the front porch, so I climbed out of the car. He stepped around the air conditioner, pulled open the screen, and knocked on the door. No answer.

He knocked again, waiting, a gust of wind sending a cluster of fallen leaves across the lawn.

Still no answer.

He knocked again, waiting, a blast of wind sending a cluster of leaves across the lawn.

Still no answer. He let the screen bang closed and jumped down into the flower bed spiked with dead stalks and a tangled green garden hose. Shading his eyes, he peered in one of the windows.

"Someone's home," he whispered. "There's a TV on in the living room."

"What are they watching?" I asked quietly, striding over the giant fallen tree trunk and then, past Elizabeth, inspecting something lying face down in the grass. It was an old teddy bear.

"Why?' whispered Cooper, glancing back at me.

"We'll be able to tell what kind of people we are dealing with. If it's hardcore Japanese anime, we've got problems. But if it's a Barbara Walters special, well…"

"It looks like The Price is Right."

"That's even worse."

Cooper stepped gingerly back up onto the porch, this time noticing a dirt-encrusted doorbell. He pressed it twice.

Suddenly there was the jumble of locks turning, a chain sliding, and the front door gaped open, revealing a middle-aged blond woman behind the screen. She was wearing baggy gray sweats, a stained blue T-shirt, her peroxide-streaked hair in a ponytail.

"Good evening, ma'am," cooper said. "Sorry to disturb you during the dinner hour. But we're looking for Stanley Dewitt."

She surveyed him suspiciously, then craned her neck to look at me.

"What do you all want with Stanley?"

"Just to chat," Cooper said with a laid back shrug. "It should only take a few minutes. We're from Mission Hills."

"He's not home," she said rudely.

"Any idea when he'll be back?"

She squinted at him. "You all get off our property or I'm callin' the cops."

She was about to slam the door when a man materialized beside her.

"What's the matter?"

He had a soft, mild-mannered voice, in startling contrast to the woman, who appeared to be his wife. He was considerably shorter than she, and looked younger, in her early thirties, stocky, wearing faded red and white plaid flannel button down tucked neatly into his jeans, the sleeves rolled up. He had brown hair in a crew cut and broad, reddish features that were neither unattractive nor handsome, only ordinary. It was the face of a million other men.

"Are you Stanley Dewitt?" asked Cooper.

"What's this about?"

"Mission Hills."

"You all got some nerve showin' up here," said the woman.

"Sarah. It's all right."

"No more communication. You heard the lawyer."

"It's fine."

"It's no fine."

"Let me handle it." He said it with a sharp, raised voice, and suddenly somewhere in a back room, a baby started to cry. The woman darted out of the doorway, though not before glaring at him.

"Get rid of them," she said.

Stanley stepped forward with an apologetic smile. As the baby wailed, he said nothing and the way he stood there, stranded behind the screen door, reminded me of my last visit to the Bronx Zoo with Kim. Kim had made a point about an ape staring dolefully out at us from behind the glass, such profound sadness.

"You guys are from Mission Hills?' he asked uncertainly.

"Not exactly," said Cooper.

"Then what's this really about?"

Cooper stared at him for a second before answering. "Gabriela."

It was surprising the knowing way he said her name. In fact, it was ingenious, implying Gabriela was some incredible experience both of them shared, so memorable, any mention of the last name was unnecessary. She was a magnificent hidden island, a secret house on a rocky cliff, visited by only a privileged few. If it was a deliberate trap on Cooper's part, it worked, because instantly a look of recognition appeared on the man's face.

Glancing furtively over his shoulder, where his wife had just disappeared to tend to the baby, he turned back to us. With a guilty smile, he extended his index finger and, careful not to make any noise, pushed it against the screen quietly opening the door.

"Out here," he whispered.

Nineteen

We followed Stanley Dewitt to the edge of the yard, where there were dense trees, close to the children's pool filled with black water and leaves. The baby was still crying, though away from the house now the wind acted as a salve on the sound, easing it, folding it into the cold shivers of the night.

"How'd you find me?" Stanley asked rather resignedly, hooking his thumbs in his jean pockets.

"Through a nurse at Mission Hills," Cooper said.

"Which one?"

"She didn't tell us her name," I said. "But she was young. Red hair and freckles."

He nodded. "Christina Granger."

"Is she a friend of yours?'

"Not really. But I heard she made a stink to administration when I got the ax."

"You used to work at Mission Hills?"

He nodded again.

"Doing what?'

"Security."

"For how long?"

"Bout seven years? Before that, I did security at the Woodlawn Condos. I had been all set for a promotion at Mission Hills. Thought I was going to be the assistant head." Smiling sadly, he looked up, staring past me at his own house. He looked bewildered as if he didn't recognize it or couldn't remember how he'd come to live there.

"Who are you guys?" he asked.

"Private investigators," said Elizabeth with evident excitement.

Somewhere Mickey Spillane just rolled over in his grave. I was certain Dewitt would call us out on this obvious lie, but he nodded.

"Who hired you?" he asked solemnly. Her family?"

He meant Gabriela.

"We work for ourselves," I said.

"Everything you tell us can be off the record," added Elizabeth.

He seemed to accept this, staring into the dark water of the pool. I realized then, he didn't care whom we were. Some people were so burdened by a secret they'd give it away free to any willing stranger.

"Sarah doesn't know a thing about it," he said. "She thinks I was fired because Mission Hills found out we're Jehovah Witnesses."

"It'll stay that way," said Cooper. "How did you know Gabriela?"

But Stanley was no longer paying attention. Something had caught his attention in the kiddie pool. Frowning, he stepped a few feet away, picked up a fallen tree branch, and extended it into the water, traveling through the decaying leaves and mud.

A bulky object was actually floating there, bobbing along the bottom. He snagged it on the branch, pulling it towards him.

I thought it was a drowned animal, perhaps a squirrel or possum. So did Elizabeth. She was staring at me with a stricken, horrified face as Stanley reached right in and pulled the thing out, dripping.

It was a plastic doll.

It was missing an eye, half bald, oozing blackened water, yet still smiling manically with puffy cheeks, what remained of its yellow hair matted with leaves. It was wearing a white ruffled dress, blotchy black, some kind of fungus growing like rancid heads of cauliflower out of the neck. It's fat little arms reached out at nothing.

"Last few weeks I turned the house upside down looking for this thing," mumbled Stanley, shaking his head. "My daughter cried for three days straight when it went missing. Couldn't find it. Was like the doll got fed up and walked right out of the house. I had to sit her down and tell her it was gone and went to heaven. The whole time it was just out here."

He chuckled at the irony of it, a tight, frustrated sound.

"How did Gabriela break out of Mission Hills?" Cooper asked, glancing at me, sensing that something was off with Stanley.

"With me," Stanley said while staring down at the doll. Cooper nodded waiting for him to go on. But he didn't.

"How?" Cooper prompted in a low voice.

Stanley glanced at us again, as if remembering we were there, smiling sadly. "It's funny how the night that changes your life forever starts out like all the others."

He let his arm fall to his side, holding the doll by its leg, its dress hanging over its head, exposing frilly underwear and dripping black water on the grass.

"I was covering for a buddy of mine," he said. "Working the graveyard shift. Seven PM to seven AM. Sarah hated when I worked all-nighters, but I liked to watch the monitors at night. It's laidback work. I'm the only one in the back rooms of the center. Patients are asleep, the corridors so still and quiet, it's like you're the last man alive." He cleared his throat. "I guess it was about three in the morning. I wasn't paying much attention. I had some magazines. Wasn't supposed to, but I had done it a million times before. Nothing ever happened. There's nothing going on except the nurses checking the Code Reds."

"And what are the Code Reds?" I asked.

"Patients on suicide watch."

"What about Code Blue?" Cooper inquired.

"Those are the patients that are kept separate because they can hurt themselves and others. I'd been watching all night. It was like every other night. Quiet. I'm flipping through a magazine when I glance up and something catches my eye on the monitor. One of those music rooms in Straffen.

There's somebody in there. As soon as I see that, it switches to another. Video feeds are on a ten-second rotation. You can break the sequence to take a longer look at any live feed. I break, go back to that music room. I see there's a girl in there. She's a patient because she's wearing the authorized white pajamas. She's at the piano. Camera's high in the corner of the ceiling, so I'm looking down on her, a little over her shoulder. All I see is her thin arms moving very fast, her hair in a braid. Never seen her before. I work day shifts mostly, and you get to know the patients. I channel in audio, turn up the speaker."

He fell silent, running a hand over the top of his head as if he couldn't believe what he was about to say.

"What?" I asked.

"It freaked me out."?"

"Why?"

"It was like a recording. Most times we got patients pounding out 'Heart and Soul.' My first thought, she had to be one of those polter...uh..."

"Poltergeist," Elizabeth interjected eagerly.

"Yeah. Something not real. She was playing violent-like, head down, hands moving' so fast. My second thought was I had to be losing it. Seeing something strange. I'm set to sound the alarm, but something makes me hesitate. She stops playing that music and starts another, and before I know it even though I got my finger on the switch to call a breach, a whole half-hour goes by, then another. When she stops playing she's quiet for a long time. Then real slow, she lifts her head. I could just see the side of her face, but it was like..."

He fell silent and shuddered uncomfortably.

"Like what?" Cooper asked.

"She knew I was there. Watching."

"What do you mean?" I asked

He gazed at me, earnestly. "She saw me."

"Did she see the camera in the ceiling?"

"It was more than that. She stood right up, and when she got to the door she turned and smiled right at me." He paused, incredulous, as he remembered. She was like nothing I'd ever seen before. A long-haired angel. She slipped right out. And I tracked her. Watched her move down the hall and outside. She moved so fast I was having trouble keeping up with her on all the different video feeds. I followed her down the paths all the way back to Membly Hall. I figured she would get caught for sure, but she enters, and for some strange reason there's no officer at the front desk."

He shook his head in disbelief. "She hurries in and up the back stairs so fast it's like her feet never touch the ground. She goes all the way up to the third floor, races inside her room. I can't believe that, either. She's Code Blue, which means she's got around the clock nurse detail. I keep watching. Twenty minutes later, I see the security officer and a nurse running to the third floor. They come upstairs from the basement, smiling, and something tells me they weren't down there doing laundry. They got a little thing going. Somehow the girl knew about it." He paused, wiping his nose. "First thing I do is wipe the tapes. They never check them anyway. Not unless there is a problem reported. But I erase them just in case. The next morning, I put in a request for extra night shifts."

"Why'd you do that?" asked Cooper with faint accusation.

"I had to see her again." He shrugged bashfully. "She went there to play piano every night. And I watched. The music. . ." He seemed unable to find the right words. "It's what you'll hear in heaven if you're lucky enough to get there. The whole time she ignored me until the very end when she looked at me." Stanley smiled to himself as he surveyed the ground. "I had to find out who she was. I wasn't to look into the files of patients. But I didn't care. I had to know."

What'd you find out?" I asked.

"She had a fear of darkness. This thing called *nycta* something or other."

"Nyctophobia?" blurted Elizabeth.

"That's it. I looked it up. People who got it go crazy in the dark. They start shaking, convulsing. Think they're dying or drowning. Sometimes they pass out. Or sometimes kill themselves.

"Hold on a minute," I interrupted. Wasn't Gabriela in the dark when you watched her on the camera?"

Stanley shook his head. "Mission Hills is very bright at night. The sidewalks and central grounds are kept lit up for security purposes. Interior building lights are on energy-saving motion detectors." They would light up around her as she came and went. Some of them are on a delay. I began to notice she'd wait for a light to go in before she'd continue. When she was outside she'd keep to the bright side of every path. Like she couldn't step on a shadow of she'd melt or something. She was really careful about it."

I frowned, trying to imagine such a manner of moving, skipping from one patch of light to another. I recalled the trip through the hanging gardens up to the roof of the warehouse in Chinatown. Had been enough weak light to step through all the way up? And yet around Lake Shore Drive, where she'd flickered in and out of the lamp lights along the jogging route in that red coat, it was mostly pitch black.

"The other thing I found out," Stanley went on, "was the doctor treating her sent out a hospital-wide memo barring her from playing the piano. Said it brought on manic episodes. The date the order went out was the first night I saw Gabriela. So, it was like she had to play. Like nothing could stop her from it."

He fell silent for a moment.

"On the eighth night I watched, on her way out of the music room, I noticed she removed something from her pocket and stopped for a second right over the top of the piano. It happened fast. I wasn't sure what I'd seen. I rewound the tape and saw she'd stuck something in there. I waited until the end of my shift and headed over to Membly hall, up to the music room on the second floor. When I walked in, the smell of her, the feel of her was still there. A perfume and like a warmth, I guess. I went over to the piano, checked under the lid. Inside, tucked in the strings, was a folded up piece of paper. I took it but waited until I was safe in my car to read it."

He paused, noticeably uneasy.

"What did it say?" I asked.

A screen door slammed.

What're you still doing here?"

Sarah was out on the front porch, cradling the baby against her chest, shading her eyes in the glare of the light. Stepping after her was another child, a little girl of about four, wearing a white nightgown covered with what appeared to be cherries.

"Why aren't they gone yet?"

"Everything is fine!" Stanley shouted. He turned to us, whispering, "Drive down the driveway and wait for me there, okay?"

He hurried back across the lawn.

"Oh my God, I told you to get rid of them!"

"They're from Human Resources. Doing some kind of survey. Hey, look what I found."

"But we're not supposed to... what is that?"

"Baby. I rescued her from the pool."

"Are you insane?"

The little girl screamed, no doubt upon taking a look at that doll.

Elizabeth and Cooper were already making their way across the grass. I headed after them, and when we climbed back into my car the Dewitt's had returned inside, though their shouting could still be heard above the wind.

Twenty

"It's obvious Stanley fell in love with Gabriela," Elizabeth said.

"Can you blame him?" I asked. "He is married to the Bride of Frankenstein.,"

"He's a freak, is what he is," said Cooper.

I turned around to him in the back seat. "You remember Gabriela having nyctophobia during your camping days?"

Glaring at me, he exhaled cigarette smoke out the window. "No way."

We were in my car, sitting at the end of Dewitt's driveway. We'd been waiting for him to reappear for forty-five minutes. Apart from my headlights illuminating the unmarked road, which twisted around the dense shrubs in front of us, it was pitch black out here, totally deserted.

The wind had picked up. It whistled insistently against the car, making the branches nervously tap the windshield.

"He's probably not coming back," I muttered. "Sarah put the guy's muzzle back on and returned him to his cage in the basement."

"She wasn't that bad," said Elizabeth, shooting me a look.

"Let me bear witness as the only person in this car who's been to the dark side of marriage and survived. She's bad. She makes my ex-wife look like Little Bo Peep."

"He's coming back," said Cooper. "He has to."

"Why?"

"He's dying to talk about her." He ground out a cigarette on the window, flicking the butt outside.

Suddenly, Elizabeth gasped as the man himself stepped onto the headlights. I didn't know how we managed not to hear his footsteps. There was something odd in the way he stood there in his faded flannel shirt, blinking at us uneasily, his head held down at a strange, shy angle. None of us said a word. Something was wrong.

But again, Cooper and Elizabeth were unlocking the doors, scrambling out. I held back to observe the guy for a few seconds longer. In spite of his sudden appearance, the ghostly pallor, he looked uncomfortable, wounded might be a better word.

I climbed out, leaving the headlights on.

"I only got five minutes," Dewitt said nervously. "Otherwise, Sarah will get out the shotgun."

It had to be a joke, yet he said it with unnerving seriousness.

Blinking, he held out a folded piece of paper.

Cooper immediately snatched it, shooting him a suspicious look as he opened it in the beam of light. When he finished reading it, his face giving away nothing, he handed it to Elizabeth, who read it with wide eyes and passed it to me.

It was torn from a legal pad.

I'm here against my will. There's nothing wrong with me. I'll do anything to get out of here.

HELP!

"It took three weeks to plan," Dewitt said. "I'd use all prerecorded tapes. They'd play, not the live feed. The time code would be wrong, but no one cared or even checked. I went down into storage, where they keep all the patient's personal belongings until they check out, and I got hers from her locker and kept it for her in a box in my house. All she had was a red-and-black coat. Real fancy."

"That was it?" I asked, noting the odd, somewhat fastidious way he'd said it. I couldn't help but imagine him silently slipping out of his bed in the middle of the night while Sarah slept, creeping down into his own dark basement to open up the cardboard box, staring in at her red coat, *that coat*.

"Yeah," he said. "She didn't have anything else."

"No cellphone? No handbag? No wallet?"

He shook his head. "No."

"What about clothing?"

"Nothing. You see her father is somewhat infamous. He is or was a big time drug lord. Well known with the authorities, he's been on the news and in the papers many times.

I figured she'd want some nice clothes, so I left her a note asking for her sizes. Then I took a day off, went up to Gurnee, and bought her some things, gray sweat pants, I knew the sweat pants would fit and a nice blue T-shirt.

Gabriela was wearing the Same clothing when she died.

"Once I had the details worked out," he went on, "I went to the music room and left Gabriela a note tucked between the piano strings right where she did. It said when she was ready, she should play "You Are My Sunshine.' That'd be the green light. It meant that the next night I would come for her at three A.M. when her nurse and the guard were getting it on in the boiler room."

"Why that particular song?" I asked.

"She'd played it before." He smiled. "It reminded me of her. That night, Sarah ended up in the hospital and was put on bed rest. I had to transfer back to days. I didn't see Gabriela for a week. I was worried I missed her playing it. But the first night I was back on the night shift she darted into that music room and I knew we were on."

As he stared at us, I could see flecks of light brightening in his eyes. He became newly animated remembering it.

"The next night around 2:00 AM, I got the prerecorded tapes going. Then I told the officer on duty who sits out front, Sarah's having another pregnancy scare and I had to head home. I go straight to Membly Hall, thinking I'm going to have to slip up to Gabriela's room to get her if she isn't already out in front waiting for me. My heart's beating like crazy. I'm nervous, like a teenager on his first date. I realized that it was the first time I'm seeing her in the flesh. She just took my hand, and together we walked across the lawn, simple as that." He grinned sheepishly. "It was like she was leading me. Like she'd planned it. I opened my trunk, she climbed in, and we drove out of there."

"But wasn't it dark inside the trunk?" Elizabeth asked. "If Gabriela had nyctophobia she wouldn't have climbed in there."

Stanley smiled proudly. "I took care of that. I had two flashlights in there so she wouldn't be afraid."

"Did they stop you at the gatehouse?" I asked.

"You bet. But I said my wife is having another emergency and he let through. As soon as we were out of sight I pulled over so Gabriela could get out of the trunk. I brought her back here so she could shower and change. I also had to put my daughter to bed. Sarah was still in the hospital, so our neighbor was watching the baby. I asked Gabriela where she wanted to go and she said the train station because she had to get to the city."

"Did she say why?" I asked

"I think she was meeting someone."

"Who?" Cooper asked.

"Don't know. She was shy. Didn't talk much. Just looked at me. She liked my little girl, Ashlynn, though. Read her a bedtime story while I was on the phone with Sarah at the hospital."

"Where was Gabriela going in the city?" I asked.

"War Allen, something like that."

"She told you this?"

He looked down cowering a little. "No. She'd asked to get on the internet while she was here. When she went to the bathroom I checked the browser to see what she looked for online. It was a website for a Hotel on Wacker Drive."

"The Warwick Allerton, on Michigan Avenue?" I suggested.

Stanley nodded. "That sounds about right. When she was dressed she put on the red coat and she looked like the prettiest thing I'd ever seen. I drove her to the station. We got there about four in the morning. I gave her some cash, then left her in the car while I went in and bought two tickets to LaSalle Street station."

"Two tickets?" I asked.

He nodded embarrassed.

"You hoped to go with her."

He stared down at the ground. "Seems crazy now. But I'm romantic. I thought we'd go together. She kept smiling at me. But when I got back to my car with the tickets, she was gone. I saw a train pulled in. I ran up to the platform, but the doors had already shut. I moved down the train, searching for her in every car, feeling sick about it until I found her. She was sitting right by the window. I knocked. And slowly, she turned to me and stared at me. I'll never forget the look she gave me, not for the rest of my life."

He said nothing for a moment, his shoulders hunched.

She didn't know me."

He exhaled, his breathing unsteady.

"You were fired shortly after?" I asked quietly.

He nodded. "Soon as Gabriela was found missing it was all traced back to me."

"When did you find out she'd died?"

He blinked. "Head of the hospital called me in. He said nothing would happen to me in terms of the law if I signed a confidentiality paper saying I'd acted alone and never, ever talk about it."

"Stanley!"

It was Sarah again. Her voice startled all of us, not just by its shrillness but its close proximity. We couldn't see her, but heavy footsteps were coming nearer, heading down the dark gravel drive.

"Stanley! Are those people still here?"

"You'd better go," Stanley hissed at us.

Before I could stop him, he's snatched the paper from my hand, racing back up the driveway.

I took off after him.

"That paper, we'd like to keep it" I shouted.

But he sprinted with remarkable speed. I could barely keep up. Sarah abruptly appeared at the top of the hill.

I froze. She wasn't brandishing a shotgun, but even more terrifyingly, she was brandishing children. The half-naked baby was still in her arms, and the girl wearing the nightgown was holding her mother's hand, sucking her thumb.

"They're going right now," Stanley said. "They needed directions to the highway." He put his arm around her, saying something inaudible as he moved them back toward the house. Shoving the paper into his back pocket.

Damn. I'd wanted to keep that paper, compare the handwriting with that on the envelope mailed to Cooper.

They moved out of sight, though I could hear them walking through the leaves, Sarah angrily saying something, the baby whimpering.

I turned, making my way back down the drive, Cooper and Elizabeth in the beam of the headlights waiting for me.

I turned around, startled, and saw I wasn't alone.

That little girl in the nightgown was following me. Her face in the darkness looked hard, her eyes hollowed black. She was barefoot. The white of her nightgown glowed purple; the cherries looked like chain links and barbed wire. She was also, I realized, holding that rotten doll Stanley had exhumed from the swimming pool, Baby, clutching it in the crook of her arm.

My first reaction was revulsion, followed by the urge to run like hell.

She suddenly extended her arm. A chill ran up my spine. Her hand was in a tight fist, her stare pointed. She was holding something black and shiny in her fingers. I couldn't see quite exactly what it was, but it looked like a tiny doll. Before I could react, she spun around and scampered back up the drive, banishing over the top in a streak of white.

I stood there, staring at the empty space on the hill, sensing, for some reason, she'd reappear. She didn't. And yet it was oddly silent. There was no trace of Sarah's harsh voice, no baby whimper, no footsteps, no screen door swinging open followed by a slam, nothing but the wind blowing through the scrubs. Even that lonely hound in the distance went quiet.

I turned, jogging the rest of the way to the car.

"What was that?" asked Cooper.

"His little girl followed me."

I unlocked the car, climbed in, and within minutes we were speeding back down Benton Hollow Road. They didn't say so, but I suspected all three of us were relieved to be rapidly putting some serious distance between ourselves and the Dewitts.

Twenty-One

"That's what happens when you marry the wrong woman," I said. "A wife sets the ambiance of a man's life. He can very easily get stuck listening to Michael Bolton, drowning in a loop of I want to slash my throat music from tin-sounding speakers for the rest of his life, if he doesn't keep his wits about him. You can't blame the guy for wanting to run."

"He was a total loser," said Cooper from the back seat.

"That's another way to put it." We were hashing over Stanley Dewitt and all we'd learned about Gabriela at Mission Hills, now driving down the Dan Ryan Expressway, minutes from the city.

That was the wonderful thing about Chicago; you might spend a few nervous hours in rural landscapes with nurses who threw themselves in front of your car and strange families, but the closer you came to the Loop and took a look at that breathtaking skyline, then took a look at the guy who just cut you off in a pimped out old Chevy bumpin to some gangsta rap, you realized that all was right with the world.

"Gabriela was playing him." Cooper went on, without looking up from his phone, buzzing with texts. "She knew someone was watching her on the camera. So, she decided, whoever he was, he was her best bet for breaking out of there."

"What about this fear of the dark?" I asked, glancing back at Elizabeth. "Which reminds me. How did you know that term, *nyctophobia?*"

She'd dismantled her hair from those long braids while absentmindedly staring out the window, untangling the ends.

"Willow Falls," she said. "A gentleman on the second floor named Ed. He used to go down this phobia list and boast about all the ones he'd had. He'd never had *nyctophobia*. He had *automaton phobia*."

"What's that?"

"Fear of ventriloquist dummies. Anything with a waxy face. He went to see Avatar and had to be hospitalized."

"He should definitely stay away from the Broadway and Clark after midnight."

"It's bullshit," said Cooper, pushing his hair out of his eyes. "Gabriela wasn't scared of the dark. She probably just put that act on for the doctors, so they'd leave her alone."

"What about the way she looked at Stanley from the train?" Asked Elizabeth. "Maybe she didn't know him. Maybe she had amnesia or short-term memory loss."

"No," Cooper shouted. "He'd served his purpose and she was done with him. That was it."

"One other thing kind of worried me," said Elizabeth.

"Only one other thing?" I asked.

"Stanley said Gabriela read his daughter a bedtime story."

"So?"

"You don't let a stranger you just broke out of a mental hospital spend time with your child. Do you?"

"He's not winning any awards for the father of the year. What about that Bride of Chucky he fished out of the kiddie pool? *Baby.* Not to mention that little *tyke* that tailed me down the drive. When she grows up she's going to need a long sojourn at Mission Hills."

Elizabeth tilted her head. "You don't think Stanley hurt Gabriela, do you? When he took her to the house to change clothes. There was something about the way he described it, just gave me the creeps."

"He didn't lay a hand on her." Interjected Cooper.

"How do you know?" Asked Elizabeth, turning around to him.

"Because if he had, he'd be severely maimed right now."

I glanced at him in the rearview mirror, startled by the tone of his voice. He stared out the window, his face gilded by lights of the passing cars. One thing I'd gathered in the past few hours was that his knowledge of Gabriela was significantly more intense than the casual acquaintance of years ago he'd claimed. He knew her better than he let on, or else he once observed her carefully, maybe even from a distance like Stanley. I was tempted to press him on it, try and get him to admit he hadn't been forthcoming, but decided against it, for the time being. He'd probably only scowl and become defense, and that wouldn't get me anywhere.

I checked the clock on the dashboard: 9:44 p.m.

"So where am I dropping you two off? I asked.

Elizabeth turned to me. "We're not done yet. We still have to go to that hotel, The Warwick Allerton, see if somebody noticed Gabriela. He said she was going there. So we should go there."

"Sounds like a plan," said Cooper, meeting my eyes in the rear view mirror.

"It's a long shot," I said. "But sure. Let's check it out."

Twenty-Two

Like most Chicagoans, I went out of my way to avoid the established, expensive hotels in the loop. Just like we all avoid a very rich, very large, and mercifully very distant great aunt who has three rolls of fat under her chin, wears taffeta and has a personality so bossy you only needed to not see her but hear about her once to have your fill of her for the next twenty years.

If you decided to venture inside, however, through the Art Deco revolving doors past the businessmen from Milwaukee and the Unitarian Church group, then took a breather before beating your way through the crowd up the carpeted stairs past the line into Starbucks and the woman rolling her carry-on suitcase over your shoes, instantly you were assaulted by the bloated luxury of the place. There were vaulted ceilings and palm trees, also gilt clocks and marble. If there was a wedding reception, and there usually was the ballroom throbbed like a gymnasium on prom night.

Cooper and Elizabeth followed me through the lobby, ducking around an extended family wearing matching Blackhawk jerseys, toward a discreet wooden doorway. It was labeled with a tiny gold plaque, *Warwick Allerton,* so tactful its obvious aim was to go unseen.

I strode down the corridor to the elevator banks, stepping inside, Elizabeth and Cooper right behind me.

"You really know your way around here," said Elizabeth, as I pressed *H.* I did, unfortunately.

The Warwick Allerton was only a distraction from the section of the hotel here the important people stayed, the more exclusive Warwick Allerton, hotel of choice to presidents, the Duke and Duchess of Windsor, Saudi princes, and various high-rolling Wall Street businessmen when the rendezvoused with their mistresses, which, sadly was something along the lines of how I know the place.

I wasn't proud of it, and I sure as hell didn't recommend it, but there was a six-month hellish stretch when, shortly after my divorce, I saddled myself with an affair with a married woman.

I met her here, at the Warwick Allerton, a total of sixteen times, though this was only after she'd sent me feedback emails in the bitter tone of an unsatisfied boss informing me the first hotel I'd chosen for our trysts, one I could actually afford, the generic Jackson hotel on Halsted, known by its clientele as *The Flop House*. But it was too close to her office, the rooms didn't get enough light, the sheets stank, and the man at reception gave her a funny look after he asked if she needed help with luggage and she announced she didn't have any, she'd be there for only forty-five minutes.

The elevator doors opened, spilling us into the Warwick lobby, small, elegant, and totally empty.

The three of us walked around the corner to the reception area, where a young man of Middle Eastern descent stood alone behind the front desk. He was tall, with a narrow build, dark eyes. His nametag read Hashem.

I briefly introduced myself. "And we were hoping you might help," I went on. "We're searching for information on a missing woman. We think she came here sometime in the last month."

He looked intrigued. He also made no sign of needing to go fetch his manager.

"Would you mind taking a look at her picture?" I asked.

"Certainly not." He replied with a bright voice, gilded with a British accent. I removed Gabriela's picture that was attached to her missing person's report. I folded the report over so only her picture was visible and handed it to him.

"When was she here?" He asked.

"A few weeks ago."

He handed it back. "I'm sorry, I've never seen her before. Of course, it's hard to tell from that picture. If you like I can make a photocopy and post it in the back, in case any other staff met her or remember her."

"Nothing was reported out of the ordinary?"

"No."

"Do you videotape the lobby?"

"We do. But that would require a warrant. I assume you've contacted the police?"

I nodded, and Hashem smiled with five-star sorrow at being unable to help me further. Now it was time for us to be on our way.

"She would have been wearing this," said Elizabeth, Pulling Gabriela's coat out and setting it on the leather desk pad.

He liked down at it and was about to shake his head when something about the coat stopped him.

"You recognize it?" I said.

He looked puzzled. "No. It's just, a member of housekeeping reported an incident. It was a while back. But I think it did have something to do with a person in a red coat. The reason I remember is the matter came up again this morning when the Same housekeeper refused to clean one of the rooms. It caused a disruption because we are at capacity."

Hashem looked up noticing all three of us were leaning with great intensity over the desk. He took a step back, alarmed.

"Why don't you leave a number and my supervisor can speak with you?"

"We don't have time for a supervisor," said Cooper, jostling Elizabeth as he moved closer to Hashem. "With a missing person, every minute counts. We need to talk to the housekeeper. I know it'd mean you bending a few rules, but…" He smiled. "We'd appreciate it."

I proposed back in the car to allege that Gabriela was missing, not dead; the missing, I have found, prompted a greater sense of haste and willingness to help. This strategy seemed to work. Or perhaps it was just Cooper's looks cranked up and turned blazingly onto the man, because Hashem stared at Cooper, a few seconds too long. And I saw the brief yet brazen look of male desire flash on his face. The man picked up the phone and tucking the receiver under his chin, swiftly dialed a number.

Sarah Hashem at the front desk. Lupe Orasco. That episode she reported a few weeks back. Wasn't there something about a red coat? What…*oh*." He fell silent, listening. "Is she still on duty tonight?" He listened. "Sixteen. All right, thank you." He hung up. "Come with me," he said with a curt smile at Cooper

Twenty-Three

We followed Hashem into the elevator, where he inserted a white keycard into the slot and pressed 16.

We rose in silence, though quite a few times Hashem glanced swiftly at Cooper, who was staring down at his Nike sneakers. I wasn't sure what was going on in this silent communication, but it was working; the doors opened, and Hashem exited briskly, making his way down the beige colored hallway. A housekeeping cart was parked at the end. We made our way toward the cart, Elizabeth hanging back to inspect the few black-and –white photographs hanging on the wall, pictures of movie stars and dignitaries. Reaching the cart, Hashem knocked sharply on the door marked 16, slightly ajar.

"Miss Orasco?" Hashem pushed the door open. We filed in after him into the suite's empty sitting room. Mauve couches, Mauve and blue plush carpeting, an extravagant mural painted on the wall, featuring old Roman columns and a gold skinned goddess.

Hashem stepped through a kitchen alcove, the three of us following. It led into a bedroom where a petit silver hair woman was in the process of making up the bed. She was Hispanic, wearing a battleship gray housekeeping dress. She didn't react because she was listening to music, a neon blue iPod strapped to her arm.

She moved around the bed, tucking the sheet, and spotted us. She cried out a short, loud shrill like a scream, clamping her hand over her mouth, eyes bulging with fear.

You'd thought we just filed in wearing hooded robes and wielding scythes.

Hashem spoke Spanish, an apology for scaring her, and the woman, Lupe Orasco, I gathered, removed the earbuds from her ears, and in a raspy voice muttered something back.

"How's your Spanish?" Hashem asked.

"Spotty at best," I replied.

Elizabeth and Cooper both shook their heads.

"I'll do my best to translate." He turned officially back to her and fired off some immaculate Spanish. She listened with keen interest. Occasionally her gaze left Hashem to study us. At one point, it must have been when Hashem explained why we were there, she nodded slowly and repeated, *Si, Si, Si.*

Then she stepped around the bed toward us slowly, nervously, as if we were three bulls that might charge her. Seeing the woman only a few feet away now, her face girlish face with the fat cheeks of a toddler, yet her caramel skin was so finely wrinkled, it looked like a brown paper bag once tightly wadded in a hand.

"Show her the picture," Hashem said.

I removed it from my pocket. She took a moment to carefully unfold her glasses, setting them on the end of her nose, before taking it. She said something in Spanish. "She recognizes her," Hashem said. Elizabeth, who'd been fumbling with Gabriela's coat, holding it up by the shoulders. The woman took one look at it and froze, whispering.

"She thinks she's seen it before," Hashem said.

"She *thinks*?" I said. "She looks pretty convinced."

He smiled uncomfortably, turning back to the woman and asking her a question. She responded, her voice serious and low, eyeing Gabriela's coat. She talked for several minutes, so dramatically at times I wondered if she were a popular telenovela actress on Telemundo. I tried to dig through the stream of Spanish to find a word I might recognize, and abruptly, I did.

Chaqueta del diablo. The Devil's coat.

"So?" I asked Hashem when she stopped talking and he made no effort to translate. He looked irritated. "It happened weeks ago," he said. "Five o'clock in the morning. She was on the thirtieth floor, starting her morning rounds."

Lupe was watching him closely. He smiled back thinly.

"She'd just unlocked a room when she noticed something at the end of the hall. A red form. She couldn't see what it was. She'd left her glasses at home. It was just a ball of red.

"She thought it was a suitcase."

He cleared his throat. "Forty-five minutes later, after she finished cleaning the room, she came out again. It was still there, this blurry red thing. Yet, it moved. Lupe wheeled her cart down the hallway and as she came nearer she realized it was a young woman. The Same one in your picture. The girl was crouched down on the floor, her back against the wall. She was wearing *that Coat.*"

"What else?" asked Cooper.

"That's it, I'm afraid."

"Did Lupe speak to her?" I asked.

"No. She tried shaking her, but the girl was in a drug-induced stupor. Lupe ran away to alert security. When they returned, the girl was gone. She hasn't been seen since."

"Can she remember the exact date this happened?" I asked. "It would be helpful."

"She can't remember. It was a few weeks ago."

Lupe smiled sadly at me, and then, seemingly recalling something new, added something, extending her right arm in front of her. It was a strange gesture, her hand forming a sort of claw as if grabbing an invisible doorknob in the air. She then pointed at her left eye, nervously shaking her head.

"What's she saying now?" I asked.

"It was all very disturbing for her," he said. "It's unusual to come across a vagrant passed out in our halls. Now, if you don't mind, we should let Lupe return to work.

His five-star customer service had deteriorated into about a one-star. Not even Cooper was enough to sway him from ending the interview. In fact, Hashem seemed to deliberately avoid looking at him.

"Downstairs you said that she wouldn't even clean her assigned floor today, I said. "What's that about?"

"The girl frightened her. We need to return to the lobby. Any further questions you should address directly with the police." He added a few words to Lupe and walked to the door.

Elizabeth grabbed the coat and put it back in the bag, as Lupe nervously watched, Cooper and I moving behind her though when Hashem continued on, I covertly darted back into the bedroom.

I waited a few private moments with Lupe, maybe get her to add something I could translate later. I found her in the bathroom, standing in front of the mirror by the beige marble sink. Spotting me in the reflection, her gaze jumped off her own face onto mine. It was such a panicked look, it shocked me. She opened her mouth to say something.

"Sir," snapped Hashem behind me. "You need to leave now, or I'm calling security."

"I was just expressing thanks to Lupe for her time."

With a last glance back at her, Hashem had scared her, because she was already crouching over the tub, her back to me. I followed him out.

Twenty-Four

"The police can be of further help," said Hashem. He took us outside of the hotel entrance, "Best of luck," he shouted as he watched us walk to the corner of Michigan Avenue and Ohio street, then said something to the doorman, undoubtedly orders to alert security in case we come back. He then went back inside.

It was after eleven now, a cold, clear night. Taxis and town cars were roaring down Michigan Avenue, though the wide sidewalks stretching north were quiet and deserted, the grand buildings nothing more than hollow cathedrals standing in the sky. In spite of the traffic, it felt lonely. As we passed over the Chicago River looking down on to lower Wacker Drive, dark immobile forms of men in bulky overcoats sleeping on cardboard boxes, looking like whales, caught unaware by a tide that suddenly receded, leaving them stranded in the alleyway.

"What do you think?" asked Elizabeth.

"Lupe? She was a bit dramatic but had to be telling the truth. Her version of it."

"Why would Gabriela be on the thirtieth floor, just sleeping there?"

"Maybe she was staying with someone. Didn't have a key. Or she was meeting someone."

"Did you see the way she stared at the coat?" It was as if she thought it was going to lunge at her or something."

"She called it the devil's coat. Hashem forgot to mention that."

"He forgot to mention a lot of things," Cooper interjected. He'd been squinting back at the entrance to the hotel, but now he stepped over to us, fumbling in his coat pockets. "He made half that shit up."

"So you speak Spanish," I said.

"I lived in Caracas for a while when I was very young. Then wandered Argentina and Peru for about a year." He said this while tapping out a cigarette, turning his back to the wind to light it.

"Like Che Guevara in Motorcycle Diaries?" asked Elizabeth.

"Not really it was hell. But I'm glad it was good for something. Like knowing when someone's trying to con me."

I was surprised, to say the least. I hadn't expected the kid to be bilingual. But then I remembered a detail he'd let slip when he was telling me about himself back at his apartment. *I'd been traveling with my mom in South America for this missionary cult shit she was into. I ran away.*

"I wanted to see if he was on the up and up. And he wasn't." Cooper exhaled a long stream of smoke. "I didn't like that guy."

"He certainly liked you."

He didn't respond, seemingly bored by the comment.

"So what did she really say?" I asked.

"It was kind of hard to follow because she was speaking in a Guatemalan dialect. And she was bat-shit crazy."

"What makes you think she was crazy?" asked Elizabeth.

"She believed in ghosts, spirits like they're all floating around us like pollen. She went on for like fifteen minutes about how she came from a long line of *curanderas*."

"What's that?" I asked.

"Some folksy medicine-woman bull crap. I've heard of them, actually. They cure bodies and souls. A one-stop shop for all your troubles."

"So, what did he lie about?"

"He was right about the housekeeper seeing Gabriela on the thirtieth floor. But the second he got to the part where she was wheeling the cart down the hall, he took all kinds of liberties. She actually called her *espiritu rojo*, a red spirit. She never thought it was a real person sitting there, but some kind of confused soul or something, trapped between life and death. The nearer she got, she felt something, like some change in the gravitational pull of the Earth.

When she crouched down in front in front of Gabriela she was *inconsciente*. Unconscious, but not from drugs. She called her *una mujer de las sombras*. A woman of shadows." He shrugged. "No clue what that meant. She touched her, and Gabriela was like ice, so she shook her by the shoulders and when she opened her eyes, she saw *la cara de la muerte* staring back at her. The face of death."

He fell silent, thinking it over. "She said Gabriela was marked," he added.

"In what way?"

"By the devil. I told you the woman was crazy. She said there was a second pupil in her left eye, and it was . . ." He tossed his cigarette to the ground. "She called it *huella del mal.*" He ground the butt out with his hell, and when he glanced up again, he seemed surprised by our expectant faces, waiting for him to translate.

"It means evil's footprint," he said.

"That's why she pointed at her left eye," I said.

Elizabeth was speechless, looking at Cooper then down at the bag she was holding that contained the coat.

"Then what happened?" uttered Elizabeth.

"Yeah what happened next. Don't tell me that Stigmata appeared on Lupe's palms."

"She was scared, ran to the basement, got her things, and went to church for the rest of the day. She didn't call security, which was why Hashem was angry. She did not follow housekeeper protocol. Hashem thought Gabriela was homeless, and he told Lupe he was going to speak to her boss about her handling of the situation. So after all that, I think we got the woman in trouble."

It made perfect sense. When I saw Lupe staring at herself in the bathroom mirror with that odd look on her face, it had to be because she feared she might lose her job. Cooper now looked rather dismissive of the entire episode. He'd taken his phone from his pocket, scrolling through messages.

"I gotta book," he said. "Catch you guys later."

Even though cars were racing down Michigan Avenue, surging toward us, he jogged right out in front of them, oblivious, or else he didn't care if he got hit. A taxi braked and honked, but he ignored it, jumping right up onto the median, waiting for the cars to pass on the other side, and then he dashed across the street, Elizabeth and I looking on in silence.

Twenty-Five

Elizabeth didn't want me to drive her home, but I insisted, so she told me to drop her off at Cermak and Canal. As I drove neither of us spoke. It's been a long day, to say the least. I hadn't eaten anything but jelly beans and Doritos. Cooper's chain-smoking had left me with a dull headache. Everything we'd uncovered about Gabriela, the escape from Mission Hills, the housekeeper's apparent sighting, was too fresh to make sense of at this hour. My immediate plan was to go home, pour myself a drink, go to bed, and see how it all looked in the morning.

I made the left onto Eighteenth, pulling in front of a Korean deli.

"Thanks for the ride," said Elizabeth, grabbing the strap of her purse and opening the door.

"Did you miss work tonight?" I asked.

"Oh, no. My last day was yesterday. The normal girl came back from maternity leave. Tomorrow I'm starting as a waitress at The Castle."

"Where's your apartment?"

"Down there." Smiling, she heaved her bag onto her shoulder, slammed the door, and took off down the sidewalk.

I stayed where I was. After she'd gone about ten yards, she glanced back, clearly checking to see if I was still there, and continued on. I pulled on to Eighteenth Street, stopping at the red light. Elizabeth was still walking down the block but slowed to glance over her shoulder again. She must have seen me because she immediately skipped up the front steps of the nearest cruddy building.

The light turned green. I floored it to get in the right-hand lane, but a bus cut me off. As usual, the bus driver drove like he owned to the road. It's common in the city for buses to bully all the other drivers on the road. I braked waiting for him to pass, then drive around the block. I pulled over behind a delivery truck and spotted Elizabeth immediately.

She was sitting back along the ledge of the front steps of the apartment building she'd seemingly disappeared into, checking her cell.

After a minute, she stood, peeked around the columns to take a reticent look at the spot where I'd just dropped her off. Seeing I was gone she skipped down the steps, heading back to the corner.

I pulled over to wait. A minute later, she emerged carrying those two giant Nordstroms bags of hers along with a funny looking, large black wire bird cylindrical birdcage.

She crossed the street with all this luggage, heading south down Eighteenth. I waited for the light to turn green and made a right, watching her jostle down the sidewalk in front of me. I slowed, so as not to pass her, a taxi behind me laying on the horn, and saw her stop at the door of a tiny, narrow storefront. Pay-O-Matic, read the sign. She pressed a button to enter, waiting and vanished inside.

I pulled over and parked in front of a fire hydrant. I locked the car and headed over to the Pay-O-Matic. The glass façade was covered in signs: Western Union, Checks Cashed, 24-hour Financial Services. The shop was tiny, with brown carpeting and a couple of folding chairs, boxes piled on the floor along the back wall was a teller window with bulletproof glass.

I rang the buzzer. After about a minute, the back door opened and a large bald man stuck his head out. He was wearing a black short-sleeved shirt and had a face like a piece of pastrami. He pressed a switch on the wall and the entrance clicked open.

As I stepped inside, he moved into the teller window, wiping his hands on the front of his shirt, which I now saw had branches of red bamboo sewn all over it. As a rule, I didn't trust men who wore embroidery.

"I'm looking for a young woman with large shopping bags and a birdcage."

He glared at me with a confused face. "Who?"

"Elizabeth Michener, young, blond."

"It's just me here." He had a thick Chicago accent.

"Then I must be Keith Richards tripping on some serious drugs because I just saw her walk in."

"You mean Anna?"

"Exactly."

He stared at me, worried. "You a cop?"

"What do you think?"."
"I don't want no trouble."

"Neither do I Where is she?"

"The back room."

"What's she doing there?"

He shrugged. "She lays two double-sawbucks on me I let her crash here."

"Forty bucks, are you kidding me."

"Hey," he said defensively. "I've got a family."

"Where's the back room?"

Without waiting for his answer, I stepped to the only door and opened it.

It led down a cluttered dark hallway.

"I don't want trouble." He was right next to me, his heavy cologne nearly knocking me over.

"I did it as a favor."

"To whom?"

"Her, she showed up here like a little-lost sheep, crying like a baby. I helped her out."

I stepped past him into the hall. Muffled rap music throbbed on the floor above, giving the building a heartbeat.

"*Bernstein!*" I shouted. There was no answer.

"It's Woodward. I need to talk to you."

At the end of the hall were two closed doors. I moved toward them, around a janitor bucket filled with dirty water, passing a kitchenette, a half-eaten peanut butter and jelly sandwich sitting on top of a folding table.

"I know you're in here somewhere," I yelled out.

The first door was slightly ajar. I pushed it open with my foot. It was a bathroom, a crumpled issue of a tabloid magazine and a ribbon of toilet paper stuck to the floor. I moved passed it knocking on the second door. I tried the handle, it was locked.

"Elizabeth."

"Leave me alone," she said sheepishly. It sounded as if she were mere inches away. Like the walls were made of cardboard.

"How about opening the door so we can talk?"

"I'd like you to leave, please."

"But I want to offer you a job."

She didn't answer.

I'm looking for a research assistant. Room and board included. You'd have to share the bedroom every few weekends with my daughter and her stuffed animal collection. But otherwise, it's yours." I glance over my shoulder. The large guy from out front was eavesdropping, his fat frame plugging the hallway.

"What's the starting salary?" she asked from behind the door.

"What?"

"Of the job. The salary."

"Three hundred a week. Cash."

"Really?"

Really. But you'll handle your own money laundering."

"What kind of health benefits?"

"Zero."

"I won't sleep with you or anything."

She noted this as if announcing a food allergy.

"No problem."

"Everything okay back here?' the guy from the front was now behind me. The door suddenly opened, and Elizabeth was there, still wearing that ice-skating shirt with her long hair down around her shoulders, her face solemn.

"Yeah Mike," she said. "I'm leaving."

"With a cop?"

"He's not a cop at the moment. Just a private investigator.

That seemed to really disturb the guy, not that I blamed him. Elizabeth smiled at me, suddenly shy, and turned back inside, leaving the door open.

It was a walk-in closet, a bare light bulb shining overhead. Spread out in the corner were a sheet and an old army blanket. Along the wall were a bag of hot dog buns, a folded pile of T-shirts, a bag of bird food, plastic forks and knives, and little mountains of salt and pepper packets, probably swiped from McDonald's. Besides the birdcage, there didn't seem to be too much in there. A blue and gold yearbook that read, Minot High School, Home of the Bison. A makeshift bed with two tiny colored photos taped to the wall, close to the spot where she'd put her head. One of a bearded man, the other a woman.

It had to be a dead mother and convict father.

I took a step inside to get a better look. Elizabeth brushed me aside and shoved a stack of shirts into a plastic bag. "If I take this job, you're not allowed to ask me tons of questions. I'm none of your business." She grabbed a pair of silver sequenced hot pants tossed in a ball in the corner and put them in the bag. "This is just till we find out about Gabriela. After that, I'm doing my own thing."

"Fine." I bent down to check out the birdcage. Inside a live red and blue macaw, the thing was so still and quiet it looked like it was stuffed. Funny looking toys were spread over the newspaper in front of him, colored ball, feathers, and bells, a full-length mirror but the bird just ignored them all.

"Who's this guy?" I asked.

"Octavius," she said. "He's an heirloom." She stepped over, smiling. "He's been inherited so many times no one remembers where he came from. Grandma Bernice got him from her next-door neighbor Gladys, when she died. And he was bequeathed to her from Jerry, when he died. And Jerry inherited him from a man named Bartholomew who died from diabetes. Who he belonged to before Bartholomew, God only knows."

"He's not a bird, he's the grim reaper."

"Some people think he has magical powers, also he is a hundred years old. Want to hold him?"

"No, I don't think so."

But she was already unlatching the door. The bird hopped over and resigned himself into her hand. She took mine and smacked the bird into it.

He was not long for this world. He looked like he had cataracts. He was also trembling faintly like an electric toothbrush. I'd have assumed he was catatonic if he didn't jolt his head to one side, staring up at me with a cloudy yellow eye that looked like an old cats-eye marble.

Elizabeth put her face up to his. "Promise not to tell anyone?" She asked quietly, glancing at me.

"About what?"

"This. I don't want anyone to feel sorry for me." Her eyes moved off the bird and onto me, her gaze steady.

"I promise."

She smiled, satisfied, and resumed packing, collecting every one of those salt and pepper packets, sprinkling them onto the Nordstroms bags.

"I actually have condiments at my place," I said.

She nodded, like I just reminded her to bring her pajamas, and set about pulling down black stockings and bras hung to dry along the top shelves, crazy leopard and zebra prints tacked down by Black & Decker drills and paint cans.

The girl was like one of those picture books with pages that unfold and unfold all the way our, which caused children's eyes to grow wide. I suspected she'd never stop unfolding.

After Elizabeth packed up her clothes, she set about peeling the odd couple's pictures off the wall. She grabbed the Minot yearbook, opened it carefully tucked the two pictures inside, and then returned Octavius to his cage.

I realized, staring at the army-green blob he'd left, the bird had taken a shit on my hand.

"It's best if you let that dry first, then flick it off," said Elizabeth, glancing at it. "I'm ready. Oh, almost forgot." She rummaged through her purse and handed me a colored photograph. I assumed she was showing me a member of her family, but then realized with surprise it was a photo of Gabriela.

Her grey-blue eyes, set deep in dark circles, seemed to fasten onto me.

"When I disappeared from the tour at Mission Hills and got in trouble? That's what I went back to get. I saw it on those bulletin boards by the dining hall under 'Weekly Picnic.' It's her, isn't it?"

La cara de ls muerte, the hotel maid had said. The face of death.

I understood what she meant.

Twenty-Six

The next morning, I was woken at 4:44 A.M. by creaks outside my bedroom door. Footsteps retreated down the hall, followed by the sound of water pipes shrieking, more creeping back into Kim's room, and then downstairs, where plates and glasses clattered in the kitchen as if someone had begun preparations for a dinner party of twenty-five.

In spite of my wondering if, when I woke up, I'd find my apartment stripped of all valuables. I fell back to sleep, only to be woken again by a soft knock on the door.

"Yeah," I mumbled.

"Oh, did I wake you?"

The door creaked open, followed by silence. I cracked open an eye. The clock read 7:35. Elizabeth was peering at me through the doorway.

"I was wondering when we were going to get started."

"I'll be right down."

"Cool."

I groggily pulled on a bathrobe and shuffled downstairs, where I found Elizabeth curled up on my living-room couch wearing a Marcel Marceau striped black and white shirt and black leggings. She was picking at the shell of a hard-boiled egg and scribbling in a leather-bound journal, which I realized, after a dazed moment of recognition, *was mine.* I'd found it in a bookbinding shop in Old-Town. A ninety-year-old man named Aristotle had crafted it by hand. It took him at least a year to finish it. It was the last of a kind because he is now dead and his shop replaced by a Ripley's Believe It or Not. I had been saving it for the day when I had something profound to write inside it.

"You like to sleep in, huh?" she stopped writing to smile up at me. I saw she'd scribbled, *Gabriela Esquivel Case Notes* at the top of the page, followed by indecipherable handwriting.

"It's not even eight o'clock in the morning. That's early."

"If Grandma Bernice were here she'd say the whole day was wasted. I made you breakfast."

With slight trepidation, I stepped into the kitchen. There was a plate of scrambled eggs and toast on the counter. She'd *cleaned*, too. Not a dirty dish or glass in the sink. I stepped out of the kitchen. "don't cook for me. Or clean. This is a black-and-white working relationship."

"It's just eggs."

"I'm forty-three. I don't need help feeding myself."

"*Not yet.* Although there was this man, Mr. Johnson, at Willow Falls. He showed sign of dementia around thirty-four.

"I think I heard that story before. He died alone?"

"Everybody dies alone."

There was little to add to that. Whenever the girl brought up Willow Falls it was like spraying Raid on the conversation, an instant killer.

I poured myself a cup of coffee and motioned for Elizabeth to follow me.

"Inside this box is everything I know about Esquivel," I told her as we stepped into my office. "Organize it by published date and subject matter. Keep all information on his suspected involvement in crimes together. Pull out anything you think might help us understand Gabriela's personality, music, hobbies, her background, any mention of family life or El Esplanade."

I noticed a thin set of papers sticking out, a photo of El Esplanade I'd found from an old time magazine article, printed and clipped to the front. I yanked it free, handing it to Elizabeth.

You can start reading this. When I began investigating Esquivel ten years ago, I went up to Nathaniel Falls, wandered around, asked locals what they'd heard about El Esplanade. Everything I found is in there. I left Elizabeth, sitting Indian-style studiously tucking her hair behind her ears as she settled in to read.

Twenty-Seven

"The number's been disconnected," said Elizabeth, hanging up. She'd tried calling the old man, Donald "Doc" Larsen, Using the number in my notes. Old Doc Larsen is Esquivel's closest neighbor. An Eighty-year-old retired naval doctor/ apple orchard owner. He claims to have never met Esquivel due to his health problems he rarely ventures into town. But he did have a few interesting incidents to tell me about his infamous neighbor. I documented them in my notes:

"We used to have street signs all around here, but the mailman told me they removed them," he said.

"Who do you mean by them?" I asked.

"The people up there."

"You mean the Esquivel family?"

He nodded.

"Why would they remove the road signs?" I asked.

"They don't want people up there. They like to keep to themselves. That's what I heard around town. I used to see all kinds of fancy cars driving in and out from midnight till all hours of the morning. Especially in the eighties and nineties. Limos. A Rolls-Royce once. A few times I heard helicopters landing in there. Music, too. But starting in early 2000, it's been quiet. Never see a soul go in or out."

According to Larsen, in early December 2004, he received a series of UPS deliveries that were intended for El Esplanade but, by mistake were delivered to him. The first was a massive box stamped with a label reading Century Scientific.

Century Scientific, Inc., based in Pittsville Pennsylvania, is a company that specializes in medical equipment. They have beds, wheelchairs, stretchers, and other therapeutic devices to private hospitals.

"My daughter sometimes sends me packages, so I signed for it," Larsen told me. "After the boy drove off, I realized it wasn't mine."

"Who was it addressed to?" I asked.

"Someone named Phil Lavallie.

And the address said 2224 County Line Road, Route 12. I'm 2242 County Line Road, Route 12. I didn't open it. But it was heavy. I could barely lift it. By the shape of the box, I'd guess it was some kind of a chair."

Larsen called and within the hour the package was picked up. A week later another delivery by a different driver for Mr. Phil Lavallie. "The return address said something or other 'Pharmaceuticals,'," Larsen said. "I told the boy he made a mistake, he apologized and said he was new on the job. And that was really about it. For about a month or two, although, once a week in the afternoon, I'd see the truck drive by and turn in there, bringing them God knows what. I'd wait a few minutes and then I'd hear the real shrill scream of the iron electronic gate opening to let the truck drive up. A piercing hinge so shrill that it hurt to listen to. You'd think it'd shattered the TV." He shook his head. "My guess is someone was sick up there. Or injured."

Larsen told me he'd probably have forgotten about the mix-up had he not noticed something else strange about a week after the accidental deliveries. He drove his garbage to the dumpster at the end of the road and noticed a strange odor emitting from the other plastic bags.

"Never smelled anything like it. It was foul. Like burned plastic." Larsen said only he and the Esquivel's used the disposal site. The week after this observation, he noticed no other trash bags had appeared, and to this day, he's the lone user of the bin.

"Now they set fire to all their garbage," he said. "You can smell it when it's hot at night. Burning. And sometimes when the wind's blowing southwest I can even see the smoke."

"Have you ever seen this Mr. Phil Lavallie?" I asked.

"No, but I looked the name up online. It seems Mr. Lavallie is quite the gangster. He used to be a big shot up there in St. Paul, Minnesota. Was in charge of all the sports gambling and eventually had got connected to the drug trade with Esquivel."

"What do the other neighbors say about Esquivel? The property?"

"No one talks about it. Don't know why. But they just don't. See, how it works around here is, everyone minds their own business.

He had nothing more to say.

On May 28, 2003, at 5:30 AM, sixty-two-year-old Diane Hartman was walking along deserted Old Plum Road in a little town just outside of Rockford, Illinois, a small resort area known as Poplar Grove, around seventy miles north of Chicago and forty-five minutes from Nathaniel Falls.

It was the end of a long night. Hartman worked at the front desk during the all-night "graveyard shift" at the forest view motel, a vacation resort south of town. Every morning, regardless of rain or snow, six days a week, Hartman hiked the two miles from the motel to Poplar Grove's main street to catch the Bluebird bus that took her twenty miles north to Janesville, Wi. where she lived with her husband and twelve-year-old grandson.

Old-Plum Road is a narrow two lane road that heads toward town at a steep incline. Its hairpin curves are notorious spots for car accidents, mostly local teenagers or tourists. Hartman told me she was two miles from town, walking on the left side of the street, facing oncoming traffic when a silver sports sedan careened past her in the right-hand lane.

"I thought it was a drunk driver because he was all over the road," she said. "He disappeared around the bend, there was silence, then came a crash, glass shattering, and a cracking noise. The horn was going off too." She hurried toward the accident, though her arthritic knees slowed her down. Less than a minute she saw what had happened. A driver miscalculating a turn and lost control of the car. Crashing into the guard rail, that prevented the car from going over a fifty-foot drop-off. The car was severely damaged and a blonde woman, about fifty years old, came crawling on her hands and knees up the dirt bank onto the street. She didn't seem to be badly hurt aside from minor cuts and scrapes on her arms and legs but noticeably shaken.

"She was crying and shaking all over. I asked if she had her phone on her but she said she'd left it at home. I've never had a cell phone. So I said I'd go straight into town and call an ambulance. I asked if there was anyone else with her, and she shook her head no."

Hartman continued down the road, but not before she stopped at the road's edge and looked inside the car again.

"This time, I noticed there was someone lying in the back seat," she said. "A large man all in black, unconscious, covered in bandages. They were all over his arms and face. They looked bloody.

I didn't stop to argue. After all, she'd just been in an accident and probably didn't know what she was saying. I decided to get help as fast as I could."

Almost an hour elapsed between the time Hartman walked the two miles, dialed 911 from a gas station, and an ambulance and police arrived at the scene. They found a woman who identified herself as Joyce Moss. The car, a pearl white 1989 Lexus, was empty.

Moss admitted she'd been speeding, submitted to a breathalyzer test, and passed. Police saw no sign anyone else had been with her in the car. She was treated at the local hospital for minor cuts and scrapes, and a few hours later released.

The following day, the Chicago Sun-Times reported that Mrs. Esquivel had been in a car accident driving home from a friend's birthday party and suffered minor injuries. The fact that El Esplanade is an hour's drive from Poplar Grove, a lengthy drive to begin at 5:00 AM, failed to alert police, though it was unclear if this was Joyce's story or simply a case of lazy reporting.

Three weeks after the accident, Hartman re-contacted police. She'd read about Joyce and her famous husband in the intervening period, "I'm not up on the big time criminal news," she explained, when I asked her why, initially, the names meant nothing to her, and she now identified the person she'd seen in the car as Carlos Esquivel. The Poplar Grove Police Department took her statement and showed her the door. Hartman's claim was never investigated further.

Obviously, I had to pay my own visit to El Esplanade. I climbed into my car and make the left turn that was the entrance to the road that led to Esquivel's compound, according to my GPS. It started out scarred with tire ruts and mud, but about fifty feet in, it flattened out into a surprisingly meticulous gravel road. Some sort of caretaker must regularly attend the path; not a stray limb, scrub, or weed blemished the way. On more than a few tree trunks, lower, offending branches had been visibly sawed off.

On my right, I passed a small but conspicuous black and yellow sign: Private Property, No Trespassing. It was a warm, unthreatening, spring afternoon. Overhead, sunlight drooled through the trees; the day had an idle, drowsy feel.

I accelerated around the bend. I was knee deep in the woods now. The foliage overhead was so dense it felt like I was inside a wool sweater: heavy, knotty, only know and then a tiny gap where you could see through to the blue sky. The air suddenly reeked of gasoline, my car in need of a tune up, probably, but something else too: a burning smell.

I accelerated past a bizarre tree, three voluptuous trunks writhed around each other either in pleasure or in pain. They looked pornographic.

My God, I asked myself, could it be this easy? I only made it a few more yards. I rounded a curve, and directly in front of me loomed a gatehouse, seemingly deserted, overrun with ivy. There was no way around it either by foot or car. Beyond the wrought-iron gate, a massive military fence cut through the forest in either direction. I inched the car closer. Two surveillance camera's hung like wasp nests at opposite corners of the gate. I rolled down the window staring at one of them. I swore I saw the lens move, that little Cyclops eye focusing in on me.

"Any chance I could come up for a cup of coffee?" Even in my thoughts, my words sounded lame.

How did he live up there? Was the property his version of Michael Jackson's Neverland Ranch, Elvis's Graceland, Walt Disney's the Magic Kingdom? Were the rumors about his lunacy all simply part of the myth and he was no dark prince, but simply an old man who hoped to live the remainder of his life in peace and solitude?

Maybe the truth was something else entirely. Maybe Diane Hartman was right; maybe she had seen Esquivel in the backseat of the car in the early morning of May 28th, 2003. Maybe he was critically injured from an accident up at El Esplanade, maybe even killed. Diane Hartman, the lone witness, was manipulated to leave the scene. Joyce probably did have a cell phone and immediately called someone, a friend or one of Esquivel's children, James or Gabriela, and in the intervening minutes, they extracted Esquivel from the car and drove him away.

Is Esquivel alive at El Esplanade, bedridden, unconscious, confined to a wheelchair? It would explain the series of medical deliveries received by Donald Doc Larsen more than a year later. I climbed out of my car, took a photo of the gatehouse, then took off, speeding back down the driveway and out onto the road leaving Nathaniel Falls. Passing Larsen's place and the garbage disposal site. My foot didn't let up until I was back in the gridlock traffic on the Edens Expressway.

Whenever the truth about Esquivel comes to light, I will be there!

Twenty-Eight

"He's probably dead," I said. "When I questioned old Mr. Larsen he could barely get up off the couch. Elizabeth said nothing, squinting as she continued to read through my notes. I went out to get a bite at the Chop House on Kinzie. When I returned, Elizabeth was in the Same position I'd left her, still at work organizing my papers. I'd brought her a chop-on-a-stick dinner. But after saying, "Gosh, thanks, that looks tasty," she'd barely touched it. I was surprised by her focus. She'd been in my office for eleven hours straight, stopping only to give some to that prehistoric bird, Octavius, whose cage she'd set on the bookshelf by the window. "He loves to people watch," she said.

Although she'd said nothing specific, I gathered Elizabeth had been raised by a pack of free-spirited geriatrics at this place she kept peppering her conversations with; *Willow Falls*. She seemed preternaturally wired to the elderly's barn-animal hours and feeding times.

She'd asked what I was doing for dinner at 4:45 P.M., the legendary hour of senior feeding time.

"How soon after you went up to Nathaniel Falls did you receive the anonymous phone call?" Elizabeth asked me, setting aside the transcript.

"A few weeks later," I was on the leather couch typing up notes on my laptop, detailing our trip to Mission Hills and the Warwick Allerton hotel.

"It had to mean what you uncovered up there was real."

"You mean Diane Hartman and old Doc Larsen?"

She nodded. "It had to be why Cooper texted you. Cordova probably got a clear picture of your face from the security camera when you drove up to his gatehouse. And Mike looked like He was the trap."

"I tend to agree, but I've never had confirmation."

"Maybe Esquivel was hurt in the car that night. And someone was sick up at El Esplanade, which was they were receiving that medical equipment."

"I didn't mention this in my notes," I said, setting aside my laptop and sitting back against the cushions. "But I always thought Diane Hartman's ID of Esquivel a little suspect. Six months after I talked to her, she tried to sell her story to the Enquirer, but they wouldn't touch it.

 There could be no corroboration for anything she said, and they didn't want to get tied up in litigation. Now, if the National Enquirer won't touch you because you're dirty, that means you're really filthy." I downed the rest of my bourbon. "Anyway, Hartman could never explain how she knew what Esquivel looked like. Because no one really knows. The Rolling Stone pictures of him appear to be doctored. The infamous close-up of him on the set of The Legacy isn't believed to be him, but a stand-in."

"Maybe he's disfigured like the Phantom of the Opera," Elizabeth whispered excitedly. "Or maybe it was a dead body Diane Hartman saw in the car."

She didn't appear to hear me. "The Esquivels might have some kind of mystical powers. There was what the Warwick maid told us yesterday. Even Stanley Dewitt mentioned it, that somehow Gabriela knew he was watching her. For a second, he thought he was watching something already dead. In your notes, Larsen says that no one will talk about El Esplanade." She picked up Gabriela's CD case, starting at the cover. "Even the music she recorded. It means "The Devil in the Night."

"You'd be shocked how many people go for the paranormal when they can't explain something," I said, striding to the bookshelf to refill my glass. "They reach for it like reaching for the remote while watching television. I, on the other hand, and hence, you as my employee will be dealing with cold hard facts."

Even though I was firmly not a believer in the paranormal, there was still the nagging remembrance of how Gabriela had appeared the night at the reservoir. I hadn't told Elizabeth about it. As a matter of fact, I hadn't told anyone. The truth is, I no longer felt certain of what I'd seen. It's as if that night could be separated from all the others as a night without logic, a night of fantasy and strangeness, born of my own lonely delusions, a night that had no place in the real world.

Elizabeth had picked up the envelope containing Gabriela's police file, the one given to me by Katie Horrigan, and pulled out the stack of papers, loosening a page from the front and handing it to me.

It was one of the colored reproductions of photos taken of Gabriela's body when she'd arrived at the medical examiner's office. There were a variety of shots, clothed and unclothed, though Katie was correct in mentioning that any pictures that would be particularly graphic, full-frontal and rear shots, were missing from the file.

This shot featured the upper portion of Gabriela's face, her gray eyes blotched red and yellow, gazing out, dulled.

"Look at her left eye," Elizabeth said.

Within the iris, there was a black freckle.

"This? It's a concentrated pigmentation in the iris. It's very common."

"Not like that. It's across from the pupil, perfectly horizontal. It has to be what Lupe talked about. Her mark. I can't remember the Spanish word Cooper said, but it meant evil's footprint."

"*Huella del mal.*"

"And then there's what happened to Esquivel's first wife."

"Gwen Esquivel."

Elizabeth nodded.

"I already looked into it." I handed her back the photo and returned to the couch. "So did the police and about a hundred other reporters and gossip columnists at the time. She'd learned to swim only two months before. Her family, a bunch of snobs from Milan who loathed Esquivel, considered him a working class heathen, even they conceded it had to be a terrible accident. Gwen had a history of being impulsive. She announced to her son's nanny she was going down to the lake to practice her swimming. She was asked to wait but refused. It was an overcast day and it began to rain, which soon became a thunderstorm. She must have become disoriented. Couldn't tell the direction of the shoreline.

After a search, she was found tangled in the reeds at the bottom of the lake. Esquivel was conveniently out of the country at the time. Elizabeth didn't appear to be listening. She was biting her lip, vigorously digging through the papers again. She pulled an article from my old notes, printed from microfiche, handing it to me. I recognized it immediately. An article about the drowning death of Gwen Esquivel.

"Even if it was an accident," said Elizabeth, "for your first wife and your daughter to die by accident, that's not a good track record in terms of karma. But what really stood out was what her friend said."

"That she was melancholy."

She nodded. "Gwen might have committed suicide. If Gabriela did, too, what does that say about Esquivel?"

"He's toxic. On the other hand, for a mother to commit suicide, orphaning her infant child, goes against the primal impulses of motherhood."

"It had to be from being around him." Elizabeth leaned forward, staring dubiously down at the stacks of papers. "I read your other notes, but you didn't get too far in terms of anyone talking about him."

"Thanks for the memo." She nibbled on her thumbnail, sighing. "We need a new direction."

"I did have something promising. But I haven't been able to crack it."

"What?"

"The Blackboards. The invisible Esquivel network. A community for the hardcore world of his criminal empire.

"What's the Blackboards?"

"The hidden internet. You download a plug-in for Firefox to access it. I managed to get the URL from a guy on death row because of being a part of the Esquivel empire. Although every time I try to log on it kicks me out." I carried my laptop over to the desk to show her, attempting to log on to the site, but again I was thrown back to the Blackboard's home page.

"Well that's your problem," Elizabeth said. "The username you're trying is *Duke of Earl*. We should try something more Esquivel related."

Elizabeth unplugged my wireless router in the corner, waited for five minutes, explaining that, this would give me a new IP address, which wouldn't be recognized and barred by the site. When she plugged it in again, she made it to the home page log in site, where she typed in new registration details.

"For a user name, let's try Lucky Luciano." We waited for the page to download, after a few minutes it kicked right back to the home page. I noticed a sign of frustration on Elizabeth's face, lost in thought. I then remembered something, "type in Salvatore Lucania, Lucky Luciano's real name." We waited again, after a few moments the page downloaded successfully, reading at the top: *Your In.*

Twenty-Nine

Elizabeth and I stayed up most of the night on the Blackboards. It was like fumbling through a pitch-black funhouse with trapdoors and tunnels, voices calling out from rooms with no doors, stumbling down rickety staircases that twisted deep into the ground with no end.

Every time I suggested we knock off for the night and continue sifting through this endless Esquivel archive with rested eyes in the morning, there was another anecdote to click onto, another uncanny incident, rumor, or strange picture of some kind.

There were quite a few pages on the site devoted to Esquivel's supposed life philosophy, which meant, in a nutshell, that he controlled everything and kept all the money. He controlled by fear and intimidation. The one common thread in drug dealing, at any level, is violence. As drug czar's go Esquivel was sovereign, top of the food chain.

In an interview by the DEA a few years back he described himself in three words, sovereign, deadly, perfect.

Sovereign; the sanctity of the individual, regarding yourself as princely, powerful, self-contained, wrestling authority for yourself away from society. Deadly; constant awareness that your own death is inevitable, which means there is no reason not to be ferocious when it comes to your life. Perfect; the understanding that life and wherever you find yourself at the present are absolutely ideal. No regret, no guilt, because even if you were stuck it was only a cocoon to break out of, setting your life on a new path, with renewed freedom.

Combing through the blackboards whispers and suspicions I realized by the sheer density of anonymous comments, which veered from reverential to the frightened to supremely twisted and depraved, only underscored what I'd long suspected, that Esquivel was not just an oddball eccentric, but a man who inspired devotion and awe in a vast number of people, not unlike a leader of a religious cult.

I can recall in my past investigation his people believed him to be an amoral enchanter, a dark acolyte who led them away from what was stale and tedious about their daily lives deep into the world's moist, tunneled underbelly, where every hour was unexpected.

By 3:45 A.M. Elizabeth and I, blank-eyed and delirious, were in the living room, digging through some old pirated files I purchased from an old friend with the F.B.I. for seventy-five bucks. We came across a CD disk

"Hey, what on this?" asked Elizabeth.

"I'm not sure, I believe it may have been some old footage of Esquivel and his family in Columbia."

"Can I play it."

"Go ahead."

Elizabeth put the CD in, as we watched Esquivel, with his family on the grounds of his prior mansion in the rolling hills of Colombia, Santo Esquivel came into view.

"Who's that? And what's happening?"

"That is Carlos Esquivel's estranged son, Santo."

I always thought Santo looked like a deranged punk: strung-out, half naked, eyes glassy, blood and what looked to be human bite marks covering his bare chest.

Elizabeth standing beside the flat screen paused it.

Frame by frame, she inched where it was possible to see that Santo was missing three fingers.

"There! Look at his hand."

"So what," I said.

"That look on his face, actual pain, I know it. Did he just lose his fingers?"

She pressed play and Santo's hand dropped out of sight.

The rest of the family got into a waiting car and barreled out of sight. Nearly running over Santo. The boys half naked body glowed in the taillights. Santo darted off the road vanishing from view.

There was no sound on the CD, but it looked like Esquivel was yelling something at Santo throughout the whole video.

Elizabeth scrambled back to the couch, pulling the wool blanket over her legs and reaching down to pick up Octavius from the coffee table as if that ancient bird would protect her from the horror about to unfold on-screen.

"Want me to make some popcorn?" I asked her.

"Abs a frikin lutly."

Once you started to get into Esquivel's head. One craved more information about him. Like an addictive opiate.

Elizabeth and I called it a day.

Thirty

The next morning, I woke up to learn Vanity Fair was reporting that they had *'the inside scoop'* on Gabriela Esquivel's death. That meant that other investigators were on the trail. It's just a matter of time before they end up at Mission Hills, and on the doorstep of Stanley Dewitt. Whatever advantage I'd had, thanks to Katie Horrigan and getting my hands on Gabriela's police file, would be gone.

And unfortunately, my own investigation had been stalled.

We'd learned about Gabriela's escape from Mission Hills and her diagnosed affliction, *nyctophobia,* a severe fear of the dark, or night, triggered by the brain's distorted perception of what would or could happen to the4 body when it's exposed to a dark environment, according to The New England Journal of Medicine. We'd had a small coup by logging successfully on to the Blackboards, able now to ransack through the rumors of his staunchest cronies.

Yet there was no new lead to follow.

Gabriela had come to the city by train after leaving Stanley Dewitt, but why. Where had she'd gone during the ten days before her death, besides the thirteenth floor of the Warwick Allerton Hotel. It was still a mystery.

I could bribe an employee at the hotel for a list of every guest staying on that floor within the time frame. From personal experience, I knew I needed something more, a filter for the names. The list would be substantial, many of the guests doubtlessly wealthy tourists who wouldn't appreciate, or feel any obligation to honestly answer questions about what they were doing at the hotel.

By the time I tracked everyone down, showing them Gabriela's picture, I'd probably have little to go on and, even worse, the maneuver would take up a hell of a lot of time.

"Maybe we could take Gabriela's picture to businesses around the Warwick," Elizabeth said after I explained some of this to her. "Ask if someone noticed her. She had to stand out with that red coat."

"I might as well take her picture to Millennium Park and ask random passersby if they noticed her. It's too vast. We need specifics."

With the feeling that we needed help Elizabeth called Cooper, inviting him to join in the fun, but he didn't respond. I actually wouldn't be surprised if we never saw him again.

I sensed from his restlessness, whatever his relationship with Gabriela, his desire to be involved in the investigation would be as erratic as his moods. He seemed to teeter between intense interest and a desire to forget the entire thing.

As we sat down to enjoy the popcorn and view more of the Esquivel mystery files the buzzer to my apartment rang. "I'll get it!" said Elizabeth.

I was in the kitchen getting drinks when I noticed nothing but silence, I stuck my head out. To my shock, Angela and my daughter Kim, were in the foyer, staring in bewilderment at Elizabeth.

It was my weekend for custody. I'd forgotten.

Seeing my ex-wife was still a jolt to the system. We always seemed to have a go-between for Kim's visits. Usually Angela's housekeeper Jeannie. The appearance of Angela in my home was akin to a grizzly wandering into my remote campsite: a life-threating scenario.

She looked stunning as usual in a cream-colored wool coat and jeans, a sweep of blown—out ash-blonde hair. She was a dealer at an exclusive contemporary art gallery in the River North area around Franklin and Superior Streets. Often scrutinizing oddly dressed strangers as if they were 99-cent airbrushed Elvis portraits.

"Hi honey," I said to Kim. "Mrs. Darcy. To what do we owe this pleasure?"

She turned to me. "You didn't get my messages? Jeannie's in the hospital. She's come down with mono and has to go home to Delaware until she's better. It'll be at least six weeks."

I looked down at Kim, tightly gripping the handle of her My Little Pony suitcase and staring, wide-eyed and opened mouthed, up at Elizabeth.

"Sweetheart, did you meet my new research assistant?" I asked. She didn't answer. She tended to become speechless out of pure awe when encountering a stranger. She took a shy step behind my ex-wife.

"Can I talk to you in private?" Angela asked me, smiling thinly.

"Certainly."

"Kim, I want you to stay here. I'll be right back."

Angela led the way down the hall. We entered my office, and she closed the door behind her.

"Who is that?" she demanded to know.

"Elizabeth. She is helping me in this investigation."

"How old is she? Sixteen?"

"Twenty-one. And extremely mature for her age." I'd have loved to imagine Angela was jealous, seeing me with another woman, but these questions had nothing to do with me. She was worried about Kim. She looked around, frowning at the papers and notes piled all over the floor, doubtlessly thinking, *some things never change.*

She was still beautiful. It was awful. I'd been waiting for Angela to venture deeper into her forties so she'd wake up to wrinkles like a maze of molehills screwing up a legendary lawn. But no, her green eyes, those high cheekbones, the expressive little mouth that broadcast her every mood with the diligence of a UN translator, were still youthful and bright.

Now Doug woke up every morning to that face. I still couldn't believe that man, fifty-eight, with a paunch, hairy wrists, and a yacht in Montego Bay named **WorkofArt,** was allowed to live daily with such a beauty. He had a knack for spotting deals in the marketplace, I'd give him that. When Angela sold him a Damien Hirst called, rather aptly, *Beautiful Bleeding Wound Over the Materialism of Money Painting,* Bruce noticed she too, was a work of art to look at for a lifetime. That she allowed herself to be bought along with the painting, **that** I didn't see coming.

When I met Angela our freshmen year at the University of Illinois, she was flighty and poor, a French studies major who quoted Simone de Beauvoir. She wiped her runny nose on her coat sleeve when it was snowing, stuck her head out of the car windows the way dogs do, the wind exploding like fireworks in her hair. That woman was gone now.

Not that it was her fault. Vast fortunes did that to people. It took them to the cleaners, cruelly starched and steam-pressed then so all their raw edges, all the dirt and hunger and guileless laughter, were ironed out. Few if any survived real money.

"So, you and that girl are only working together," Angela said, turning her back to me.

"Yes. She's my research assistant."

"Well, research assistant to you can mean any number of things."

I let that one hit me square in the gut. It was true, after our divorce, I'd ended up in a slight relationship with my last research assistant, Sharilee Beck, age thirty-nine, though, let me state for the record, it was not as hot as it sounded. Making love to Sharilee was like rummaging through a card catalog in a deserted library, searching for one very obscure, rarely read the entry on Slovenian poetry. It was dead silent, no one gave me any direction, and nothing was where it was supposed to be.

"It's all very G-rated around here, so what's really the problem?"

"You didn't even remember Kim was coming today."

"That's not true. She'll have a great time. If there's any trouble, I'll call you and you can airlift her out by Black Hawk."

"What about Bethany?"

"*Elizabeth. She'll be out of here by ten.*" *It wasn't the time to mention Kim had a roommate.*

Angela sighed, a familiar look of surrender on her face. "Have her home by six on Sunday. Keep in mind Doug and I rescheduled our Santa Barbara trip for next week, so you'll have Kim for a long weekend." She eyed me skeptically. "Unless you can't handle it."

"I can handle it."

"We're going with friends, so you can't suddenly change your mind."

"You have my word. I want the extra time with her."

She seemed to accept this, sweeping her blond hair over her shoulder, staring at me expectantly, waiting for me to say something more.

This had been one of the great enigmas of our marriage. In the sixteen years, we were together, Angela often waited for me to say something more as if there were very specific words that would unlock her, a state-of-the-art vault that she was. I never came close to deciphering the combination. *I love you* did not work. Neither did, *what are you thinking?* Or *Tell me what you want to hear.*

She'd wait a minute, maybe longer, and when she understood she was going to remain locked until further notice, she'd walk away, lost in sealed-tight silence. This was what she did now, opening the door and striding back down the hall.

I was about to head after her when I felt me cell ringing in my pocket. It was Cooper.

"Come to Twenty-Sixth and California," he shouted as a police siren ripped into the receiver, *"Now."*

"What?"

"I found someone who saw Gabriela a few days before she died."

"Give me twenty-five minutes," I said and hung up.

So Cooper couldn't stay away after all. The kid was proving to be quite the trump card.

Thirty-One

Kim stared sullenly back at me. Even though I'd just explained, crouched down on her level with as much drama as I could muster, that her dad had some top-secret business to attend to and needed to run, so she was staying with Mommy. She didn't say a word.

"Next weekend we'll be spending four days together," I said. "Just the two of us, okay?"

Still, the silence. But then, seemingly thinking something quite serious, she reached her right-hand way up and patted me on my head. She'd never done that before. Angela, her face flushed, shot me a look, *Great Parenting,* smiling agreeably for Kim's sake, she extended the handle of the My Little Pony suitcase, handing it off to Kim, who dutifully wheeled it to the door like a tired stewardess learning she had to fly an extra leg to Cleveland.

"Bye sweetheart," I said. "I love you more than, *what was it again?*"

"The moon and all the stars," she answered, heading down the hall.

"I'll make it up to her," I said to Angela.

"Of course." She swept her hair over her shoulder and smiled, stepping after her. "We'll put it on your tab."

I strode to the hall closet, trying to ignore the tsunami of guilt flooding through me."

"Cooper called," I said to Elizabeth over my shoulder. "We're meeting him by the county jail now.

He has a lead."

I grabbed my keys, but Elizabeth didn't move from the living-room doorway. She was staring at me, wide-eyed.

"What's the matter?" I asked.

"That was bad."

"What was bad?"

"That."

"My ex-wife? Yes, I know. Can you believe that woman used to live to karaoke on a Saturday night? In college, we called her Bangles. You couldn't pay her to stop singing 'Just Another Maniac Monday', in public."

"She's not what I'm talking about."

I was helping Elizabeth into her coat. "Then what are you talking about? And please tell me quickly, because we need to get going."

"You think your subtle, but you're not."

I was jostling her into the hallway, locking the door. "Subtle about what?"

"That you're crazy mad in love with her."

"Hey, No one's crazy or mad or in love with anyone here."

She put a hand on my shoulder, a look of evident pity.

"You need to move on with your life. She's happy." And with that, she took off merrily down the hall, leaving me staring after her.

Thirty-Two

Cooper was waiting for us on the corner, smoking a cigarette, a hollowed out expression on his face suggesting that he'd barely slept in the two days since we'd seen him.

"What are we doing here? I asked him.

"Remember what Stanley Dewitt said? He thought Gabriela had to play the piano every day."

"Sure."

"Yesterday I started thinking if Gabriela came into the city to track someone down if she wanted to play, where would she go?"

"Jazz clubs, Buddy Guy's, a hotel lobby? It's hard to say."

"None of those places would let a stranger off the street just sit down and start playing, uninterrupted. But I remembered. I got a friend who's big into the classical music scene. If you're really good, the showrooms on Piano Row let you came in and play as long as you like. This afternoon I went for a brunch, asked around, and a manager in one of the shops actually recognized her. Gabriela came in twice the week before she died."

"Nice work," I said.

"Right now he's waiting to talk to us. But we have to hurry because they're about to close." He chucked the cigarette onto the pavement and took off down the sidewalk.

I never heard of Piano Row. It was a splinter off Printers Row by Clark and Harrison Streets, where delicate piano stores had tucked themselves between the chic lofts, like a few sparrows living among hippos. We hurried past a small shop called Steinway Pianos, posters taped in the windows advertising Vivaldi concerts and voice lessons. Inside, identical shiny baby grands were lined up, lids open, like hefty chorus girls awaiting a cue. Cooper shuffled past Maxwell's Polish Sausage stand and crossed the street, passing a fire station, and then pausing in front of a shop with a dirty green awning that read *Onofrio Classic Piano's*.

    I held the door open for Elizabeth and we entered. Unlike Steinway Pianos, there were only three pianos on display. The store was empty, without a single customer or employee. It appeared on the Internet as pianos, like physical books, were fast becoming culturally extinct. They'd probably stay that way unless Apple invented the iPiano, which fit inside your pocket, and could be mastered via text message. *With the iPiano anyone can be an iMozart. Then, you could compose your own iRequiem for your own iFuneral attended by millions of your iFriends who iLoved you.*

    Cooper emerged from the back with a middle-aged wisp of a man sporting brown corduroys and a black turtleneck, a weedy patch of gray hair sprouting from his balding head. He looked like a classical man-child. You could spot these guys within a ten-block radius the Civic Opera House. They tended to wear earth tones, and have all of public television's Great Performances series on DVD, live alone in apartments in the River North area, and have potted plants that they talk too daily.

    "This is Caesar DePasquale," Said Cooper.

    "The manager of Onofrio Classic Piano's," Caesar added with pride.

Elizabeth and I introduced ourselves. "I understand Gabriela Esquivel came in here a few weeks ago," I said.

"I had no idea who she was at the time," Caesar said eagerly, clasping his hands together. "But based on Mr. Jones's description, yes, I believe she came to Onofrio's."

HE was one of those people you initially believed had a foreign accent, though it turned out he was a natural born American, only spoke delicately as if every word were something to be carefully dusted off and held up to the light.

"Did the police come here to ask about her?"

"No, no. We've had no police. I had no inkling who she was until Mr. Jones came in this afternoon. He gave me her description, and I recognized her immediately." Caesar glanced at Cooper. "The hair and that red coat, unmistakable. She's a beauty."

"When exactly did she come in?" I asked.

"You need the precise date?"

"It'd be helpful."

Caesar hurried into the administrative alcove along the opposite wall. After fumbling down behind the counter, he produced a large leather calendar stuffed with papers.

"It was almost certainly a *Tuesday* because we'd just had our weekly concert," he mumbled, flipping open the cover. "Usually, it's over by ten o'clock. On this night, around eleven, I was in the back cleaning up when suddenly I heard the most exciting interpretation of *Ludwig Van Beethoven, Fur Elise*. I'm sure you know it?"

We shook our heads, which seemed to concern him.

"Well. I'd forgotten to lock the door." Scrutinizing t4he calendar, he frowned, thoughtfully pressing a finger to his lips. "It was October fourth. Yes. That has to be it."

Smiling, he slid the calendar around for us to take a look, tapping the day in question with his index finger.

"I hurried into the showroom, and saw her at the piano."

"Which one and where?" I asked.

He pointed toward the front. "The Fazioli. There in the window."

I strolled over to it. Elizabeth following me.

"Is it a good one?" I asked.

Caesar chuckled as if I'd made a joke, heading after us. "Faziolis are the best in the world. Many professionals find them superior to Steinways."

I studied it. Even by my amateur eyes, it was a gorgeous, intimidating instrument.

"Pianos are like people," Caesar noted softly. Everyone has a different personality. They take the time to get to know. And they can get lonely."

"What personality does this one have?" Elizabeth asked.

"Her? Oh, she's a bit of a diva. If she were in high school, she'd be a prom queen. She can be moody, imperious. Take over if you're not careful. But show her a firm hand and she'll dazzle you. All piano soundboards are made of spruce. Well, Fazioli uses spruce from the Valdi Feimme forest in Northern Italy."

He awaited our amazed reaction, but we could only stare back blankly.

"It's the Same timber the Stradivari family used to craft their legendary violins in the seventeenth century. It produced an opulent velvet sound that can't be replicated by any other manufacturer today. It's why Stradivarius violins today sell in the millions."

"What did you do when you heard her?" I asked.

"I intended to tell her she'd have to come back tomorrow. We've closed after all. But her playing was," he shut his eyes and shook his head, "*electrifying.* I could tell she'd been trained by a European, due to her take-no-prisoners, blustery articulation perfectly balanced with profound intimacy, which brought to mind some of the greatest pianists of all time. Argerich, Pascal Roge. I couldn't bear to interrupt. Genius doesn't keep to business hours, *n'est-ce pas?* I didn't speak to her until she was finished.

"How long was that?" I asked.

"Approximately a minute and a half. She looked so familiar, in a very distant way. Like a tune, you suddenly recall from childhood and yet you can't remember the lyrics or really anything beyond a handful of mysterious notes." He sighed. "Now I realize it was Gabriela Derouin, grown up. I'd heard from one of our owners, Lenzi, that she used to come in here and play years ago, as a teenager. But I didn't make the connection." He paused, his face pensive. "When she finished, she asked me politely if she could play the entire suite, *the Assez Lent* through the *Epilogue*. The performance takes about fifteen minutes. Naturally, I said yes." He smiled. "If she'd asked to play every one of Beethoven's sonatas, I'd have agreed. When she finished, she raised her head, gazing at me. She had a very piercing stare."

"Did she say anything?"

"She thanked me. She had a low voice. Hoarse. A sort of swanlike way of moving. Immaculate surface. No idea what's going on beneath. She sat there a moment saying nothing. I sensed it was difficult for her to speak. I wondered if English wasn't her first language.

She picked up her bag, and then . . ." His eyes drifted away from the piano as if imagining Gabriela there now, walking to the door. "I tried getting her to stay, but when I asked her name she said, '*No one.*' And then she left."

"What was her demeanor?" I asked

"Demeanor?"

"Did she seem depressed? Mentally unwell?"

"Apart from her hesitation with talking? No not this time. This time, she was quite satisfied when she finished. The way one might feel after a vigorous swim in the Atlantic. Musicians feel that way after a good practice." He cleared his throat, turning to stare out the window at the empty street. "I watched her drift down the sidewalk as if she weren't quite sure where she was going. Finally, she moved west toward Milwaukee Avenue and was gone. That might be when I got home, I remember very distinctly I couldn't sleep, not the whole night. Yet I felt great calm. I'd been dealing with some personal issues of late, the details of which I'll certainly spare you. But her sudden appearance for was a gift. Or a figment of my imagination. One of Debuussy's *demoiselles*. I doubted I'd ever see her again."

"When did she come back?" I asked. He seemed saddened by the question. "Three days later."

"That would be the seventh," I said, making a note of it in my BlackBerry. "Do you remember the time of day?"

"An hour after closing. Seven o'clock? Again, I was the last one here. Even our intern had disappeared." He turned, gesturing at the large antique-looking leather notebook open on a table along the back wall.

We ask everyone who comes into Onofrio's to sign the guestbook, it's believed to help future recitals and technique. A sort of baptism, if you will. We've had all the legends sign it. Zimmerman, Brendel, Lang-Lang, Horowitz."

When it was clear the names meant little to us, he inhaled sharply, disheartened, and pointed over his shoulder to the administration alcove.

"I was typing up the addresses and names when there was a knock on the glass.

Technically, we were closed. But when I saw who it was, of course, I let her in. As soon as I unlocked the door, however, I realized something was terribly wrong."

"What?" asked Cooper.

Caesar looked uncomfortable. "I don't think she'd had a shower, perhaps, hadn't even taken off that coat since I'd last seen her. Her hair was disheveled. She reeked of dirt and sweat. The cuffs of her jeans were filthy. *Mud from the country*, I thought to myself. She seemed drugged. It occurred to me she must be homeless. We've had quite a few vagrants enter the shop. They wander down here after sleeping down on Lower

Wacker Drive. The music draws them in." He sighed. "She asked if it was all right if she played. I said yes. And she sat down right there." He indicated the Same lustrous Fazioli piano, gazing down at the empty brown leather seat. "She ran her hands over the keys and said, 'I think Debussy today. He's not so mad at me.' Something to the effect. And then she…"

"Wait a minute," I interrupted. "she talked about the composer as if he were an *acquaintance?*"

"Sure," Caesar said with a slight nod.

"Isn't that a little strange?"

"Not at all. Concert pianists get to be quite chummy with dead composers. They can't help it. Classical music isn't just music. It's a personal diary. An uncensored confession in the dead of night. A baring of the soul. Take a modern example. Florence and the Machine? In the song 'Cosmic Love,' she catalogs the way in which the world has gone dark, disorienting her, when she, a rather intense young woman, was left bereft by a love affair. The stars, the moon, they have all been blown out.' Well, it's no different with Beethoven and Ravel. Into their music, these composers poured their fiercest beings. When a pianist remembers a piece, he or she gets to know the dead man intimately, giving rise to all the pleasures and difficulties such an intense relationship implies. You learn Mozart's trickery, his ADD attention span. Bach's yearning for acceptance, his intolerance for shortcuts. Liszt's explosive temper. Chopin's insecurity. And thus when you set out to make their music come alive in concert, on stage, in front of thousands, you very much need the dead man on your side. Because you're bringing him back to life. It's a bit like Frankenstein resuscitation his monster, do you understand? It can be an astonishing miracle. Or it can all go horribly wrong."

I glanced at Cooper. He continued to stare at Caesar, the look on his face something between absorption and skepticism. Elizabeth was spellbound.

"What happened this time?" I asked.

"she began playing. The opening parallel fifths of *La Cathedrale Engloutie*."

"The opening parallel what?" interjected Elizabeth, frowning.

"*La Cathedrale Engloutie*. The Sunken Cathedral."

Caesar, noting our obvious ignorance, beamed, unable to restrain his delight.

"Claude Debussy. The French impressionist. It's one of my very favorite preludes. It tells the story of a cathedral submerged at the bottom of the sea. On a clear day, it rises up out of the churning waves and fog, bells chiming ecstatically, to rest for mere seconds in the air, shimmering in the sun, before sinking down again into the fathomless depths, out of sight. Debussy instructs the musician to play the final chords pianissimo, at the half pedal, so it truly sounds as if there are church bells deep underwater, notes colliding, before fading and ending as all things do, as we all do, with a few reverberating chords and then silence." He paused, his face darkening.

"She couldn't do it. Her playing, so revelatory before, such melting, lyricism, such romance, was disturbing now. She tore into the music, but the notes eluded her. It was erratic. *Despairing*. And when she looked up at me, I . . ." He looked shaken. "Her eyes were bloodshot. They actually looked to be bleeding. I was filled with such horror by her face, how it had transformed so from the time I'd seen her before. I instantly left to phone the police. I left her playing here, in front. But just as I entered the back room, she stopped. There was only silence. I peeked my head out. She was sitting very still, watching me with those eyes, like she knew what I was going to do. Suddenly she grabbed her bag and left. Just like *that*." He snapped his fingers. "It was truly frightening.

"Why?" I asked.

He rubbed his hands together, uneasily. "She moved like an animal."

"An **animal**?" cooped repeated.

Caesar nodded. "It was too fast. It certainly wasn't normal."

"Which direction did she go?" I asked.

"I don't know. I returned to the front, but there was no sign of her. I even stepped outside to take a look. She wasn't anywhere to be seen. I locked up the store immediately. I didn't want to be in the shop alone."

He lapsed into a melancholic silence, staring at the floor. "she never came back. I thought about her. But I never told anyone, until you came in." He looked at Cooper.

"I was relieved when you came in and asked about her, so happy to know that I hadn't dreamt her up out of thin air. I've . . . I 've been under some pressure of late." He flushed. "To say the least, it nice to know I wasn't going crazy." His gaze returned back to the piano. "she was a bit like that cathedral. Rising up, stunning me, decaying, and then vanishing, leaving only her echo. And me, so uncertain of what I'd seen."

"So you have video surveillance in the store?" I asked.

"We have an alarm system. But no cameras."

"Did she mention anything else? Where she was staying?"

"Oh, no. We didn't speak beyond what I told you."

"And she left nothing behind? No personal items?"

"I'm afraid not."

Elizabeth had moved over to the small table along the wall with the open guestbook, turning back the pages.

"That's really all, Oh, *do* be careful with that." Caesar scurried after her. "The pages are quite fragile, and it's our only copy."

"I'm just wondering if she signed it," said Elizabeth, Caesar looking on nervously over her shoulder.

Cooper had stepped up to the Fazioli that Gabriela had played, solemnly running his hand along the gleaming keys, playing a few sharp notes.

I strode over to Elizabeth. Having found the page marked the day, she was running her finger down the list of scribbled names and addresses. As she got to the bottom of the page, nothing sticking out to her. She turned the page rather roughly, and Caesar touched his forehead as if he might faint. "Heidi Carter. Daniel Katalinic. Claire Tr..."

"What did you say?" I asked.

"Daniel Katalinic."

"Before that."

"Heidi Carter."

I stepped closer, incredulous, staring down at the page. It was scribbled in black pen, that familiar handwriting, identical, I was certain, to the note that Stanley Dewitt had shown us, and maybe even that package mailed to Cooper.

"That's her," I shouted.

Thirty-Three

The streets were narrow, shriveled bodegas and faded walk-ups packed shoulder to shoulder. Upstairs windows, filled with plants and shampoo bottles, were lit up like dirty fish tanks in electric greens and blues. Every now and then we passed someone walking alone, usually Chinese, carrying orange plastic shopping bags or hurrying along in a down jacket. Almost everyone turned to stare in at us as if they know, probably because we were riding in a taxi, we were trespassing.

"There's fourteen twenty-one," said Elizabeth, leaning forward to survey the deserted street. "Fourteen twenty-seven is coming up on the right."

Gabriela had written in the Onofrio guestbook, and Caesar was at a loss to explain when exactly she had done so:

Onofrio

Guestbook

Heidi Carter, 1427 S. Normal Avenue, Apt 16, Chicago, IL. 60616

Heidi Carter was the name of a missing El Esplanade matron. One of Esquivel's trusted bookkeepers and babysitters for Gabriela. I'd only recognized the name from the Blackboards, the website was rife with theories and the occasional shrine to the elusive Heidi Carter. The question of what happened to her was an Esquivel trademark. Time magazine said in an article about Esquivel titled, "The World's Number One Drug Czar," that mention's Heidi Carter, *aka Shadow,* as someone who is a mystery in our lives, It's something unseen, lurking about like a darkness that gives our lives dimension.

The fact that out of all the potential pseudonyms, Gabriela had chosen that one, a missing woman from her Father's inner circle. Perhaps Heidi became of Gabriela's daily life, maybe even overshadowed her sense of self. What was her response when Caesar had asked her who she was?"

No one, she'd said.

It reminded me of the profile in the Amherst newsletter. *It's wonderful to get lost in a piece of music, she'd said. To forget your name for a while.*

Our taxi eased down the deserted street. In front of us, the overpass viaduct of the Stevenson Expressway. Dingy walk-ups had sprouted up around it. Graffiti actually brightened up the rusted girders.

"There," Cooper said, indicating the building on our right. The awning out front read 1427 S. Normal Avenue in white letters, followed by a few Chinese characters. Metal grates had been pulled down on either side of the front entrance, a green door with a small rectangular window.

I paid the driver, and we climbed out.

It was oddly silent and still, the only sound the faint moans of unseen cars racing across the expressway. I stepped up to the door, looking through the window.

Inside, a derelict hallway spray-painted with more graffiti extended beyond a row of mailboxes.

"Look," Elizabeth whispered, pointing at the label beside the buzzer for #16. It read H. Carter.

"Don't press it," I said. I stepped back to the curb, staring up at the building: five stories, crumbling red brick, a rusted fire escape. All of the windows were dark except two on the second floor, another on the fifth with frilly pink curtains.

"Someone's coming," Cooper whispered, moving away from the door, darting around the corner, where there was a parking lot. Elizabeth lurched backward, hurrying down the sidewalk. I stepped around the trash bags piled on the curb, heading across the street.

Seconds later, I heard the door open behind me, rapid footsteps. An Asian man wearing a blue jacket had exited, walking toward S. Normal Avenue. He didn't appear to have seen us, not even Cooper, who'd slipped past him and managed to catch the door before it closed.

"Nice," Elizabeth whispered excitedly, rushing inside after him. "Number sixteen must be the top floor."

"Hold on a minute," I said, stepping after them. But Cooper was already racing down the hall and out of sight, Elizabeth right behind him. I held back, inspecting the mailboxes. Apart from Carter at #16, there was only J. Mergener in #1 and R. Mergener in #13.

I slipped down the hall, a TV babbling somewhere close by. Cooper and Elizabeth could already be heard clanging upstairs. Because of a bright light somewhere beyond the corridor, their dark, elongated shadows were suddenly tossed against the wall in front of me, like two long black tongues sliding down, licking the cracked brown tiles and vanishing.

I headed after them, the steps strewn with trash and ads for Asian escorts, mostly in Chinese. One flier wedged into a filthy window-pane, **Asian Girl Massage** and featured a naked Korean wearing rubber chaps shyly peering over her shoulder. **Meet Yumi,** it read.

Cooper and Elizabeth disappeared somewhere on the top floor. As I started u the next flight, kicking aside a Tsingtao beer can, there was a sudden bang somewhere below me.

I stared over the railing. No one was visible. Yet I swore I could hear breathing.

"Hello?" I called out, my voice echoing through her stairwell.

There was no answer.

I moved up the remaining flights, pulling open the door marked 5, spotting Cooper and Elizabeth at the end of a long dim hallway outside #16. As I caught up, they both turned, startled, at something behind me.

A woman had just appeared at the opposite end.

Thirty-Four

The single neon bulb on the ceiling drenched her wide nose and forehead in the sickly yellow light. She was quite heavy, wearing a long green skirt and black T-shirt, straggly brown hair covering her shoulders.

"What do you think you're doing?" the behemoth croaked in a masculine voice.

"Checking on a friend," I said.

She scurried toward us, hunched shoulders, flip-flops rapidly slapping her bare feet.

"What friend?"

"Gabriela."

"Who?"

"Heidi," Elizabeth interjected. "He means Heidi."

The name made the woman stop short, unwilling to approach further. She had to be in her fifties, with mottled skin, also missing some teeth, giving her face the countenance of a crumbling statue.

"Where the hell *is* Heidi?" she demanded. "You tell her she owes me three weeks rent. I'm not running a free shelter here."

Cooper reached into his coat pocket, unfolding a piece of paper. "Is this her?" he asked.

It was a black-and-white photograph of Gabriela. He must have printed it off the Internet because I'd never seen it before unless it was from his own collection, a snapshot taken at Gateway Wilderness Therapy. The woman didn't move to look at it, only jutted out her chin.

"Yawl cops?"

"No," I said. "We're friends of Heidi's."

"When was the last time you saw her?" blurted Elizabeth.

The woman glared at us. "I don't talk to cops."

"We're *not* cops," said Cooper, removing his wallet. The instant he flipped it open, the woman's small black eyes began scanning the contents like flies swarming over a turd. "answer our questions, we'll make it worth your while." He held out three twenties, which she grabbed instantly, counting them, then sticking them down the front of her T-shirt.

"Is this Heidi?" asked Cooper again, holding out the picture.

"Sure looks like her."

"When did you last see her?" I asked.

"*Week*s ago. That's how come I came up. Heard all the creeping around, thought she came back to get her stuff and was trying to sneak past me. Any idea when Her Highness plans to show?"

"Not really."

The news infuriated her. "I coulda rented this room five times over. Now I gotta get a locksmith up here. Clean out her shit."

"Why a locksmith?" I asked.

She nodded at the door. "I don' got the key to her room. She changed the locks on me."

"Why?"

"Hell if I know."

"What was she like?" asked Elizabeth.

The woman grimaced. "Had duchess airs, if you ask me. Had a way of demanding things, like she was the queen of England. Wanted me to fix the lights in the bathroom 'cuz it was too dark for her, then the hot and cold tap. Musta mistook this place for a damn Merriott."

"Do you know what else she was doing in the city?" asked Elizabeth.

The woman squinted faintly as if insulted. "You pay me on time, what you do in the room is your business. She *did* do me a favor once.

I had to run out, and she watched my nephew for coupla hours. That I did appreciate. But then she changes the locks, runs out, stiffs me on the rent. I'm running a business. Not a charity." She stared resentfully at the door again. "Now I gotta pay for a locksmith."

"How long has she been living here?" I asked.

"Bout a month. But I haven't seen her for weeks."

"And how did she hear about it?"

"Answered my ads. I got fliers posted around the area."

"How much to break down the door down?" Cooper asked, running his hands along the jamb.

"We'll also cover whatever Heidi owed you in rent."

"Uh, well that'd be, oh, one-fifty. Plus, any damage to the door."

"Here's three-hundred." He shoved a wad of bills at the woman, which she hastily grabbed, then he strode to the end of the hall, where there was a door with a grimy pane of glass, sort of a communal bathroom, and a fire extinguisher. He pulled the extinguisher free and moved back, raising it over his head and slamming it hard against the deadbolt.

He did this five times, the wood splintering, and then, with a laid-back ease that hinted he'd done this before, he tossed aside the canister, took a few steps back, and side-kicked the door. It flew open, cracking against the wall, and then close, stopping so it was ajar about an inch.

For a moment, no one moved. Cooper pushed the door wider. It was pitch-dark inside, light from the hallway barely illuminating the scarred concrete floor, walls of flaking beige paint. There was also a noticeable stench, something rotten. I turned, intending to ask the landlady when she'd last been inside Heidi's room, but she'd actually backed away.

"Gotta go downstairs," she mumbled, then turned, flip-flops hammering her feet as she hurried down the hall. "Gotta check on my nephew." She darted out, and within seconds could be heard clanging back downstairs.

"She's afraid of something," I said.

"It's that smell," whispered Elizabeth.

Thirty-Five

Cooper took a step inside. I followed, sliding my hands along the wall, trying to find a light switch. "*Shit,*" he said, coughing. "The smell's really bad."

There was a grating screech as he accidentally tripped on something, a metal folding chair, then fumbling with a lamp, the room was suddenly drenched in pale light.

It was small and stark, with a faded brown rug, a window with a torn shade, a metal cot in a corner. Something about the way the sheets were thrown back, a blue blanket dangling on the floor, a discernable dent in the pillow, seemed to suggest Gabriela had just climbed out of it, moments ago. In fact, the entire shabby room hinted she'd just been here, the musty air still filled with her breathing.

The rank stench, a combination of sewage and burning, seemed to seep out of the walls. A brown stain covered the ceiling by the window as if something had been slaughtered on the roof, then left to slowly bleed down into the rafters. The floor, strewn with a few plastic wrappers, was sticky from some type of dark soda that had spilled.

"Didn't Dewitt say Gabriela was wearing white pajamas when he broke her out of Mission Hills?" Cooper asked.

"Yes," I said.

"They're right here."

Sure enough, a pair of white cotton drawstring pants and a top had been tossed in a heap on the sheets.

Cooper seemed reluctant to touch them. I picked up the pants, noting with surprise not just that L. Esquivel, MH-*350,* her room number at Mission Hills, had been printed along the inner waistband, but the legs still held her form. So did the top; cut in the boxy shape of surgical scrubs, the left sleeve still twisted around her elbow.

I put them back on the bed, stopping toward a small closet. There was nothing in there, just four wire hangers on a wooden rod.

"Something's under here," Cooper shouted. He was looking under the bed.

We grabbed the cat, carrying it to the center of the room, and then all three of us stared, bewildered, at what had just been exposed. None of us said a word.

Thirty-Six

My first thought was that it was some type of target. And if I ever found such a thing under my own bed, I probably couldn't help but wonder if the Grim Reaper had put it there. A reminder that I was due to be picked up in a matter of days, or *I had enemies who wanted to scare the daylights out of me.*

Four concentric circles made out of black ashes had been meticulously laid out on the floor. At the center, almost directly beneath where Gabriela's torso or heart would be, I noticed, if she were lying flat on the bed, was a pyramid of charcoal, the concrete beneath it charred black.

"What is it?" Elizabeth whispered.

"The ashes are what smells," said Cooper, crouching beside it.

After taking photos, Elizabeth found a sandwich bag in her purse, and turning it inside out, we collected a sample of the powder. It looked like finely chopped leaves, dirt, and bone. I sealed the bag and tucked it into my coat pocket.

"Holy shit," Cooper whispered behind us. "Check this out."

He was by the door, staring at something lodged above it, a cluster of twigs. They'd been carefully positioned deep in the corner *as if to deliberately escape notice.*

Cooper pulled them down, holding them in the light from the hallway. They looked like some roots, some thick, others thin, others tightly coiled in spirals, though they all looked to be from the same plant. Each one had been knotted neatly with white string and tied to another.

"Looks like some kind of occult practice," I said, carefully taking the bunch from Cooper. I'd come across some bizarre religious customs over the years, baby tossing in India; Jain monks who walked around naked, wearing the air; tribal boys forced to wear gloves filled with bullet ants, a ritual to enter adulthood. This seemed to be something along those lines.

"Why would it be over the doorway?" asked Elizabeth.

I looked at Cooper. "You remember Gabriela being involved in any unusual practices or beliefs?"

"No."

"Let's do another walk through. See if there's anything we missed. Then let's get the hell out of here."

Elizabeth and Cooper nodded, glancing warily around the room. I was about to head over to the bedside table when out of the corner of my eye I saw something green streaking past the doorway followed by staccato slapping. *Flip-flops.*

I stuck my head out. The landlord was scampering down the hall. *The old crone had been spying.*

"Wait a minute!" I shouted, stepping after her.

I don't know nothing," she growled.

"You must have noticed that smell coming out of her room."

She stopped dead at the end of the hallway, turning, her skin glistening with sweat.

"I don't know what that girl did to herself."

"Have any of the residents said anything?"

She didn't respond. She had an off-putting, *lizard-like* way of moving, remaining very still, as if knowing she'd be camouflaged by the grim light and cracked walls around her, then hastily scuttling away. Now she was absolutely immobile, staring at me with her head cocked.

"She scared people." She grinned. "Don't know how, because she's a skinny thing. And some of a' the people who take my rooms, they're usually the ones who do the scaring. But I don't make it my business. People can do what they want, long as they pay me."

I was half way down the hall now but stopped because of a small boy, no more than five or six years old, was peering at me through the stairwell door. After a pause, he slipped out, standing sullenly behind the woman. He was in a dirty T-shirt, cotton pants too short in the leg, and socks meant for much larger feet.

"Is that your nephew?" I asked.

She looked him up and down, coldly, and turned back to me, can he tell me anything about her?"

She pointed at me. "For a friend, you don't know too much."

I noticed then a shard of light was coming out of a room beside me, the door moving. Someone was eavesdropping. Before I could see who it was, there was a loud clanging noise. The landlord and boy had just disappeared into the stairwell. I took off after them.

"Hold on!"

"You leave us alone."

I raced down the steps, tripping on fliers, catching up on the next landing. Without thinking, I grabbed the boy by the arm. He emitted a blood-curdling squeal as if I'd branded him with an iron.

Startled I let him go, yet he continued to scream as he watched something, some kind of action figure he'd just dropped, careen down through the metal railings, bouncing on the steps, skidding across the tiles on the ground floor. With a whimper, he took off after it.

"Look what you've done now." The woman said furiously, heading after him. "Take your friends and get out of here. We don't know nothin'."

When I reached the ground floor, I found the two of them frantically scouring the hallway. The boy stood up, turning to the woman, his fingers working fast in the air. He was speaking in sign language. He was deaf. *And I'd traumatized him.*

Guilty, I turned, searching the tiled floor, kicking aside fliers and wrappers. I soon found it in a rectangle of light under the stairwell. It was a tiny wood carving of a snake, three inches long, mouth open, tongue extended, twisted body. It felt oddly heavy.

Suddenly beside me, the landlord snatched it, handing it back to the boy. She then seized his arm, hauled him toward an apartment door. I caught a glimpse of a cluttered room, a TV playing cartoons, as she shoved the boy inside, darted in after him, the door slamming.

Elizabeth and Cooper were racing downstairs, the building growling with noise. They ran straight down the hall, Elizabeth turning, silently beckoning me to hurry. I exited after her into the cool night, realizing I was gasping for breath, as if I'd just wrenched free of something, something that, without my knowledge, had been suffocating me.

Thirty-Seven

"Did you take the boots over the door?" I asked when I caught up with Elizabeth and Cooper across the street.

"Yep," she said, opening up her purse to show me.

"Okay, let's grab a cab."

"We can't. A neighbor of Gabriela's is coming down to talk to us."

I recalled a shard of light I'd seen outside room #13.

"While you chased the landlady, this other woman stuck her head out, upset by all the commotion. Cooper showed her Gabriela's picture, and she recognized her. She's coming down to talk to us in two seconds."

"Nice work."

"Here she comes," whispered Elizabeth, as a figure emerged from Seventy-Five Normal Street, an apartment building. The woman was tall, wearing a white zip-up sweatshirt and sneakers. She carried a black duffel bag over her shoulder, and whatever was in there, *assault rifles,* by the shape of it, appeared to be quite heavy, making her walk stooped over. She hurried across the street toward us.

"Sorry I took so long," she said breathlessly, skipping up onto the curb in a potent blast of perfume. "Couldn't find my keys. I'm off to work, so I don't have much time. What'd you want to ask me?" Her face was quite pretty, fringed with bleached blond curls, though wearing so much makeup, it was difficult to know where she ended and her illusion began. She looked about thirty, though I noticed she stood deliberately away from the streetlight and kept her hands shoved in the pockets of her hoodie, shoulders hunched, as if not entirely at ease with people getting a close look at her.

"Just a few questions about your neighbor Heidi."

She smiled. "Oh, yeah. How's she doing? Haven't seen her lately."

"Fine," I answered, ignoring Elizabeth's look. "We're friends of hers and want to know about her stay here. What's she doing with herself?"

"Gee, I wouldn't know. We barely talked." Setting the duffel bag down on the sidewalk, *mysterious metallic clangs*, the woman removed a ball of Kleenex from her pocket and blew her nose. *"Sorry.* I'm just getting over a bad cold. I only saw Heidi, like once."

"When?" I asked.

"A month ago? I was just getting in from work. About five, six in the morning. I went into the bathroom to take my make-up off. There's only one per floor. Everyone shares. I was in there, like, forty-five minutes, brushing my teeth, probably even talking to myself, when all of a sudden there was a *splash* behind me." She shuddered. "Scared the shit out of me. I screamed. Probably woke up the whole building."

"Why?" I asked when she didn't go on but paused to blow her nose again.

"She was right there," she said, giggling, a high pitched, jingle bell sound. "**Heidi.**"

"Where?"

"In the bathtub. She'd been behind me taking a bath the whole time."

I glanced at Elizabeth and Cooper. They seemed to be thinking what I was, *the disturbing nature of the scene she'd just described was entirely lost on the woman.*

"I introduced myself", she went of sniffling. "She told me her name but leaned her head back against the tub, closing her eyes like she'd bad a long day and didn't feel like talking. I finished putting on my wrinkle cream, said good night. After I heard her leave the bathroom, I want back because I'd left my toothpaste on the sink. She hadn't drained the tub, so I stuck my hand in to unplug it." She shook her head. "I don't know how she was in there without her legs and arms freezing off. It was **like ice**"

"You never saw Heidi again?" I asked.

"No, I heard her, though. The walls are like paper. She seemed to keep the same hours as I did."

"What hours are those?"

"I work nights." She said it vaguely, gazing past us at the deserted street.

"You know what? There was another time. Sorry. My head's a little stuffy from this cold medicine. It was my night off, so it musta been on a Saturday. I was coming back from the supermarket and passed Heidi on the stairwell. She was on her way to a club. I don't remember the name." She shook her head.

"It was feminine. Kinda French? I *think* she said it was being held in an old warehouse on South Halsted. She wanted to know if I had ever been there, but I hadn't."

"An old jail?" I repeated.

She shrugged. "It was a five-second conversation. You know what? Last week U dud see two guys outside her door. They stared at me like they wanted me to mind my own business, so I did."

"What did they look like?"

"Just guys. One was older, the other in his thirties? Later I heard Dot come upstairs and get rid of them. She doesn't like strangers."

"Dot?"

"Yeah. You were talking to her."

"A little boy lives with her."

"Lucian. He's her nephew."

"How long has he been living here?"

"Long as I've been at this place. About a year." She sniffed and pulled back her sleeve, checking her watch. "Shit. I gotta run." She grabbed the duffel, heaving it, clanging, over her shoulder. "You'll tell Heidi I said hello?"

"Of-course."

"How can we get in touch if we have more questions?" asked Elizabeth. After a slight hesitation, the woman unzipped her satchel, handing Elizabeth a black business card. Then smiled and took off down the sidewalk toward State Street. Elizabeth handed the business card to me without a word.

Lexi, it read **Bachelor Party Entertainment.**

Thirty-Eight

"A nightclub in the River North," I said, "It has a French name. It might be held in an old jail or abandoned building. Ring any bells?"

I was on the phone with Katie Horrigan, standing outside **Chez Paul,** a temperamental little French restaurant on the corner of Erie and Rush. Every time I come near this place I crack up, recalling the scene John Belushi and Dan Ackroid performed here in the classic Blues Brothers movie.

After leaving Gabriela's apartment, we'd taken a cab here to grab a bite and debrief. When a Google search of clubs, River North, French, and abandoned warehouse elicited on breakthrough. I decided to call Katie on the off chance she knew what the club could be.

"Don't tell me you're harassing me because you need help with your social life," said Horrigan on the other end.

I could hear phones wailing, a TV droning Chicago Tonight, which meant she was still at her desk at the police station, sitting in her beat-up swivel chair, poring over the details of a case her colleagues had long given up on, glasses perched on the tip of her nose.

"Not actually," I said. "It's a lead."

"I know River North like I know my kitchen. I understand it's there for my pleasure and enjoyment, but somehow I never manage to go there. Can't help you. Can I get back to work now?"

"What about occult worship in the city? How prevalent is it?"

"Does worshiping money count as the occult?"

"I mean, strange practices, rituals. How often do you come across that kind of thing at a crime scene? Would it surprise you?"

"McCarthy, I got stabbings. I got gunshot wounds. I got a rich kid who knifed his mother in the neck, a six-month-old baby shaken to death., a man who was castrated in the International Terminal at Ohare. Sure we got occultism. We got it all.

There might be a Starbucks on every corner and an iPhone at every ear, but don't worry, people are still stark raving mad. Anything else?"

I was about to say no and apologize for bothering her when I thought of something.

"I might have a case for Child Protective Services."

She didn't immediately respond, though I could practically see her jerking upright, unearthing a yellow legal pad out of the piles of witness testimonies and lab photos, flipping through her illegible scribbles to a blank page, grabbing a pen.

"I'm listening," she said.

"I just left a woman who's the guardian of a young deaf boy. It doesn't look right. The building's a shithole, might be a brothel."

"What's the address?"

"Fourteen twenty-seven South Normal Avenue. The woman's name is Dot. She runs the place."

"I'll have someone look into it."

"Thank you. Now, when am I taking you out for a drink?"

"When the city gets all fuzzy and warm inside."

"So, never?"

"I keep hoping." A phone bleated on her end. "I gotta take…"

She hung up.

It was after ten o'clock now, a Friday night. Groups of twentysomethings crowded the sidewalk, stumbling toward bars and hookups. Across the street, where the sloping red brick wall surrounding Saint Patrick's old cathedral cut sharply around the corner, I noticed a man in a black leather jacket talking on a cellphone, his hand cupped over the receiver.

He was staring at me and I couldn't shake the feeling it was me he was speaking about. He looked away, past the Ralph Lauren store on the corner, still muttering into his phone. I headed back into Chez Paul. *I was just being paranoid.*

Thirty-Nine

"I was just telling Cooper," said Elizabeth, as I sat down in the window seat beside her. "I found a receipt in Gabriela's trash-can.

After Cooper's inspection of the small piece of yellow paper, with a doubtful look, he handed it to me.

It was a handwritten receipt from Dragon Master Tattoos, located at 5050 West Lawrence Avenue. Someone, I could only assume Gabriela, though no name was listed, had paid $360.22 in cash for an "American flag portrait tat" on October 5, at 8:21 p.m. I knew from the coroner's photos that the tattoo Gabriela had on her right foot predated this receipt. So it was a mystery what American flag/ portrait tat referred to.

"We'll go there tomorrow," I said. "See if someone there recognizes her picture."

We'll also have to find someone who can tell us what those circles are that she put under her bed," said Elizabeth, taking a bite of avocado toast.

"We don't know she put that down there," interjected Cooper. "Any kook could have planted that."

"I agree," I said. "The landlord eavesdropping, she could have easily been lying about the key. There are also the two men Lexi saw outside Gabriela's door. I wonder if she was hiding from somebody, possibly her family. Why else would she take the room under a pseudonym and change the locks?"

"It's almost like there are two Gabriela's," said Elizabeth thoughtfully.

"Meaning?" I asked.

She shoved her fork through the tower of couscous on her plate. "There's the pianist. The woman who was fearless and wild. The girl Cooper met at Gateway Wilderness Therapy camp. Then there's this other one people keep talking about. This creature with supernatural tendencies."

"Supernatural tendencies," I repeated.

She nodded, her face serious. "There's what Lupe said at the Warwick Allerton. That she was marked." She looked at Cooper.

"In the coroner's photo, we saw a black dot in her left eye just like she said. Think of how she manipulated Stanley Dewitt without saying a word. She hypnotized him. And then Caesar at Onofrio? He said she moved like an animal."

"She was admitted against her will to a mental hospital," said Cooper, sitting low in his seat. "Who knows what meds they gave her? I've seen people on that shit, trying to come off that shit. They don't know what they're doing half the time."

"One other thing I noticed," Elizabeth continued in a subdued voice. "Gabriela had some kind of weird interest in children."

I was impressed, I noticed the same thread myself.

"Gabriela read Stanley Dewitt's daughter a bedtime story," she went on. "She also babysat the landlord's nephew. If she came to the city, hoping to meet someone at the Warwick, and now this nightclub, why would she take the time to do that?"

"Maybe she liked kids," said Cooper.

"That's some serious interaction with children in a span of just a few days. Remember that doll Stanley Dewitt fished out of the pool? He told us it'd been missing for a few weeks"

"So?" said cooper.

"That'd be around the time Gabriela was at his house."

"You think Gabriela hid the doll in the pool?"

"Maybe. Why would she put that dirt in circles under her bed? Or those roots over her door?

"We already established she probably didn't do that." He said it so angrily, a couple of models at the table beside us stopped speaking to stare at him. He leaned in, lowering his voice. "I'm sure you love the idea that Gabriela was some kind of Blair Witch, cooking up stews with puppy-dog tails and little kids toes or whatever the hell. But it's a joke. Her family's responsible. They're the wackjobs who put her in Mission Hills. She wanted to get away from them. Probably died trying." He muttered these last words to himself, shoving his hair out of his eyes and stabbing his fork into his baked eggs, too irritated to eat.

Elizabeth shot me a look and mutely resumed eating. I said nothing. The way she phrased it, Gabriela had some kind of weird interest in children, reminded me of my anonymous caller from five years ago. *John. There's something he does to the children,* he'd said, words that had haunted me.

What did it mean? That the entire family, or at least father and daughter, had a fixation on children? *Why?*

Simply asking such a question, the mind automatically answered with the darkest responses imaginable. This dichotomy was a major theme in Esquivel's work: the malignancy of drug addiction, the purity of youth, and the collision of these two charges. Where the debts of the father get handed down to the son. Thus fester hatred and revenge. *Better to murder an innocent child and be done with it, then give rise to a monster.*

I thought of Stanley Dewitt's daughter, Ashlynn, how she'd silently tiptoed after me down the driveway and held out her hand, holding something black.

Had I misread her? Had she silently been pleading for help, begging me not to leave? I was glad I'd told Katie Horrigan about that boy on Normal Avenue. With a little more research, I wouldn't hesitate to make the same call for the Dewitt children. The thought was so unsettling, I found myself sending Angela a text, apologizing for the change in plan, telling her I was looking forward to having Kim for the weekend while she was in Santa Barbara.

"That's the third time that guy's walked by looking in at us," Cooper said, staring out the window behind me. I turned following his gaze. It was the same man I'd noticed before, tall, dark hair, black leather jacket. He was across the street again, a few yards from where I'd first spotted him.

"He was watching me before when I was outside," I said.

Cooper suddenly leaped out of his chair, jostling a waitress, who nearly dropped her tray of food as he ran past her and outside. Seeing him coming, the man darted around the corner. I stood up and took off after them.

Forty

Cooper was halfway down the block, running in the middle of the street. I caught up with him at the corner of Rush.

"He just took off," he yelled, pointing at a cab accelerating toward Erie Street. Cooper stepped into the street trying to flag down another, and I headed after the taxi.

Far ahead at the intersection, the light turned yellow, and the cab, swerving into the center lane, was flooring it. *He was going to fly right through, and that would be that.* But then suddenly the taxi slammed on its brakes, coming to an abrupt halt at the red light.

I had seconds. I weaved between the cars, darting along the right-hand side. I could see the man, a dark silhouette in the backseat, looking over his shoulder, probably to see if Cooper was behind him. I tried the door.

He whipped around, startled. His shock quickly gave way to cold calm as he realized the doors were locked. He looked instantly familiar.

"Who are you?" I shouted. "What do you want?"

He shook his head, shrugging as if he had no idea who I was. *Did I have the wrong taxi?* The cab crept forward, the man's face slipping into the shadows. Then the light turned green and the taxi shot across Division Street, cars honking as they swerved around me.

Just as the cab pulled away, his left hand had slipped into the light. The man was missing three fingers.

Forty-One

Back at Chez Paul, I explained to Cooper and Elizabeth what had happened, that I was certain it was Santo Esquivel who'd been watching us.

"It changes everything," I said. "The family is on to us now, so we'll have to assume our every move is being watched."

They responded with somber acceptance. Cooper almost immediately throwing a few crumpled bills on the table and taking off in answer to a text, Elizabeth and I headed home. She went to bed, though I poured myself a Maker's Mark and looked up Santo Esquivel.

There were at least a thousand returns in Google images, almost everyone a reference to Santo's father Carlos. Photos of the family scurrying into limo's, some of the family outings. The more I scrutinized the photos, the more certain I was that it was the same man, the same long, thin nose, same pale brown eyes. I checked my notes for his birthdate: born in Northwestern Hospital, Chicago on March 12, 1981, which made him thirty-four.

There was little more about Santo on the Blackboards. In the world of Esquivel, it appeared the man's son was basically an afterthought. According to one source, for the past eleven years, he'd been living a life of total obscurity in rural Indiana, working as a landscaper, and had changed his name to Johnson.

After scrolling through a few more pages, I had an idea. I set up a simple post in the talk to stranger's section, asking for assistance identifying and privately accessing a mysterious club in River North with a French name, "held in a very old former jail or forgotten prison."

Then I put the computer to sleep and headed to bed.

Forty-Two

Exhausted yet still, sleep escaped me. I had the gnawing feeling that he was still out there somewhere, watching me.

Santo Esquivel. The feeling was so grave I climbed out of bed, yanked up the shade, and looked out the window. But the street remained silent and solemn, packed with shadows, no movement except the trees trembling in a faint cold breeze. *Now I was turning into some paranoid nutcase straight out of Dostoyevsky.*

I went back to bed, pulling the sheet up over my face, furiously willing sleep. Shoving my pillow over to the cool side. Within seconds it was hot and clammy. The sheets were scalding, too, untucking from the mattress so they bunched around my waist like carnivorous plants trying to strangle me. Whenever I closed my eyes, Santo's face was there, half-drowned in the shadows of the taxi, his dull eyes and deformed hand pressing against the window as if trying to tell me something, plead with me, warn me, as disturbing and elusive a presence as Gabriela that night at the Reservoir.

Somehow, around three in the morning, I must have fallen asleep because I was awakened by soft knocking on my door.

I cracked open an eye. The clock read 3:45 A.M.

"Can I come in?" whispered Elizabeth.

Without waiting for an answer, thank God I had on pajama bottoms, she crept inside. I couldn't see much of her in the dark, but she appeared to be wearing a white long-sleeved nightgown, which made her look like a ghost that had just wafted into my room. Now hovering at the end of my bed, sizing my up, trying to decide if I was worth haunting.

"I was just thinking…" she began but didn't continue.

"Why are you thinking at four in the morning?" I asked, bunching the pillows underneath me and leaning back against the headboard. "This better be good."

"It's Cooper. Before I couldn't put my finger on it, but. . ." she propped her feet on the railing of the bed, slipping the nightgown over her knees. "How did he know to go to that piano store? Out of the whole city, he found the one place she went to? It's too incredible."

I agreed with her. It's been such a stroke of luck, Cooper chancing upon an eyewitness for Gabriela at Onofrio. When something appeared to be a wild coincidence, nine times out of ten it wasn't.

"And when I suggested that Gabriela put that stuff under her bed, he got so mad."

"I noticed."

She bit her thumbnail. "You think he's responsible in some way for what happened to her?"

"Not sure yet. But he's definitely hiding something."

"I don't think he likes us, either."

A terrible flaw. There's also the chain-smoking, the morose scowling, the bad-boy hair. It's like he thinks he's the rebel in a John Hughes movie."

She giggled.

"We'll pull a choice move from the McCarthy playbook. The Corleone. We keep him close. Eventually, he'll reveal himself. Works every time."

She tucked her hair behind her ears, making the bed shake, but said nothing.

"May I ask you something?" I asked.

She turned to me, her face a blur in the dark.

"Willow Falls. How were you allowed to live there? Surely there was some kind of age requirement."

"Oh, it was illegal. But I couldn't leave Bernice. She raised me. The worst day of my life up till then was when she fell in the parking lot of Church's Fried Chicken and the doctors said she had to go into a home."

"How old were you when you moved in?"

"Fourteen."

"What about your parents?"

She fiddled with the frilly sleeves of her nightgown. "My mom died when I was three. She had a heart problem. My dad had been put away for twenty years by then."

"What has he been put away for?"

"Mail fraud, wire fraud, identity theft, credit cards. He was real hardworking at being illegal. Bernice used to say if my dad put half the energy he did into cutting corners into just driving around the corner, he'd be a billionaire."

I nodded. I'd known such men, had investigated more than a few.

"For a while I'd spend the day there, leave, then sneak back in at night. But after I got caught, I was all set to go into foster care. But Bernice got together with the other seniors on their floor, and they made a big stink. The president ended up surprising everyone because she didn't want a senior uprising. She said if I stayed out of sight when the state evaluators came I could live there till I finished high school. There was always a room coming available because someone was always dead.

When Bernice died of cancer I left without saying a word to anyone. I figured if I didn't do it then. I never would."

She paused, clearing her throat. "She died in the hospital on a Sunday, and I went back to her room to collect her things. There's a waiting list, so I knew someone was going to be moving in. If the family doesn't take away the personal items they just chuck them, and within seconds the room looks like you were never there in the first place. Just an old bed and chair, a window waiting to be gazed out of by the next person. I was getting her stuff together when all of a sudden Old Grubby Bill who lived right across the hall whistle at me through his teeth."

"*Old Grubby Bill?* You haven't mentioned him."

"Everyone called him Grubby Bill because he always had black dirt under his fingernails. He'd fought in World War Two, and He bragged to everyone he stood right beside Hitler's bunker just before it exploded. So, people used to whisper some of that debris for that bunker was still under his fingernails, which was why they were so filthy."

She paused sniffling. "He whistled at me to come into his room. He was always whistling at people. I was scared to go in there. Nobody did because it smelled. But he dug under his bed and pulled out a Rockport shoebox. He told me he's been saving money for my dreams. He had six hundred dollars in there. He handed it to me and said, *'Now's your chance to make something of yourself, Scram kid.'* So I scrammed. I walked to the Kissimmee station and got on a bus to Chicago. People don't realize how easy life is to change. You just get on the bus."

She fell silent. For a while, neither of us spoke, letting her story drift like a raft on a river between us.

"I was lucky," she went on. "Most people just get one mom and dad. I got a whole crowd."

"You were very lucky."

She seemed pleased, tucking her hands inside long white sleeves. "It's easy to be yourself in the dark. Ever notice that? Guess we should get some sleep." The bed shook as she hopped off and darted out of the room. "Night Woodward."

"Night Bernstein."

Forty-Three

I had just picked up today's copy of Fascinations. The front page read **"Underworld's most famous daughter, *Suicide or?*"**

Fascinations, reporter Denise Cambridge tracks down Gabriela Esquivel's freshman roommate at Wesleyan University, Middletown, Conn. and learns that the wild-spirited daughter leaves in her wake as many alarming questions as her notorious father.

"We lived together almost the entire year and I can't say that I knew her." Says Emma Starks, Gabriela's roommate freshman year at Wesleyan from 2005 to 2006. "She was wild. I am from Milford, Illinois, population 1200. We didn't have girls like Gabriela in my town. I mean, she had a crazy Japanese tattoo on the back of her neck and drank whiskey while she wrote her term papers.

The fact that I am sitting in Starbucks on a Tuesday morning, having scones with a woman who actually knew Gabriela Esquivel, feels a bit surreal. Ever since news broke of her alleged suicide in a run-down Chinatown warehouse, the first report of anything Esquivel related in years, notwithstanding the slander scandal surrounding detective Shawn McCarthy some five years ago, I've been trying to track down Gabriela's friends, neighbors, people she worked with, to hear what they had to say about her, if they could explain such a tragedy, to no avail.

Gabriela used no social media, which in this day and age means you don't exist. Google gives rise only to her childhood music career. So far my wild goose chase leads me only to Emma Starks, 25, formerly of Milford, Illinois, currently of Battery Park, New York City. She now works as an analyst at JPMorgan Chase.

"Gabriela read things: Interview and Lord Byron," Starks continues, thoughtfully pulling apart a croissant. "Sometimes she stayed up all night composing music. I'd wake up at four in the morning and see she was awake in bed with a flashlight, her pencil scratching away. The rest of us freshmen wandered around in big awkward groups, you know, worried about grades, who our friends would be, fitting in. She already knew who she was. And nothing scared her."

When I ask what she means by this, Starks tells me about an incident halfway into the fall semester when she and a friend attended an off-campus party.

When they arrived, there was a commotion in the back room. Making her way through the crowd, Starks saw everyone watching a strip poker-drinking game, which consisted of Gabriela Esquivel and eight men, all seniors.

"I would have been so intimidated," says Starks. "They were on the lacrosse team, economic majors, super-arrogant. All of them thought they were the next George Soros. Gabriela drank them under the table. Four had to excuse themselves to go throw up on the lawn. Soon it was just her and this rich kid named Carson. He was a third, a total asshole. You know those guys who use words like attenuate in conversation and talk about summers on the Vineyard? Well within an hour, he was stripped to nothing but his tightie-whities, so wasted he staggered out of his chair and fell to the floor unconscious. Gabriela was totally sober. That was the moment every guy on campus fell in love with her."

Starks describes another incident when she came home late one night from the library to find Gabriela holding a "Truth or Dare?" party in their room. "Gabriela refused to do truth, only dares," says Starks. "The dares became more and more insane, and she wouldn't hesitate. At one point, someone dares her to put out a cigarette with her fingers.

She did it with her tongue. When they were daring her to climb onto the roof and she climbed right out, walking along the edge, I felt sick and had to leave the room. When I came back an hour later, the party had broken up and she was in bed, reading. Like nothing happened."

I asked Starks if Gabriela ever talked about her home life, her father, in particular. "No, she was private. But at a party just before Christmas break, I remember seeing her making out with this junior soccer player, Matt, who every girl on campus was obsessed with. She went off with him, I think because she didn't come back to the room for three days. When she did, she was curled up on her bed, sobbing. It scared me because I'd never seen her like that, so I asked what was wrong and she said, 'A demolished heart.' That was so Gabriela. Her heart wasn't just broken, it was demolished, you know? She said she was in love with someone and there was no hope. I figured Matt had blown her off. But Matt started calling all the time, trying to see her, so I don't think it had anything to do with him. It was someone else, something else, I never knew who."

Starks was an economics major and spent most nights in the library. Soon she had a boyfriend and rarely spent time in the room, though when she was there, Gabriela never was.

"I think she was taking the train into the city, doing her own thing, as well as her school work. In spite of all her running around, she made better grades than me. I remember seeing her semester average printed out on her desk and it was all A's. She did everything to the max. she hated things that were wishy-washy, half-assed, weak and cautious, which she probably saw in me.

Starks knew nothing about Gabriela's family, except that they called regularly, like her own parents. "Most times it was her mom. She had a thick French accent. Very glamorous.

But one time I picked up when Gabriela wasn't there and a man with a deep voice asked for her. I asked who was calling, and he said, 'her father.' That was it.

This state of affairs continued until about spring semester when Gabriela disappeared from school, with no word as to why.

"There were a series of phone calls for her," Starks tells me. "I didn't recognize the voice. It was a man. And suddenly Gabriela was gone. This Hispanic woman came a week later to pack up her stuff. I wasn't there, but people saw her. I came back to the room and found it stripped bare. The only thing left were three photos I found months later when I was moving out for the summer. They'd fallen down behind her dresser. She had an old 1970's Polaroid camera she was always taking pictures with. It was three of them."

I asked Starks where she thought Gabriela had gone.

"People whispered that she'd gotten pregnant," she tells me. "Or she'd done something illegal or was into hard drugs and had to go to rehab. No one knew. But then, spring of my sophomore year she was back. She'd gotten permission to live off campus. I'd lost contact with her. But I remember seeing her once alone in the library reading at the end of senior year. I wanted to go up to her to say hi but I didn't. I guess I was still intimidated."

Starks says she was saddened to hear of Gabriela's death. (At the time of this article's publication, the Chicago Police Department have yet to release the medical examiner's official ruling, though preliminary inquiries point to suicide.) Starks admits her stunning, free-spirited roommate awed her. Now she feels only regret, wishing she'd taken the time to get to know her, see what was behind Gabriela's daredevil attitude and thirst for living.

"If I learned anything about her it was that she lived with a passion most of us never have the courage for," Starks tells me. "But there was something about her that precluded an ordinary existence. In some ways, I'm not surprised she's dead. A job, husband, kids, a beach house? That wasn't her. I can't explain why, except she was more like a force that whipped through life, defying logic, scaring you, even hurting you because she was everything you wanted to be, but you knew you'd never have the guts, and then she was gone. That was my experience of Gabriela Esquivel."

Starks fell silent, her uneaten croissant pulled to flaky bits on her plate.

"It was many and many a year ago, in a kingdom by the lake, that a maiden there lived whom you may know by the name of Gabriela E."

She smiles with embarrassment. "Spring semester, after she was gone so suddenly, someone on our floor, I never found out who, wrote that on the dry eraser board hanging outside our door. I left it up because it was amazing. No one would ever rewrite an Edgar Allen Poe poem for me, you know?"

Starks checks her watch. She pulls on her gray jacket and slings her JPMorgan Chase bag over her shoulder. "That's all I know," she says, draining the rest of her cappuccino and gently returning the cup to the saucer. She sighs. "Guess I have to get back to my life now."

Forty-four

I put down the paper, looked at my watch and noticed it's after ten A.M., and we were in a taxi speeding down Wells Street. I was actually reassured by the article published in this morning's paper that Denise hadn't made much headway in the investigation into Gabriela's suicide. And a google search of news for Gabriela Esquivel revealed no other reporter had uncovered the critical lead, that Gabriela had been admitted to Mission Hills, which meant we were still ahead of the game. *At least for now.*

I made a quick note of one odd detail: Gabriela's unexpected leave from Wesleyan during her freshman year.

"There it is," Elizabeth said suddenly, and the driver pulled over. We'd turned down an alley off Lake street and Wells, Elizabeth indicating a narrow storefront sunken some five feet down from the sidewalk, a black gate and a beat-up metal awning, a single word painted on it in purple letters:

FASCINATIONS

On its website, Fascinations called itself *Chicago's Oldest and Largest Witchcraft and Goddess Supple Store.* We climbed out of the cab, heading down front steps encrusted with dead leaves and cigarette butts, stepping inside.

Immediately, a tall freckled-faced orange-haired kid moved out from behind the cash register, shouting, "Septimus, come back here!" Septimus being a white angora cat that had run toward the open door, though I closed the door before it could escape.

"Thanks, man," said the kid.

There was an overpowering smell of incense, the ceiling low, narrow brick walls slanting inward like a corridor the old row houses on Fullerton Parkway. They were lined with wooden shelves crammed with mystical knick-knacks. In Fascinations it seemed all holy items were created equal. The store arranged as if Buddha, Mohammed, Vishnu, plus a couple of pagans all got together to hold a garage sale.

Mini witch cauldrons (in Tall, Grande, and Venti) were brazenly stacked next to Saint Francis, Mary, and a few other Catholic saints. Beside them sat a much paged-through paperback on display, *Jewish Kabbal Magic,* which rested next to a Bible.

An array of Tarot cards, sachets of potpourri called *Luck & Happiness Ouanga Bags*, a basket of carved wax crucifixes, ceramic frogs, and plastic vials of holy Water (on sale for $4.95) also adorned the shelves.

Apparently, many Chicagoans had given up on shrinks and yoga and thought, *hell, let's try magic* because the store was crowded. Toward the back, a group of thirtysomething women was swarming around a tall bookcase crammed with hundreds of colored candles, choosing them with a frantic intensity. A tired middle-aged man in a blue button-down, he looked alarmingly like my stockbroker, was carefully reading the directions on the back of an Ouija board.

I stepped around Elizabeth and a solemn boy with stringy brown hair paging through a pamphlet, I glanced at the title over his shoulder: *Guide to Planetary and Magical significance,* and walked over to the display case. Inside were silver necklaces, pendants, and charms carved with hieroglyphics and other symbols I didn't recognize. Hanging from the ceiling above the cash register was a five-pointed surrounded by a circle, a pentagram, the symbol for Satanists if I remembered correctly from my college days. Beyond that on the back wall were framed 8 x 10 black-and-white headshots of men and women who had the severe expressions and dead raisin eyes of serial killers, legendary witches, and warlocks, no doubt

A small faded handwritten sign was taped beside them.

WE DO NOT SELL BLACK MAGIC SUPPLIES, SO DON'T EVEN ASK.

The orange haired kid who'd chased Septimus to the back of the store shuffled over to us.

"Need some help?"

"Yes," said Elizabeth, setting a book she'd been leafing through, *Signs, Symbols, & Omens,*

Back down on the stand. "We were hoping someone could help us identify some herbs and roots that we found in strange patterns in our friend's room."

He nodded, totally unsurprised, and pointed his thumb toward the back.

"Ask the witches on call," he said. "They know everything."

I hadn't noticed it when we'd entered, but in the back of the store, there was a wooden counter, a young Hispanic kid sitting behind it.

Elizabeth and I made our way to him, navigating around the women fussing over the colored candles. One with frizzy red hair holding a purple, a yellow, an orange, and a green. "Should I get Saint Elijah and San Miguel, too?" she asked her friend.

"Don't mess this up," Elizabeth whispered. "I know you don't believe in this stuff, but it doesn't mean you can be rude."

"Me? What are you talking about?"

She shot me a look of warning before stepping behind a young woman quietly discussing something with the Hispanic kid. He was perched on a tall stool, industriously carving into a green handle with a large bowie knife.

He didn't look like a witch, but that was probably the same dim observation as a neighbor telling the *evening news* old Jimmy who lived in his mother's basement and was rarely seen in daylight didn't look like a homicidal maniac. This male witch had shaggy black hair and was wearing a faded green army work shirt, the kind popularized by Fidel Castro and Che Guevara, giving him a sort of socialist tropical authority.

Cluttering the wooden counter in front of him were colored candles, sachets of herbs, bottles of oils and dark liquids, box cutters, string, switchblades. On a clipboard hanging off the side of the counter by a rope was a cluster of tattered pages. I grabbed it, **Fascinations Custom Carved Menu**, it read, flipping through.

"*Win at Court. This candle allows you to win in all legal matters great and small.*"

"*Purple Wisdom. Used for overcoming obstacles, known or unknown, and for prophetic decisions. It is for gaining wisdom* in the ancient sciences such as astrology, hermetic magic, Qabbalism, and other magical systems."

"Come to me. This candle works on people who are full of sexual desire and brings them together. It is a **<u>Very Powerful Sexual</u>** candle and should be used with caution."

I should have come here years ago.

The woman in front of us stepped aside, and we moved to the counter.

"How can I help you?" the kid asked without glancing up. Elizabeth, in a lower voice, tactfully explained why we were there, removing two Ziploc bags from her purse, one containing the dirt Kimple, the other with the cluster of roots tied together with white string.

"We found this under our friend's bed in a series of strange circles," she said, holding up the dirt Kimple. "We need help identifying what it is and why it was put there."

The kid set down the knife, taking the time to carefully wipe his hands between his fingers, inspecting it under the small desk lamp in front of him. He then opened it, sniffing, blinking from the stench. He resealed it, set it down, hopping off the stool. He grabbed a small stepladder shoved into the corner and set it down in front of the shelves to our right. They spanned all the way to the ceiling and were jam-packed with row upon row of giant glass jars filled with herbs, each one with a faded label.

I stepped forward to read a few.

ARROWROOT. BALM OF GILEAD. BLADDERWRACK. DEER'S TONGUE. DRAGON'S BLOOD CHUNKS. FIVE FINGER GRASS. HIGH JOHN THE CONQUEROR ROOT. QUEEN OF THE MEADOW. JOB'S TEARS.

The kid climbed the ladder, reaching up on his tiptoes to collect a jar from the top shelf.

VALEERIAN ROOT, read the label.

He returned to the counter with it, opened the lid, using a spoon to scoop some of the dirt like substance into his palm. He compared it to the contents of the Ziploc bag.

"Same texture, same smell," he whispered to himself.

"What is it?" asked Elizabeth.

"Vandal root."

"What's that?" I asked.

"A herb. Its magical reputation is pretty dark."

"It's *magical reputation?*"

He nodded, unperturbed by my skepticism. "Sure. Vandal is used a lot in black magic. Hexing. Forcing love. Uncrossing. It's kind of like coming across a gimp costume in your best friend's closet. There's no explaining that shit away, know what I mean?"

I wasn't sure I did, but I nodded anyway.

"You said it was laid out in a specific pattern?" he asked.

"Yes." I showed him the photos on my BlackBerry.

"We also found these twigs tied together," added Elizabeth, indicating the other bag on the counter. "They were hidden along the doorjamb of her front door." The kid, frowning at it, reached into a box on his left, donning a pair of latex gloves, and pulled out the clump of sticks.

"Where'd you find all this," he asked uncertainly.

"In a friend's room that she was renting," I answered.

He squinted at the root in the light, twirling it in his fingers. "This looks like some really high-level shit, so you should talk to Cleopatra. Let me see if she's available."

He yanked aside a heavy black curtain on the back wall, and as he disappeared, I caught a glimpse of another room with dim red light and a few candles.

"Hang on to your wallet," I said to Elizabeth. "We've been marked as whales. We're about to be granted access to the high-rollers room. They're going to be offering us glimpses of our future, contact with the dead, and other soul-cleaning paraphernalia that's going to save us from bad vibes and set us back a couple thousand bucks."

"Shhh," she admonished as the Hispanic kid stuck his head out.

"She'll see you," he said and held aside the curtain for us.

Elizabeth grabbed the plastic bags, eagerly stepping after him like she'd just been granted one-on-one with the pope in the Vatican's inner chambers.

With a silent Hail Mary, I followed.

Forty-Five

It was a small back room lit with gloomy red light, crumbling brick walls draped with black fabric, a circular wooden table with a few folding chairs, a red stained-glass lamp suspended over it.

A woman, Cleopatra, I could only assume was standing in the back beside a messy counter, talking on a cordless phone, her back to us. She was tall and pudgy, wearing a black peasant blouse, jeans, old red Doc Martins. Her shoulder-length jet black hair, streaked with chunks of purple, sat atop her shoulders like a lampshade.

"Have a seat," the Hispanic kid said, pulling out the chairs for us around the table. "I'm Dexter, by the way."

"Yeah, let's try that on him," Cleopatra said into the phone, her voice flat and clinical. "The Juniper berries. See how he treats. If he doesn't call you to set up the third date, we'll try something more potent." She set the phone down then turned toward us. She was Asian, Korean, I guessed, with a stark, clubby face, in her late forties. She wore a long clip of bluebird feathers in her hair and so many silver bracelets, cuffs, dangly skull earrings, necklaces, one pendant a four-inch tooth from the mouth of a tiger, as she strode toward us, she rattled and clanged.

"I'm Cleo," she announced flatly. "Hear you found evidence of a black trick."

"We don't know what it is," said Elizabeth.

Cleo, clearly having heard this many times, pulled an upholstered armchair set against the wall over to the table, foam crumbling out of the seat. She sat down, folding one leg under her, the other knee up, linking her arm around it, so when she was finally still she was in a warped pose, something between an extreme level yoga position and a dead twisted insect one finds along a windowsill.

"Get me up to speed," she asked Dex with a touch of impatience. He picked up the Ziploc bags and my BlackBerry and walked her through the evidence like an intern showing a specialist a confounding MRI.

"But see this?" he murmured, pointing at something. "And here? I didn't understand the symmetry. First I thought anvil dust or maybe rabbit feces? But then that? I've never seen . . ."

His voice trailed off into a doubtful silence. She grabbed the phone, narrowing her eyes as she zoomed in on one of the pictures.

"I got it," she said with a glance at Dex. "You can go now."

He nodded, and with a final look back at us, what appeared to be a genuine worry, he darted around the curtain back into the store. Cleo inspected the pictures for another minute, ignoring us. She picked up the herbs, sniffing them, unaffected by the rank smell, and then studied the roots, the strand of feathers clipped into her hair rolling along her cheek as she leaned over the table.

"Tell me where you found all of this," she said in a low voice.

"Inside the room that a friend of ours was renting," said Elizabeth. "The circles and the charcoal were under her cot."

"Who is this friend?"

We'd like that to remain anonymous," I said.

"Man or woman?"

Woman." Answered Elizabeth.

"And where is she now?"

"That is something we don't dare discuss," I said.

"How is she?"

"Fine," I answered. "Why?"

Cleo had been closely inspecting the bouquet of roots, but now she looked up at me. She had black eyes, so deeply embedded in her plump face I couldn't see the whites, only the black irises sparkling with light in spite of the dimness of the room.

"Your friend has a pretty severe curse on her."

She didn't elaborate, only set down the branches and sat back in the chair, patiently waiting for us to say something. I stared back at her in silence. So did Elizabeth.

Normally I would have shrugged off such a pronouncement, thinking it was pure superstition. Yet something about Cleopatra, her point blank certainty, that wasn't so easy to shrug off.

First of all, the woman looked like Confucius's punk sister. She also spoke in a bland expert neurosurgeon's monotone.

"What type of curse?' I asked her.

"Not sure," Cleo answered. "It wasn't a simple jinx." She grabbed my BlackBerry, holding up one of the pictures. "She performed a high-level uncrossing ritual. Vandal root in a circle mixed with sulfur, salt, insect chitin, dried human bones, probably some other stuff that'd make your stomach turn. All of that encircling asafetida burned on a perfect pyramid of charcoal. There was probably a really repulsive smell."

"Yes," Elizabeth answered quickly.

"That was the Devil's dung. Asafetida. It repels evil and brings harm to enemies. Another way to undo a spell is to mix it with vandal root, black hen feathers, black arts powder, and a strand of hair off the person who cursed you. You urinate into it, put the mixture into a glass jar, and bury it in a place you know they'll walk over again and again, like their front porch or garage. After that, they'll pretty much leave you alone for the rest of your life."

"Does it work on ex-wives?" I asked. "If she lives in a posh condo on the Magnificent Mile, can I just leave it with the doorman?"

Elizabeth shot me a look of rebuke, but Cleopatra only cleared her throat.

"If you don't have access to a location where they'll be," she went on patiently, "you do what your friend did. Set up a Vandal Circle."

"Did it work?" asked Elizabeth. "Did it remove the curse from her?"

"No idea. Spells are like really crude antibiotics. You have to try different ones to see the response. Super-spells can be resistant just like a strain of bacteria, one that constantly morphs to stay firmly attached to and thriving on the host. Have you talked to your friend lately? How's she feeling?"

Elizabeth eyed me uncomfortably.

"What about these twigs we found over the door?" I asked.

Cleo reclined in the chair as she considered the cluster on the table. "It's Devil's Shoestring. A natural-occurring root from the honeysuckle family. It grows in wild fields and forests. It's used for protection. In the deep American-South, people make anklets out of it. Or they douse them in whiskey and bury then in the ground. You can also do what your friend did. Take nine pieces, some white string, tie a single knot around each piece, nine roots, nine knots. Then you stick it somewhere by your front door or under your porch. Some people bury it in their front yard."

"What does it do?" I asked.

She stared at me for a moment before answering, her face unreadable.

"It trips up the devil."

"*Trips* him?"

"Stops him. Gives him pause."

"I see," I said, picking up the roots. "I don't know why the U.S. spends six billion on national defense. We could just make sure every American family had a set of these."

Cleo was clearly used to, and totally unfazed by, skeptics and non-believers. She didn't react only interlaced her ring-laden fingers, skulls, Egyptian ankhs, a cat's head, atop her raised knee.

"Did your friend take baths before sunrise?" she asked.

"Yes," said Elizabeth. "In really icy water."

I was about to ask Elizabeth what she was talking about when I suddenly remembered the strange incident Lexi had described, the early morning when she'd come upon Gabriela bathing it the tub.

"So she did cleansing rituals," said Cleo, nodding.

"What are they for?" I asked.

"They grant purification from evil. For a time. They're not permanent. More of a temporary Band-Aid. Did she wash her floors?"

Elizabeth glanced at me. "We don't know."

"Was she cold to the touch?"

"No idea," I answered.

"Did you notice if she had difficulty communicating? almost as if she had a mouthful of peanut butter or sand?"

"We wouldn't know."

"What about alarming heaviness?"

"Meaning?"

Cleo shrugged. "I've heard of some people, if they're under a particularly severe curse for an extended period of time, when they step onto an ordinary scale they can weigh up to three hundred, sometimes even four hundred pounds, even though visibly they've grown very, very thin."

"We wouldn't know that either," I answered, though I had a sudden, unnerving vision of the first and only time I'd ever seen Gabriela in person when she was wandering around the Reservoir, that strange, trancelike bearing, the heavy sound of her footsteps cutting resoundingly through the rain.

Cleo, suddenly struck by a new thought, grabbed my BlackBerry again, frowning as she scrolled through the pictures.

"One thing I don't see here is a reversal. When you're dealing with black magic, you have to uncross but also reverse, so the curse boomerangs back onto the perpetrator." She glanced up at us. "Spells are nothing more than energy. Think of it as charged particles that you've attracted to one concentrated place. You have to put them somewhere. Energy is neither created nor destroyed but transferred. It's the transfer I don't see evidence of, and that's troubling." She tilted her head, thinking, twirling the tooth pendant in her fingers. "Notice any reversing candles in the room?"

"What are reversing candles?" Elizabeth asked.

"White wax on the bottom, black at the top."

Elizabeth shook her head.

"What about a cardboard box filled with objects?"

"No."

"No mirror box," whispered Cleo to herself.

"What's a mirror box? I asked.

She looked at me. "For straightforward reversals. You get a black candle, inscribe the enemy's name onto it, bury it in a graveyard with pieces of a broken mirror. Whatever negativity or evil aimed at you will reflect back onto them." She cleared her throat, raising an inky black eyebrow. "Let's go back to her room. Were there any powders or chalk marks on the floor?"

"It was dark inside," Elizabeth said. "But no. We would have noticed something like that."

"But the floor was sticky," I added.

Cleo looked at me. "Sticky?"

"As if a soft drink had been spilled all over it, Plus a couple of plastic wrappers."

Cleo unwound herself from the twisted way she was sitting, leaning across the table, jutting her chin out. "did you pick up one of the wrappers?" She demanded t so intensely I caught a whiff of her breath, hot and garlicky and pungent like she'd been drinking some strange herbal tea. She had small tobacco-stained teeth crowded together, quite a few in the back capped in gold.

"No," I said.

"Then how do you know they were plastic wrappers?"

"That's what they sounded like."

She took a deep agitated breath. "Did you go inside the room?" she asked, sitting back in the chair.

"Of course. How do you think we found that thing under her bed?"

"How long ago was this?"

"Just last night."

She looked underneath the table. "Are those the shoes you were wearing?"

She stood up and strode to the back counter, returning with a pair of latex gloves and a pile of faded newspaper across the table's surface.

"Take one shoe off and slowly hand it to me, please."

Looking at Elizabeth, she was visibly stricken, I pulled off one or my black leather boots, handing it to Cleo.

Carefully as if handling a rabid animal, she placed the boot on its side on the newspaper, the sole facing her. She fumbled in her jean pocket and produced a four-inch pocket knife, the handle intricately carved out of some type of animal bone. She opened the blade with her teeth and holding down the boot with her other hand, scraping it slowly along the sole. She did this for minutes, ignoring us, and when she stopped, inspecting the blade inches from her nose, there was a thick brownish-black paste collected along the edge. It looked like dried molasses.

"This is the reversal," she whispered. "It's a sophisticated foot-track spell. I've never seen anything like it."

"What's a foot-track spell?" asked Elizabeth.

"Something for your enemy to walk through, a trap."

"But we walked through it," I said.

Cleo's eyes darted from the knife to me.

"Does she have any reason to believe you're her enemy?" she asked.

"No," I said, though as soon as I did, I felt an uneasy chill. I had the sudden memory of Gabriela stalking me at the Reservoir, her hard face staring down at me when she'd appeared abruptly by the gatehouse. Had she considered me a threat? *But what have I ever done to her, to her father, except seek the truth?* Maybe that alone made me an adversary.

"Whatever her reasoning," Cleo whispered, as if reading my mind, her gaze returning to the dark glue coating the knife, "one thing is clear."

"What?" I asked, my mouth suddenly dry.

"You've been crossed."

Forty-Six

"Would you mind Expounding on that?"

Cleo only carefully set down the knife and stood up, striding to the bookcase at the back of the room.

"Look," Whispered Elizabeth, inspecting the cracked soles of her own motorcycle boots. They were spangled with the same dark blotches, like wads of black gum. She yanked off one, scrutinizing the sole in the overhead light. I could see sand and thread, maybe even fingernails, mixed into the paste, glittering splinters of what looked like glass.

Cleo returned with a hulking stack of encyclopedias. *Hoodoo, Conjuration, Witchcraft, Rootwork* by Evan J Jones, read the spines. They looked ancient, with orange covers tied together with a frayed black ribbon. She sat down, picking up volume one and flipping to the contents page, slipping her index finger down the entries. When she came to the end, apparently not finding what she was looking for she slammed it shut, moving on to volume two.

I grabbed the book she'd just put down. It reeked of mildew, the pages yellowed. It was published in 1970, and a splotch of red liquid, tomato sauce or *blood*, had dried along the seam of the title page. *Hoodoo, Conjuration, Witchcraft, Rootwork. Beliefs accepted by many nationalities, these being orally recorded among blacks and whites.*

General Description of beliefs p. 1. Belief in spirits, ghosts, the Devil, and the like p. 19. The timing of spells and recurrence of the effects of spells over time p. 348.

The book appeared to be an encyclopedia of spells, some of the entries short, others extensive. They have transcribed interviews with backwater southerners with thick accents, their accounts were written phonetically. For example, on P. 521 under the heading *Mojo hands grouped somewhat alphabetically according to their major ingredient (e.g. buckeye nuts, needles, black cat bone) was the following entry* 668.

Jest git ya a snake, ya can take a rattlesnake en dry his haid up, pound it up, en den yo kin go ta work en use dat as goofer dust. Kill anybody.

"I found something similar," muttered Cleo, inspecting the bottom of my boot before returning her attention to the page in front of her. I craned my neck to read what she was looking at.

Volume four, *more conjuring type work utilizing human body parts and waste.*

"'The Black Bone Trick'," she whispered, tucking a chunk of purple hair behind ears. "'Frayed hemp rope, gum Arabic and goofer dust.' Your friend used a slight variation. I see some dark brown sand in here, some seaweed, too. She must have picked this up someplace exotic. You put it down on the floor in a Quincunx, which is a makeshift crossroads. Your enemy unknowingly walks through it. Immediately it sticks to his shoes, and within hours it's eating away at his life."

"Eating away," I asked. "What does that mean?"

She shrugged. "I've heard of a coma. Heart attacks. Abruptly losing everything you love, like your job or family. Sudden paralysis from the neck down." She raised an eyebrow. "Have you felt any strange sensations in your legs?"

"I woke up with my foot asleep this morning," Elizabeth said worriedly. Cleo nodded as if expecting this bad news. She then tilted her head, grabbing that tiger tooth pendant around her neck, rolling it in her fingers.

"One thing that bothers me is something you said before. The plastic wrappers all over the floor. I don't think they were plastic wrappers."

"What were they?"

"Probably snakeskins. If they were filled with graveyard dirt, she combined all of this with a killing curse."

"And that's . . ."

"Like it sounds. It'll kill you."

"The surgeon general says the same thing about cigarettes."

She only stared at me. "With cigarettes death takes decades. With this, you could be dead within weeks."

Elizabeth looked somewhat stricken.

"Anyone told you your *witchside* manner is a little harsh?" I asked.

"There's no point in sugarcoating black magic."

I tried smiling at Elizabeth for reassurance, but she ignored me, staring at the curse-riddled sole of her shoe as if it were a cluster of malignant tumors.

"Graveyard dirt," I said. "That means our friend collected dirt from a graveyard?"

"Yeah. And it's not easy to get. You have to do it at a certain time of night. Under a certain moon. You have to know whose grave you're taking it from. How the person dies. Some witches believe the best dirt to use comes from either a murderer, a baby less than six months old, or someone who loved you beyond all reason. You also have to know where you're digging in relation to the body if it's above the head, heart, or at the feet. You have to leave something behind, too, as a token of appreciation. Money or whiskey usually works. You mix the dirt into the snake sheds and goofer dust."

"What's goofer dust?" asked Elizabeth.

"The H-bomb of spell materials. When you goofer someone, You're spiritually poisoning them. It comes from the Congo, the word *kufwa*, which means to die. The powder is usually a yellowish color, but you mix in the graveyard dirt so it's dark and can't be spotted. It's really powerful because it eats away at your mind without you even realizing it, poisoning your reasoning and your love. It pulls apart the closest friends, isolates you, pits you against the world so you're driven to the margins, the periphery of life. It'll drive you mad, which in some ways is worse than death.

"So our friend had something like a Ph.D. in witchcraft," I said.

"She had a major proficiency in dark magic. Absolutely."

"And what is dark magic? Voodoo, Hoodoo?"

"It can mean any number of things. It's a blanket term for all magic that's used for evil purposes. I'm not an expert. My training is in Earth goddess, fertility spells, spiritual cleansing, that kind of thing. A lot of the black stuff's underground. Passed down through generations. Secret meetings in the middle of the night. Old leather-bound journals filled with spells written backward. Attics stockpiled with the really obscure ingredients, like deer fetuses, lizard feces, baby blood. This stuff is not for people with queasy stomachs. But it works. Does your friend come from a family of occultists?"

"It's possible," I said.

Well, she *thought* she was cursed. She tried hard to stop it, reverse it back onto the executioner. She wanted to kill him. That's what it looks like to me. So maybe she didn't expect you to walk through it, but someone else, maybe someone who put the curse on her. I suggest tracking your friend down and asking her."

Elizabeth shot me a wary look.

"Here's what I can tell you," Cleo went on, clearing her throat. "Scrape the trick off with a knife or razor blade. Make sure it doesn't touch your skin. Wrap it in the old newspaper and throw the materials away at a crossroads or a freshwater river."

"Guess that rules out the Des Plaines, or the Cal-Sag."

"I'll give you some reversing candles." She headed to the back again, crouching beside a cabinet, digging through shelves. "Again, I really don't have experience with this. You should consult a witch doctor with a specialty in black magic."

"Where do we find one of those/ Disney World?"

"Google it. Some names will come up. But all the really legit ones are in the Louisiana bayou." Cleo returned to the table, handing Elizabeth two candles, black by the wick, white at the base.

"How much are those setting us back? A couple hundred bucks?"

"No charge. It's unethical to charge people who came in suffering from dark magic, kind of like someone coming into the emergency room with a fatal gunshot wound. You do what you can to save their like. Money's irrelevant."

Thoughtfully rolling her tiger's tooth pendant between her fingers, Cleo watched us pull on our shows. Elizabeth, collecting the candles, explained that it had actually been three of us who'd been inside the room. So Cleo dug out a third reversing candle and then escorted us back through the store.

It was even more crowded. A dapper elderly couple inspected the skull candles. Four teenage girls browse incense. A young man with the desperately preppy look of an unemployed Wall Street analyst perused a pamphlet: *Fascinations fall class schedule.*

Magic was all fun and games until you had the H-bomb of spell materials on the bottom of your shoes.

Dexter must have given the orange-haired kid at the register the lowdown because they stared in fascination as we filed past them. Cleo opened the door for us, shooing away the Persian cat.

"Good luck," she said.

"Thanks," said Elizabeth bleakly, stepping outside. I paused.

"What if I don't buy any of this? I was raised Catholic."

Cleo stared at me blankly, through for a moment, I swore I caught an amused gleam in her black eyes.

"Then I guess you have nothing to worry about."

She slammed the door closed with a preoccupied expression, darting through the milling crowd, doubtlessly racing to her red-light den at the back of the shop.

Forty-Seven

"You think we're going to die?" asked Elizabeth nervously as we moved up the Fascinations steps.

"Everyone tends to."

"In the next few days. That goofer stuff she was talking about. She said it can kill you without you even realizing it."

"Ex-wives do the exact same thing. The most interesting thing she said was the knowledge of dark magic passed from generation to generation."

"You think that's what the Esquivels are hiding? That they're all witches or something?"

I said nothing, the notion sounding absurd. But then, Esquivel was a creative multi-millionaire holed up in an isolated estate, basically a petri dish for cultivating the weird and outlandish. Cleo had testified that Gabriela was quite proficient in spells. She'd learned how to assemble those materials from someone.

But for whom had she intended this Black Bone killing curse, *me?* Had she laid it knowing I'd investigate her death and eventually show up at Normal Street? What about Cooper? He'd been sent that stuffed parrot and had somehow known she'd frequented Onofrio. *Or did she intend it for someone else entirely?* Lexi, if she could be believed, claimed she'd seen two men outside Gabriela's door. One might have Santo Esquivel. Maybe it was her family Gabriela considered the enemy and she'd put down the killing curse for them. Cooper's inclination was to hold them accountable. Maybe they'd been chasing her, trying to find her, fearing she was on the verge of exposing them.

She had, after all, been following me, which doubtless would have made the family extremely nervous.

Elizabeth was thinking it over, nibbling her thumbnail. "It could be why Gabriela took her life. She couldn't handle the guilt of what the family had done for years, practicing black magic." She wrinkled her nose. "Maybe that's what the housekeeper at the Warwick noticed when she saw that mark in her eye. Maybe she could tell Gabriela practiced black magic."

"At this point, it's all conjecture."

Closing the metal gate behind us. I noticed my phone was buzzing. I assumed it was Cooper, but instead it was an email notification from the Blackboards, indicating someone had answered my post, though to read the response I needed my laptop with the Tor browser.

"You might think this magic stuff is hogwash, but I don't," Elizabeth said, scraping the soles of her boots on the curb. "This curse is like cement."

"We need to go back to the apartment." I stepped onto the street, hailing an approaching cab.

"What about going to Dragon Master tattoos and asking about that receipt?"

"We'll do it later. Someone on the Blackboards answered my post."

> *I need assistance identifying and privately accessing a mysterious private club on the north shore. I'm told it has a French name and is held in a former jail or forgotten prison.*

Any direction offered much appreciated. Thanks.

Reply to Help: Les Silencio

Posted by Special Agent Wolf

It's called Les Silencio
The party you seek.
The butterflies that swarm there
Make decent men weep.

Women are verboten
In this cellar of sickness.
The sentences carried out
No good girl should witness.

If you were a Member, such a question
You wouldn't bother to pose.
My guess is you're a fraud
The lost way in I'll now disclose:

Drive midnight tonight to Zion
Walk east along the shore.
When you spot Duchamp's staircase
Proceed to the door.

Les Silencio is a madhouse
A hell, an attack.
Partaking or gawking
You must watch your back.

If you're exposed or you're weak
You'll be lost from the day.
And all those who love you
Will be left to pray.

Forty-Eight

Les Silencio, there was no mention of it as a private nightclub on the Internet, nothing to verify the Claims of Special Agent Wolf. According to Les Silencio is known as an Oubliette, which is derived from the French verb *oublier* which means *forgotten place*. Historically, an oubliette was the most claustrophobic and hidden section of a castle dungeon, where there was only an iron trapdoor in the ceiling and no light, a cell so small, it was often impossible for the prisoner to turn around or even move, a casket for the alive but damned. It was reserved for the most reviled prisoners, those the captors wanted to forget.

My guess was it was some type of sex club. It didn't appear to make for a particularly *fun-filled* Saturday night, but Lexi had claimed Gabriela was going to the club, so it was certainly worth a shot to try and find someone there who'd encountered her.

At eight o'clock that night, the October weather chilly and overcast, Elizabeth and I left to pick up Cooper. He'd finally responded to our messages and wanted to join, which was fine by me; with that coup he'd produced at Onofrio, he was proving to be an unexpected asset to the investigation.

He told us to pick him up on the corner of Sacramento and Archer, in Brighton Park. I said to Elizabeth, "Make sure and keep your door locked." We waited more than twenty minutes, and just when I thought we'd have to leave without him, cooper emerged from the Blue Moon hotel.

It was an infamous place, one of the city's last flophouses where rooms, more like stalls suited for barnyard animals, went for $17.50 a night. I could only assume cooper had been doing business there, dropping off candy for a few customers with a sweet tooth, because the men around the entrance smiled with jittery appreciation as he ambled past them.

"How's the Blue Moon?" I asked as he sank into the backseat.

Not bothering to acknowledge us, he took out a wad of crumpled bills, counted them, and then tucked them into his coat pocket.

"Awesome," he muttered.

Within minutes, we were speeding down the Dan Ryan, Elizabeth breathlessly filling Cooper in on everything we'd learned at Fascinations, including the Black Bone killing curse we'd stepped on, thanks to Gabriela.

She pointed out the splotches on Cooper's own Converse sneakers, he had a sizable black wad on his left heel. His reaction was little more than cynical disbelief.

"What about that tattoo parlor?" he asked her. "Master Dragon."

"We didn't get there yet," she said. "When we saw we'd gotten a response on the Blackboards about Les Silencio, we headed back home to regroup."

Cooper said nothing, squinting thoughtfully out the window. Three hours later, Cooper was passed out cold in the backseat and Elizabeth was scanning satellite radio. I was doing eighty on the Edens heading up to Zion. I knew they had some private lakeshore homes near Illinois State Beach Park, or as the locals called it Zion Beach Park. I had been out quite a few times back in my married days, but never after Midnight on a mission like this.

"I want to come," said Elizabeth.

"We went over this," I said.

"But Gabriela went. I can easily pass for a boy. I brought pants to change into and a baseball cap."

"This isn't *Boys Don't Cry*. And after your performance at Mission Hills, we've established you're no Hilary Swank."

Within minutes, we were driving through Zion, so dark, and still it looked like an evacuated fairground, the brightly lit sidewalks strewn with sand and empty plastic bottles, deserted. Shingle roofed beach cottages, so cheerful in the summer, now hunched sullenly on the hill, dark and dour, bracing themselves for the winter. Even the locals were nowhere to be found.

I made a right onto South Emery Street and a left onto Emerson, accelerating past darkened shops and inns, Lakeside Resort, Free Flow Motel, signs reading see you next year, and then: The Lake Haven Diner, its blue twenty-four-hour neon sign bright in the window, a few cars parked in the lot out front. I sped past it and turned onto Coho Way, edging past a cluster of beach condos and pulling up behind a dented pickup.

When I cut the engine, I could hear the roar of the lake, somewhere in the dark in front of us.

"Okay, troops," I said. "Let's move."

We climbed out, Cooper yawning and stretching. I locked the car and handed the keys to Elizabeth as we headed back to Emerson Street.

"You want Cooper to go in with you?" I asked her.

I can handle it," she said, incensed. Slinging her gray purse onto her shoulder, she spun on her heel and shuffled away.

We watched her go, her footsteps crunching down the sidewalk, the hem of her dress flashing green as she passed under the streetlight, she was dressed like Lily Munster meets Cinderella by way of *punk* in an emerald green velvet dress, black crocheted tights, black motorcycle boots, and black fingerless gloves.

"Maybe you should catch up with her," I said. "Make sure she's okay waiting in there."

Cooper shrugged. "She'll be fine."

"Glad to know chivalry's not dead."

He only squinted after her. Elizabeth pulled open the door to the diner, disappearing inside. When she didn't emerge, I zipped up my jacket.

"Let's get going," I said.

Forty-Nine

We walked Coho Way, along with the wood fence to the beach, beyond the reach of the streetlamps. I took out a small flashlight from my pocket. We trudged through the sand and up the sloping hill, a freezing headland wind hitting us hard, slicing right through my clothes. Not knowing Les Silencio's dress code, I was wearing all black, leather jacket, slacks, button-down, hoping the Russian look would be enough for people to sense I should be left alone.

The wind grew stronger, the rumble of Lake Michigan deafening as we crested the knoll. The beach looked deserted. The lake was rough choppy with whitecaps, the waves crashing along the shore violently, their white explosions the only interruption in the dome of darkness surrounding us.

Staring eastward, far ahead of us down the coast, were condos and houses, all of them looked dark, boarded-up for the winter, and beyond the streetlights of town, Zion's steep dunes rising along the shore.

Duchamp's staircase.

It was an ambiguous clue, to say the least. I knew the modernist Cubist painting of 1912 it seemed to refer to: Marcel Duchamp's Nude descending staircase, No 2. Elizabeth, I googled the work before leaving home, though how I was going to associate that with something on this beach, I had no idea.

I turned to Cooper, but he'd wandered down to the water, standing there, immobile, his coat whiplashing behind him, water frothing inches from his feet. He looked so dark and melancholy, contemplating the huge waves, I wondered if he was considering walking right into them, letting them overtake him.

"It's this way!" I shouted, my voice scarcely audible above the wind. He must have heard me because he turned and started after me. The walk was slow going.

The sand was littered with debris after a recent storm, tangled clumps of weeds, plastic bottles, bony arms of driftwood reaching out of the sand. The wind picked up as we trudged on, trying to shove us back. We hiked past blocks of boxy condos with empty porches and parking lots, motels with dark welcome signs. I scrutinized every battered flight of stairs leading down to the beach, looking for some sign of life, but there was nothing.

We were out here alone.

After twenty minutes, we'd walked beyond the town of Zion and had reached Zion Beach Park. It was empty, nothing but a few lost beach chairs and some faded towels strewn about the beach. As I scaled some rocks, I didn't move out of the way in time as a wave crashed to shore and I got soaked up to my shins in icy water. I could forget about a hard looking Russian, I know like Tom Hanks in *Cast Away*.

Here the beach narrowed considerably, the massive dunes like muscular knotted shoulders bulging down the coast. Ahead, there were only multimillion-dollar beachfront estates, and it certainly wasn't a stretch to imagine that a secret party took place at one. But looking far ahead, my eyes watering in the fierce wind, I could see black silhouettes of beach houses perched high on the bluffs, but not a single light. *Les Silencio*. The forgotten place.

Maybe that meant they partied in the dark.

Cooper had moved ahead of me. He'd been silently striding along with dogged resolve, starting at the sand, unaware, it seemed, of the cold or the high water drenching his sneakers, the hem of his coat now soaked. I picked up my pace to catch up, my flashlight whipping over the rocks, empty crab shells, the chains of seaweed. I could see he'd stopped and was waiting for me beside a flight of wooden steps. The stretched from the sand up a steep hill to the house, hidden high above us over the precipice.

"Think this is it?" he yelled.

There was nothing about these stairs that reminded me of the painting.

I shook my head. "Let's keep going!"

We moved on, within ten minutes, we reached the next flight, this one-half demolished. Though at first glance I saw nothing here either that brought to mind *Duchamp,* I inspected it with the beam of the flashlight and saw with surprise that the steps above actually did look Cubist. Pieces of splintered driftwood had been nailed crudely over the top. It wasn't like *stairs* more like a rickety ladder barely attached to the rock.

It was, however, the second staircase we'd passed. The title of the painting included *No.2.*

"This might be it," I shouted.

Cooper nodded and leaped up onto the first step. It was five feet off the ground, the lower stairs, including part of the railing, strewn in mangled pieces across the sand. The structure shuddered dangerously under his weight as he climbed farther up, eventually reaching a part where the handrail was intact so he could use that to balance himself.

I stepped up onto the first platform, making a mental note not to look down, took off after him. Every wooden plank felt damp and rotten, sagging under my feet. At one point, a plank Cooper stepped onto snapped in half, his leg going through two more rotten planks below that, so he hung by the railings and I had to duck so the wood didn't nail me in the face as it flew past, crashing onto the beach below.

He managed to scramble onto the next step, which held his weight, and began climbing up again. Within minutes Cooper had vanished over the top. When I got to the top, it was a white-knuckled pull-up, as the last few steps were completely out. I stood up in tall beach grass, switching off the flashlight.

We were in someone's backyard.

Beyond manicured grass, a covered swimming pool, and clusters of black cherry trees sat a massive cedar-shingled mansion, entirely dark and still.

I checked my watch. It was after one.

"Maybe we're too late," I whispered.

Cooper eyed me. "Sounds like you need to get out more."

He took off deliberately through the shadbush onto the path, making his way toward the house. I followed him, though when we were some twenty yards from the back patio, without warning, a door opened. Dense, throbbing music filled the air. Pale white light flooded the flagstones.

Cooper and I froze, pressing our backs into the hedge along the path.

A lanky kid sporting a black bar apron emerged, dragging numerous garbage bags. He hauled them across the patio, tossing each one against a low wall stretching around the side of the house, the sound of shattering glass bottles exploding through the night. After he tossed the last bag, he retreated back into the mansion, slamming the door hard.

Silence again engulfed the house.

Cooper and I waited for a minute, the only noise the wind, the faint roar of the ocean far below. With a nod to each other, we sprinted the final distance to the patio and up the steps. Cooper tried the door. It opened easily, and we slipped inside.

Fifty

It was some kind of backroom storage area. The overhead lights had been switched off, and it was freezing inside. WE appeared to be alone. Stacked all around us were large wooden crates and boxes, a two-wheeled cart propped against the wall. I stepped over to the crates and read the labels. **Remy Martin, Chateau Lafite, Wray and Nephew LTD. Jamaican Rum.**

Not too shabby. Spanning the wall was a row of oversized steel refrigerators, and beyond that in an alcove, hanging from a line of hooks, black pants and shirts, some type of waiter's uniform. There was a long wooden table at the center of the room cluttered with supplies, and I stepped over. Piled across it were cellophane-wrapped blacks of what had to be cocaine, each one about a kilo. There were at least a hundred, plus four padlocked cash boxes chained by a metal cable to the table legs.

"It's an airport duty-free shop in Cartagena," I muttered.

Cooper stepped beside me, raising his eyebrows. "Or some billionaire's outfitted his bunker really nicely for the end of the world." He grabbed one of the bricks of cocaine, tossed it into the air like it was a football, he a seasoned quarterback. He caught it and stuffed it into his coat pocket.

"Are you nuts?"

"What?"

"Put it back!"

He shrugged, wandering over to the refrigerators. "It's market research." He wrenched open one of the steel fridge doors, the shelves packed with foam cartons and trays.

"I've crashed parties like this before." He rummaged through the containers. "It's underwritten by a Saudi prince, maybe a Russian. All this shit for them is like Bud Lite and pretzels for us. Would you give a shit if a couple of bags of Fritos go missing?"

I picked a box of Cuban cigars. *Cohiba's*

Cooper, scrutinizing a black glass jar, returned it to the shelf.

"There's more caviar here than the Black Sea."

"Help yourself. I'm getting out of here before the Saudi prince needs a pick-me-up." I stepped over to the door on the opposite side of the room. I could hear house music, throbbing like the gears on a Caterpillar tractor, grinding, shimmering, relentless.

I opened the door a crack and peered out. It took a moment of adjustment to understand what I was seeing.

It was a party. And yet the floor, black and white geometric inlaid tiles, rippled like a sea. It spanned an immense circular atrium, ringed with Corinthian pillars, yet no ceiling, just a bright blue cloud-filled sky. *How in the hell could it be a perfect summer day in here?* In the distance, beyond stone arches covered in ivy and dark doorways leading down dirt paths, there was a luscious bloom-fitted garden where stone Greek statues reclined in the sun. An egret waded in a shining stream. Red-and-green parrots soared through the jungle, sunlight filtering divinely through the canopy.

As my eyes madly searched for some semblance of reality, my mind short-circuited, both entranced and trying to form some rational conclusion as to what the hell it was: *a biosphere, a staged play, an adult Disney World, a portal to another planet.* Suddenly I caught a flaw in the in the tropical paradise: Along the floor, about a foot from where I stood, here was a light socket.

All of it was painted, a photorealist masterpiece of such detail and beauty, in the dimmed amber light it was all somehow alive, thriving. At the sunken center of the room, seated on the leather couches, standing around the marble tables, gathered a dense crowd. I was certain they were real. They were middle-aged men, most had the battered gargoyle faces of self-made tycoons (a few with the flabby dimensions of those who'd inherited their wealth), most of them Caucasian, a few Japanese. Women drifted among them, dripping in gowns and jewels, though due to the liquid floor, they seemed to float in a pool of water, snagging on a group of men like scraps of paper caught on a branch before spinning across the room on another mysterious current.

There was a strict dress code, which the person who'd answered my post on the Blackboards had failed to mention. The men were in suits and ties. Cooper and I were certainly going to stick out, not to mention the fact that I had dried water rings on my pants. Cooper moved behind me, and I stepped aside so he could take a look.

"Holy shit," he whispered.

"It's got to be some kind of cult. Anyone offers you Kool-Aid or a hot shower, just say *no.* "And don't forget the reason we're here. Find someone who saw Gabriela."

He turned to me with a deep foreboding stare. "See you on the other side."

Fifty-One

A black marble bar spanned the far wall, a handful of men seated there, one vacant red stool on the farthest right side. That would be a perfect vantage point for me to wait until I understood just what I was dealing with, so I strode casually toward it around the atrium, passing the columns, those were real, feeling slight vertigo from the shifting floors and the teeming landscapes surrounding me.

The ceiling high as a cathedral's and the mural of the sky so realistically painted, it looked infinite, glaringly blue. Staring up make me light-headed, and I nearly collided with a short, fat man with thinning black hair who'd abruptly crossed in front of me. He expressly avoided eye contact, making a beeline toward the stone garden wall. He pushed a moss covered urn and it smoothly turned into a door. I caught a glimpse of a black-and-white tiled bathroom, a make attendant in a black uniform standing beside the sinks, hands clasped, eyes discreetly on the ground before it all vanished again into that empty garden.

I slid onto the vacant stool at the very end of the bar, relieved to feel it was sturdy and real, then I turned to observe the scene.

Waiters in black slacks and Asian tunics moved among the marble tables, balancing drinks on silver trays. There was a deejay up high in a bell tower. Adorned in a purple T-shirt, headphones around his neck, his hair in dreads that reached down to his waist. He looked relatively normal, straight King Solomon's Mines on Halsted Street. I noticed he kept his eyes averted from the crowd below as he worked the controls of the synthesizer and two MacBooks.

He must have been instructed not to stare at the guests.

I returned my attention to the crowd. The women were stunning. They were all different races, many of them dark-skinned and exotic, their unifying attributes a height of about six feet and a thinness that made them resemble insects swarming, feeding ravenously on the dark suits and balding heads. They looked young. As one turned, her blond hair so pale it seemed to float like a gleaming white halo around her face, she tipped her head back, smiling, and I caught sight of a prominent Adam's apple.

Geez, holy-moly. She is a man.

Ignoring an irrational feeling of alarm, I scrutinized another wandering through the crowd in a blue sequin dress. After speaking with a group of men, she, or he, touched one on the shoulder. She had long fingernails painted black, her arms laden with jewelry. Very slowly, as if to move suddenly in this place was prohibited, would puncture the dream, they detached from the group.

She took him by the wrists, led him up the stairs along a crumbling stone wall. They slipped through an arched doorway and down a dirt path, vanishing. There were at least twelve identical entrances around the room. They led to…*what? A crying game.*

It had to be a high-end bondage club. *Never underestimate the desire for wildly successful men to torture themselves for fun.*

"May I bring you something. Mr.?"

I turned to see the bartender across from me. Though he was dressed in a slick gray suit like everyone else, a Double-Windsor blue silk tie, he was muscular, with a crew cut, craggy features, and an iron-rod posture that make me guess he was ex-military.

"Scotch, straight up," I said.

He didn't move, the friendliness draining from his face. I was doing something wrong, revealing myself and a sham. I didn't react. Neither did he. He was so brawny from anabolic steroids he looked like an action figure as if his arms might not bend at the elbows and his head could pop off from heavy play.

"Any preference of scotch?" he asked.

"Your choice."

He grabbed the bottle of Glenfiddich from the shelves. As he poured my drink, a hidden door opened beside the bar, a pastoral scene of a Tuscan landscape, and the young kid I'd seen outside hauling trash slipped in carrying a crate of glasses. His head lowered, he also seemed to have been told not to make eye contact, he began stacking them on the mirrored shelves.

The bartender returned with my drink and stood there expectantly.

"Your card?" he prompted.

"Which one?" I make a production of fumbling for my wallet.

"Membership."

"Yeah, I don't have one of those. I'm a guest."

"Whose guest?"

"Harry, can I have a glass of water, quick? I feel dizzy."

I couldn't have timed it better. One of the women, *or boys*, if that's what they were, had slunk up beside me.

She had a pouting doll profile, long blond hair, a purple silk dress so tight it looked like it's been poured over her.

The bartender, harry, he looked more like Biff, shot her a furious look, indicating she was breaching serious protocol by asking such a thing.

"Try downstairs," he said with a tight smile.

"I can't. I just need some water and I'll be fine."

He glared at her, and with a hard look at me, *I'm not done with you yet*, he stepped away.

"He's fun," I said turning to her.

She eyed me uncertainly, her hands had those long black painted fingernails, tightly holding the edge of the bar as to keep herself moored there, otherwise, so skinny, she'd waft to the ceiling like a helium balloon. Her blue eyes, heavily made up, looked watery, the pupils dilated. She'd done something to her mouth to make it puffy, injected it with something, which makes it exaggerated and sad like a clown's.

"What's your name?" I asked.

That prompted an immediate *Game Over.* She cast me an icy look. I was sure she was going to move away, but instead she tilted her head.

"You're a friend of Assad's," she said.

"Where is Assad? Haven't seen him."

"Back in France, isn't he?"

Harry banged the glass of water onto the bar. She grabbed it, gulping it down, a drop of water trickling out the edge of her red mouth, sliding down her chin. She set the empty glass down, wobbling unsteadily on her heels, and the bartender wordlessly moved away to refill it. *He'd been through this drill with her before.*

She wiped her mouth with the back of her fingers.

"Sure your all right?" I asked in a low voice.

She didn't answer me, instead inspected the plunging V-neckline of her dress, her puffy mouth in a clown like frown as she straightened the fabric.

"You should eat something. Or go home. Get a decent night's sleep."

She glanced at me in drowsy confusion as if I'd again said something taboo. Harry shoved the second glass in front of her, and without a word she guzzled it.

I cleared my throat, smiling at him. "As I was saying, I'm a friend of Assad's". The name, Arabic, meant something to him. He nodded grudgingly and moved to the other end of the bar, where a short, fat man signaled to him.

I leaned in toward the woman. "Maybe you can help me."

But her attention was on the young busboy stacking glasses under the bar in front of us. With shaggy brown hair, freckles, he liked no older than sixteen, like he'd just popped out of a Norman Rockwell painting.

"Hey," she whispered. "Do me a favor? Get me a vodka cranberry?"

He ignored her.

"Oh, *shit.* Don't worry about Harry. He's a pussycat. I'm dying."

Her pleading, threatening to get shrill, caused the boy to look up at her reluctantly, then down to the other end of the bar, where Harry was busy fixing another drink. The kid must have felt sorry for her because he turned, grabbing a bottle of Grey Goose.

"You're an angel," she whispered in a low sexy voice.

He added the juice, set it in front of her, and resumed stacking the glasses.

"Any chance I can get some ice?" I asked, sliding my drink forward.

He nodded. When he brought it back, I slid a folded fifty-dollar bill into his hand. He looked at me startled.

"Don't react," I said, glancing down the bar at Harry. "I need some information." I took out a picture of Gabriela from my pocket, slipping it across the bar.

"You recognize her?"

He kept his head lowered, stacking the glasses.

"Take it off the bar," he whispered. "They got cameras."

I stuck it back into my wallet. If someone was watching, I hoped they'd assume I'd just showed the kid a picture of my daughter, or, given the clientele here, my jailbait Eastern European girlfriend who spoke no English.

"Can you help me out?" I asked.

The boy squinted off to his right and scratched his check. "Uh, *yeah*, she was the breach."

"The *what?*"

He resumed arranging the glasses. "She was the security breach from a few weeks ago. They got her picture posted downstairs."

"What happened?"

"I'm sorry. I can't do this. I'll be up shit creek if . . ."

"This is life or death."

The kid eyed me nervously. He looked better suited for a paper route, leading a band of Boy Scouts, then working in this place. I reached into my pocket for another fifty-dollar bill, leaned over the bar to grab a black drink stir, and dropped it at his feet.

He bent down and picked it up, then started organizing the stacks of red cocktail napkins emblazoned with lips open and screaming.

"She attacked a guest," the kid said under his breath.

"Attacked?"

"She, like, went after him. That's what I heard."

"How?"

He didn't seem to want to elaborate or didn't know.

"Which guest?"

He looked apprehensively at Harry and picked up a towel, wiping down the bar.

"He's called the Tarantula"

"What?"

He shrugged. "That's his nickname."

The words had an odd effect on the girl. She'd been sucking down her drink, ignoring us, but now she swiveled around on the stool, trying to focus her bleary eyes on me.

I turned back to the kid, now replenishing with tongs the crystal jar of maraschino cherries on the bar. The cherries, I noticed with surprise, were entirely black, including the stems, and everyone was a connected twin, one tied to another.

"What's his real name?" I said casually sipping my drink.

The kid shook his head. *He didn't know.*

"Is he here tonight? Can you point him out to me?"

He nervously licked his lips, was on the verge of answering me, but then spotted something over my shoulder. He turned, grabbing the empty crate on the counter, and scooted out the door with it, eyes averted, vanishing into the countryside.

I looked to see what make him bolt.

A middle-aged man with spiky silver hair was striding through the crowd, his eyes glued to the woman beside me. He stepped right behind her and said something quietly into her ear.

She jerked upright I shook. He then grabbed her arm and wrenched her off the stool so hard she spilled her drink, leaving an ugly dark wound stain down the front of her dress. She sullenly mumbled something in a foreign language, the music too loud to hear what it was.

Then she sprang away, lurching into the main lounge, fighting through the crowd and up the steps, fleeing down one of the dark pathways. I turned back to the bar, sipping my scotch, ignoring the man, still standing behind me, his attention now squarely on me.

I don't think we've met," he said.

Fifty-Two

"You think right," I answered.

"Let's remedy that."

"I'm a friend of Assad's."

He hesitated, taken aback. He had to bb the manager of the place. He wore an expensive suit, an earpiece, and had the overinflated posture of all short, insecure men in positions of power. I sensed he was about to leave me alone, but then, looking me over, frowned at the saltwater ring on my pants.

"How are you acquainted with Mr. Masood?" he asked.

"Ask him."

"Come with me, please."

"Well, I'd like to finish my drink."

"Come with me or we're going to have a serious problem."

I studied him with bored indignation. "You sure?"

"Do I look like it?"

I shrugged, taking the time to down the rest of my scotch, and stood up.

"It's your funeral," I said.

If this unnerved him even a little, the man gave no indignation. He stepped stiffly to the steps leading down into the main lounge, waiting for me to follow.

This isn't going to end well. I headed after him and as we moved down into the crowd I felt another unnerving surge of vertigo. It was like sinking into another dimension, hitting a snag in reality. The trompe l'oeil, which is French for *'deceive the eye'*, paintings must have been painted to be viewed from this central vantage point, because everyone came into greater focus. Coastal towns bustled. Sunflower fields ripped in the wind, a flock of crows exploding over them, yet unable to fly away. Jungle bromeliads shook, a dark animal stalking through them. A snake writhed over a wall. Even the pulsing music seemed to converge onto me. I could actually feel the sun beating down on my neck.

As we jostled our way through the crowd, the suits, and ties, the girls, the *boys* in those dresses, which down here looked to be made not of fabric but fish scales, I caught snippets of conversations over the music; *be here, sometimes I agree, scuba diving.*

I had to stay calm and make an exit, pronto. We appeared to be heading toward one of those dark passageways and I'd be damned if I was going to follow him down there and get my legs broken, maybe worse.

My eyes scanned to atrium's periphery for the door back to the storage room, but it was lost in the glinting scenes around me.

The manager was a few feet ahead, glaring as he waited for me to catch up. But suddenly a tall, blond man tapped him on the shoulder, greeting him, shaking his hand.

I held back a few seconds. *This was most likely my best chance.* The man introduced a friend beside him. The manager turned and I hastily turned away from him, elbowing my way through a large group, accidentally ramming the back of a waiter. A cocktail slid out of his hands, exploding onto the floor.

I picked up my pace, my eyes averted. The women were wearing stilettos, and their toenails were painted black, filed into points, like bizarre thorns. Abruptly, I spotted something out of place: *dirty white Converse sneakers.* A waiter was warring them.

Cooper.

He'd actually put on one of the uniforms from the storage room. He was wielding a silver tray, wandering among the guests like he owned the place. I slipped beside him.

"Hey, I need to get the hell out of here fast. I've been caught."

He nodded. "Follow me."

We cut sharply left, elbowing through the crowd, skipping up the marble steps, Cooper striding deliberately toward the crumbling stone wall that ringed the entire plaza. There was no visible door. But he extended his hand, pressing the weathered statue's arms, legs, bare feet, trying to find whatever the hell opened the door.

I glanced over my shoulder.

Two guests sitting in the lounge were watching us, alarmed. One of them turned around, signing to a waiter. And then I saw the manager. He was pushing aggressively through the crowd, whispering into his earpiece, scanning the atrium's perimeter. He was seconds from spotting me.

"Any chance we can speed this up?" I muttered.

I stepped beside him, sliding my hands over the wall, and Cooper moved left toward another reclining statue. He pressed her hands, face, breasts, eyes, and *thank God,* she unexpectedly gave way into a regular rectangular door, which led into a long corridor with white walls and orange linoleum.

We sprinted down it, two stainless-steel doors visible at the end.

"And you thought I was getting our asses kicked," Cooper said over his shoulder.

"Fallout from obtaining vital information."

"Oh, yeah, what's that?"

"Gabriela crashed this party a few weeks ago. She went after a member known as the Tarantula. That's what you call skills."

"The Tarantula? What's his real name?"

"Didn't get that."

We charged through the swinging doors into an industrial kitchen. It was lively, with cooks in uniform, bubbling pots, smells of roasted meat and garlic. A few glanced up curiously as Cooper and I raced around the counters, the stoves with sizzling pans, wheeled carts, dessert trays.

We flew out of a second swinging door into another empty corridor. Cooper stopped, panting, pointing.

"Take it all the way to the end, make a right, the door leads outside."

I took off, turning around when he didn't follow.

"You're staying?"

He was heading back into the kitchen. "Just getting started."

"Be careful. And thanks for saving my ass."

He smiled. "It's not saved yet."

Fifty-Three

I reached the end of the hall, followed it right, running toward the emergency exit door at the end. An alarm began to sound from an intercom.

The manager must have alerted a security breach.

I shoved it open, sprinting outside. It was a brightly lit loading area, the driveway packed with supply trucks, two black Escalades. A lone waiter sat on a crate, smoking a cigarette. He smiled as I walked casually past and jogged down some steps, then along a stone pathway winding around the side of the house. *It had to be the eastern side.*

Rounded the corner, I stopped dead. In front of me was the mansion's entrance, an elaborate columned porte-cochere crowded with security guards dressed in black. A silver Range Rover was parked out front, the backseat window unrolled *whoever* sat there clearly being checked on a guest list. The driveway curved left through dense trees, probably heading north toward Old Fort Sheridan and *the way out of here.* Visible farther to my left beyond the foliage was a lawn, quite a few cars parked there.

I couldn't make it out this way. The guards had obviously been alerted, because they were fanning out, heading inside. One turned in my direction, motioned to another, *both coming toward me.*

I backtracked and broke into a sprint, dashing past the loading dock again and the lone waiter. He stood up, shouting something as I raced past, veering around the next rambling wing of the mansion, the windows dark, though for a split second, maybe it was the wind through the brush, I swore I heard a man's dull, prolonged moan.

Ohhhh Shit. I kept going, racing toward the backyard through flower beds and shrubs, rounding the corner. I froze.

The back lawn was flooded with light. Guards were milling around the patio and pool, two of them far across the lawn, inspecting the stairs where Cooper and I had climbed up. I whipped around, checking behind me. I could hear the guard's footsteps getting closer.

I scrambled past the piles of garbage bags, piled up onto the stone wall, racing across the strip of grass into a tall hedge, forcing my way through. The branches so dense it was like fighting through a tightly woven net.

I crouched down, breaking the limbs with my hands, crawling through headfirst. I heard shouting behind me, cutting through the roar of the ocean. I tore free on the other side and stumbled to my feet.

I wasn't in another backyard as I'd hoped, but in an empty expanse of moorland, no house or lawn, only darkness and tangled shrubbery shoulder high, impossible to walk through. I slipped along the hedge I'd just crawled out of, where the undergrowth wasn't as thick, fighting through what felt like holly or rosebushes, heading in the direction of Lake Michigan.

I had to find another flight of stairs to the beach. I reached the bluff, squalls of wind barreling off the lake. I headed unsteadily along it, but could see within minutes there were no stairs. *This had to be a wildlife preserve. I was trapped.* There wouldn't be another flight of steps or a house for miles.

I checked behind me. The hedge was shaking, black forms emerging through the branches, flashlight beams sweeping the gnarled thickets, heading in my direction. *They were still coming.* The manager had probably declared a fatwa on my ass.

I scrambled to the edge of the cliff. It wasn't a sheer drop to the water, but a slight incline, jagged with shrubs. Grabbing a plant to brace myself. I began to climb down it, feet first, creating an avalanche of loose rocks and sand. Flashlights were already inspecting the vegetation directly above me, the men's shouts barely audible above the roaring waves of the lake. I pressed my back against the rocks, waiting until they moved farther down, then hurriedly continued on, many of the shrubs so loosely rooted were pulling out in my hands so I dropped to a free fall until I managed to seize a root that held my weight.

I reached a rock outcrop jutting out over the water. There was no beach, only five-foot waves, which receded for a few seething seconds, exposing sharp rocky crags along the cliff's base, before the waves folded over aggressively forward, erupting in wild explosions against the rocks.

I waited, checking above me for movement. *No one would be idiotic enough to follow me down here.* Yet the instant I figured I was safe, I could see two dark figures bending down, clamoring after me.

I groped my way down a few more feet, reaching some boulders. I began crawling between them, heading westward, moving quickly. After a few minutes, I could make out the spindly skeleton of what had to be Duchamp's staircase, far ahead, rising out of the waves.

I edged toward it. Flashlights suddenly appeared at the top of the cliff, searching the shoreline, the beams of light sliding along the rocks just a few feet from where I was crouched.

They were waiting. The light slipped right over me. Loud voices cut through the waves. I took off again, faster, half expecting a ricochet of bullets clattering against the rocks around me. When I reached the bottom of the stairs, I wedged my boots between two rocks to steady myself and looked up. A guard was actually attempting to climb down, the whole structure trembling under his weight. I seized the weakest of the beams and after a few attempts managed to wrench it free, a large section of the railing detaching with it. I threw it into the water behind me and took off across the rocks, drenched by another onslaught of waves.

After another few yards, I quickly checked behind me. The guard on the staircase had fallen through a section of the stairs above what I'd dismantled and was clinging to the cliff face, seemingly awaiting help. I moved up, scaling a precarious section of the cliffs where there wasn't much to hold on to and had just started to let myself think that I might be home free when a massive wave suddenly lobbed itself against the rocks.

I lost my grip. Falling backward, my ears filled with deafening thunder as I was tossed upside down, choking on water. I managed to fight my way to the surface, gasping for air, but within seconds, another wave surged forward, pulling me back before throwing me toward the cliffs. Kicking as hard as I could, I was alone in a narrow inlet. I sat crouched on the rock, waiting for one of the guards to appear.

No one came.

When the sky was turning a silvered gray, I saw as, I squinted down the beach, a ribbon of sand. I dropped down onto it, breaking into a jog, trekking past silent condos and along the wooden fence bordering Coho Way, the deserted alley coming into washed-out focus in the pale morning.

I stopped, staring at the empty parking space.

My car was gone.

Bewildered, I headed to Emerson Street and the Lake Haven diner, scanning the parking lot. There was no sign of my car, only a silver pickup, and an Audi. Entering, I saw the place was empty, apart from an old man in a back booth and a redheaded waitress slumped over the counter, reading a magazine.

"You look shipwrecked," she said as I approached.

"I'm looking for a young woman, Blond. Green dress. Was she here?"

She smiled in recognition. "You mean Elizabeth?"

"Exactly."

"Sure, she was here."

"Well, where the hell is she?"

"Beats me. Got up and left about an hour ago."

I slid onto one of the counter stools, pulling off my leather jacket, still drooling lake water.

"I'll have some coffee, three eggs over easy, bacon, toast, orange juice."

The waitress disappeared through the swinging doors. When she returned with my coffee, she sighed heavily, crossing her arms.

"She got a call from some guy. Ran out of here real fast."

I glanced at her, taking a drink of coffee. "A call on her cell?"

"No. Cell service sucks out here. Just one bar. He called the restaurant, asked for her by name. you're her dad, I take it, coming to pick her up?"

She didn't wait for my response, only nodded knowingly. "I don't know how you dads put up with it. Girls always going after the bad boys. Then there's the internet, which makes it ten times worse with the stalkers and the sex predators."

My breakfast came quickly, *thank God.*

A few locals wandered in, but there was no sign of Cooper of Elizabeth. After I ate, I tried calling them. I was surprised to see my cell still worked, but the waitress was right: no service. I used the phone at the cash register, but for both of them it rang and went to voicemail.

When I boarded the 9:45 A.M. Amtrak, taking me back to civilization, if you call Chicago civilization, I conked out cold before we left the station.

Fifty-Four

When I arrived in the city, it was afternoon. Yet still no word from Cooper or Elizabeth. I took a cab back to my apartment. Elizabeth had a spare set of keys, so I wondered if she'd somehow been unable to get in touch and had beaten me home. But the place had been untouched, no messages on my home phone.

I took a shower, considered going back to bed, but felt too uneasy, too stoked, too annoyed.

They'd left the general for dead on the battlefield. Or had something happened? I didn't have time to worry about it, because my cell phone buzzed, reminding me that Julie Mergener, one of Esquivel's former mules, would be at Garfield Park for a Drug Addiction Seminar tonight at 6:00 P.M. It was the lead Horrigan had given me almost a weeks ago.

I headed to my office, feeding Octavius some birdseed, and pulled Julie Mergener's 1995 rap sheet out of my record file. She was just sixteen when first arrested, a strategy employed by many drug lords. Minors get released to their parents or guardians, and they always had their people registered as legal guardians over all their mules.

I recall Horrigan telling me Mergener had become very loyal to Esquivel. Her mistake was becoming addicted to the drug she was smuggling. Esquivel must have taken a liking to her or else she would just be another dead junkie found in the lower south side. The fact that she was still alive spoke volumes. I needed to see if there is anything she could tell me about Gabriela.

I checked my watch. It was almost five. I needed to get going. But a detective wandering an addiction meeting in Garfield Park being friendly, asking too many questions would set off all kinds of alarms.

I needed a decoy.

Fifty-five

"Mrs. Quincy called to alert me you'd be here," announced Dorothy, surveying me skeptically over the rim of her glasses.

"But not a half-hour early, Kim's in the midst of her *Nutcracker* audition."

Dorothy was the gray-haired czarina who ruled the Goodman Theater Ballet School with an iron fist. I'd encountered her before, and every time she treated me like I was a fugitive from a Siberian gulag.

"Okay, but we have a reservation at Morton's for a father-daughter dinner."

"If you pull her out now, she won't be in the running for getting a doll from Herr Drosselmeyer. She might not even make it to the party scene."

"Come on, Dorothy. Kim has to make the party scene. She is the party scene."

Dorothy sighed, relenting. "Go ahead."

Winking at her, I turned, striding down the hall to the ballroom where they held the classes, the wood floors creaking under my feet. I'd called Angela to ask if I might spend a few quality hours with Kim this evening, to make up for my postponing it, and miraculously, she'd agreed to it. I didn't exactly go into detail as to what we'd be doing during these quality hours, but no matter what happened with Julie Mergener, Kim would enjoy the dog run, and afterward I'd treat her to a dinner and a hot-fudge sundae at Baskin Robbins.

I found Kim at the end of the hall in a sunlit studio blaring Tchaikovsky. She was dancing in a flock of five-year-olds. They were all holding their arms over their heads, jumping. Kim looked ready for the Bolshoi: leotard firebird red, white tights, slippers, and white tutu. She was right in front, watching the ballet mistress demonstrate the steps.

I knocked on the glass door. The children froze. The mistress craned her long neck, surveying me imperiously.

"Yes, sir? May I help you?"

I stepped inside. "I'm here for Kim."

Fifty-Six

Even though I was getting dark, Garfield Park was crowded with teenagers on skateboards, a few couples walking hand in hand, break-dancers performing on a sheet of plywood while an eighties boombox blasted out the beats. Most of the people stopped mid-conversation to stare, dazed and enchanted, as Kim nimbly plodded past them, tightly holding my hand. Though she'd agreed to put on her black coat and pink Rapunzel backpack, she'd refused to take off her tutu, tights, or ballet slippers.

"She's a very nice woman," I said. "We're going to chat with her and visit her dog for a few minutes. Okay?"

Kim nodded, brushing her gold curls off her face. "What's wrong with your hand?" she asked. After my Cliffside escape from Les Silencio, my hands were cut up badly.

"Don't have to worry. Your dad's tough. Now give me the four-one-one on Mommy is she still working at the gallery?"

Kim thought it over. "Mommy has a problem with Sue," she answered.

"The manager. They've always butted heads. What about your step-dad?"

"Bruce?" she clarified.

Good. Still a proper noun like me. Thank God he wasn't Dad.

"Yes, Bruce. Has the SEC investigated him yet? Is there anything about Amy's arrest for insider trading that I should know about?"

She squinted at me. "Bruce has a spare tire."

"Mommy said that?"

Kim nodded, hanging heavily on my arm. "Mommy makes him drink green juice, and Bruce goes to bed hungry."

So Old Man Quincy had put on a couple of pounds and was suffering through one of Angela's infamous juice cleanses. Suddenly I felt fantastic.

"Does Mommy ever mention me?"

Kim considered this for a minute and then nodded.

"Oh, yeah? What does she say?"

"You need some serious help." She even mimicked Angela's self-righteous inflection. "And your elevator isn't going all the way to the top floor and you're acting out a teenage fantasy."

I should have stopped asking questions after the *spare tire*.

I bent down, scooping Kim into my arms because we'd reached the dog run, a fenced in area along the south perimeter of the park. It was packed with romping dogs and their owners, who hovered around the periphery like overbearing stage parents, nervously watching, armed and ready with leashes, balls, pooper-scoopers, and treats.

"Okay, toots. We're looking for a big black dog and a lady with red hair, mid-thirties. When you spot them, keep it on the down low. No pointing. No screaming. Be cool. Ya got it?"

Kim nodded again.

Sure enough, in the remotest section of the dog run, there was a gaunt woman with red hair and an old black Lab hunched on the bench beside her.

"Stellar surveillance work, honey. They could use you at Homeland Security."

I took a moment to glance behind us, making sure there was no one watching. I'd been keeping a vigilant eye out, ever since I'd been back in the city, in case there was a further sign of Santo Esquivel, but I'd noticed nothing out of the ordinary.

I unlatched the gate, and we stepped inside.

Fifty-Seven

I watched Kim carry out her orders with precision and poise. *The girl would make one hell of a Green Beret.* She actually made the whole thing look random. First, on her way around to Julie Mergener, she stopped and crouched next to a white teacup Chihuahua decked in more bling than a Las Vegas hooker. She said hello to that dog for a minute before stepping over to the black Lab. Angela had clearly drilled into her that she must ask permission before she touched any strange animal because I heard her politely ask both Martin and then the dog himself if they minded her petting him.

Both must have said no, because very gently and respectfully Kim began to touch the top of the dog's old grayed head, his eyes weary and unblinking. She started with just her pinkie, stroking the quarter inch right between the dog's eyebrows.

I strolled past the other owners standing around the fence and moved toward them.

"It's alright if she pets him?" I asked, approaching Julie Mergener.

"Of course," she answered, glancing at me.

"He doesn't bite?"

Her attention was back on the dogs in front of her.

"No."

It was Julie Mergener, all right.

Her hair was thinner, dyed a synthetic shade of red, something between dying autumn leaves and beets. She'd been such a vibrant, beautiful girl until the addiction took over.

"What's your name?" Kim asked the dog, though he didn't respond.

"What's his name? I asked Julie.

She looked irritated to be addressed again.

"Leopold."

"Leopold," said Kim. She was petting the top of his head with her hand rigidly flat like a spatula. Like she might have been carefully spreading icing.

"You look familiar," I said glancing at Julie. "You don't teach Sunday school at Saint Joseph's, do you?"

She looked flustered.

"Uh, no. That definitely wouldn't be me."

"My mistake."

She smiled thinly, returning her attention to the dogs.

I took a minute to watch them, too, so as not to appear forward. A hyper Dalmatian was the leader of the pack. That brown hoochie-mama Chihuahua was making her rounds, yipping, desperate for a john, but every dog accepting, overwhelming happiness with a soggy tennis ball.

"Okay," I said. "This is a long shot, and you're probably going to think I'm crazy."

She looked at me, wary.

"Now don't run off please just hear me out. I'm Shawn McCarthy, the detective that has been assigned to the Carlos Esquivel investigation."

"What! Didn't you get thrown off the force for something you said to the press?" she inquired.

"No. Just suspended," I answered. "I got news that his daughter Gabriela committed suicide. And I have been looking into the circumstances of her death. I haven't been able to locate Mr. Esquivel to tell him the situation."

Looking into her eyes, "I have to ask, what he was like? Esquivel."

The light in her eyes vanished like a match blown out. Glancing at her watch, she grabbed the strap of her backpack, pulling it into the crook of her arm, about to leave. But then, to my relief, Kim had managed to fully woo Leopold. He was wagging his tail.

It moved like a windshield wiper. Seeing this, and Kim, quietly discussing something of great importance with the dog, she hesitated.

"It's tragic what happened to his daughter," I noted.

Julie scratched her nose.

"But then, I'm not surprised," I went on. "To create a safe zone for one's self in that lifestyle. Working for Esquivel must have been terrifying. The man had to be horrifying in his personal life. Only the greatest of personal strength can separate you from working for him and keep some semblance of a sane life.

I figured if I steamrolled the woman with words she might not get up and leave. She was sitting with her back against the bench, studying me with an absorbed expression.

"Maybe," she said. "You can never tell how a family is from the outside. But I just. . ."

She fell silent because that damn tennis ball had just rolled exactly behind her feet. She bent down, grabbing it, the dogs freezing in incredulity, mouths closed, ears perked. She threw it, sitting back again as they took off in a stampede across the gravel.

"You just . . . ?" I prompted quietly.

"When I first met Mr. Esquivel," she said. He invited me and my boyfriend up to El Esplanade. He rarely did things like that, he was private. At least that is what I heard.

He was private. She actually meant Esquivel. I turned my gaze back to the dogs so she wouldn't realize I was hanging on her every word.

"It was surreal. Granted, any family that was together, not shouting or stumbling-down drunk, would have been surreal to me. But even now I think there had been more love and joy in that family than I've ever seen before or since." She shook her head in disbelief. "They had their own language."

I gawked. "What?"

"Esquivel's son, Santo, invented a language for the family. They spoke it to each other, telling jokes and laughing, which make them even more intimidating. I remember the housekeeper trying to explain it to me like it was yesterday. 'the Russians have sixteen words for love.

Our language has twenty.' She brought out all of these notebooks Santo had. He'd written his own dictionary as thick as a Webster's dictionary, filled with grammar rules, conjunctive irregular verbs, nouns that he'd made up. I will always remember some of the words. One was *terulya*. It meant deep-diving love, a love that excavates you. It's something you have to have before you die in order to have lived. I remember being shocked that a teenage boy came up with this stuff. But that's how they all were. They soaked up life with themselves. None of them were encumbered by anything. There were no limits."

She fell silent, wistful, maybe even slightly jealous of this family she was describing. She crossed her arms, frowning out at the dogs again.

"A *picnic*," I repeated, a prompt for her to keep talking.

"It was a bright day. Once you turned onto the property you continued along a long drive through woods. And at the end, the house rose up, an enormous mansion commanding the hill like a castle out of a fairy tale. It was deserted. I knocked on the door and wandered around the house and the gardens. There was no sign of anyone. Finally, after twenty minutes, the massive front door opened and a Japanese man stood there. He was wearing a silk green kimono with a sword around his waist. He said something in Japanese, as beckoning for us to follow him. He led us down to the lake. That's where everyone was. Everyone except Mr. Esquivel. A group sitting on white blankets under white umbrellas.

"Where was Mr. Esquivel?" I asked.

"They said, he was in the house taking care of business. It was like walking into a dream world, everyone looked like movie stars. People laughing, enjoying each other. I wanted to be a part of this family in the worst way. Billy and I were sitting at a little table when the Japanese man in the green kimono came up to us and said that Mr. Esquivel wanted to see me in the house, alone. I began shaking at the thought of meeting him one on one."

She stared off toward the dogs again with that thousand-mile stare.

"Sounds like Shangri-La," I said when she didn't go on.

She looked at me distractedly, saying nothing, and I regretted speaking, for fear I'd punctured the spell she'd been under, recounting that day. The words had sputtered, then to my immense surprise blasted out of her like a fountain, one that's been dry for years.

Now she seemed sorry that she'd said anything at all.

"When I returned to the party after discussing my part in the Esquivel empire. Billy was gone. I was informed that Billy had gotten a call and had to leave. They said don't worry they would make sure I got home safely. I never saw Billy again."

"What year was this?" I asked nonchalantly.

"It was Gabriela's sixth birthday party, so that would have been 1993."

"Did you meet Gabriela?" I asked.

Julie nodded, reluctant to go on, but then, it seemed she couldn't leave such a vibrant question dangling in the air.

"She was beautiful. Short dark hair, almost black. Like a sprite. Pale gray eyes." She smiled, suddenly animated. "I was seventeen. Wasn't into kids at all. But totally out of the blue,

Gabriela took my hand and brought me down to a deserted part of the lake where there stood a willow tree and tall grass, the water emerald green. She asked me if I could see the trolls. I still remember their names. Limdaka and Dorizin. By the time she let go of my hand and took off across the fields chasing a butterfly, a huge butterfly, bright red and orange, like this property had their own insects, I believed in trolls. I still do."

She fell silent, seemingly embarrassed by her zeal. Kim, I noticed, was staring at Julie, listening intently. It was dark now in the park, the strangers standing along the fence, faceless. The giant I

Elm trees with their outstretched limbs were sinking deeper into the darkness, slipping away. The pack of dogs was still going strong, a white-and-brown blurry squall of gasping and flying gravel.

"I've held on to that day," Julie continued in a thin voice," like some faded postcard. Something you put in a scrapbook to remind yourself of perfect happiness, that it does exist, for one moment, like a sudden streak of lightning through the sky. When I read what happened to Gabriela, I couldn't believe it. I didn't know her at all, but . . . it seemed so sudden and wrong. If you have a family like that and you still can't withstand this world what hope is there for the rest of us?"

She smiled sadly, looking away.

What was he like to work for?" Silently I cringed at the probing question. Thankfully, she just shrugged.

"I had such a small part in the Esquivel empire. I understood nothing that was going on, really, because the crew was Columbian and Esquivel's main assistant gave them all their directions in Spanish."

"His main assistant, you're talking about Marissa Garcia?"

"Yeah. But the crew all called her *Jaguar*."

"Jaguar? Why?"

"No idea," she answered.

"Do you still keep in touch with Esquivel? Or anyone from that time?"

Julie shook her head. "After he'd gotten all he needed from you, like a surgeon harvesting organs, he was done with you. After two weeks of traveling back and forth to Columbia, that was it for me."

She turned away from me to unzip her backpack, taking out a dog's leash, clipping it to Leopold's collar.

"I actually got to get going."

She was seconds from walking away. I wanted more time, was tempted to throw caution to the wind and keep riddling the woman with questions, anything to get her to keep talking, to tell me more. Yet I sensed her candor was fleeting, the moment already departed.

She stood up, stooping over to help her dog off the bench. He moved like an old man with arthritis. She actually picked up his back legs for him, placing them on the ground, and turned to me with a perfunctory smile.

"Take care."

"You too," I said.

And then she and Leopold were walking away, two slow-moving figures impervious to the pack of dogs charging past them.

"Is she a nice lady?" Kim asked me, pushing her curls out of her eyes.

"Very nice."

Kim climbed up onto the bench beside me, sitting close, staring fixed on my face.

"Is she feeling sad?" she asked.

"No honey. She's a little confused."

Kim seemed to accept this. It was one of the things I loved about her. I could make some ambiguous observation about human beings, about their failings or hypocrisies, their deep-seated pain, and she took the comment like an old diamond dealer handed a raw stone, turning it over in her palm, then pocketing the gem to be examined and cut later, moving on.

Kim scratched her cheek and interlaced her fingers in her lap, copying the way my fingers were interlaced, and we watched them go in silence.

Fifty-Eight

"Ms. Quincy is coming down," said the doorman, hanging up the phone.

I bent down to Kim. Her ballet slippers were scruffy and her tutu was slightly crushed, but otherwise she looked all right.

"I'm proud of you toots," I told her.

The elevator doors opened, Angela emerging in a crisp white blouse, jeans, dazzling swish of gold hair, Suede driving loafers. I could see that smiling face that she was furious.

"Hi, love," she said to Kim. "Go wait for Mommy by the elevators."

Kim blinked up at her and padded obediently across the marble lobby.

Angela turned to me. "I said six."

"I know . . ."

"She was auditioning for The Nutcracker."

"I worked it out with Dorothy. She's going to make the party scene."

She sighed, heading back across the lobby. "Just don't forget Thursday," she added over her shoulder.

"Thursday?"

She turned. "Bruce and I are going to Santa Barbara?"

"Right. Kim is staying with me for the weekend."

Shooting me a warning look, *don't mess this up,* she took Kim's hand and they stepped into the elevators. I held up a hand, waving, and Kim smiled just as the doors closed.

Fifty-Nine

The afternoon Julie Mergener had described at El Esplanade sounded almost too idyllic to be real. But she'd been only seventeen at the time, doubtlessly insecure and impressionable, so it was possible she'd taken creative liberties with the memory without even realizing it. Given Esquivel's terrifying reputation, for his home and workplace to be such a blissful paradise seemed unlikely.

How close was an artist real life to his work? Doctoral students wrote dissertations on the subject. Yet when Julie had described Gabriela leading her down to the lake where the *trolls* lived, there was something undeniably honest about the episode, also when she described Esquivel as a surgeon harvesting organs, leaving his mules for dead.

Within every elaborate lie, a kernel of truth.

I let myself into my apartment, noticing music coming from the living room. I threw my coat on the chair, striding into the living room, finding Elizabeth curled up in the leather club chair, Octavius perched on her knee. Cooper was slouched on the couch, looking over some papers. The three reversing candles Cleo had given us at Fascinations were burning on the coffee table in front of them beside a pizza box.

"Your home!" Elizabeth announced brightly.

"Don't tell me, I said. "You both lost your cell phones and gale-force winds uprooted every landline in the state."

"We're sorry. But we had a good reason for going MIA." She looked meaningful at Cooper and he smiled some shared excitement between them.

He held out papers, and I took them. It was fifteen pages, about two thousand names. Many were LLC's or bizarre aliases like Marquis de Roche.

"It's the membership list for Les Silencio, said Elizabeth.

"I can see that. How did you get it?"

"It wasn't easy," said Cooper proudly, stretching his hands behind his head. "The place turned into the Gaza Strip after you took off. Bur I was in the waiter uniform, so no one looked at me twice.

I talked to one of the girls, at least I think it was a girl. She told me how to get down to the basement where the offices are. I found an empty one, got on the computer, searched the hard drive for membership. Some Excel files came up. I logged on to my email, sent the files to myself, cleared the folder, and go out. Only they'd apparently reviewed the security footage and saw me saving your ass, so two guards chased me outside onto a neighbor's property. I had to break into the house, called Elizabeth to come pick me up. I managed to explain to her exactly where I was."

"It was a real getaway," Elizabeth chimed in. "Tires squealing. I felt like Thelma and Louise."

"I thought you were Bernstein," I said.

"Elizabeth pulled up, headlights off," Cooper went on. "I climbed out a window, ran across the yard, and we got the hell out of there."

"What time was this?"

Elizabeth looked at Cooper uncertainly. "Four?"

"I waited at the restaurant until nine. What'd you do for five hours?"

"We went back to Les Silencio because I wanted to look," she blurted out. "We hid next door hoping to talk to some guest's when they were leaving, ask them if they recognized Gabriela. But we couldn't approach any of them. They all looked exhausted, shuttled away by housekeepers in expensive cars and limos. One guy in a wheelchair looked dead. There were too many guards, anyway."

"You didn't think to call? You abandoned the boss, *El Jefe,* in the field without a single communication?"

Cooper stood up, yawning and stretching. "I'll see you guys bright and early tomorrow."

"Bright and early?" I asked.

Elizabeth nodded, "Tomorrow we're posting missing-person signs for Gabriela around Normal Street and Onofrio." She handed me a flier with the scanned picture of Gabriela that Elizabeth found at Mission Hills.

Have you seen this girl? Serious reward offered for real information. Please call ASAP.

"We'll weed through the phony reports by asking what color coat Gabriela was wearing."

Cooper took off, and I headed into my office, leaving Elizabeth scribbling in her notebook. Cooper obtaining a copy of the guest list was stellar investigative work, much better than anything I had come up with lately, *not that I was going to admit it.* I spent the next few hours cross-referencing the Les Silencio guest list with anyone associated with the Esquivel empire, in the off chance that one name appeared on both, to no avail. But it did rule out one possibility: The person Gabriela had gone to Les Silencio to find, *this Tarantula,* was probably not associated with her father's work. *Was he a friend of hers? A stranger? Someone connected to her death?*

I switched off the lamp, rubbing my eyes, heading back down the hall. The apartment was quiet. Elizabeth had blown out the reversing candles before going upstairs, but oddly enough, I noticed the wicks were still smoldering orange as if they refused to be extinguished, three orange pinpricks in the dark. I grabbed them and dumped them in the kitchen sink, running water over them until I was certain they were out, then headed to bed.

Sixty

"Cooper promised to be here," said Elizabeth, squinting down the street. "Posting fliers was his idea."

It was 9:00 A.M., and we were back on the block that Onofrio was on with a hundred missing-person fliers. We decided to split up to cover more ground. The neighbor was predominantly Asian, so I didn't think our English language flier would get us very far. Posting leaflets, as if Gabriela were a lost cat, wasn't exactly my style, but it couldn't hurt. With Santo Esquivel following us, I could no longer hope to keep the investigation quiet. So why not go in the opposite direction, brazenly carper-bombing the neighborhood with Gabriela's picture, and see where that gets us?

I taped fliers to lampposts and mailboxes, bus stops, store windows. A Chinese woman on a bike, orange shopping bags swinging from the handlebars, braked to see what I was doing, scowled at me, and rode on. Quite a few men in shops along the way refused to let me post the missing poster after they saw what it was saying, shaking their heads shooing me away.

When this happened for the seventh time, I wondered if they were worried a missing Caucasian woman would bring them bad luck, or if they'd seen something in Gabriela's photo they didn't like. Or perhaps there was an even more disturbing reason: *I looked like I worked for Immigration and Customs.*

It was the opposite reaction at Ling-Ling's Hair Salon on Archer Avenue. The teenage receptionist, the female manager, two stylists, and I client (pink robe, hair in tinfoil) surrounded me, smiling, and speaking in excited Cantonese. They took great care taping Gabriela's flier to the window beside a faded poster for eyebrow threading, and when I left, they waved as if I were a beloved relative they wouldn't see for the next fifty years.

And yet the longer I walked the streets, past Asian restaurants, gift stores, unisex hair salons, orange and white koi drifting in pet store windows, I had a sense I was being watched. Yet every time I checked behind me, once even popping into a Laundromat and scanning the area, I noticed nothing suspicious.

I wondered if the feeling came from the strength of Gabriela's stare, so alive and insistent, gazing out from the white page. All "missing" fliers were unsettling, the lost person smiling out from some candid photo taken at a birthday party or happy hour, so ignorant of their fate.

Yet Gabriela, alone on that picnic table at Mission Hills, had a gravity, an understanding as if she knew what awaited her within weeks.

As I walked on, however, I realized I was absolutely right. I was being watched, by the entire neighborhood. Cooper's idea to post these fliers wasn't so simplistic, because if I stood our this much, attracted this many hostile looks and slow drive-bys. Once I looked and saw an old woman had pulled aside her lace curtains to stare down at me. Gabriela had been noticed also.

They all must have seen her, watched her, wondered about her as she wandered their sidewalks in her red coat.

Now all we needed was one of them having the courage to call.

Sixty-One

"Eh-Tommy!" The guy at the front desk bellowed in a thick Chicago accent, turning toward the dozen tattoo artists at work behind him. "These guys here got a question for ya!"

Dragon Master was a fluorescent, spacious tattoo parlor on the second floor of a walk-up on Lawrence Avenue. It was cheerful inside, without the aggressive *Hells Angels* feel that most of the shops in the city offered, where the handle-jawed thugs wielding the tattoo guns looked like tattooing is just a side job, their main work, contract killings.

The light was clean and clinical, walls decorated with tracing paper and framed stencils of full-bodied tattoos, skulls, Buddhas and warriors, Maori tribal patterns, shelves cluttered with bottles of colored ink and iodine. The Rolling Stones "Jumping Jack Flash" playing loudly from the speakers.

"Ask 'em if they're cops!" The answering male voice cut through the buzzing of the tattoo guns. Yet every artist remained bent over a client. I had no clue who had just spoken.

"Are ya cops?" the guy asked us, wincing at the awful thought. He had peroxide white-blonde hair and the permanently stunned face of a Malibu surfer facing an unexpectedly large wave. Dragon Master tattoos snarled all over his biceps.

"No," I said.

The kid turning around yelled, "They're no cops!"

"Tell them to come over."

The kid, bobbing his head to the music, pointed to an alcove in the farthest corner.

"You can go talk to Tommy, the manager."

Tommy my appeared to be a large middle-aged man wearing black latex gloves. He was doing an autopsy on a sperm whale. His client was face down on a black massage table and was at least three hundred pounds, bald, naked, whiter than bleached snow. As I stepped into the shop toward them, Elizabeth right behind me.

The tattoo in progress was a massive lotus tree, a gnarled trunk growing out of the guy's ass crack, up his spine, twisting all over his back, flourishing branches reaching around his chest, a couple of birds, not yet colored in, perched on his forearms.

"What can I do for you?" asked Tommy, without looking up.

"Do you recognize her?" I asked, holding out the picture of Gabriela.

"She came into your shop a few weeks ago."

He ignored me until he'd finished coloring in a pink lotus blossom.

Grown men with youngish names, Bobby, Johnny, Freddy, there had to be some unspoken law that they looked meaner than the rest of us. He had a wide, thuggish face, salt-and-pepper hair. Unidentifiable tattoos peeked out of the neck and sleeves of his skintight silver polyester shirt.

He had an easy confidence as if she were used to people filing through the store to get to his station in the very back, *tattoo parlor equivalent of the chairman's corner office in the sky.* Asking for his take on things as we were now.

He uninterestingly looked us over, then the photo, and leaned back to his client.

"Sure. She came in a few weeks back."

"What color coat was she wearing?" Elizabeth asked.

"Red coat. Black on the sleeves."

Elizabeth shot me an astonished look.

"Did she come in for a tattoo?" I asked him.

"Nah. She wanted her after picture."

Her after picture? What's that?"

Tommy stopped working to stare up at me. "After we finish your tat, we take your freaking picture." He gestured toward a far wall, covered with photographs of smiling people showing off with their completed tattoos.

"She had a tight twofold of an Orichi on her ankle," he went on, resuming his work. "She wanted to know if we still had the after."

"A twofold?"

One tat on two people. When they're apart it doesn't look like much. But together, when their arms are around each other, hand to hand, lovesick and shit, it turns into somethin'. A very Jerry Maguire' you complete me' kinda thing."

Of course, Gabriela's tattoo on her ankle featured only half of the animal, the head, and front legs.

"You said her tat was of an Orichi?" I asked.

"It's popular with Jap tattoo fanatics. A mystical beast."

"Did she say who had the other half?" asked Elizabeth.

"Nah. But it's big with lovers, newlyweds, prom dates, couples 'bout to be split up like one's gotta serve time. I did one last week. A couple in their seventies. They drove up here from Key West for their fiftieth wedding anniversary. I got the after picture somewhere."

Turning off the ink gun, he spun around in his swivel chair to search the messy desk behind him, the black latex gloves making his every gesture faintly dramatic, like a cat burglar or mime. He found the photo, handed it to Elizabeth, turning on the gun again, he bent over to inspect his client's face under the massage table.

"How you doin' down there, Mel?"

"I'm cool."

Mel didn't look cool. He was drooling on the floor.

Elizabeth handed me the photograph. It featured two grinning retirees, their arms around each other, wearing matching yellow polo shirts and Khaki Bermuda shorts. On the top of her right foot and his left was a tattoo of a red heart with wings. With their feet side by side, it was whole.

It was a bit schmaltzy for my taste, but Elizabeth was enraptured.

"I tell all my clients who come in wanting a twofold," Tommy went on cheerfully, "be a hundred and ten percent sure. Can't tell you how many times girls come in cryin' a month later, want the work redone 'cuz her true love ran off with her best friend. At first, that's what I thought your friend wanted." He nodded at the photo of Gabriela. "But she just wanted the picture."

"Did she say why?" I asked.

"Nah."

"And did she get it?" asked Elizabeth.

"Uh-uh. She had the art done a while ago, 2004, when I was at my old location at the Jackson Hotel, near Greek town. With the move, things got lost. I let her go through our files in the back. She stayed coupla hours, lookin'. But she couldn't find it."

"We have the receipt stating that she bought something," I said, removing it from my coat pocket.

He didn't bother to look up.

"There was a young soldier in here on leave. Wanted a portrait of his wife over his heart. She was also a soldier and got killed in Afghanistan. He was a mess, but what he wanted was a real job. Didn't have the cash. We decided on just her name. But your friend took care of it. Didn't make a big deal about it."

Elizabeth looked at me, astonished.

"Did she behave strangely?" I asked him.

"Apart from not talking much? Not really."

"Did she look unwell?"

"A little pale."

"Do you know who did her tattoo back in 2004?"

"One of my old employees. Norman. I could tell from the work."

"And where can we find Norman?"

Tommy chuckled. "Somewhere between heaven and hell."

He wiped the finished blossom with a tissue, closely inspecting it, and moved on to the next.

"One minute Norman was slingin' ink? Next minute he's passed out on my floor, blood shooting outta his nose like the Buckingham fountains. Died in the ambulance. An aneurysm." He frowned, bending to survey his client. "Sure you're all right, Mel? You're like a cadaver down there."

"I'm listening," said Mel.

Tommy frowned, tilting his head up at us and sighing.

"So, this is the thing, I go home the night after your friend came in. and I think back to what happened to Norman coupla weeks before he died. This is back, like summer of 04. Now for you to understand what I'm about to tell you, you got to understand Norman. He was a big husky man. Bigger than a fridge, bigger than a Barcalounger, I swear on a stack of Bibles."

"Bigger than me?" asked Mel in a muffled voice from under the table.

"Not bigger than you. But close." Tommy resumed his work. "He was a helluva artist. Studied in Yokohama under a Horiyoshi. The guy could pound skin, grind with the best of 'em. He could do a mean *Tebori, Horimono, Irezumi,* you name it, which was how come I had him in the shop. Because he was an asshole. I'm sayin' nothin' I wouldn't say to his face. He embraced hi assholeness. Hated kids. Called 'em larvae. Had four girlfriends. None of them knew about each other. His whole life was like that. Buncha lies and dodges, unreturned calls and letdowns. So, one day I come in and the shop's quiet. All the lights are off and Norman's just sitting in the dark by himself like he felt sick or somethin'. I ask him what's the matter and he's all down and shit, tells me his life's crap. He's a coward, he tells me. He's a cheat. Says he's made so many mistakes. He says he's going to change his *priorities*. The first time I ever heard him use a four-syllable word. So I humor him. Ask what the hell brought on his salvation. He said he'd just done a Japanese twofold for two teenagers. They'd just left the shop ten minutes before. He said they were in love and it was like an electric current. Like that lightning that comes out of the blue when there's not even a storm going on, just a crazy crack in the sky.

With something like that right in front of you, you can't help but feel there are new possibilities out there. He started goin' on about life, love, and promise." Tommy looked up at us, grimacing. "Suddenly, he was Shakespeare. I'm not payin' attention. I'm pissed as hell 'cuz he did an illegal tattoo on two kids, which means I could get my license revoked. And anyway this is Norman were talkin' about.

He'll go back to being an asshole in a few days, guaranfrickinteed. A week later I come into the shop." Tommy shook his head, rubbing his chin. "And there's a kid in here. I don't allow kids in here, but there's a kid in here. She's real weird-lookin'. Big. Arms and legs so long they got tangled when she walked. Braces. Frizzy hair out to here." He gestured a foot off his head. "Freckles everywhere like something exploded on her. I ask who she belongs to. She's Norman's. turns out she's the daughter he skipped out on a coupla years before when he was slingin' ink in Kentucky. He tells me he's gonna be a real dad now." Grinning, Tommy shook his head, returning to the tattoo. "*A real dad.* It was a coupla day's before he croaked. Who knows if those two teenagers actually turned him around? I like to think they did. I like to think it was forever. Why not? Sometimes people can surprise the hell outta you. Sometimes they can tear your heart out and turn it to putty, can't they?"

He asked this so adamantly, his voice cracked. He fell silent for a moment, faltering, clearing his throat, and, bending over his work again, began to ink the last pink blossom.

"That night after your friend came in I went home, thought about it. I wondered if she was one a' those kids Norman talked about. One a' the runaways. 'Cause that's what he called them. They were goin' somewhere together. Where I don't know. Probably Timbuktu."

Tommy stopped working and looked up at us, a surprisingly tender expression on his face.

"So, who was she?" he asked.

Sixty-Two

<u>Orichi</u>

The Japanese Orichi is believed to be the most powerful creature that has ever lived, mightier than dragons, the minotaur, the phoenix, and even man. While physically powerful, the Orichi's true supremacy lies in its kindness, for it uses its strength only to defend the innocent. The Orichi is a guardian and protector, the champion of all that is good. It is so kind that it doesn't hunt, but thrives on the wind and the rain, and when it walks it does so without disturbing the grass under its feet.

In the face of malevolence and deceit, however, the Orichi unleashes a devastation that knows no bounds. It lights the sky on fire, creating the reddest of sunsets, and leaping into the air, emits a roar so deafening birds go hoarse, oceans freeze. The ground has been known to shake for a year.

They have the head of a dragon, the body of a deer, the scales of a fish, the legs of a horse, and the tail of a bull. They usually have antlers or a single horn. The Orichi is often depicted with fire all over its body.

In repose, the Orichi is quiet, allowing itself to be seen only by the pure of heart. Those who have had an Orichi sighting claim it is a lightning-quick creature, with dragon's head and horse's body, often covered in the luminescent scales of a fish. By all accounts it *is an incredible creature to behold, for in whatever spot on Earth it has just left, observers swear that the clouds are always parting, revealing golden sky and sun.*

I handed the printed page to Elizabeth.

"Why would Gabriela go back to Dragon Master for the photo?" Elizabeth asked. She was sitting on the couch. Octavius fluttering along the armrest.

"Maybe the photo had a clue in it," I said. "Something to help her track down this Tarantula."

"This Tarantula might have the missing half of the tattoo."

I leaned forward, scanning the timeline of Gabriela's movements I'd typed on my laptop. "Dewitt broke Gabriela out of mission Hills on September thirtieth. She turned up at Onofrio and played a Fazioli piano of October fourth, Dragon Master Tattoos on the fifth. Two days later, on the seventh, she reappeared at Onofrio.

According to the manager, Caesar DePasquale, she looked unkempt and behaved strangely. On the tenth, she sent Cooper the package, and hours later fell or jumped or was pushed to her death that night. Somewhere in this eleven-day time span she checked into the Normal Street apartment, and appeared at Les Silencio and the Warwick Allerton."

And last but not least, *she went to the reservoir.*

"It's almost as if she was visiting important places a final time," Elizabeth said, "tying up loose ends, taking a last look around, just before she . . ."

Unable to finish the thought.

"Before she killed herself," I finished.

"Or before someone she was hiding from, or chasing, caught up to her."

"Someone like the Tarantula," Elizabeth said.

There had to be some hidden reason that would give perfect logic to Gabriela's wanderings, a reason that wasn't a resolve to commit suicide. What had Julie Mergener said about the family? *They mopped life up with themselves. None of them were encumbered by anything. There were no limits.* A desire to die at twenty-four wasn't in keeping with that or anything we learned about Gabriela. *And if the Esquivels weren't afraid of what I might uncover, Santo Esquivel wouldn't have been following me.*

I grabbed my phone, buzzing with an incoming email.

To: Shawn McCarthy

From: Stu

McCarthy
This morning I received an interesting request.
See below
Fondly,
Stu

P.S. Are you still alive?

To: Stuart Laughton
From Assistant
Subject: your client

Dear Mr. Laughton;

Mrs. Olivia Wainscott Pierre would like to speak with your client,

The detective, Shawn McCarthy. Could you forward this email to him so he might get in touch?

Ms. Pierre has a matter of the utmost importance she would like to discuss with him.

Very truly yours,
Louise Bourne

Personal assistant to Mrs. Olivia E. Pierre (312) 779-2951

I hadn't heard from my attorney, Stu Laughton since I was marooned at that charity cocktail party weeks ago. He's sent me a text alerting me to the news of Gabriela's death, asking me to call him.

I hadn't. Stu was a British aristocrat and extremely gabby, and if I gave him the slightest hint that I might be returning to my investigation of Esquivel, everyone from here to McMurdo Station, Antarctica, would know.

I dialed his office.

His assistant answered. After putting me on hold, she informed me, "Mr. Laughton is in a meeting," which meant Stu was sitting at his desk eating an egg-salad sandwich, playing computer solitaire, and would call me back when he was in the mood.

To my surprise, it was just two minutes later.

Sixty-Three

"You talked," I said.

"Haven't said a word," insisted Stu on the other end.

"You must have mentioned my name in connection with Esquivel at one of your power lunches because nothing else explains this."

"You may find this difficult to fathom, McCarthy, but I have other clients and I don't always discuss you at every hour of every day, though I admit, it's terribly tricky to pull off, you're so damn captivating."

It was always a mental adjustment talking to you Stu. As a posh Englishman, he was so well educated, with such an expansive vocabulary, his briefest conversations peppered with irony and wit and deep knowledge of current events, it was like communicating with Jeeves if he ever anchored for the BBC.

"How do you explain it, then?" I asked.

"Damned if I know, if by some miracle of God, Olivia Wainscott wants you to do some investigative work for her, take the job. To quote Captain Smith, 'Grab what you can and fight your way to a lifeboat.' Most people associated with outcast detectives are fast becoming the Great Crested Newt of the culture. Surviving on the brink of extinction.

"Is that supposed to make me nervous?"

"Grab the work when it comes, my man. Your competition is now a fourteen-year-old in pajamas with the username freedom-fighter-21 who believes thinking before speaking. Be afraid, be very afraid.

Pledging Stu, I'd call Wainscott, I hung up.

"A means to track down Madelyn Hughes just fell into our lap," I said to Elizabeth, rearing back in my chair. "The timing can't be a coincidence. Someone's been talkin. Someone we've talked to or bribed."

Elizabeth looked bewildered.

"Olivia Wainscott Pierre wants to meet with me."

Elizabeth frowned. "Who's Olivia Wainscott Pierre?"

Sixty-four

"They were sisters. They were wealthy, and as far apart as the east from the west. And they loathed each other."

"Who is sisters? What are you talking about?" asked Elizabeth.

"Madelyn Olivia wasn't *born* Madelyn Olivia. She was born Jean-Louise "J.L." Wainscott on February 1, 1949, in Tokyo. J.L. was a loose cannon. She had a gargantuan *girls gone wild* kind of teenage life. I arrested her many times, drug possession, prostitution, retail theft, all the usual drug-related offenses. Although none of the charges ever made it to court. With her family's connections and money, she avoided all the consequences. That is until she got caught with a shit load of cocaine coming across Lake Michigan headed for Chicago, coming from Detroit."

"And let me guess, those were Esquivel's drugs," said Elizabeth staring at me.

"That's right, and after months of back and forth with the Federal Lawyers. They finally reached an agreement. If Jean-Louise would help them with the Esquivel investigation no charges would be filed against her. She would have to continue to work for the Esquivel empire and get as close to him as she could. They explained that she would be under constant watch and perfectly safe. They thought they had the first real chance of getting to Esquivel."

"What happened," Elizabeth asked.

I moved over to my file cabinet and pulled out my old files on Madelyn Olivia. Thumbing through until I came across the file about her marriage to Esquivel.

"They put their plan into action, letting her escape and putting the word out that she is on the top ten fugitive list. That naturally caught Esquivel's attention. As things, progressed communication between the feds and Madelyn became less frequent." I shook my head wondering how they could not see this coming.

"As fate would have it, during the empire infiltration Madelyn or "J.L." fell in love with Esquivel. And to make matters worse He fell for her. They were married. Well, that blew the case against Esquivel right out the window. Then a few months later she died in a so-called drowning accident. J.L.'s family always thought it was suicide or worse, they hated Esquivel and considered him the scum of the earth."

I smiled sitting back. "That is the common thread between me and Mrs. Wainscott."

"Call Olivia. Immediately."

I dialed the number.

"Of course, Mr. McCarthy," said the secretary on the other end. "If you can be available tomorrow? Ms. Pierre is off to Saint Moritz the following day. She was hoping you'd forgive her for the late notice and squeeze her into your busy schedule, as she won't be back for four months."

I agreed to meet Olivia at her apartment at noon the following day. The Building on the Magnificent Mile, downtown is about as posh as it gets in chi-town, 540 North Michigan Avenue.

As I hung up, I realized that my cell phone was buzzing. I didn't recognize the number, Walton Street Market, Inc.

"Who is it? Asked Elizabeth.

"I suspect it's the first person calling about Gabriela's missing-person flier."

Sixty-five

Golden Way Chinese grocery is a store that ignored the English language so aggressively, standing in one of the narrow aisles, pungent with smells of fish and sesame, I could convince myself I was in China's Chongqing province.

There were shriveled whole chickens strung up by their talons, trillions of noodles, black teas, and lethal-looking produce, red chilies that'd numb your tongue for a year; greens so spiky, they looked like an underworld heavy lurking on the sidewalk, a dirty red awning pulled low over its cruddy windows and stands of bruised fruit.

I headed after Elizabeth, who'd disappeared in the back, finding her alone in front of a table piled with what appeared to be packets of potato chips, until I read the label; **roast dried squid shavings.**

She shrugged, puzzled. "I just spoke to a man, but he disappeared through there." She pointed at a set of steel doors beside a few fish tanks, fish drifting inside.

When I'd answered the call, a man who barely spoke English announced he had *information*, though he was unable to explain what exactly it was. Finally, a woman came on the line to bark an address; 11 Market Street. The address was near Archer Avenue, only a block, and a half from Normal Street, so it was feasible Gabriela had come in.

At this moment, a slight middle-aged Chinese man emerged, followed by what had to be his entire extended family; his wife, his daughter of about eight, and a grandmother who looked to date back to the ancient Ming Dynasty.

Hell, maybe it Mao Tse-Tung. She had a long forehead, his tired face and gray workman's pants, the flip-flops on her bare feet, which resembled two dry chipped rocks that'd fallen off the Great Wall.

The family all smiled eagerly at us and set about getting a stool for the old woman, helping her sit. The wife then handed her a piece of crumpled paper, which I recognized as the missing-person flier.

"We have information," the little girl announced in perfect English.

"About the girl on the poster?" I clarified.

"Did you meet her?" Elizabeth asked.

"Yes, said the little girl. "She came here."

"What was she wearing?" I asked.

The family conferred heatedly in Cantonese.

"A bright orange coat."

That was close enough.

"And what did she do when she was here?" I asked.

"She talked with my grandmother." The little girl pointed to Mao, who was carefully inspecting the flier as if it were a speech she was about to present in class.

"In English?"

The little girl giggled as if I'd made a joke. "My grandmother doesn't speak English."

"She spoke to her in Chinese?"

The girl nodded. *Gabriela spoke Chinese*. That was unexpected.

"What did they talk about?" I asked.

For the next few minutes, there was so much wild Cantonese flying back and forth Elizabeth and I could do nothing but watch. Finally, the entire family hushed quickly because Mao had at last spoken, her parched voice scarcely audible.

"She asked my grandmother where she was born," explained the girl. "If she missed her home. She brought chewing gum. And then she talked to a taxi driver who comes in here for dinner. He said he'd take her where she wanted to go. My grandmother liked her very much. But your friend was very tired."

"Tired in what way?" I asked.

The girl conferred with Grandmother Mao. "She was sleepy," she answered.

"This taxi driver, do you know who he is?"

She nodded. "He comes in here to eat dinner."

"What time?"

This resulted in more debate, during which the girl's mother did most of the talking.

"Nine o'clock."

"Will he come in tonight?" asked Elizabeth.

"Sometimes he comes in. Sometimes he doesn't."

I checked my watch. It was eight.

"Might as well wait," I said to Elizabeth. "See if he shows up."

I explained this to the girl, who relayed it to her family. I thanked them, smiling, the whole family came forward to shake our hands, moving aside so we could shake Mao's hand, too.

Removing my wallet, I thanked the father and tried to give him a hundred dollars, but he refused to take it. This back and forth went on for a good ten minutes, though I noticed his wife's eyes were glued to the money. I had to get the guy to take it; if I didn't, judging from the look on his wife's face, he wouldn't survive the night.

He finally relented and I turned back to Grandmother Mao with the intention of asking her a few more questions. Evidently, the old woman had silently moved off the stool, disappearing through the doors and into the back of the store.

Sixty-six

"Ah, Shit man," said the taxi driver, "you scared the shit outta me. I thought you were here to deport me." He cackled with laughter, revealing a blinding set of white teeth, a few capped in gold. He scratched his red-and-yellow Rasta cap as he studied Gabriela's picture.

"Yah mon, sure. I did pick her up here."

"When?" I asked."

"Coupla weeks ago."

"What color coat was she wearing?" interjected Elizabeth.

He thought it over, rubbing the gray stubble on his chin.

"Greenish brown? But I'm color blind, mon."

He called himself Ziggy. He was black, from Jamaica I guessed from his accent, 6'6", lean yet disheveled, and slouched like a palm tree after a mild hurricane.

During the past hour, as Elizabeth and I waited, we'd managed to stitch together some basic information. He came to Golden Way five nights a week for dinner. He ate outside, leaning against the hood of his cab, playing loud music with the windows unrolled, and then took off, doubtlessly resuming his all-night driving shift, which ended at 7 a.m.

"When I got here," Ziggy went on, scratching his head, "she was in da back talkin' to da old lady, I got my dinner. She followed me outside."

"And you drove her somewhere?"

"Yah."

"Do you remember where?"

He thought it over. "Some big-ass house on the North Shore."

"Could you take us there now?"

"Oh, no." He held up a hand. "Da stops and starts all bleed together when you drive."

"We'll pay you," blurted Elizabeth.

He perked up. "You'll pay da meter?"

Elizabeth nodded.

"Okay, sure mon. We can do that."

Grinning, as if he couldn't believe his luck, Ziggy cheerfully grabbed a foam container and loaded it with noodles, egg rolls, sesame chicken, if it was chicken; *the gray meat looked like the Siamese cat in a steamed bun I'd once eaten by accident in Hong Kong. Astonishing how quickly money jogged a man's memory.*

Elizabeth and I headed outside to wait.

"This is going to be expensive," I muttered, squinting farther down Fulton Street, where a lone man was shuffling toward us. Instantly I recognized the gray wool coat and the cigarette.

"Look who decided to make an appearance."

Elizabeth, unabashedly worried, grilled Cooper on why he'd stood us up this morning. "We waited for you. I almost called the police."

"I had things to do," Cooper said unconvincingly.

He looked like he'd been up all night. I was beginning to realize the key to his behavior could be found in his own description of Stanley Dewitt: *He's coming back. He has to. He's dying to talk about her.*

Elizabeth eagerly filled him in on the latest. In no time, the three of us were tearing up Michigan Avenue crammed into the backseat of a taxi decorated with more gold bling-bling than Mr. T. I leaned forward to study Ziggy's picture ID. His full name was Ziggy Akapudo, noticing a worn-out paperback, *Taxi Driver,* on the passenger seat beside him.

"Did you notice anything unusual about the girl?" I asked Ziggy through the bulletproof window.

He shrugged. "She was a white girl. They all kinda look alike." He guffawed happily, stopping only to take a bite of his food.

"Did she talk to you? Anything you can tell us about her?"

"No way, mon. I got one rule as a driver."

"What's that?"

"Never look in da rearview mirror."

"Never?" We drifted into the left-hand lane, cutting off a cab.

"It's not healthy to keep a watching what you leavin' behind."

Ten minutes later, we were weaving our way up and down every street on the North Shore, starting at Ohio Street moving up Lake Shore Drive. The meter clicked from twenty dollars to thirty, forty.

"Oh ya mon, dis is right," Ziggy would say, leaning, forward to scrutinize the quiet rows of townhouses until he'd reach the end of the block. "Shit. I got it wrong." He'd sigh in apparent frustration, then cheerfully help himself to more sesame chicken. "No worries, mon. It's da next block."

But the same thing happened on the next block. And the next. After another fifteen minutes, the meter was $80.25. Elizabeth was gnawing her fingernails, and Cooper hadn't said a word the entire ride, slumped against the seat, staring out the window.

I was about to call it off when, as we were cruising down North Sheridan Road, Ziggy abruptly slammed on the brakes.

"*Dat's it!*" He indicated the building on the left. It sat entirely in the dark, a massive townhouse that looked more like an embassy than a residence, pale gray limestone, eighty-five feet wide. It was weathered and run-down, dead leaves strewn across the front steps, the double doors littered with takeout menus, a sure indication no one had been there for weeks.

"We already drove down here," I said.

"I'm telling you. Dat's *the house.*"

"All right." I opened the door, and we climbed out. I handed Ziggy a hundred bucks.

"Peace out, brother."

Ziggy happily tucked the money into his shirt pocket, alongside what looked to be a gigantic half smoked joint. He turned up the radio, and though there was a yellow light at the intersection. He barreled out into Lake Shore Drive, as if yellow lights were signals to floor it and pray, in a noisy clanging of loose parts and a stuttering transmission, the trunk thudded as he blasted over a pothole and swerved south, leaving us alone on the quiet street.

Sixty-Seven

We crossed the street to get a better view. It was dim on that side, with just a streetlamp and a high-rise apartment building, its entrance around the corner on Lake Shore Drive, so it afforded some privacy to watch the townhouse.

It was after eleven o'clock, the neighborhood deserted. Chicago might be the city that never slept, but the well-heeled residents of the Upper North Shore got tucked into their silk satin sheets around ten.

"Doesn't look like anyone's lived there for years," I stated.

I noticed Cooper staring intently at the place, the expression on his face unreadable, though I sensed a sort of deep-seated hostility as if within its hulking grandeur he saw something he detested.

It stood unapologetic in its opulence, five stories, a garden on the roof, tree branches could be seen reaching over the top cornice. Every window was dark, a few adorned with heavy curtains, the window panes dirty. A narrow covered balcony extended outside the windows on the second floor, detailed with an oxidized copper roof, black iron latticework along the sides and railing. And yet in spite of its lavishness, or because of it, the townhouse had a cold, lonely demeanor.

"Are we going to knock?" whispered Elizabeth.

"You two stay here," I said.

I skipped up the marble steps strewn with leaves and bits of trash, a deli napkin, a cigarette butt. I rang the bell, noting the black bubble of a security camera above the intercom. A strident clanging straight out of nineteenth-century England rang inside. I waited silently listening, no response.

I pulled out the papers wedged through the mail slot, a Burger King menu, and two ads for a twenty-four security system. They were faded, warped from the rain.

I looked back to Elizabeth and Cooper. "These have been here for months," I said.

"Only one way to find out," said Cooper. He took the last drag of his cigarette, chucked it to the ground, and, pulling up the collar of his coat, crossed the street.

"What's he doing?" whispered Elizabeth.

Cooper stepped right up to the townhouse, grabbed the black iron grating over the arched window on the ground floor, and began to climb. Within seconds, he was twelve feet off the ground. He paused for a minute, looking down, then stepped on top of an old lantern flanking the front doors and, straddled about five feet of space, grabbing hold of the concrete ledge of the second-floor balcony.

He hoisted himself higher, dangling there for a few seconds, his gray coat floating around him like a cape. He hiked his right leg over the railing and fell sideways onto the balcony. Immediately, he scrambled to his feet and with a cautious glance down at the sidewalk, crept along the narrow veranda to the window on the farthest right. Crouching, he shielded his eyes to look through the glass, then fumbled inside his coat for what appeared to be his wallet. He cracked the casement, probably using a credit card, slid the window open, and without the slightest hesitation, he crawled inside.

There was a moment of stillness. He reappeared as a silhouette, slid the window closed and disappeared. I felt stunned, expecting at any moment a maid's bloodcurdling scream or sirens. But the street remained silent.

"What the hell? What do we do now?" whispered Elizabeth, clamping a hand over her chest.

"Nothing. We wait."

As it turned out, we didn't have to wait long. Cooper had been inside not ten minutes when a lone taxi coasted down the street toward us, slowing and stopping directly in front of the townhouse.

"Oh, no," whispered Elizabeth.

The rear door opened and a heavyset woman emerged.

"Text Cooper," I said. "Tell him to get the hell out of there."

As Elizabeth fumbled for her phone, I slipped between the parked cars, aiming for the woman who was moving up the townhouse steps, digging through her purse, trying to find her keys.

Sixty-Eight

"Excuse me?"

She didn't turn around. She jammed the key in the lock, pushing open one of the doors.

"Ma'am, I'm looking for the nearest Metra station."

She darted inside, switching on a light. I caught a fleeting glimpse of the entryway, a black and white checked floor, and as she whisked around, the woman herself, before she slammed the door, hard.

A deadbolt clicked, followed by the five-digit beep of an alarm.

I froze in shock. I knew her.

Suddenly, the lamps over the entrance switched on, bathing me in bright light. *She probably wanted to get a good look at me in the security camera.*

I moved up the steps and rang the doorbell. There was no response. I rang it a second time, then a third. Not that I expected her to open the door, it was to alert Cooper to get the hell out. I jogged swiftly down the steps, looking back to the house. Elizabeth and I jogged across the street looking for a place to hide and still see the front of the house.

"He's still inside," she whispered. "I texted him but haven't heard back."

"You're not going to believe this. That was Marissa Garcia. Esquivel's personal assistant for years. The Esquivels must own this place."

It's unbelievable, not just that Cooper had broken in, but he was now trapped inside a personal residence of Esquivel's.

Elizabeth, amazed, turned back to the townhouse, where a bright light had just illuminated the second floor, revealing a dark, wood-paneled library, the shelves lined with books.

"Now he has no way out," said Elizabeth. "Should we call nine-one-one?"

"Not, yet."

"But we have to do something. She might shoot him."

"We need to give him time to find a way out."

"How long?"

Distant wails of sirens answered her question. They grew louder, and suddenly three police cars came barreling down the street, screeching to a halt in front of the townhouse. Four policemen jumped out, hastening up the steps, Garcia opening the door, and they disappeared inside. Two cops remained on the front steps, staring suspiciously down the street.

"Time to get the hell out of here," I said.

"But we have to make sure he's okay"

"We'll be more help to him out of jail."

But suddenly there were loud voices, and the cops reemerged, leading Cooper down the steps.

He was handcuffed, his gray coat had been confiscated, but otherwise, in his faded blue T-shirt and jeans, he looked rather undaunted by the proceedings. His eyes purposefully avoided our direction, although I swore I caught a faint smile on his face as they shoved his head down and pushed him forcefully into the backseat.

Sixty-Nine

At home, I called an old friend, a criminal defense attorney named Saul Feinstein. I'd never needed him, not yet, anyway, but he's pulled plenty of people I knew out of rocks and hard places. Apparently, you could call Feinstein a couple of hours after killing your wife and, in a voice silkier than a Hermes scarf, he'd assure you everything was going to be fine. Then he'd tell you exactly what to say and do as if the issue were simply that you'd lost your driver's license.

I left a message with his answering service: Someone assisting me with some research had gotten carried away and broken into a private residence, though he'd been unarmed and stole nothing, and was now in police custody.

The woman assured me she'd have Feinstein call me back. Elizabeth and I then moved into my office to research Marissa Garcia.

"What do we know about her?" asked Elizabeth, curling up on the couch beside the box of research.

"Not much," I said. "She was supposedly Esquivel's longtime assistant."

After digging through the papers, I pulled out Marissa Garcia's wedding photo. The picture always turned up whenever her name appeared in the press. In it, she looked like every other beaming newlywed, which only make it tragic. Years later, she'd abandon this very husband and her two children to go work alongside Esquivel.

"We also found that page on the Blackboards," noted Elizabeth. "The one that contends she and Esquivel are the same person. They both have a tiny wheel tattoo on their left hands. Are you sure it was a woman?"

"Positive."

We dug around YouTube and found a grainy film clip of Garcia in front of the courthouse, during a segment of Crime Watch Chicago. The camera's focused on Marissa Garcia, who was quickly making her way down the steps. Garcia was black-haired and heavy set, with strong, brawny features, undeniably similar to Esquivel's in his early photographs, dressed in a black T-shirt and combat boots. Later, when the Crime Watch asked her questions about Esquivel, she focused her discussion to the extent of the rumors about the exact nature of her relationship to Esquivel.

The rumors on the Blackboards suggested Marissa was his sister, his puppeteer, and Svengali, his female doppelganger, an obsessive caretaker and enabler who catered to Esquivel's every need and desire, a custodian who cleaned up his every mess.

Combing through one rumor after the next, Elizabeth's eyes were closing, so she headed to bed, though I stayed up a few more hours reading. Maybe it was simply my shock at encountering her, but there had been something unaccountably bizarre about Garcia's wide chiseled face, the hard features, the embittered voice.

Maybe the key to all of this was exactly what Cleo had said at Fascinations: *Dark magic passed from generation to generation.*

I searched on the Blackboards for the mention of it, *witchcraft* and *Marissa Garcia,* or another reference to the wheel tattoo that both she and Esquivel supposedly had on their left hands. Other than a brief mention of her being from Puebla, Mexico, and her selfless devotion to the drug lord being the stuff of legend (There's nothing Garcia wouldn't do to protect him," claimed one post).

    There was nothing else there.

Seventy

"Woodward?"

I cracked open an eye. The clock read 4:05 A.M.

"Are you asleep?"

"Yes."

"Can you talk?"

"Sure."

Elizabeth opened the door, slipping through the darkness. She was again wearing that ghostly nightgown, a pale blur perched on the end of my bed.

"What's the matter?" I asked, propping myself up on the pillows.

She said nothing. She seemed nervous. She had a way of being quite talkative, then suddenly growing silent and still, so you studied her face like some hard blue desert sky, waiting for some sign of life, however distant.

"You're going to have to give me more to go on," I said, after a moment. "I'm a guy. I'm illiterate when it comes to reading between lines."

"Well . . . "She sighed as if it were the end of the conversation rather than the beginning. This meant, because she was a woman, she'd probably already had this discussion umpteen times in her head.

"Is it about Cooper?" I asked. "Are you worried about him spending the night in jail? Because he'll be fine, trust me." The bed jerked. "Did you nod out? It's too dark to see in here."

"It's nothing to do with him. It's something I said that I feel bad about."

"What?"

"That I wouldn't sleep with you."

"No need to clarify it. It goes unsaid. And it's nothing I haven't heard before." I did not know where Bernstein was going with this, but I had a bad feeling. It was crucial to get the girl out of my room, back to her own bed, *stat!* Adding sex to ongoing investigations was as inspired an idea as Ford unveiling *the Pinto*. What was meant to be fun, sexy, and practical was actually a nightmare, causing great personal injury on all sides.

"You're very handsome," Elizabeth said. "If you were at Willow Falls, the ladies would *die*."

"Isn't that what they do anyway?"

"I didn't want any professional lines to be crossed."

"You were right. I can't tell you how many women I've crossed all kinds of lines with and afterward felt terrible."

"*Really?*"

"Like I'd just been given a prognosis of a few weeks left to live."

She giggled.

"Started my very first time when I was fifteen, Maureen Wilson. Talk about lines; she played pinochle with my mother. I got carried away. She fell into a shower curtain. You know that little soap holder in bathtubs?"

"Sure."

"Her face smashed into it. She lost two teeth. Blood everywhere. Maureen went from a perfectly attractive fortysomething divorcee to a lead character on *Night of the Living Dead.*"

"My first time was Ronnie Bailey."

I waited for more information. None came.

"Don't tell me he was a resident of Willow Falls."

"Oh, no. He worked at Wolf's Pool Cleaners. He cleaned the pool every Friday."

"How old was he?"

"Twenty-eight."

"How old were you?"

"Sixteen. But an old sixteen. He had a wife and two kids. I felt awful about it. It's a terrible thing, to lie. It's a field you keep seeding, watering and plowing, but nothing will ever grow on it." She wrapped her arms around her knees, fidgeting her shoulders. "I tried to end it a couple times, but Ronnie and I would go out behind the kitchen when everyone was at Wine and Cheese, and he'd dance with me to the country music coming through the kitchen window. He was a good dancer. He was also sad. He dreamed of just taking off and starting over, pretending his life never happened in the first place."

"Did he?"

"Don't know. Can I tell you something?"

"Of course."

"You won't make a big deal out of it?"

"I promise."

When I first got to Chicago, at the greyhound bus terminal, it was three in the morning. Octavius got stolen." She paused clasping her hands between her knees.

"One of the people on the bus did it. I knew who it was. He got on the South Dakota station, and he sat behind me and Octavius the whole way. He smelled like alcohol, and he tried hard to make conversation during the ride, but I just put on my headphones and pretended to be asleep. Something was wrong with him. Mentally, you know? But when we got to Chicago, I let my guard down when we were all getting off. This lady needed help getting one of her kids into a stroller. I helped her, then went to the underneath part to get my bag, and when I went back to the curb Octavius wasn't there. His cage was gone. I went crazy. I told the driver, and he told me to report it to the main office, I thought I was going to die without Octavius. I couldn't think, thoughts racing so fast. By then all the other passengers had left. I exited the lot into the part where all the shops are and it was quiet. The next thing I knew, that same man was walking behind me. He whispered he had my bird. He said he wanted to give him back. All I had to do was give him um. . . you know. . . *sex* in the bathroom."

I stared at her. I felt as if the wind had been kicked out of me, so sudden was this confession. I was careful not to do anything at all, not even to move.

"I said I didn't believe him, so he brought me behind a Pizza shop and into the women's bathroom. Octavius's cage was there on the floor, but it was empty. And then I saw the man had stuck him in one of those silver containers in the stalls. You know, where you throw stuff away? He was fluttering around in there, going crazy. Because he hates the dark. Always has. You're supposed to put a sheet over the cage to calm a bird, but Octavius doesn't like it. He has to be able to see. The man said all I had to do was *that* and he'd let him go. I got into the stall with him.

There was a lady getting dressed in the back, but she didn't say anything when I called out to her. He unzipped his pants and started to overpower me, punching me. So I told him to close his eyes and lean back. When he did I kicked him as hard as I could right in the balls, grabbed Octavius put him in the cage and ran with everything I had, when I finally stopped the place was deserted, all the shops were closed up, only a few people staring at nothing like a bunch of ghosts. I took the escalator up to the street. I went over to the taxi stand, climbed in, and I asked the driver to take me to the center of everything. Madonna did it when she came to the big city, she asked the cab driver to take her to the center of everything.

She looked at me as if to ask a question.

"He didn't know where that was. I said State and Madison. He took me right there. There were people everywhere, lights made it seem like the middle of the afternoon. And I knew I was going to be fine. Because I was right where I was supposed to be. I'd spent my whole life feeling like I was waiting to be someplace else. For the first time, I didn't." Elizabeth turned to me, her hands clasped over her knees. "I never told anybody."

"I'm glad you told me," I said.

It took a moment to hear it all; the story seemed like a toxic vapor wafting through the room that needed time to dissolve. I felt sick to my stomach and an overwhelming need to make sure she was all right, to extract the memory of such a thing from her head. It was never the act itself but our own understanding of it that defeated us over and over again.

"You didn't want to go to the police?"

She shook her head. "I didn't want to waste another minute on it. My life was meant to begin. The bad things that happen to you don't have to mean anything at all. And anyway, he'll answer to God for what he did."

She announced this with great certainty. For a girl with nothing to her name but a crazy old bird, to have such unwavering belief in the reckoning of evil in the world, a belief I could never bring myself to have, having seen, time and time again, depravity go unchecked, it awed me, and it was some time before I could bring myself to speak.

Outside, a car cruised down the street, and the night's stillness made it sound drowsy and relaxed; it might have been a rowboat wafting by.

"You are a magnificent and powerful person," I said.

I hadn't intended to say that, *exactly*, it's never been my strong suit, whipping out the right words heal that ever-present wound in a woman's heart, but it made Elizabeth smile. She slipped toward me, mattress creaking, kissed me on the cheek, and hopped off the bed, a blurred bluish figure floating through the dark.

"I'm a fan," I added. "And that's an unconditional lifetime warranty. I'm like Samsonite Luggage and Carhart jackets."

She laughed sleepily, slipping out of the room. "Night, Woodward," she whispered over her shoulder. "Thanks for listening."

I don't know how long I sat there, staring into the darkness, the hardened shadows thawing as the minutes passed, the only sounds night-shivers of the city outside. After a while, when I was half asleep, her presence lingered as if some wild creature had been inside my room, a fawn or iridescent bird, or maybe *an Orichi.*

Seventy-One

"He was held overnight at the precinct," Feinstein informed me over the phone. "I sent a junior associate downtown to get him out. They dropped burglary in the second degree, but he's facing criminal trespass. Bail will be around five thousand dollars."

"Why so high?' I asked, wedging the phone against my ear as I pulled my coat out of the closet and pulled it on.

"He has three priors. Assault of a police officer in Peoria, Illinois, petty theft in Key West, Florida."

"Florida?"

"And two years ago. Possession of a controlled substance with intent to sell. That was in Los Angeles."

"What was the substance?"

"Marijuana and cocaine. He served eighteen months, did a hundred hour's community service."

I told Feinstein I'd cover the bail, then, hanging up, quickly relayed the story to Elizabeth as we prepared to leave for the meeting with Oliva Wainscott. I'd made Elizabeth an omelet, but as soon as she saw it, she said she wasn't hungry her face red. I chalked this up to that bizarre Pandora's box of feminine behavior that defied explanation, until I realized, cursing my stupidity, it was because of what she'd told me last night. She didn't want me to treat her with kid gloves, didn't want to be handled like some fragile thing with a crack through it. So I forcefully through the omelet and announced that Moe Gulazar's black sequin leggings and that Captain Jack Sparrow blouse didn't suit a meeting with one of Chicago's most elegant swans. I ordered her to change her clothes., which made her smile with relief as she raced upstairs to do so. Within minutes, we were out the door.

It was a gray day, the sky threatening rain. We headed for the Metra, we were already late. And if there was one thing I knew about Chicago's wealthiest, they loved to keep you waiting, not the other way around.

Seventy-Two

"Mr. McCarthy. Welcome." The woman who greeted us at the door was in her fifties, dressed in a dust-gray suit. She had the dimmed-bulb face of someone who'd lived a life of servitude. Her eyes moved inquiringly to Elizabeth.

"This is my assistant. I hope it's all right if she joins us."

"Certainly."

Smiling, the woman ushered us into the foyer, where an old codger wearing a rumpled burgundy jacket appeared, seemingly from the walls, to take our coats. Wordlessly he drifted with them back down another dim hall.

"Right this way."

She led us in the other direction down a dark a gallery. The wine-colored walls were plastered with paintings, the way scaffolding downtown was covered with ads for concerts: only these happened to be Matisses and Schieles, Clementes, the odd Magritte, each painting sporting its own bronze lamp like a miner's helmet. Between these masterpieces were dark open hallways, and I slowed to glance inside. Every room looked like a grotto, dank and stalactite with brocade curtains and Louis XIV chairs, vases and Tiffany lamps, busts in marble, ebony sculpture, books. We passed a formal dining room. The windows framed a northwestern view, turning the city into a serene concrete still life with a gray sky. A helicopter hovered over the lake front like an errant fly.

The woman gestured for us to sit on the yellow chintz couch in front of a coffee table covered in miniatures: porcelain schnauzers, sheep—herders, finger bowls. Fresh yellow and red tulips exploded out of a Chinese vase. They matched the yellow walls and the red jackets of the riders in the giant foxhunt oil painting looming behind us.

Elizabeth sat down stiffly beside me, folding her hands in her lap. She looked nervous.

"May I offer you some tea while you wait? Mrs. Pierre is finishing up with a telephone call."

"Tea would be nice," I said. "Thank you."

The woman slipped out of the room.

"This is what you call *super rich*," I whispered to Elizabeth. "These people are a strange breed in themselves. Don't try to understand them."

"Did you see the shining armor on the way in? Real shining armor just standing there, waiting for a knight."

"Two percent of the world's richest people have over half of the world's wealth. I think it's all in this apartment."

Elizabeth, biting her lip, pointed at the small end table on my right, where there was a black-and-white photograph in an antique silver frame. It was Oliva standing with her husband, Knightly, probably some twenty years ago. They had their arms around each other, posing beside an antique Bentley in front of a colossal country manor. They looked happy, but of course, that didn't say much. *Everyone smile for a picture.*

Abruptly, Elizabeth sat up.

A woman was entering the room. I stood up immediately, Elizabeth following my lead, fidgeting to straighten her skirt.

It was Olivia. She didn't walk as much as float, three Pekingese dogs shuffling alongside her feet. The room had obviously been designed with her in worn in a rich candy swirl around her face, matched the Persian rug, the carved lion paw legs of the table, even the silver cigarette case with the elegant initials engraved on the lid, OPE, the fine lettering like tangled strands of hair clogging a shower drain.

I wasn't sure what I'd expected, some grand dame, blistering with jewelry, but she was surprisingly light and airy, devoid of ornamentation. She wore a simple gray-and-black dress, plump pearls wrapped twice around her neck. Her oval face was attractive and soft, neatly made up, long, splinters of eyebrows framing her bright brown eyes, an elegant neck like a stalk of a flower just starting to wilt. *How many times had Madelyn dreamed of wringing that thing?*

As Olivia moved toward us, smiling, I realized her right arm hung limply in a sling fashioned out of a black-and-red floral scarf. The hand hung there like a broken wing, but she seemed resolved to pull off this handicap gamely. The fingernails on that withered hand were perfectly painted fire-engine red.

On the ring finger on her functioning hand, which she now extended to us, a pale blue diamond, at least twelve karats stuck out, unblinking, like the mesmerizing eye of Mordor.

"Olivia Pierre. I'm so pleased you could come, Mr. McCarthy."

"My pleasure."

After shaking her hand, we all sat down, including her three Pekingese, which resembled gat girls stuffed into fursuits. Olivia steeled into the white couch opposite, extending an arm over the white throw draped across the back, and the dogs piled around her as if to form some sort of fluffy stronghold, then stared at us expectantly as if we were meant to entertain.

"I'm sorry to have kept you waiting. It's quite mad around here with the move."

"You're leaving the city?" I asked.

"Just for the season. We spend the winter in Switzerland. The whole family comes out. My grandchildren love to ski and hike, though Mike and I tend to just laze around. We really sit down in front of the fire and don't budge for four months."

She laughed, a crisp, elegant sound, bringing to mind a spoon tapping a crystal glass before some dignitary made a toast. *Boy-oh-boy* had the apple fallen far from the tree. It was astounding how a woman when she struck marital gold, procured not just a new wardrobe and new friends but a now voice straight out of a 1930's gramophone Victrola and a vocabulary that reliably included *laze, season, and terribly sorry.* I had to actively remind myself Olivia was an army brat who'd grown up so impoverished, her mother had a third job cleaning the bathrooms of the very public high school she attended. Now Olivia probably had six estates and a yacht as big as a city block.

"My grandson, Jackson, is a huge fan of yours, Mr. McCarthy."

"Shawn. Please."

"Jackson's in the eighth grade at Mount Carmel. He read all the newspapers during your investigation of Mr. Esquivel. He is quite taken be your expressive feelings about the case." She adjusted her position on the sofa, then looked me in the eye. "I never doubted you, you know," Olivia said, arching an eyebrow.

"That hoopla a few years back about you and Esquivel, your fictitious chauffeur, the outrageous assertions you made on television. I knew exactly what was going on."

"*Did* you? Because it was a *mystery* to me."

"You'd done something to provoke him." She smiled at my look of surprise.

"Surely you've noticed that the space surrounding Esquivel *distorts*. The closer you get to him, the speed of light slackens, information gets scrambled, rational minds grow illogical, Hysterical. It's warped space-time, like the mass of a giant sun bending the area surrounding it. You reach out to seize something so close to finding it was never actually there. I've witnessed it firsthand myself."

She fell silent, pensive, just as her three uniformed maids entered with the tea. They set about arranging it before us on the coffee table, fine china, a five-tiered silver tower laden with cakes, mini-cupcakes, and triangular sandwiches. Olivia slipped off her silver heels, from Stubbs & Wootton. I noticed, *the billionaire's Nike,* curling her black stocking feet underneath her. As the maids poured the tea, I noticed Elizabeth was blinking in shock at the elaborate setup.

"Thank you, Charlotte."

Charlotte and the other girls nodded demurely and darted away, their shoe's silent on the carpet.

"You must be wondering why on earth you're here," said Olivia, sipping her tea. "You've resumed work on your investigation of Esquivel, have you not?" Her eyes met mine as he set down the teacup. They were bright like a little kid waiting for a big piece of cake.

"How did you hear that?"

"Christine Plath."

The name rang a bell.

"The director of Mission Hills? I've done some charity work for them. She told me she caught you digging rather shamelessly around the grounds last week. Posing as a potential guest."

Of course, Plath had hauled me into the Security Center and threatened to have me arrested.

"How is the investigation going?" she asked.

"It hasn't been easy getting people to talk."

Returning the teacup to the saucer, she sat back, staring at me.

"I'll talk," she announced.

I couldn't help but smile, amused by her directness. "About?"

"What I know. It's quite a lot, believe me."

"Because of your sister?"

Her smile faltered. That was unexpected; I'd have assumed she'd gotten over Madelyn long ago, that she'd put her in some safe-deposit box of childhood memories and locked it, and tossing the key. But the mention of her sister visibly upset her.

"I haven't spoken to Madelyn in forty-seven years. I don't know what she thought of Carlos or what her experiences were. I had my own encounters. And I've never wanted to speak about them. Until now."

"Why the change of heart?"

"Gabriela."

She said it matter-of-factly. Elizabeth was leaning forward, nervously eyeing the mini cupcakes, as if worried they'd scurry away if she went for one.

"Police think it was suicide," I said.

Olivia nodded. "Perhaps. But there's more to it."

"How do you know?"

"I met her once." She paused to sip her tea, and when she set the tea cup down, she looked at me, her eyes piercing. "Do you believe in the supernatural world, Mr. McCarthy? Ghosts and the paranormal, unexplained forces we can't see yet nonetheless affect us?"

"No, not really. But I do believe in the human mind's ability to make something like that seem very real."

Carlos and his third wife, Delores, have an estate in the northeastern part of Illinois, near Deer Lake."

"Yes, I know. El Esplanade."

She arched an eyebrow. "You've been?"

"I tried stopping by to pay my respects five years ago. Never got past the security gate."

Olivia smiled knowingly, sitting back on the couch. "I went there the first week of June in 1977. I was struggling and thought I could maybe make some quick money working for

Esquivel. His assistant Marissa Garcia met with me for an interview." She smiled with visible embarrassment. "It was a rather pitiful display, but yet his assistant seemed to think I might be able to work for him." Olivia stood and looked a little shaken for some reason. "She invited me to travel up to el Esplanade and stay the weekend so we might discuss my role in his operations."

She paused for a moment, her hand idly stroking one of the dogs.

"When you drive past the security gate's, it becomes a leisurely drive through oak trees and undulating hills. There wasn't a soul around. The sun was out, it was bright, hot and yet I remember feeling so anxious, it soon slipped into terror, as if I were entering a graveyard in the dead of night. Every now and then I could hear flocks of birds, crows, screeching overhead. But when I slowed the car and looked up, there was nothing in the sky or the trees. *Nothing.*"

She sipped her tea.

"When I arrived at the house, a dark colossal mansion straight out of, I don't know, an Edgar Allen Poe story. I parked by the other cars. There were quite a few as if other potential workers had been summoned as well. Yet I found myself unable to get out of my car. It was a terrible feeling. But I wanted that job. I needed it. She paused to smile ironically at this last comment.

"I climbed out and knocked at the front entrance and immediately found myself greeted by a stunning Italian woman who acted oddly withdrawn. Without saying a thing to me. She beckoned me to lunch, already under way outside on a loggia draped with wisteria. There was a large group eating there, no one I recognized. Esquivel's groupies, I imagined. But there was no sign of the man himself. Not that I had a clear picture of what he looked like. I asked someone where he was and someone informed me that he was working. They pulled up a chair for me to sit at the table. They were all talking about this object someone had just purchased at a private auction.

They were passing this object around. Eventually, it came to me. And for some reason when I had it everyone went silent, and they asked me what I thought it was. It looked odd. It looked like some sort of dagger. The bronze handle was intricately carved, the blade narrow, about five inches long, with a strange loop in the middle of it. A young blond man in clerical garb sitting at the very end of the table, he was beautiful, like Adonis, suggested that I should stick it in my wrist to see what happened, and they all erupted in loud laughter.

The only person who didn't immediately go in. she looked at me, her face somber. "A pricking needle. They were used in European witch-hunts of the sixteenth and seventeenth centuries. They're made of precious metals, artfully engraved. The pricker would use it to stab the accused woman, usually bare naked, all over her body. When he, at last, found a spot that didn't bleed or cause pain, he'd found the witch's mark. If he found such a place, it was of course because she could no longer scream. She'd been stabbed by this needle some three hundred times and was unconscious, slowly bleeding to death. These things, archaic instruments of torture, have a vibrant market today for certain willing collectors."

Elizabeth was so captivated she'd forgotten to chew the rather large piece of cake in her mouth. A crumb fell from her lips, which she hastily collected from the hem of her sweater. She swallowed with a loud gulp.

"But I soon put the bizarre lunch out of my head, because of someone, a masculine looking maid with a sweaty face and gleaming black eyes, announced that Esquivel was ready to meet with me.

I was escorted through various hallways, into a large room filled with filing cabinets and a long dining room table. A man sat at the very end. He was like a king on a throne, stacks of papers and photographs of locations, spread-sheets piled all around him. He was rather large but not obese. His massiveness looked distinguished. He had a round face with thick black hair, and he wore glasses, the lenses oval and black as ink. He was handsome. At least I think he was. He had one of those faces that captivated you. And yet you couldn't memorize it a minute later as if your brain just would not memorize the features, the way it can't memorize an infinite number. Possibly this was due to the glasses, the lack of eyes. For a moment I thought he was blind, but he wasn't, because he stared at me without saying a word and then informed me I had parsley on my lip. I did, much to my chagrin.

He then started to interrogate me. It began with a series of pointed questions, all of which became increasingly personal and unsettling. He asked if I had a family, a boyfriend, if I was sexually active, how regularly I went to the doctor, who was my next of kin. Was I healthy? Was I easily spooked? He wanted to know if I was afraid of heights, Tarantulas, drowning at sea. How much physical pain had I ever endured? What was my worst nightmare? I began to suspect the underlying purpose of the questions was to find out how isolated of a person I am. To know who would notice if I ever vanished or changed in some way. I kept asking what the reason was for all the questions.

He greeted such requests with silence and a smile. Finally, another person came in a woman and escorted me out. It felt like I'd been grilled for over an hour. It was only fifteen minutes.

Olivia took a deep breath and poured us more tea with her functioning hand. When she grabbed the tongs for a sugar cube and dropped it into her cup, I noticed with surprise her fingers were trembling. *She was nervous.*

"It became clear," she went on, "that there would be further discussion on my duties after supper. I agreed. A maid brought me to a room. It was an enormous house, and my room a suite, a wall of windows with gauzy curtains like long bridal veils and a view of a lake far down the hill. I'd never seen such a beautiful room. I lay down on the bed, intending to shut my eyes for just a moment, but fell into a deep sleep. I must have been exhausted from the drive than I realized. Three hours later, I woke up very suddenly in the dark, gasping for air, my throat hurting as if someone had been strangling me. My wrists and arms felt as if they'd somehow been pinned down. They ached. But there was no one, no sign of any restraints. Then I saw horror, my suitcase was empty. All of my clothes had been neatly hung up in the closet. Even my underwear had been folded into meticulous piles in the dresser drawer. A dress of mine that I was seemingly meant to wear down for dinner was laid out for me, including earrings and a silver comb for my hair.

The windows were open, the curtains blowing every which way. They'd been closed when I fell asleep. Every hair on my arms was standing up as if I were about to be struck by lightning. I had only on thought. *I had to escape.* Dinner was starting at eight o'clock, and there was more guest arriving. I didn't care. I threw my clothes into the suitcase and hurried our, managing to find a back staircase, running outside into the night. My car was exactly where I'd left it, and I drove out without turning on my headlights. At first, I thought someone was following me. There were headlights a few turns in the road behind me. But they were gone by the time I reached the gate. It was closed. I got out, unlocked it myself, and frantically drove away. I didn't stop for six hours. But that feeling, a weight, a suffocation as if my entire body had been put in some sort of vise. It didn't go away for days. I came very close to checking myself into a hospital."

Olivia paused to take two of the mini cupcakes from the tea stand, feeding one to herself, the other to a Pekinese. When she looked back at us, she smiled ruefully.

"Of course, the more time that went by, when I thought back to that incident I felt humiliated. Time leeches most horror and pain from our memories. All that so-called terror I'd felt, I reasoned it's been my youth, an overwrought imagination. I'd gotten mixed up. I'd confused fantasy with reality.

I wrote Esquivel three pages of apology after the episode and heard nothing back from him except a very churlish response."

"What did it say?"

"Something to the effect of, if I was the last person on Earth, He'd never use me for any venture in his holdings. I suppose the invitation to El Esplanade was my audition and I'd blown it."

I couldn't help but smile. What she said corroborated seamlessly with what I already knew.

She shrugged dismissively. "It was fine by me. Two years later I was a married woman. I had a family, real love, a real life. I'd long given up on being a part of that lifestyle. I understood that the whole culture of those women was nothing more than consigning oneself to a cheap carnival where one lives forever in a cage, applauded and ridiculed by equal measure. Then, in 1999, I received an invitation quite out of the blue. It was from Esquivel. He was inviting me to a private dinner at his home, this time in the city. This was long after he buried himself underground when he was more secretive and chilling a figure than ever before. I was hesitant to accept, but then again, it was Esquivel.

I was still enamored. To me, he was more of a magician, a hypnotist in the vein of Rasputin. Not a criminal. All these years later, I still felt unrequited about him. It gnawed at me, ever so slightly, this question about him I needed to be answered. The location of the dinner was almost next door, just across Michigan Avenue on East Lake Shore Drive. If I felt uncomfortable I could leave at any time and simply walk home."

I glanced at Elizabeth, and she nodded imperceptibly, making the same connection I was. The townhouse cooper had broken into last night was on the upper north shore; Olivia had to be referring to that very house. I also recognized the sentiments she described, the unrequited feeling about Esquivel, the need for a resolution, for an end, how it nibbled at you over the years; I had it myself.

"By then, I was fifty years old, no longer a skittish young girl. I'd been married for twenty years, had raised three boys. It would take a hell of a more to terrify me."

She leaned forward, taking another cake. The three Pekingese's eyes were glued to it. To their evident heartbreak, she played it in her own mouth, chewing.

"It was a beautiful dinner, but oddly enough Esquivel wasn't even there. His wife Delores, who explained her husband had gotten waylaid working out of the country and wouldn't be able to make it. I was thrown by this. I suspected something was wrong as if it were a trap. And yet it was a wonderful mix of people. Whatever reservations I had about being there soon dissipated.

A Russian opera star, a Danish scientist, a French actress known for her immense beauty, and yet the unmistakable center of attention was Esquivel's daughter, Gabriela. She was cultivating a rather stellar piano career at the time. She was twelve, the most beautiful child I'd ever seen, eyes almost clear. She played for us. Shubert, a Bach concerto, a movement from Stravinsky's *Petrushka,* and then she joined us for dinner. Oddly enough, she chose to sit right beside me. Immediately, I felt disconcerted. Her eyes, they were so beautiful and yet so . . ."

Olivia clasped her hands, frowning.

"What?" I prompted.

Her eyes met mine. "Old. They'd seen too much."

She paused to take a deep breath, smiling ruefully.

"Dinner was fantastic. The conversation, fascinating. Gabriela was charming. And yet when she fell silent she seemed absent as if she'd slipped off somewhere else, into some other world. When dinner was over, Delores suggested we play a Japanese game that she claimed the family often played after dinner, having learned it from a real Japanese Samurai who apparently lived with the family. It was called The Game of One Hundred Candles. Later, I looked up the Japanese term. *Hyakumonogatare Kaidankai* is what it's called. Have you heard of it?"

"No," I said, shaking my head.

"It's an old Japanese parlor game. It dates back to the Edo period. The seventeenth, eighteenth centuries. One hundred candles are lit, and each candle is blown out after someone tells a short kaidan. Kaidan is Japanese for ghost stories. This continues, the room gradually getting darker and darker, until the final candle is blown out. It's at this moment that a supernatural entity is finally inside the room. It's usually an *Ouryo,* a Japanese ghost who seeks vengeance."

Seventy-Three

Olivia took a long breath, exhaling.

"We began to play, all of us fairly drunk on port and French wine, each of us grasping at our stories, but when Gabriela told hers they were perfectly succinct tales. I assumed she'd memorized them, unless at twelve she could speak so eloquently, right off the top of her head. Her voice was leisurely and low, and at times it sounded like it was coming from somewhere else in the room. Every story she told was riveting, some disturbingly violent. One I remember described a master raping a poor servant girl and leaving her for dead on the side of the road. I was amazed at how easily her lips formed the words ass if she were talking about something perfectly natural. At times I had a sense of being outside myself as she talked.

And then, I don't know how exactly it turned out that way, there was one candle left and Gabriela was up to tell the final story. It was a tale of unrequited love, a Romeo and Juliet tale of illness and hope, a young girl dying, thereby setting her lover free. Everyone was mesmerized. She blew out the candle, and it was pitch-black in the room. Too dark. People were giggling. Someone told a dirty joke. Suddenly, there was a sucking noise and I felt a cold finger touching my forehead. I was certain Gabriela had reached over and touched me. I shrieked, tried to stand, yet both of my legs had fallen asleep. To my utter humiliation, I tumbled out of my chair, right onto the floor.

Delores, apologizing, helped me to my feet and turned the lights on. Everyone was laughing. Gabriela sat there, without looking at me, but smiling. That feeling I'd had all those years ago when I was at El Esplanade, that pressing as if my insides were being taken hold of, it was there again. I went home, fixed myself some tea, and went to bed. But hours later, when Mike woke up beside me, I was in a coma. I'd had a stroke. I regained consciousness in the hospital and realized I'd lost the use of my right arm."

Olivia looked down at her limp arm cradled in the scarf, almost as if it were separate from her, the gnarled albatross she was forced to carry.

"I'd had a brain aneurysm. Doctors said it was my stress over the incident that must have triggered it. I'm a practical woman, Mr. McCarthy. I am not prone to drawing hysterical conclusions. What I do know is that they did something to her, to Gabriela, to make her behave in such a way."

"Who?"

"Her family. Esquivel."

"And what exactly do you think they did?"

She liked thoughtful. "Do you have children?"

"A daughter."

"Then you know she was born innocent, yet soaks up everything around her like a sponge. Their way of life at El Esplanade, my own encounter there, years ago, and all the questions he asked me. It's as if I were an experiment. They must have done that to Gabriela. Except, unlike me, she couldn't run away. At least not as a child."

I observed Elizabeth. She looked spellbound. What Olivia said fit in with my assumption, that at the time of her death Gabriela had been on bad terms with her family, hiding under an assumed name, searching for someone known as the Tarantula.

What I couldn't understand was why she returned to the townhouse, unless it was to meet with Marissa Garcia. Perhaps Garcia lived there.

"Have you heard of someone connected to Esquivel with the nickname the Tarantula?" I asked.

"The Tarantula." Olivia frowned leaning forward. "No."

"What about Marissa Garcia? It wouldn't be her nickname, would it?"

"Esquivel's assistant? Not to my knowledge. But I don't know anything about her, except I believe she was the woman who escorted me in to see Esquivel. And while she interviewed me, she sat on his right side, as if she were his henchman or bodyguard, or perhaps his subconscious."

I nodded. This subservient, losing position certainly backed up what was written about Marissa Garcia on the Blackboards.

"Why doesn't anybody talk about Esquivel?" I asked.

"They're terrified. They ascribe a power to him, real or imagined. I don't know. What I do know is that within that family's history there are atrocious acts. I'm certain of it."

"Why haven't you looked into it? You're obviously quite passionate about the matter. Surely you'd have a vast array of resources at your disposal." I asked.

"I made a promise to my husband. He wanted me to put the business behind me, given what happened. If I ruffled feathers, trying to get to the bottom of it, would I lose the use of my other arm? And then my legs? Because a part of me actually believes, you see, that yes, there was something in that room summoned by that girl, and what I was brought there for, an act of revenge, had happened exactly as they'd planned. I'd been made to pay for some perceived offense I'd done against my sister."

I couldn't help but think of the killing curse. Technically, my life had grown more hazardous since we'd walked through it; I'd nearly drowned. It eats away at your mind without you even realizing it, Cleo had told us. *It . . . isolates you, pits you against the world so you're driven to the margins, the periphery of life.* I could actually understand such a phenomenon happening to someone going after Esquivel.

Olivia sighed. She looked tired, the intensity went from her face, leaving it drained of color.

"I'm afraid I don't have much more time," she noted, glancing across the room at the doorway. I followed her gaze and realized I'd been listening so attentively I hadn't noticed that the woman in the gray suit who'd greeted us, Olivia's secretary, I assumed, had struck her head into the doorway, silently alerting her mistress to her next pressing appointment.

"You mentioned Mrs. Plath," I said. "Gabriela was a patient at Mission Hills prior to her death. I wanted to know the circumstances of her being admitted there, but Plath gave me a hard time. Any way you could help me out with her?"

Olivia smiled, bemused. "Mrs. Plath assured me Gabriela was never a patient there. But I'll certainly ask again. We'll be in Saint Moritz through March." She sat forward, slipping her feet into her shoes. "The number you have reaches my secretary directly. Contact her if you need me for anything at all. She'll be able to get me a message."

"I appreciate that."

She stood up from the couch, her three Pekingese plopping onto the carpet around her feet, and arranged the silk scarf around her immobile arm. As Elizabeth and I rose, Olivia reached out and took my hand with a disarmingly warm smile, her brown eyes gleaming.

"It's certainly been a pleasure, Mr. McCarthy."

"Pleasure's been all mine."

We started for the door.

"But one last thing, I said.

She stopped, turning. "Of course."

"If I wanted to speak to your sister, Madelyn, where might I find her?

She looked irritated. "She can't help you," she said. "She can't even help herself."

"She was married to Esquivel."

"And the whole time she was addicted to barbiturates. I doubt she remembers a thing about the marriage, except maybe screwing Esquivel a few times."

There it was, beneath the flawless elegance, the scrappy army brat.

"It would still be invaluable to talk to her about what she saw up there, what the man was like, how he lived. She was an insider."

Olivia stared me down imperiously, not accustomed to being disagreed with. Or perhaps it was exasperation that again, even after all these years, her sister's name still came up in her presence.

"Even if I gave you're the address, she'd never see you. She doesn't see anyone except her maid and her drug dealer."

She took a deep breath. "Her maid comes here every week to give me her bills and an update on her health. My sister doesn't know she's bankrupt, that I've been paying for her care and drugs for the last twenty years. And if you're wondering why I haven't sent her away to Betty Ford or Gateway, or Mission Hills, I assure you I have. Eleven times. It's no use. Some people don't want to be sober. They don't want reality. Afterlife trips them, they choose to stay face down in the mud."

"All right," I said. "But if what you told us is true."

"It is," she snapped.

"Madelyn might be able to give me more. The most unreliable witness still has the truth inside them."

Olivia surveyed me challengingly, then sighed.

"The Dearborn Plaza. 1030 Dearborn Street, apartment 1421." She turned, swiftly gliding to the door, her furry entourage panting to keep up. "Speak to the doorman, Ernest," she added over her shoulder. "I'll phone him this afternoon. He'll make the arrangements."

"I appreciate that."

"When you do see her, don't mention me. For your own well-being." I swore I caught a faint satisfied smile on her face as she said this.

"You have my word."

She escorted us through the gallery to the entrance hall, the old codger already waiting with our coats. He looked so stiff I couldn't help but imagine he'd been standing there for more than an hour.

"Thank you," I said to Olivia, "for everything. It's been invaluable."

"Hopefully, you can do something about it. Avenge that girl. She was special."

Elizabeth stepped inside the elevator, and though I entered behind her, I stuck out my hand to prevent the doors from closing.

"One more question, if you don't mind, Mrs. Pierre."

She turned her head inclined at that artful angle between curiosity and superiority.

"How did you meet Mr. Pierre? I've always wondered."

She stared me down. I thought she was going to icily pronounce it was none of my business. But to my surprise, after a moment, she smiled.

"Rush University Medical Center on Congress. We got into the same elevator. We were both on our way to visit Madelyn on the eighth floor. The elevator got stuck. Something to do with a bad fuse. When it got unstuck an hour later, Mike on longer wished to go up to the eighth floor to visit Madelyn."

She met my eyes with a look of triumph.

"He wanted to come down to the lobby with me."

With a warm smile, Olivia turned slowly on her heel and vanished down the shadowy hall, her dogs at her feet.

Seventy-Four

When Elizabeth and I stepped outside under the pale gray awning onto Michigan Avenue, I was surprised to find it raining quite hard. I hadn't noticed it upstairs with Olivia, probably because I'd been so absorbed by what she was saying. Unless her apartment was so elegant it simply edited out bad weather as if it were a terrible faux pas.

The doorman handed me a golf umbrella and, opening one for himself, raced into the street to hail a taxi.

"She wasn't what I expected," all I could think about was Nathan."

"The tattoo artist?"

She nodded vigorously. "Remember what happened to him?"

"He died."

"Of a brain aneurysm. Don't you see? It's a trend. Olivia had one, and Norman. Both after they'd encountered Gabriela."

"So what are you saying, she's the Angel of Death?" I meant it facetiously, though suddenly I recalled the incident Cooper had described at Gateway Wilderness, the rattlesnake found in the counselor's sleeping bag, the widespread belief that Gabriela had put it there. And, of course, her appearance at the Reservoir."

"Olivia described the same thing Julie Mergener did," I said. "A visit to El Esplanade. But their experiences were so different. One was petrifying. The other was some kind of childhood fantasy dream sequence."

"Wonder which one's is true."

"Maybe both. The incidents occurred almost twenty years apart. Olivia said she went in June 1977. That's a year after Esquivel had purchased El Esplanade with Gwen and a month before she drowned. Julie Mergener's picnic at the estate was in 1993."

"It was scary how Olivia described Gwen, his first wife, don't you think?"

"The prisoner too terrified to speak."

She nodded. "and what about that witch-pricking needle?"

"It actually corroborates what Cleo back at Fascinations suggested, that Gabriela comes from a dynasty of black-magic practitioners."

Elizabeth nibbled her fingernails, apprehensive. "I bet if we ever broke into El Esplanade, that's what we'd find up there."

I knew exactly what she was thinking; somehow Cleo's words had engrained themselves in my head when she'd described the lurid realities of those working with black magic. Old leather-bound journals filled with spells written backward. Attics stockpiled with the really obscure ingredients, like deer fetuses, lizard feces, baby blood. This stuff is not for people with queasy stomachs. But it works.

The doorman had found a taxi, so we raced out from the awning, scrambled into the backseat. I saw I had a missed call from Feinstein and two from Cooper. He'd also sent a text.

I'm out on bail. A million thanks. Heading to your apt.

Good. I couldn't wait to ask him what he'd seen inside the townhouse, not to mention, how in the hell had he known how to break in.

Seventy-Five

As Elizabeth and I entered my building, she stopped in alarm and grabbed my arm, pointing at the lock on my front door.

It was smashed, the wood splintered.

Slowly I pushed the door. It was dark inside, no noise but the pounding of the rain. I stepped into the foyer.

"Don't," whispered Elizabeth. "Someone might still be here."

I pressed a finger to my lips and crept farther down the hall, my every step creaking on the wooden floors. Suddenly I heard a muffled thud coming from the living room.

I raced to the doorway just in time to see a man climbing out the window, violent rain pummeling his black coat and knit cap as he scrambled over the flower box and jumped out of sight.

I wheeled past Elizabeth and back down the hallway, seeing the intruder streak past the building, heading west down Erie. I ran outside and took off after him. He was already halfway down the block, charging past a pedestrian, who I realized was Cooper.

"Catch that guy!" I shouted.

Seeing me barreling toward him. Cooper spun around and took off after the man, who'd just disappeared onto Rush Street.

The intruder was too short to be Santo.

Cooper disappeared around the corner. When I reached the intersection seconds later, he was already chasing the man around the block onto Huron. I ran after them, dodging cars, chained bicycles, people hauling shopping bags. The intruder made the light at Wabash, Cooper racing after him, shouting through the resounding cracks of thunder drowned out the words. Within minutes, I'd made it to the West side of State Street, though I had to wait for the light to turn green.

The man was hightailing it north down the bike path along LaSalle Street, suddenly he turned right, heading toward Navy Pier, and then vanished.

The light turned yellow, and with a break in the traffic, I sprinted across, catching up to Cooper on the bike path.

"I lost him," he said, panting.

I gazed down the track, shielding my eyes from the rain. Apart from a couple walking a German shepherd, it was deserted. But the pier, a popular recreational spot, was busy, some fifty or sixty people strolling the promenade, armed with ponchos and umbrellas.

"He's on the pier," I said. "I'll check this end. You search the other side."

I took off, passing a family of tourist in plastic ponchos; a young man walking a German Shepard; a pair of teenagers giggling, huddled under a brown coat.

No sign of him.

I moved past a crowd of joggers in raingear stretching on the railing and spotted a lone man at the very end of the pier.

He was seated on a bench, staring at Lake Michigan, his back to me. He wore a khaki coat, a bright red umbrella over his shoulder over his head. Yet there was something about him, and as I approached I saw what it was: Not only was his thinning gray hair disheveled as if he'd just yanked a stocking cap off his head. But his shoulders were rising and falling like he was out of breath.

Casually, I stepped alongside the bench beside a trashcan, some six feet away, and turned to see his face. It was just an old man, his hand resting atop the handle of a quad orthopedic cane, his jeans soaked. There was a large blue JanSport backpack beside him, and the remains of a Subway sandwich.

I must have seemed brazen, studying him so intently, but he only glanced at me and smiled, muttering something.

"What was that?" I shouted.

"Think we'll need Noah's Ark?"

I smiled blandly and stepped in front of him, walking to the end of the pier. The downpour was so severe now, there was barely a difference between the swelling green Chicago river and the rain.

I turned to check out the old man again, just to be sure.

But he was still hunched there harmlessly, the rain streaming in a gurgling waterfall off the red umbrella around him.

He smiled again, beckoning me to approach, and I realized from his excited expression he'd actually mistaken my gazes for some kind of sexual overture.

He was some old gay geezer, out here cruising. For Christ's sake.

"Would you like to share?' he shouted at me, looking up at his red umbrella, which made his complexion pink. "Actually, I think I have an extra." Licking his lips, he unzipped the backpack, fumbling inside. I held up a hand, waving him off, and moved quickly down the walkway just as a resounding crack of lightning struck, followed by another rumble of thunder. As I reached the northern side of the pier, I saw that there was a commotion, a small crowd forming back along the bike path. I sprinted toward it, jostling through the onlookers to find Cooper, as well as another man, helping an elderly African American woman to her feet.

The poor woman was sobbing and completely drenched, wearing only a thin pink housedress, clutching her arm in pain.

"What happened?" I asked a woman next to me.

"She just got mugged. The asshole even stole her cane."

No sooner had she said the words, I was fighting my way through the crowd, racing as fast as I could back along the pathway.

The old man was already gone.

When I reached the empty bench, I could only stare down at it in anger. There, abandoned, was the red umbrella, the backpack, the orthopedic cane and trench coat, the Subway sandwich wrappers. *The cunning son of a bitch had probably taken them out of the trashcan so he'd appear to be enjoying a leisurely lunch.*

Exactly where he'd been sitting was a small white card, face down on the bench. I picked it up. It was my business card.

Seventy-Six

I returned the belongings to the woman. Each item was hers: the blue JanSport backpack, the red umbrella, the cane, and coat. No money was missing. Her assailant had come from behind her, brutally wrenching her things away, shoving her down on the sidewalk.

"No way that was an old man!" Cooper shouted over the downpour as we jogged across Ontario Street, heading back to my apartment.

"I'm telling you. It was."

"Then he's been eating his friggin' Wheaties because he had the torque of a Suzuki. What did he steal?"

"We're about to find out."

We picked up our pace. I could hardly calm myself to think, it had happened so quickly. I had a feeling I shouldn't have been so cavalier about leaving Elizabeth alone. I hadn't stopped to consider if the intruder had an accomplice.

We raced into my building. She wasn't in the hallway.

"Elizabeth!"

I shoved the door open, racing through the foyer. Nothing in the living room had been disturbed. I hurried down the hall to my office and stopped dead. It looked like there'd been an earthquake. Papers and boxes, files, entire shelves had been ransacked and dumped on the floor. A window was open, rain pouring in. Elizabeth was moving frantically around the wreckage.

"What's the matter? Are you hurt?"

"He's gone."

"What?"

She was panicked. "Octavius. I can't find him."

I spotted the empty birdcage on the floor.

"Where the hell's my laptop?" I shouted.

"Everything's been stolen. Someone else was here. I heard him go out the window, but I didn't see him." She moved to the closet, the wooden door hanging off the runner.

I scaled through the mess to the window, angrily slamming it closed. My filing cabinets were pulled open, the papers looted. My old framed awards had been pulled off the wall.

I righted some of the frames, grabbed the leather cushions, and threw them back on the couch. I grabbed one of the fallen shelves and heaved it upright, stepping on a picture frame lying face down. I picked it up, seeing with a twinge of horror that it was my favorite shot of Kim, taken when she was hours old. The glass had been smashed. I shook out the shards, set it on my desk, then stepped over to the overturned box of Esquivel research.

I almost laughed.

It was empty, except for the Meet Yumi escort flier that I'd pocketed back at Normal Street. The half-naked girl stared mischievously at me as if to whisper. *Are you really that surprised?*

I couldn't fathom my incompetence. I'd known we were being followed, yet like some reckless fool, I'd taken no precautions, which now seemed galactically stupid. Considering the last time, I'd gone after Esquivel, my life had collapsed around me like a cheap vaudeville set. Now my notes were in the hands of the very subject of my investigation. Esquivel would be reading my every note, every brainstormed thought, and scrawl. He'd be perusing my head like a department store. My laptop had a password, but any decent hacker could override it. Now Esquivel would know everything we know about Gabriela's final days.

Whatever edge we might have had after breaking into Les Silencio, the Warwick, Mission hills, knowing that Gabriela had been searching for this person called the Tarantula, it was gone.

I picked up my stereo, putting the receiver back on the shelf, and saw with disbelief Gabriela's CD was gone, too. This gave way to another alarming thought.

"Where's Gabriela's police file?"

Elizabeth was still digging through the closet.

"Gabriela's file that I got illegally from Katie Horrigan, you were reading it two days ago. Where is it?"

She turned, her face distraught.

"I don't know."

She began to cry, so I started trawling through the rubble myself. I couldn't imagine the ripple effect of that file going public: Katie losing her job; her career ending in disgrace due to my own folly; my name appearing in print yet again as something toxic. It made me so furious. We found him in the kitchen, standing by the open oven door. The macaw was inside, frantically fluttering around the fan. Elizabeth rushed forward, gently capturing the bird. He was alive but trembling violently.

"Was the oven on?" she asked Cooper.

"No."

As she tended to the bird, Cooper looked meaningfully at me. He was thinking the same as I. This was no act of clemency. It was a threat. leaving the bird alone sent a clear message: They were in control. They wanted to toy with the bird, play with it, petrify the fragile thing a little longer. But if they'd wanted to, they could have killed it.

And so the same was true for us.

Seventy-Seven

We spent the next few hours cleaning up my office, while a locksmith replaced the bolt on the front door. Everything about Gabriela and Carlos Esquivel had been taken, with a few exceptions, some of my old notes concerning the neighbors. We found these items on the couch, which suggested that my study had been trashed first, then scoured for information on the Esquivels.

In another stroke of luck, they'd left behind Gabriela's coat. We found it still crammed into the plastic bag behind the door, probably assumed to be garbage. We also found Katie Horrigan's police file. Two days ago, Elizabeth had taken it upstairs to review before bed. It was still on her bedside table; a sign the intruders had never made it upstairs. I kept thinking about Olivia Wainscott. It was certainly convenient that while we were uptown listening to her, the intruders had unmitigated access to my apartment. I couldn't help but wonder if I'd misread her. Had she been in on the whole thing from the start and tipped them off to the appointment? *Why? What motivation did Olivia have to protect Esquivel?*

There was also an unsettling symmetry to what had happened. We were following Gabriela's footsteps; Santo Esquivel had followed ours. Cooper broke into their house last night; today, they broke into mine. Searching for the man on the pier, I'd only encountered myself, my business card. Were they genuinely threatened by what we were doing? Or were they treating it as a game, mirroring our actions, boomeranging them back onto us, one violation of the Esquivels privacy resulting in one of mine, one invasion for another?

I didn't know what any of it meant, but at least one thing Olivia said made sense: The space around Esquivel distorts . . . the speed slackens, information gets scrambled, rational minds grow illogical, hysterical.

I went upstairs and took a shower, gave Cooper some towels so he could, too. I was planning to order some Chinese food and then quiz him about the townhouse, he'd briefly mentioned he hadn't seen very much before he was caught. I left Elizabeth monitoring Octavius and retreated to my bedroom to clean out the old safe in my closet. I hadn't used it in years, but going forward, all notes and evidence would have to be locked inside. I was clearing out dome old redacted files when there was a knock behind me.

Elizabeth was in the doorway, her face ashen.

"What's the matter? Is it Octavius"

She shook her head, beckoning me to follow her. She'd put on deafening music in the living room, the volume turned up so loud it drowned out our footsteps. She crept to the very end of the hallway, pointing at the bathroom door, open just a crack.

Cooper was inside, the faucet running. I wasn't in the habit of spying on men in bathrooms, but she animatedly gestured that I take a look.

I leaned forward. Cooper was at the sink, brushing his teeth, a towel around his waist.

And then I saw it.

Seventy-Eight

"What's going on?" asked Cooper, stepping into the living room.

"Have a seat," I said. "we're going to have a little chat."

"Right. The townhouse."

"Not the townhouse," said Elizabeth crossly. "The tattoo on your foot."

He froze, astonished. "What?"

"Gabriela's Orichi," she said. "You have the other half."

He eyed the door.

"Cooper, we saw it. You lied to us."

He glared at her, then suddenly darted for the doorway, but I was ready. I grabbed him by the back of his T-shirt and shoved him hard into a club chair.

"That tattoo on your frigging ankle. Start talking."

He appeared to be too shocked to speak, or else was trying to think up another excuse. After a minute, Elizabeth rose and poured him a glass of scotch.

"Thanks," he muttered sullenly. He took a sip, staring into the glass.

"To know her and then not," he said, his voice low, "is like serving a life sentence. You see everything at a distance, through thick glass and telephones and visiting hours. Nothing tastes like anything. Bars everywhere you look." He smiled softly. "You can never get out."

He raised his head, gazing at us intently as if remembering we were there. He actually looked relieved. And just like that, he began to tell us all about her as the rain beat the windows like an army trying to get in.

Seventy-Nine

"I didn't lie to you," Cooper said. "Gateway Wilderness was how I met Gabriela. And it's true, that bet we made. She did blow me off. And that incident with that kid everyone made fun of, Mondo. When he took the ecstasy and Gabriela took the blame for all of us. That happened, okay? What I didn't tell you was I'd been planning to break the hell out."

"Of Gateway Wilderness Therapy?" I asked.

He nodded. "I'd had it with the entire operation. Even after the rattlesnake incident, we still had another six weeks. I wasn't about to keep eating all their bullshit. Sure, thanks to Gabriela, the head of the camp leaders was scared, but so what? Every day it was a hundred degrees. The kids were fledgling Ted Bundy's, the therapists, perverted shitheads. At night you could hear one of them, Wall Walker, jerking off in his tent. It was only a matter of time before he tried to get someone to join him. The only girl worth talking to, Gabriela, didn't give me the time of day. So I thought, screw it. One of the female counselors, this headshrinker, Horsehair, she was always checking out this map she kept hidden in her backpack, thinking she was covert about it. One night, when she was having a one-on-one with one of the girls, I stole it. I saw on the map that if you made it out of Zion National Park, there was an interstate pretty close that could take you west into Nevada. If I got to the road I could easily hitch a ride with a truck driver. I'd traveled with truckers before. Most hate cops, so they're trustworthy as hell. The others are so hyped up on meth they don't know who the hell's tagging along with them. My plan was to get to Vegas."

Cooper sat down and lit up a cigarette, he exhaled and took a deep breath, while looking up with those far away eye's he continued. "Horsehair made a big stink about her stolen map and there was a major inquisition around the campfire. People's backpacks got searched, but they didn't find a thing. The counselors figured Horsehair had lost it. But I'd hidden it under the foot insert in my hiking boot. I came up with an escape plan. I'd wait for us to reach the camping spot in closest proximity to that highway. From what I calculated, we'd reach it in three days. From there, the highway was half a day's hike. I'd sneak off after everyone was asleep. This one counselor, Four Crows, was supposed to keep an all-night watch, but she secretly fell asleep around one, so I'd have no problem. But there was one thing I hadn't considered. Mondo."

Cooper ran his hands through his hair. "We shared a tent. You get assigned a tent mate at the start of the trip. Mondo was mine. One night I was up studying the map, and all of a sudden I heard in the dark, 'Cooper whatcha looking at?' He'd woken up and was spying on me. I didn't know for how long. I told him I thought I saw a lizard and to go back to sleep. But he was a cunning kid. He was used to people lying to him. The next morning when I woke up he'd gone through all my things and found the map. He said he know I was planning to run away, and if I didn't take him with me, he was going to tell the counselors."

He paused to take a long sip of scotch.

"I don't think he'd ever had anyone be nice to him without him having to blackmail them into it. He wanted me to promise on Jesus Christ, he was from North Carolina, his parent's born-again Baptists. He was always mentioning Jesus like he was his next-door neighbor, someone he did a little yard work for. So I said "Cool no problem."

I swore in the name of Jesus Christ I'd take him with me. I swore that we were a team. Like Frodo and Sam."

He seemed anxious saying this, brushing his hair out of his eyes, resuming his concentrated stare at the coffee table.

"Within days, it was the night. We'd set up our camp in the exact location I needed to be. And I remember when everyone went to bed there was a clear night sky and a silence I'll never forget. Usually, the insects and shit screaming in your ears all night. But on this night it was still, like everything alive had run away. I set my watch to wake up at midnight. Instead, I was woken up by a counselor. The entire group was awake. There was a torrential downpour. The whole campsite was flooded, all of us sleeping in about three inches of rain. It was mayhem. The counselors were yelling at everyone to pack up their tents. We had to move to higher elevation because they were worried about flash floods. Not that they gave a shit about our well-being, they just didn't want to end up dead themselves. People were screaming, freaking out. No one could find anything. I realized it was a blessing, because, in the chaos, it'd be easy to slip away. I knew where I had to go, where the path began. I helped Mondo pack up the tent, but as I did, I noticed Gabriela. She already had her tent together, was waiting for the rest of us. The beam of someone's flashlight slipped onto her face, and I saw she was across the campsite, just staring at me. The look on her face, it was like she knew what I was about to do. I didn't have time to think about it. Some of the kids were starting to make their way up the path to the next campsite.

I fell in behind them. I held back, and when they were far enough ahead, I turned off my flashlight and stepped off the path, heading down a slope in the rocks, waiting. I could see some of the kids walking along the ridge, others still freaking out over the tents. The rain was coming down so hard in the pitch-black dark you couldn't see more than a foot in front of you. They wouldn't notice I was missing until morning. I turned my flashlight back on and took off."

He paused to light up a cigarette and take another drink.

"I hadn't walked ten minutes when I turned and saw another flashlight right behind me. It was Mondo. I was pissed. I shouted at him to go back, but he refused. He kept saying, 'You promised. You promised to take me.' He wouldn't stop. I lost it. I said I couldn't stand him. I told him he was fat, that everyone made fun of him. I said he was pathetic and weak, and even his own mother secretly didn't love him. I said no one in the whole world loved him and no one ever would."

Cooper began to sob, uncontrollably, a tortured choking sound that seemed to tear through him. "I wanted him to hate me. So he'd go back. I didn't want him to like me. I didn't want him to look up to me."

He gasped a deep breath and fell silent, his head in his hands. After a minute, he wiped his face in the crook of his arm, hunching forward in the chair, visibly determined to keep talking, fighting his way through the story or he'd get lost in it, drown inside of it.

"I took off. A minute later, when I looked back I could see his flashlight, a tiny white light in the dark behind me, so far away. It looked like it was getting smaller like he was heading back up the path. But then I actually couldn't tell if it was moving toward me or away. It looked like it was getting smaller like he was heading back up the path. But then I actually couldn't tell if it was moving toward me or away. Maybe he was still coming after me. I continued on. But an hour later, I realized I had no way out. The trail I was supposed to follow was through a canyon called The Narrows, and as I came into it, slipping in the mud, I saw there was a raging river where the trail was supposed to be. There was no way across. I had to turn back. It took forever because the path was pretty much a mudslide. I wasn't even sure I'd make it, and I probably wouldn't have if I hadn't had the map. It felt like I stumbled forever through the dark. Three hours later, I made it to the ridge and the new campsite. It was about five in the morning, still pouring. Everyone was asleep. No one had noticed I was gone.

I unrolled my sleeping bag, slipped into one of the other tents, and collapsed. When I woke up the counselors had taken a head count. There was no sign of Mondo. By the afternoon they'd called the National Guard. I remember it was this beautiful day. A huge blue sky, so bright and beautiful."

He leaned forward, taking another deep, uneven breath, staring at the floor.

"They found him eleven miles away, drowned in a river. Everyone thought it was an accident, that he'd gotten lost in the commotion. But I knew the truth. It was because of what I'd said. He was walking and saw the river, and he threw himself in. I did it. I killed that sweet kid who hadn't done anything except be himself. There was nothing wrong with him. It was me. I was the loser. I was the waste of flesh. I was the one that no one loved. And no one ever would. See, Gabriela had saved Mondo," he whispered. "And I destroyed him."

Eighty

He closed his eyes. He looked so anguished whispering this, it was as if the words cut into him. After a moment, he forced himself to look up, his eyes watery and bloodshot.

"They helicoptered us out, back to base camp," he continues. "The outraged parents descended. The counselors faced negligence charges. Two served jail time. Some of their discipline methods came out, and the camp changed its name to, Silver Lakes Retreat a year later. No one knew I had anything to do with what happened. Except Gabriela. She didn't say anything. I just could tell from the way she looked at me. We were the last two to leave. A black SUV came for her, no parents, just a woman driver wearing a suit. Before she climbed into the backseat, she turned and she looked in at me, where I was watching inside the cabin. It would've been impossible for her to actually see me, but somehow she did. She knew everything."

He seemed on the verge of crying but wouldn't let himself, angrily wiping his eyes in the crook of his arm.

"You were supposed to be checked out by your parents," he said, his voice hoarse. "My uncle couldn't make it. But things were nuts with police, the local news, Mondo's family; finally, the cops just turned to me and said, 'Go.' I could just walk out. And that's what I did."

I'd been so absorbed listening to him, I'd hardly noticed Elizabeth had darted across the living room. She retrieved the box of Kleenex off the bookshelf, smiling as she handed it to Cooper, slipping back to the couch.

"The next five months were a blackout," he said, pausing to blow his nose. "Or a black hole. I hitchhiked. I went into Oregon and up into Canada. Most the time I didn't know where I was. I just walked. I spent nights in motels and parking lots, strip malls. I stole money and food. I bought some heroin once and locked myself in a motel room for weeks at a time, floating away in a haze, hoping I'd find the end of the Earth and just float off. When I reached Alaska, I went into this one town, Fritz Creek, and stole a six-pack of Budweiser from a convenience store. I didn't know every mom-n-pop store in Alaska keeps a shotgun behind the counter. The owner shot two inches from my ear, right into a display of potato chips, then pointed the barrel right at my head. I asked him to please pull the trigger. He'd be doing me a favor. Only goading him like that, like a madman.

I probably scared the shit out of him, because he lowered it and, visibly freaked out, he called the police. A month later. I was at Peterson Long, a military school in Texas. I'd been there about a week, and I remember I was in the library, it had bars on the windows, wondering how the hell I was going to break out when I got this email out of the blue."

He smiled reluctantly, staring off somewhere as if even now surprised by it.

"All it said in the subject line was 'Do I dare?' I didn't know what that meant or who the hell sent it. Until I read the email address. Gabriela Esquivel. I thought it was a joke."

"Do I dare?" I repeated.

Cooper looked up at me, his face darkening. "It's from Prufrock."

Of course. "The Love Song of J. Alfred Prufrock." It was a T. S. Eliot poem, a crushing description of paralysis and unrequited romantic longing in the modern world. I hadn't read the poem since college, though I still remembered some of the lines as they burned into your head the moment you read them; *In the room, the women come and go / Talking of Michelangelo.*

"That's kind of how our friendship started," Cooper said simply. "Writing to each other. she didn't talk about her family. Sometimes she mentioned her brother. Or her dogs, a couple of rescued mutts. Her letters were the reason I didn't break out of there. I worried we'd somehow lose touch if I did. Once she wrote that maybe I should stop running from myself and try standing still. So that's what I did." He shook his head. 'When spring break came, I was dying to see her. I think a part of me didn't think it was actually Gabriela that I'd been writing to, but some figment of my imagination. I knew she was in the city, so I went online and found a spot in Grant Park, by the fountain. I told her to meet me there, April the second, seven o'clock sharp. Cheesy as hell. I didn't care. She didn't answer my email for two days. And when it came, her response was one word. The best word in the English language."

"What's that?" I asked when he didn't immediately go on.

"Yes." He smiled sheepishly. "I took three buses to get to Chicago. I arrived a day early, slept on a park bench. I was so damn nervous. Like I'd never been with a girl before. But she wasn't a girl. She was a goddess. Finally, it was seven o'clock, seven-thirty, eight. She didn't show. Blew me off. I was friggin embarrassed for myself, and I was about to take off when all of a sudden I hear right behind me in her low voice, 'Hello, Tiger Foot.'" He glanced up, wryly shaking his head. "It was my damn tribe name from Gateway Wilderness. I turn around and, of course, she was there."

He fell silent, thinking about it, amazed.

"And that was it," he noted quietly. "We were up the whole night just talking, walking the city streets. You can walk those blocks forever, take a break on the edge of a fountain, eat pizza and snow cones, awed by the human carnival all around you. She was the most incredible person. To be next to her was to have everything. When it was dawn, we'd been sitting on the concrete wall by the Planetarium, watching the light come upon the lake. She mentioned the light took eight minutes to leave the sun and reach us. You couldn't help but love that light, traveling so far through to loneliest of spaces to get here, to come so far. It was like we were the only two people in the world."

He paused, looking up at me with a penetration stare. "She told me her father taught her to live life way beyond the cusp of it, way out in outer reaches where most people never had the guts to go, where you get hurt. Where there are unimaginable beauty and pain. She was always demanding of herself, *Do I Dare? Do I dare disturb the universe?* From *Prufrock*. Her dad revered the poem, I guess, and the entire family lived in answer to it. They were always reminding themselves to stop swimming way, way down to the bottom of the ocean to find where the mermaids sang, one to another. Where there were danger and beauty and light. Stay in the now. Gabriela said it was the only way to live."

After the feverish outpouring of words, cooper paused to collect himself, taking a deep breath.

"It was how she was. Gabriela not only rode on the waves and dove of every day down to where the mermaids sang, she was a mermaid herself. By the time I walked her home, I loved her. Body and soul."

He admitted this evenly, his face naked and unafraid. I sensed it was the first time he had truly talked about her. There was a feeling in his unsteady voice, in the words used to describe her, like they'd been submerged inside him for years; they were musty and purpled and fragile, practically dissolving as soon as they hit the air.

"You walked her back to 107 Normal street?" I asked.

He eyed me. "Where we were last night."

"That's why you knew how to get in," whispered Elizabeth. "You'd climbed in before."

"After the first night we were together, when she didn't come home, her parents were furious. They kept a pretty tight rein on her. They insisted she be home by one in the morning or they were going to take her away or something, to their house upstate. So, every night that week, I'd drop Gabriela off at her house at one, wait for her across the street, where we stood last night. At about one-thirty, Gabriela would climb out and we'd take off, heading to Navy Pier, or Millennium Park. At six in the morning, she'd climb back in. She'd cut the wires to the sensors on that window, so the alarm became disabled. Nobody ever knew about it. When I saw the place last night it looked exactly the same. I half expected to see Gabriela come climbing out."

He dropped his gaze to the floor and drained the glass of scotch.

"When that week was over," he went off quietly, "I went back to school and the first I did was write a letter to Mondo's parents, telling them what had happened. She'd given me the courage, even though she never said a work. When I put it in the mail, I felt like a noose had been removed from my neck. It took them a few weeks to write back to me, but the letter, when it finally arrived, it awed me, I guess. They blessed me for coming forward, telling the truth. They asked me to forgive myself, said that they'd pray for me and I'd always have a place in their home."

Cooper, still awed by this, shook his head. "For the next couple of weeks, Gabriela and I wrote every day," he went on. "In later May, for a week I didn't hear from her. I went crazy, worried something had happened. Then I got a phone call. It was Gabriela. I'll never forget how she sounded. She was desperate, sobbing. She said she couldn't find her. She asked if I'd come away with her. And I said, well, I said the best word in the English language."

"Yes," I whispered.

He nodded. "I borrowed money from one of my teachers to buy the tickets. June the tenth, 2004. Nine-thirty-five P.M. United flight 7057 Ohare to Rio de Janeiro, Brazil. There was a city way in the south of Santa Catarina Island that I'd been to once, Florianopolis. The most beautiful place I'd ever seen, second to her. A buddy of mine ran a bar down there on the beach. He said he'd help us out with work until we knew what our plan was. Summer break arrived, and I traveled on those three Greyhound buses all the way back to Chicago to see her. The moment I did I knew it was on. We were going to leave it all behind. Best night of my life was when we got those tattoos. I'd heard about Dragon Master. But the Orichi was her idea."

"Did Norman do it?" asked Elizabeth.

"Yeah, he was a big guy. It was just the three of us in the shop. The design was intricate. You were supposed to do that kind of thing over a month's time to handle the pain. But our flight was the next day, so it was that night or never. When it was over, she threw her arms around me, laughing, like it hadn't hurt at all, and she said she'd see me tomorrow. Tomorrow it would all begin."

Cooper took a deep breath, interlacing his fingers, staring beyond us and out the window, where the rain still whipped against the glass. He seemed suddenly very far away, lost in a bottomless crevice of the past he couldn't pull himself out of. Or perhaps he was recalling a detail he chose not to disclose to us, words she'd said or something she'd done, that would remain forever amongst them.

When he looked back at us, he seemed reluctant to continue.

"Mind if I smoke?" he asked quietly.

I shook my head. He stood up to retrieve his cigarettes from his coat pocket, and I glanced at Elizabeth. She was so mesmerized, she hadn't moved a muscle in fifteen minutes, elbow on the armrest, chin planted in her hand.

He sat down and got out a cigarette, lighting it quickly. There was a long silence, his face dark and pensive, cigarette smoke clinging to the empty space around him.'

"That was the last time I ever saw her," he said.

Eighty-One

"The next day, we were due to leave," he went on. "June the tenth. Gabriela was meeting me at six P.M. at The Coffee Studio, on Clark Street. Then together we'd head to Ohare. Six o'clock came and went. There was no word from her. Time went on seven, eight, I called her cell phone, no answer. I went to her house and rang the bell. Usually, there were lights on. It was dark. I knocked, no one came to the door. I climbed up there, exactly the way Gabriela did, up the iron bars to the second-floor balcony and in the far right window. The place was luxurious, a palace, but it's been packed up, and in a hurry. Like a bunch of criminals had decided to run for the border. The furniture, covered with sheets, randomly, so they were half on the floor. Beds stripped.

Milk and fruit and bread tossed out on the sidewalk in piles of garbage bags. I found Gabriela's room on the third floor. There were a few photographs, books, but a lot of her things had obviously been taken, thrown in bags really fast. The lamp was tipped over on the nightstand next to bed. But inside her closet, hidden beneath blankets on the top shelf, I found a small leather suitcase. I pulled it down, unzipped it. It was packed with her clothes, sundresses, T-shirts, cash, sheet music, a Frommer's guide to Brazil. She was planning to go. I knew then that her father had found out, and they'd taken her away, probably to that estate where she'd been homeschooled her entire life." He paused, anxiously twiddling his fingers, looking around nervously.

"I was all set to go to the police when I heard from her. She sent me an e-mail. She was sorry, but she'd made a mistake. We were just a couple of delusional kids, caught up in the moment. She didn't want to be tied down to anyone. She said she loved our time together, but it was over, simple as that. She told me to keep riding the waves seaward, keep searching for the chambers of the sea, where the mermaids sang . . ."

He irritably cut himself off, taking a long drag on his cigarette.

"I was sure her father had put her up to it," he continued, exhaling smoke in a fast stream. "I wrote back; said I didn't believe her. I was going to find her and she could say it to my face. She asked me not to contact her. I wrote back again. If this was my Gabriela, what was the address of the stoop we'd sat on that first night when the watched the sunrise? She wrote back instantly.

It was the correct address, she also wrote, *and I am no one's Gabriela*, it was a dagger to my heart. A year later, I found out she was attending Amherst. So she was fine. It had been her decision."

He brushed his hair out of his eyes, leaning back in the chair, his face calm, even slightly dazed.

"Did you ever hear from her again?" Elizabeth softly asked him.

He nodded faintly, his eyes shifting to her, but said nothing.

"What did she say?" asked Elizabeth.

"Nothing," he answered tersely. "She sent me a stuffed parrot."

Of course, the parrot, that faded toy with loose stitching, covered in dried mud. I'd almost forgotten about it.

"Why?" I asked.

He stared at me. "It was Mondo's. He slept with it. I don't know how Gabriela had it or where she'd found it. But when I pulled it out of that envelope, I was sick. She was sick, sending it, when she knew every day I thought about that kid, lived every day with the horror of this thing thinking I'd find a reason why she did such a thing." He looked at me. "That's when I ran into you."

"No wonder you didn't trust me," I said.

He shrugged. "I thought you might be working for her family."

"How did you know to go to Onofrio?" asked Elizabeth.

"I went there with Gabriela once. She used to practice there."

Elizabeth bit her fingernails, frowning. It was a long time ago, but . . . I didn't want to take the chance. Or be reminded." He gaped with resentment down at the tattoo. "I used to have dreams about cutting off my foot so I wouldn't have to look at that thing."

"Why didn't you tell us?" I asked. "At some point, you must have noticed we were just as ignorant as you were as to what was going on."

He shook his head. "I didn't know what to think. I didn't recognize the Gabriela I knew in any of this, this witch we've been tracking. Curses on the floor? Nyctophobia? Gabriela wasn't afraid of the dark. She wasn't afraid of anything."

"Maybe she didn't send it," Elizabeth suggested.

"It's her handwriting on the envelope."

"Someone in her family might have copied it. Maybe they're afraid of something she told you and they sent it to scare you off."

"I've been racking my brain for weeks. Trying to think of something she told me. But I never met anyone in her family, and she rarely talked about them, though I definitely sensed, particularly from that one phone call, she and her father did not get along."

"Nothing about witchcraft?" I suggested.

He looked puzzled. "The idea Gabriela would be involved in something like that is crazy."

"What about why she was sent to Gateway Wilderness Therapy Camp?"

"She told me she lost her temper and burned herself on a candle. She had a bad burn scar on her left hand. That was it."

"What about when you were in the townhouse last night?"

He stared at me with evident unease before answering. "It was the same. Like no one had set foot there since I'd broken in seven years ago. Same exact sheets tossed randomly over the furniture. Same Chopin music on Gabriela's piano, the lid open. The same rugs rolled up, same books piled on top of the tables, same drinking glass on the mantel above the fireplace, only there were about three inches of dust on everything. And this mildew smell made things feel like a tomb. I was heading up to Gabriela's bedroom to see if she'd ever come back. I honestly expected to find her suitcase still packed and hidden in the closet where I'd left them. That was when the doorbell rang and I had to turn back. I was almost at the window when the lights came on and I heard a woman ordering me to put my hands up. She was wielding a friggin shotgun."

"Marissa Garcia," I said. "Had you ever seen her before?"

He frowned. "I thought for a second I recognized her as the driver who picked up Gabriela back at Gateway Wilderness. But I'm not positive."

Gabriela went back to Master Dragon for the picture of you together," said Elizabeth. "She wanted to have it, even though it was lost."

He stared at her. "It's not." Slowly he reached into his back pocket and took out his wallet, removing paper from the billfold.

He handed it to me.

It was a photograph, crinkled and worn, taken out and stared at a thousand times.

Even now, after everything he told us, it was startling to see them together, as if two people from two different worlds had collided. They sat in one folding chair, hands clasped. It was a captured moment of youth, of joy, a moment so free the camera couldn't even hold on to it. Rendering them in streaks and blurs, hinting that they were so new and so full of life, there were no words to describe them, their ankles forming that fighting creature on fire, leaping to its death or its life.

Eighty-Two

I gave Cooper a pillow and blanket so he could crash on the couch. The rain was still coming down, and he didn't seem to want to go home.

Elizabeth drowsily said good night, slipping into Kim's room.

I headed to bed myself. I was mentally and physically drained, though before turning out the light, I looked up Gateway Wilderness on my BlackBerry, just to verify the details of Cooper's story. There were quite a few articles about the drowning, which had occurred July 2003, many of the actual newspaper clippings scanned and posted on a site called Thelostangels.com.

Investigation under way in Zion Wilderness camp death

Zion National Park, Utah. Five counselors at a private camp for troubled youngsters heave been arrested and a sixth resigned after a 15-year0old boy died in a flash flood in the park late Monday.

Counselors of Gateway Wilderness Therapy failed to account for Mondo Kimono, 15 during a campsite move away from Canyon Overlook trail during a heavy storm late Monday. Kimono was not discovered missing for seven hours as more than five inches of rain fell on the area, causing flash flooding. Park dispatch received an emergency call just after 7 A. M. Tuesday. After a widespread search, the boy's body was recovered by the Park's SAR team, from the North Fork of the Virgin River.

The counselors are facing criminal charges of negligence and mistreatment and have refused to take a polygraph test.

I read the other articles, everyone confirming what Cooper had told us.
So, he had loved her. Of course, I'd known it already.

Gabriela.

How elusive she was, how she shape-shifted, seemed composed of as many rival creatures as the tattoo, head of a dragon, body of a deer. Inclinations of a witch. She was Mondo's flashlight in the dark behind us, a pinprick of light in the violent downpour, dogging Cooper, dogging me. She was a beacon of mysterious origin and intention, impossible to determine if heading toward me or away.

What, really, was the difference between something hounding you and something leading you somewhere?

I turned out the light, closing my eyes.

Do I dare?

I jerked upright, my heart pounding. The bedroom was dark, empty, and yet I had the distinct feeling someone had just whispered those words in my ear.

I grabbed the phone off the table, Googling Prufrock, my eyes blearily reading the poem.

It was as searing and sad as I'd found it to be in college, maybe more so, now that I was no longer an arrogant young man on nineteen, now that the lines about time and I grow old . . . I grow old . . . meant something. The poem's narrator, Prufrock, was a sort of insect specimen, mounted and pinned, still squirming, to his tedious little life, a world of endless social get-togethers and parties and inane observations; the modern equivalent world probably be man alone with his phones and screens, Tweeting and friending and status updating, the ceaseless chatter of Internet culture. The man's thoughts veered between resignation, the stuttering, delusional belief that he had time, and a profound longing for more, for murder and creation.

The whole family lived in answer to that poem, Cooper had said.

If that were true, it was doubtlessly a ferocious, powerful way to live. It even corroborated the mystical afternoon Julie Mergener had described at the dog run and some of those early stories about Gabriela. But it could also be an enslavement, a hell, to keep searching for the enchanted, keep plunging down, down to the lonely chambers of the sea. *To seek mermaids.*

It was a tragic thing to do, like looking for Eden.

I closed my eyes, my limbs so heavy they seemed to melt onto the bed, my mind untying all thoughts so they flew into the air, unattached and disordered.

She attacked a guest. He's called Tarantula. Knowledge of darkness in the most extreme form. You've no respect for darkness, McCarthy. The black darkness unexplained. Within that family's history there are atrocious acts. I'm certain of it. Sovereign. Deadly. Perfect.

The only sound was the rain, playing like an exhausted orchestra on the windows. Only when I was drifting to sleep did the storm let slip a few delicate notes, strands of some new song, and abruptly disperse.

Eighty-Three

"That's him," I said.

I left Elizabeth and Cooper seated on the guardrail at the dead end of an alley by Dearborn Street, The Dearborn Plaza, an elegant limestone apartment building overlooking the Chicago River, and walked swiftly down the sidewalk toward the approaching man wearing the gray doorman's uniform.

He was very short and very bald, carrying a small deli coffee cup, an impish spring in his step. He might have been Danny DeVito's cousin. I caught up to him under a maroon awning. "You must be Harold."

He smiled cheerfully. "That's me."

I introduced myself. He nodded an immediate recognition. "Oh, right. The sarcastic detective. Mrs. Pierre said you'd be stopping by. So, you, uh . . ." He raised his chin to glance over my shoulder, lowering his voice. "You want to get in to see Madelyn."

"Olivia said you could arrange a time for me to talk to her."

He smirked. "You don't talk to Madelyn."

"What do you do?" What do you do with any man-eating beast? Tiptoe around and pray they're not hungry." He laughed again and then sobered when he saw my confusion. "Come back tonight. Eleven o'clock sharp. I'll take you up. But, uh, then you're on your own."

"What's that supposed to mean?'

"I made a rule never to go past the laundry room."

"I'd like to speak to Madelyn. Not break into her apartment."

"Yeah, yeah, that's how you speak to Madelyn. It's how Mrs. Pierre visits.

Mrs. Pierre pays for the whole spread, so technically she's sneaking into her own place."

"Olivia sneaks into her sister's apartment in the middle of the night?"

I find it difficult to imagine Olivia Pierre sneaking into anything.

"Oh, yeah. Madelyn and daylight is a bad combo. At night she's, uh, much more mellow.

"And why is she so mellow only at night?"

"Her dealer comes at eight. Coupla hours later, she's riding a magic carpet over Shangri-La." He grinned, but then, seeing my reaction, shook his head defensively. "I swear it's the only safe way to enter. That's when we do repairs, take out her trash, make sure she hasn't left on a gas burner or clogged the toilet with her fan mail. Once a week Mrs. Pierre takes up fresh food and flowers. If she did it during the day, there'd be carnage. This way, when Madelyn wakes up, she thinks she's been visited be Santa's little elves."

He took a sip of coffee, squinted at something over my shoulder. I noticed one of the other doormen at The Dearborn Plaza had wandered outside.

"Artie needs to go on break. Just, uh, come by at eleven and I'll get you up there. But . . . " He squinted. "You know those electric prods they use in circuses? You might want to bring one." He chuckled heartily at his own joke, taking off down the sidewalk. "Of course, it proved ineffective for Siegfried and Roy," he added over his should, "but no promises."

Eighty-Four

Fifteen minutes later, we were sitting in the window of a downtown Starbucks.

"It's an ideal situation," said Cooper. "If Madelyn is out cold, we'll have plenty of time to look through her place."

I was relieved to see this morning Cooper seemed to be all right after everything he'd told us. After disclosures such as his, it was difficult to gauge how the person would react afterward. But he appeared to be more focused.

"It's like having secret access to Marilyn Monroe's house," said Elizabeth. "Or Elizabeth Taylor's. Think of the photos and letters and love affairs with presidents no one knows about. She might even know where Esquivel is."

"As enticing as it sounds to ransack Madelyn's home while she's in a drug-induced coma," I said, "this operation is possible because of Olivia. I don't want her to find out I rummaged through her sister's apartment like a yard sale."

"We'll work fast," said Cooper, "leave the place exactly as we find it."

I said nothing, squinting across the street. A few yards from a restaurant, Luigi's Ristorante, a suspicious looking white haired man wearing a black coat was loitering by a brick wall. For the past five minutes, he'd been standing there, having an intense argument on the phone, but every now and then he glanced pointedly right at us.

"It's time to get the Warwick's guest list," I said, keeping an eye on him. "we'll get the name of every guest who stayed on the thirtieth floor between September and October the tenth, the days Gabriela was in the city. We'll compare that to the Les Silencio membership. If one name appears on both, that's the person Gabriela was looking for. That's the Tarantula."

The white-haired man outside hung up and took off, heading north on LaSalle. I wanted to see if he'd circle back or cross the street, but he appeared to be gone.

"But how do we get the names?" asked Elizabeth.

"But only way." I drained the fest of my coffee. "Corruption and intimidation."

Eighty-Five

I strolled into the Warwick Allerton lobby to do some reconnaissance. Today, behind the front desk there was an attractive woman, thirties, with long shiny black hair, He name tag read Monica, and a young Japanese man, Masato. After answering the phone a few times, Monica fumbled around under the desk and produced a large Louis Vuitton bag, a good sign, it meant she liked luxury goods, and would welcome some extra cash to buy more. This, while Masato stood stoically at the other side of the desk, doing and saying nothing, like a Kendo warrior proficient in the Way of the Sword.

The single girl and the last samurai, it didn't take a genius to decide who'd be amenable to bribery.

I caught up to Elizabeth and Cooper on the steps of Saint Patrick's across from the hotel. I gave then Monica's description and put the three of us on a surveillance rotation, so we could catch her alone as soon as she left the hotel. One of us monitored the employee's entrance from Saint Pat's while the other two waited at a Starbucks down the block.

Four hours passed. And though quite a few employees departed, crossing the street to discreetly smoke a cigarette, Monica never appeared.

At four, I did another drive-by and realized Monica must have ducked out another entrance because only Masato remained.

"Everyone has their price," Cooper said when I explained this unfortunate development.

"Yeah, well, from the look of this guy, his price is three hundred beheadings and a Katana sword."

At the stroke of six, Elizabeth alerted us that Masato was leaving the hotel. I managed to flag him down.

"Sure, I'll do it," he announced in a flawless American accent after I explained. "For three thousand dollars. Cash."

I laughed. "Five hundred."

He stood and walked out of the Starbucks. I was certain he was bluffing, but then he was on the subway escalator descending into the dense crowd.

"Eight hundred," I said, fighting shopping bags, women giving me dirty looks, trying to reach him. Masato didn't turn. "One thousand." I jostled an owl-looking girl in tortoiseshell glasses to get beside him. "Complete with home addresses."

Masato only put large blue deejay headphones over his ears.

"Twelve hundred. My final offer. And at that price we should know what nuts they ate from the minibar."

The deal was official. Minutes later, Masato, displaying a fairly impressive poker face, ducked back inside the Warwick, I went around the corner to an ATM, and then returned to the Starbucks. An hour passed, the crowd of commuters, once a flash flood, had drained to a meager trickle of women with tired faces and men in rumpled suits. Another half-hour and there was still no sign of Masato. I was beginning to think something had happened, when suddenly she entered, pulled a thick envelope out of his bag.

There were more than two hundred names, alphabetized according to date, complete with calls made from the hotel phone. I handed him the cash, which he counted in plain sight. Apparently, this Starbucks was used to underworld transactions, because the employees behind the counter who'd witnessed us skulking in the window all day mind-numbingly carried on taking orders.

"Quad venti soy latte!"

Masato stuck the envelope into his shoulder bag and left without a word, donning his headphones and vanishing into the subway.

The three of us ordered coffees, sat down at a table in the back corner, and started combing through the names, checking them against the Les Silencio membership.

We'd been doing this for more than an hour, taking turns reading aloud, when Elizabeth excitedly jerked forward in her seat, eyes wide.

"How do you spell that? The last name you just said?"

"Paulino," Cooper repeated. "P-A-U-L-I-N-O."

"It's here," she whispered in amazement, holding out the paper.

I stared down at the name on the Les Silencio list.

Steven Gregory Paulino III.

On the Warwick list, he was Steven Paulino. Paulino was a guest in room 3010 for one night on October the first. He made no phone calls. His home address was in Humboldt Park, on the corner of Augusta and Homan. I Googled the name on my Blackberry. Not a single result came up.

"That's the scariest result of all," said Elizabeth.

"Try Googling his address," said Cooper.

A business listing came up, a shop called The Broken Door. It had no website, only a bare-bones listing on Yelp.com, which described it as a shop for "discerning connoisseurs of peculiar antiques."

"Open Thursday and Friday, four to six," Elizabeth read over my shoulder. "Those are weird hours."

"We'll go tomorrow when it opens," I said.

Staring down at the single name on both pages, I felt a wave of exhilaration and relief. At long last, a decent break, a minute crack to wedge my fingers into to pry the whole thing wide open: *the man Gabriela had been searching for in the days before she died.*

Eighty-Six

"You have nothing to worry about," Harold explained, stopping on the tenth-floor landing to wipe his bald forehead, drenched with sweat, before continuing up the flight behind us. "Her dealer came by at eight tonight so she's deep in Candy Land."

"Does she stay conked out the whole night?" Elizabeth asked him.

"If you keep quiet. Coupla months ago we sent up a workman to do some repairs. She sat up in bed and started talking to him like he was her ex-husband. Accused the poor guy of screwing around. All he wanted to do was replace a furnace filter. But she's weak and needs a wheelchair to move even a few feet, so don't worry about her getting physical. "I stopped to make sure he was joking, but he was only wheezing heavily as he cleared the last step onto the eleventh-floor landing, catching up to us. He dug in his pants pockets for the keys and stepped toward one of two white doors marked 1102.

"If you need me for an emergency, there's an intercom in the kitchen."

"What kind of emergency?" I asked.

"Just be careful. Try not to touch anything. She hates her things moved." He twisted the knob, gently opening the door, but it was locked from the inside with a chain.

"She must be extra-paranoid tonight," he muttered, slipping his hand through and nimbly sliding the chain loose. "Lock the door from the inside when you leave." He took off back down the stairs. "Good luck to you."

The three of us exchanged bewildered glances.

"I feel sorry for her," said Elizabeth. "Locked up in here."

The only sound was the neon sizzle of the bulb in the stairwell, the steady thuds of Harold's footsteps retreating below.

We slipped inside, entering a dim laundry room reeking of body odor and baby powder. I switched on the overhead light. Mountains of silk robes and pajamas were piled everywhere, on top of the washing machine, spilling out of laundry baskets, heaped on the floor. One looked like something worn by the King of Siam, billowing sleeves, a red sash. I cracked the door opposite, staring into a long, dark hall.

It was silent. The only light came from an open doorway at the very end, Madelyn's bedroom, according to Harold's instructions.

"She must sleep with the lights on," whispered Elizabeth.

"We'll check in on her," I said. "Then take a look around."

We moved into the hall, the walls covered, salon style, with framed photos. There was just enough light to make them out: Madelyn reclining poolside surrounded by palm trees, a wide-brimmed black hat on her head; Madelyn at the premiere of the Godfather, *how apropos,* she was wearing a puffed sleeved eighties style wedding dress, smiling up at a nondescript groom who looked rather shell-shocked to be marrying such a knockout. It had to be the veterinarian she'd married after Esquivel.

Anderson had just one thing to say about him: "A man so far out of his league he suffered from altitude sickness." I looked, but there was no evident shot of Esquivel or her at El Esplanade.

We passed three dark open doorways, though I couldn't see anything. The curtains had to be pulled.

Outside Madelyn's bedroom, we stopped, stunned by the vision in front of us. Never before had I seen such decayed tropical splendor. It looked like a dried up lagoon, a flamingo habitat for a zoo that had gone bankrupt years ago. Two giant fake palms dolefully touched the ceiling. Black mold spangled the faded pink floral wallpaper, giving the room a five-o'clock shadow. There was a strong stench of Glade air freshener on top of mildew on top of chlorine from a motel pool. A tiny brass lamp drenched rose light all over antique wooden dressers and end tables carved and gilded. Porcelain figurines were sprinkled everywhere, drummer boys and pugs and swans with chipped beaks. Vases bulged with fake flowers that made no attempt to look real, the leaves shiny and plastic, the giant blooms colored like synthetic candy. Dominating the far side of the room, floating there like an old docked ferry, was a baroque king-size bed.

Right in the center, submerged under ripples of pink satin sheets, was a tiny curled-up form.

Madelyn. *The last flamingo.*

She was so small and bony, it was almost inconceivable there was actually a woman under there, certainly not the one life magazine had proclaimed "a swimming pool in the Gobi."

Spiky tufts of platinum blond hair sprouted out of the sheets like dune grass.

I tiptoed inside, Cooper behind me, out footsteps silenced by the carpet, which looked to have once been pale cream, now browned in deeply tread pathways around the room. Stepped over to the bedside table on the left, littered with orange prescription bottles; a glass bottle filled with a strange, neon yellow liquid, an ashtray filled with cigarette butts, many smudged with maroon lipstick. A red fire extinguisher stood beside the bed. In case she accidentally incinerated herself.

Her face was entirely concealed under the sheet. There was something so vulnerable about that immobile, deflated mound, I couldn't help but feel a twinge of guilt about what we were doing.

"Madelyn?" I whispered.

She didn't move a muscle.

"What does she look like?" said Elizabeth anxiously from the doorway. "Is she okay?"

"As okay as a blown-out tire on the side of the highway."

"Seriously. Is she asleep?"

"I think so."

Cooper, who'd moved to the other nightstand, was inspecting the label of a prescription bottle.

"Nembutal," he whispered, shaking it, pills rattling, setting it down. "Very retro."

He wandered over to the chest of drawers along the wall between the windows, concealed under bloated pink curtains, which looked like faded bridesmaid dresses from the early eighties. He pulled open the top drawer, staring inside, and pulled out a piece of paper.

"'My dear Madelyn,'" he read quietly. "'Let me start out by saying I am your number one fan. I love looking at all your pictures from the papers.'"

I moved beside him. Inside the drawer were stacks upon stacks of envelopes, some loose and crumpled, others bound with rubber bands. I pulled out an envelope. It read Stateville Penitentiary, B-House. In the return address, the stamp reading May 20, 1980. The letter was crudely typed on thin paper. Dear Miss Madelyn, On July 4th,1975 I shot and killed a man in the parking lot of the Cook county jail. Could you talk to your husband for me about a job. . .

I refolded it and put it back. Cooper was scrutinizing another letter, Elizabeth was bent over the vanity table strewn with old perfume bottles and jewelry boxes, inspecting what looked to be sepia baby pictures tucked along the dappled mirror.

"Let's get moving," I whispered. "You guys check those rooms off of the hall. I'll look around here and keep an eye on her."

They seemed reluctant to leave. The room itself had a sort of barbiturate effect; it'd be easy to browse forever around this Pompeii of lost promise. But Elizabeth nodded, re-tucking a picture into the mirror, and with a last look at me, they filed out, closing the door. I glanced back at that mound on the bed. It hadn't stirred.

Across the room, beyond the vanity, another doorway became visible. I crept over to it, gently pushed it open, switching on the light. It was a large walk in dressing room bloated in clothes, warped pumps, and stilettos lined up in rows, a door opposite leading into a bathroom.

There was a strong smell of mothballs. The clothes looked to be mostly from the seventies and eighties. Toward the very back of a rack noticed a set of pale purple garment bags peeking out from a cluster of sequined evening gowns, as if hoping to remain unseen. There were nine of them. For the hell of it, I yanked back the dresses, pulled down the first bag, and unzipped it.

To my surprise, it was the chic white suit, the one Esquivel wore to all his court appearances. I pulled down the next, unzipping it. It was the same suit. I unzipped the bag behind it. It was identical, though this one had what looked like blood splattered all over it. I scratched at the rusty brown streaks. They looked convincingly real.

I took out my phone and took a few pictures of the clothes, zipped up the garment bags and returned them to their original spots, switched off the lights.

As I stepped back into the bedroom, however, I stared in disbelief.

The bed was empty.

That shriveled lump was no longer there. The pink satin sheets had been flung aside.

"Madelyn, hello, Madelyn?"

There was no response. *Shit!*

Eighty-Seven

She had to be hiding somewhere in here. The wheelchair remained folded beside the bookshelf, the bedroom door still closed. I lifted up the pink taffeta bed skirt. Nothing but a few balls of Kleenex.

I strode to the curtains, jerking them aside, then checked the bathroom. It was empty. Only two working bulbs above a dirty mirror, a counter littered with old makeup, blushes and chalky powders, fake eyelashes in plastic cases, behind the door, a limp red robe. I flung back the shower curtain. A filthy loofah hung from a rusty showerhead, a caddy laden with cruddy bottles. Prell, Breck Silk 'n Hold. I hope those don't date back to the last time she washed her hair.

I slipped out into the hall, finding Elizabeth in the next room, which was cluttered with suitcases and old boxes. She'd switched on a lamp and going through the closet.

"I lost Madelyn."

"What?"

"She slipped out of bed when I wasn't looking."

"But Harold said she needed a wheelchair to move."

"Harold is mistaken. The woman moves like the Vietcong."

I darted out. Elizabeth right behind me. We searched the next room, an ornate living room that looked like a rotten terrarium, then headed into a dated kitchen, where we found Cooper taking pictures of clippings magnetized to the fridge, all of them faded photo spreads of Madelyn.

"She couldn't be in here," he said after I explained. "I've been here the whole time."

As he said it, I spotted, right behind him, the kitchen door moving.

"Madelyn?" I called out. "Don't be alarmed. We just want to talk."

As I stepped toward the door, it banged forward and a diminutive figure shrouded in black satin, a voluminous hood hiding her face, jumped down from a countertop with a whoosh and came lunging to me, wielding a meat cleaver.

I easily deflected it, she had the strength of a dandelion, the knife clattering to the floor. Her shoulder was shockingly brittle, like grabbing a spike in a railing. I instinctively let go as she wheeled around, kicking me hard in the groin before darting out, the kitchen door swinging wildly. We lurched after her, Cooper snatching the hood of her robe.

She shrieked as he clamped his arms around her, hauling her, flailing, into the living room and setting her down in a purple velvet chair underneath some fake palms.

"Calm down," he said. "We're not going to hurt you."

Elizabeth switched on the overhead lights, and Madelyn immediately curled up into a fetal position, burying her face in her knees as if she were some light-sensitive night bloom. Her tomato red silk robe covered her, so she was little more than a heap of fabric slumped on the chair.

"Turn the light off." She said in a husky voice. "Turn it **off!**"

I felt an icy chill on the back of my neck. It was her voice. Madelyn had a very distinct voice, one that lounges in its bathrobe all day.

I motioned to Elizabeth, and she turned off the lights. I opened the curtains, and the orange neon light along Lake Shore Drive lit the room, softening the décor, transforming the gaudiness into a garden at midnight. Fake roses, gilt chairs, a floral couch became mysterious tree stumps tangled with overgrowth and wildflowers.

Slowly Madelyn raised her head and the pale light caught the side of her face.

All three of us stared in awe, in shock. The famous cleft chin, the valentine face, the wide set eyes were still there, yet so eroded as to be nearly unrecognizable. She was a temple in ruins. She'd had terrible plastic surgery, the kind that wasn't a nip and tuck but vandalism; bulging cheekbones, her eyes, and skin stretched as if life had literally pulled her apart at the seams. Her skin was waxy and ashen, her eyebrows drawn in shaky dark lines with what looked like a felt-tip pen.

If there was ever evidence that nothing lasted, that time ravaged all roses, it was here. My first thought was from a sci-fi movie, that her immense beauty had been an alien thing that had feasted upon her, eaten her alive, and when it had moved on, it left this ravaged skeleton.

"Have you come here to kill me?" Madelyn whispered gleefully, maybe even with hope, tilting her head as if posing for a camera, her profile gilded in the light. It had the same slopes and angles of her youth, *a profile you'd love to ski down,* but now it was a sluggish sketch of what it'd once been.

"No," I said calmly, sitting on a chair in front of her. "We're here because we want to know about Carlos Esquivel."

"Carlos Esquivel."

She said it with wonder as if she hadn't intoned the word in years, almost sucking on his name hungrily like a hard candy.

"His daughter's dead as a doornail," she blurted.

"What do you know about it?" I asked, surprised. Obviously, we didn't have the full picture of Madelyn's mental state; she knew Gabriela was dead.

"Girl never stood a chance," she muttered under her breath.

"What did you say?' Cooper demanded, stepping toward her. I wanted to kill him for interrupting her. She was gazing at him with a knowing smile as he sat down on an adjacent velvet chair.

"This must be Tarzan, Greystoke, Lord of the Apes. You're missing a grunt and a club. Can't wait to see you in your loincloth. Now, who else do we have here?" Enunciating this acidly, she leaned forward to survey Elizabeth. "A chorus girl. You won't be able to screw your way to the middle, Debbie. And you." She turned to me. "a wannabe Warren straight from Reds. Every one of you, the farting demeanor of the artfully clueless. You people demand to know about Esquivel?" She scoffed dramatically, though it sounded like a handful of pebbles rasping in her throat. "And so fleas look up at the sky and wonder why stars."

"Drop the crazy actress shtick," Cooper said.

"It's not shtick," whispered Elizabeth, sitting stiffly on the couch.

"We're not leaving until you start talking."

"Cooper," I cautioned.

"Then I suppose we'll be shacking up together. You'll sleep in the guest room. My days of bull riding are over. Though I warn you. The sheets haven't been changed since I bedded Hans, so they'll be sticky."

Abruptly, Cooper stood up, strode to a lamp in the corner, and, switching it on, drenched the room suddenly in blue light. It was as if he'd thrown acid on her. Madelyn hunched forward, gasping, burying her face in her knees.

"Turn it off," I said to him, though he didn't appear to hear me. I realized this situation was swiftly eroding, though the more I reprimanded Cooper, the more it seemed to invigorate Madelyn.

"Gabriela Esquivel. What do you know?" he demanded, looming over her.

"Diddly-squat! You deaf, Romeo?"

"Cooper." I stood up.

"Poop," chirped Madelyn. "Zilch. Goose egg. From the day she was born, she was toast."

"She doesn't know what she's saying," said Elizabeth.

"Are you going to shake it out of me? Murder me? Good. I'll finally get my postage stamp. Unlike Gabriela. No one will ever remember her. She died for nothing."

Before I could react, Cooper bent over her, roughly shaking her by the shoulders.

"You couldn't hold a candle to her!"

I leaped forward and wrenched Cooper away from her, shoving him back onto the couch.

"What's the matter with you?" I shouted.

Cooper appeared to be as stunned by what he'd just done as I. Turning back to Madelyn, she slumped in the chair, motionless. It looked like he'd just shaken the last bit of life out of her. Now we were all going to meet Old Sparky.

Elizabeth raced back over to the lamp, switching it off, and the room again melted into dark drowsy vines and sharp rocks, Madelyn a slippery black animal lying wounded in the chair. After a moment, I realized with a wave of horror that Madelyn was whimpering, frail moans that sounded as if they were trickling out of some dark corner inside of her.

"We're sorry," Elizabeth whispered, crouching beside her, putting a hand on her knee. "He didn't mean to hurt you. Can we bring you something to drink? Some water, or. . .?"

Abruptly Madelyn stopped crying like someone had flicked an off switch. She lifted her head.

"Oh, yes, child. There's some, uh, club soda just," she twisted around the armchair, craning her neck toward the other side of the room, "there in the bookcase, second shelf; behind Treasure Island, you'll find some water. If you could just fetch it for me, dearie."

She was emphatically pointing at the shelves lining the far side of the room, around then a painted fresco of trellised roses climbing to the ceiling. Elizabeth ran to it, fumbling behind the rows of books.

"There's just booze here," Elizabeth said, pulling out a large bottle of Makers Mark.

"Really? What a shame. Lucille must have confiscated my Evian water. She's always riding me about my water drinking. Wants me to go to meetings for it. Hydrated Anonymous or whatever the hell. I'll have to make do with that, uh, bourbon, child. Bring me my Makers Mark. And don't drag your feet."

Elizabeth was reluctant.

"Give it to her," I said.

"What if it mixes with the pills she's taken?"

My gut told me old Madelyn wasn't on pills or anything at all. When she'd jumped down from that countertop like a flying monkey out of The Wizard of Oz she'd had superb reflexes. Whatever irrational phrases she was spewing seemed purely mental, a side effect of being alone and locked inside this apartment for a couple of years. For all of her feigned terror at our break-in, I could see, too, she was eager for a live audience.

"Give it to her."

Madelyn practically lurched out of the chair to snatch the bottle from Elizabeth. Her hands moving faster than a blackjack dealer's in Vegas, she unscrewed it and chugged. There was a soft clink of metal against the glass, and I noticed her Tarantula looking white fingers had slipped out of the long sleeve. She was wearing a single piece of jewelry, a ring with a large black pearl.

It was what her old fiancé Knightly had allegedly given her the day he'd broken off their engagement. Though I'd fact-checked the story before, it was staggering to see evidence of that emblem of heartbreak, here, now, right in front of me.

Madelyn pulled the bottle from her lips with a gasp, wiping her mouth. She sat back, settling comfortably into the chair. She looked calm now and oddly lucid, clutching the bottle like a swaddled child in her arms.

"So, you'd like to know about Esquivel, dearies," Madelyn whispered.

"Yes," said Elizabeth.

"You sure?" Some knowledge, it eats you alive."

"We'll take our chances," I said, sitting in the chair across from her. She seemed very pleased by this response, gearing up for something, preparing.

It was at least two or three minutes before she spoke again, her low voice, rutted with rocks and potholes only moments before, suddenly smoothly paved, winding its way effortlessly through the dark.

"What do you want to know about El Esplanade?" she said softly.

Eighty-Eight

"It's Esquivel's legendary estate," I said. "It sits north of Crystal Lake in the wilderness."

"Did you know it was built on a Mohawk massacre site?"

"No, I didn't know that."

She excitedly licked her lips. "Sixty-eight woman and children were slaughter there, their bodies were thrown into a pit on a hill and set fire to. This was where they constructed the foundation for the house. Carlos naturally didn't know that when he bought the place. He told me all he knew was that the couple living there, some British lord and his idiot wife, had gone bankrupt. But they failed to disclose the wife went completely loony living there. Where they sold the estate, returning to England, the lord had no choice to put his poor mad wife into an institution. Within days, she stabbed a doctor in the ear with scissors. She was transferred to Broadmoor, hospital for the criminally insane. Shortly thereafter, the lord dropped dead of a heart attack. And that, as they say, is a wrap."

She paused to take another long drink from the bottle. It was as if with every swig she was resuscitating herself, coming slowly back to life. She even seemed to grow less bony, filling in.

"My Carlos," she went on, clearing her throat, "without knowing a thing about any of this, moved right into his lovely mansion with his lovely wife, and his baby son. Now, I'm a cynical old bitch, if you haven't noticed. I don't believe. Religion? Humans desperate to take out infinity insurance. Death? The great big nada. Love? Dopamine released in the brain, which gets depleted over time, leaving contempt. Nevertheless, knowledge of those two simple facts, massacre, and madness? It would have kept even me away."

She took another swig, wiping her mouth with her sleeve.

"Carlos told me, the very first day they arrived after the movers had gone, his wife disappeared to take a nap upstairs and he went for one of his long walks. He always walked alone in the woods when he needed a break from the stress of his business.

She paused, her bony hands crawling out of the sleeves to fiddle with the red wax still on the top of the Makers Mark bottle.

"He'd been walking for an hour, following one path and then another deep into the forest when he noticed a knotted red string dangling from a tree branch. A single red string. Do you know what it means?"

Elizabeth shook her head. Madelyn nodded, with a wave of her hand. "He untied it, thinking nothing of it, and continued on until the trail opened up into a circular clearing beside a wild rushing river. Within the clearing, nothing grew. Not a stray leaf, nor a pinecone or twig. Only dirt in a perfect, inhuman, circle. Outside of it on the ground, he found a sheet of plastic, letters were written backward across it, the words indecipherable. There was a naked, headless doll with its feet nailed to a wooden board, its wrists tied with more red string. Carlos assumed it had been left by local pranksters who frequented his property. He collected the junk and threw it away. But when he checked the same area three weeks later, he saw black charred circles on the ground where there had been evident burning. It smelled recent. He complained to local police. They wrote up a report and assured him they'd patrol the area and let locals know the house was no longer vacant. Carlos put up no-trespassing signs along the perimeter of his property a month later, he and his wife woke to piercing screams in the dead of night. They didn't know if they were animal or human. In the morning he went to the area. There, at the center of a perfect circle, was an altar with a newborn fawn on it, the fawn's eyes gouged out, its mouth tied shut. Carved into its dappled body with a knife were strange symbols. Carlos became livid. He even reported it to the local police. Again they wrote up the report. And yet? There was something in their expression, the way they glanced at each other. Carlos realized they not only already knew who was doing such things, they were in on it themselves. They, along with countless people in the town, were using his property for sadistic rituals. Not the Carlos should have been surprised. He was living amongst country kooks, after all, white-trash crazies inbred Deliverance freakazoids."

    She grinned impishly, her eyes bright.

    "You get the idea. And you can imagine what Carlos dear wife, Gwen, from a swank Milanese family, thought about such backwoods heathens. She pleaded with him to erect a fence around the property for protection, to keep them out. So he did. He put up a twenty-foot electric fence, spent a fortune on it. The problem was, what he'd actually done was, rather than keeping them out, he'd barricaded himself and his family in."

    She fell silent for a moment.

    "I don't know how he fell into experimenting with it," she went on. "He never told me. Carlos wasn't afraid of the unknown. Within the universe. Within ourselves. It was the subject he followed endlessly. He took submarines down there.

He went down, down into the dark crags and muck of human desire and longing into the ugly unconscious. No one knew when he'd come back if he ever would. When he was working on a project he disappeared. He breathed it. He'd always invent ways to prosper in his business, a treacherous business, full of violence, lies, deceit from within. He could be pure agony to live with. I, of course, experienced it firsthand, up close and personal."

Visibly proud of this pronouncement, she gulped down the Makers Mark, a drop sliding off her chin.

"The problem with Carlos," she went on wiping her mouth, "as with so many gazillionaires, was his insatiable needs. For life, for learning, for devouring. For understanding why people did the things they did. He never judged you see. Nothing was categorically wrong. It was all human in his eyes and thus worthy of inquiry, of examining from all sides."

She squinted at us.

"Your fans of his, are you not?"

I couldn't immediately answer. I was too stunned, not just by what she was saying but by her sudden energy and sanity, both of which she was saying but by her sudden energy and sanity, both of which seemed to increase in direct proportion to how much Makers Mark she guzzled, now almost half the bottle.

"What do you know about his early life?" she demanded.

"He was the only child of a single mother," I said. "Grew up in the streets of Colombia, then moved to the south side of Chicago."

Madelyn sighed a deep breath. "His mother Sencha knew a great deal about Strega Ria. You've heard of it?"

"No," Elizabeth shook her head.

"It's an ancient Colombian word for witchcraft. A seven-hundred-year-old tradition, passed along mostly in wives' tales, yarns to scare children, make them go to sleep and eat all their vegetables. Esquivel's Grandmother told him about bruixeria, the tradition of witchcraft in southern Columbia. He told me that she told him on New Year's Eve witches have the utmost power, and that's when they kidnap children. She told him to put the fire tongs in the form of a cross over the embers in the fireplace, sprinkle them with salt, and he would prevent a witch's entry via the chimney. So, you see, my dears, Carlos grew up with superstition. Certainly not taken seriously, yet it was nevertheless, it was a part of his young life. And Carlos's imagination on the worst of days is stronger than our realities. I think with a background like that, he was sadly predisposed to it, susceptible, you might say.

She gazed at us, her fingers fiddling with the pearl ring, twisting it around and around her finger.

"He never told me how it happened. But shortly after building the fence around the property, he realized the townspeople were still trespassing."

"How?" I asked.

"They came by boat. The estate is north of Fox Lake. If you leave from the public coastline and make your way to the northern side and along a narrow river, eventually it will feed into a lake on El Esplanade property. When Carlos found this breach, he had his men build a chain-link patch straight down to the bottom of the riverbed so only a thimble could get past. A week later he and his wife woke up to the sound of drumming. Voices. Screams. The next morning, he went back to the fence and saw that the spot barring the way by the river had been sawed straight through. And he could see from the way the wires were cut it'd been done by somebody on the inside of the property."

"Someone living there," I said.

She nodded but didn't elaborate.

"Who? A servant?"

"Every paradise has a viper." She smiled. "If Carlos had one weakness it was his belief that personality was fluid. He didn't believe people could be evil, no in the pure form. He always liked a lot of people around him. Hangers-on, groupies, you'd call them, though he called then his allies. He hadn't been living at El Esplanade a month when he met in town, quite by accident, a handsome young priest who'd just moved to Nathaniel Falls to set up his parish.

Carlos needed a religious adviser for redemption, because of the things he partakes in because of the drug trade. Within weeks the priest was shacked up at El Esplanade. Gwen was furious. She loathed the man. He was hot as hell, a brawny Rock Hudson type with gold hair, blue eyes. Probably had one hell of a der schwanz, if you catch my drift. He claimed to have been raised in the Iowa cornfields. But something was rancid about the man. Gwen tried to convince Carlos he was dangerous. An impostor. A leech. She was Italian, a staunch Catholic, and had noticed rather gaping holes in the man's knowledge of the Church. She also believed he was unnaturally obsessed with her husband. Carlos told her to relax, that the man was fascinating, an inspiration."

Madelyn took another long drink.

"I don't know how it happened," she said. "I suspect one night Carlos went down to the crossroads to confront these townspeople and ended up hiding, watching them. By the time he returned to the mansion at dawn, he had a wildly different perspective on the entire business. I don't know what he saw, of what they did. Nothing was proven, but Gwen always believed that the priest had everything to do with it. That he'd made some kind of deal with these people, or even perhaps, one of them."

She sighed.

"So Carlos began his life there. Strangely, he came into his own. His hyper-vigilance became over the top, out of hand. He thought everyone was a spy for the feds.

She fumbled with her long satin sleeves, smoothing the fabric over her knees. I didn't say anything, mesmerized by what she was telling us about Esquivel, and also by Madelyn herself. She'd grown so lucid and animated, she seemed entirely different from the woman we'd encountered before.

"Eventually, there was no need for him ever to leave that property," she continued. "Everything, everybody, came to him. He had three hundred acres. He built a processing plant there for drugs. It was as if he'd come to believe his power could be God-like when on those grounds. And it was true. The energy he possessed was astounding. His workers turned their lives over to him, mind, body, and soul. When you put yourself in his hands you were changed."

"He sounds like Charles Manson," Cooper stated loudly.

She looked amused by his vehemence, narrowing her eyes at him.

"There's the human desire to exert free will, yes. But there's an equally strong desire to be tied up, gagged, and bound. Naturally, there was the fearful respect that came with being a part of the Esquivel empire. People knew who you were associated with, and they gave you a certain respect, mostly out of fear, nonetheless it felt titillating.

"Is that why you fell in love with him?" Elizabeth asked tentatively.

Madelyn sat up, jolted by the question, jutting out her chin. "Everyone fell in love with him, child. You'd be mere putty in his presence. That goes for every one of you. Who can resist the man who understands and dominates your every thought?" She looked sad and with the wave of her hand, staring down at the Makers Mark bottle, now almost empty.

"We married," she paused, quietly taking a deep breath. "Let's just say, when it was over, I saw that our love was a hothouse flower. Thriving and vivid indoors, in very specific conditions; outside the enclave, in the real world, dead. I couldn't live at El Esplanade, not forever. Because Carlos refused to leave it. It was his private dimension, his personal netherworld. He wanted to remain forever on this magical planet. I had to get back to earth."

"He really refused to leave?" Elizabeth whispered, incredulous.

Madelyn stared her down. "Zeus was loathed to leave Olympus, was he not, unless he had mortals to torment?

Occasionally Carlos would vanish for weeks at a time, couldn't be found anywhere. So we often wondered if there was some other place he went. The secret place within the secret place. When he did finally show up again, he had strange rocky sand in his boots and he reeked of the open sea. He was also especially voracious in the sack, if you catch my drift, like he'd sailed away for a time on his pirate ship, invaded villages, burned them to the ground, raped and stole and murdered, and them he came back to El Esplanade with the salt still encrusting his hair, and all that mist, sweat, and blood soaked into his skin." She smiled dreamily. "Those were the nights he totally overpowered me."

"Hold on," Cooper interjected, sitting forward, elbows on his knees. "These intruders from town. You're saying Esquivel became one of them?"

Madelyn looked exasperated. "I said I didn't know the exact nature of his involvement, Tarzan. But at some point, he was doing more than just observing. It was the reason for his wife's suicide. Gwen. He never told me exactly what happened. But I imagine that the poor, rather fragile woman found out about his nightly activities.

You see, that priest, he was still there, hanging on, silently waiting at the perimeter. An oily shadow, always around. It was too much for her mentally. One gray afternoon, she drowned herself in a lake on the property. The police ruled it an accident, but Carlos knew the truth. Gwen hadn't gone swimming. She got in a small boat, rowed out to the center of the lake, and jumped out, pockets of her dress filled with rocks. They found the boat later, destroyed it. Carlos adored her, of course. But not enough to be ordinary. He couldn't be contained by one woman. You'll find that great minds don't love, live, laugh, or even die like ordinary people. Because they always have their imagination. It nourishes them more than any connection to people. Whatever human tragedy befalls them, they're never to gutted, because they need only to pour that tragedy into their vat, stir in the other lured ingredients, blast it over a fire. What emerges will be even more magnificent than if the tragedy had never occurred."

Madelyn fell silent, abruptly weary. For a minute, she did nothing but fumbled with the robe, pinching at the fabric.

"Rumors about what Esquivel did at El Esplanade swirled, of course. Especially amongst the help. One story I heard from Rueben Garcia. Rueben was head of security at El Esplanade. One night while walking through the gardens He saw a figure hurrying to the front entrance, up the steps, vanishing inside the manor. It was Carlos. He appeared to be coming back from the woods, and He was carrying a black bundle in his arms. When Rueben followed he noticed on the handle of the front doors there were reddish-brown streaks. It was blood. Tiny droplets trailed through the marble foyer and up the stairs. Rueben went to bed. By morning the droplets had all been cleaned up."

Madelyn drank down the last drop of Makers Mark.

"People did whisper," she went on, eyeing me. "But the whispers quickly were silenced out of fear of retribution."

"They were afraid?" Elizabeth asked.

She smiled wryly. "They didn't have the balls. As long as Carlos made all the decisions and money.

Paid them a hundred times what any other employer would have paid them, they didn't dare say anything about Carlos's personal life. If he drank blood? Chanted? Decapitated animals? They'd dealt with trouble before.

There was an incident they had to hush up involving one house maids, apparently, she went mad working for Carlos. So scared out of her mind, the poor girl climbed out of her fourth-floor bedroom window in the dead of night, scaled to the ground like a centipede, and was never seen again."

"Who was she?" asked Elizabeth.

Madelyn shrugged. "Her name escapes me. You see, whatever he was doing to unleash this creativity in getting his empire to the top, no one saw anything. It was business as usual, everyone kept their mouths shut.

"Everyone but Gabriela" Cooper whispered it, his voice so quiet and resolute, it sliced through the room, through Madelyn herself, rendering her silent, even a little unnerved.

"She'd never look the other way," he said.

"No," Madelyn answered.

Eighty-Nine

"It happened on a devil's bridge," Madelyn continued, staring at Cooper, anxiously clutching at her shoulders and chest to make sure she was fully covered by the robe. "You've heard of them?"

"No," said Elizabeth.

"They're medieval bridges. Steeped in folklore. Most are in Europe, from England to Slovenia, built between one thousand and sixteen hundred A.D. Through the stories of each bridge vary, the underlying premise is that the Satan agrees to help build the bridge in exchange for the first human soul to cross it. I don't know the specifics. But somehow there came to be such a bridge on El Esplanade property. They built it, I imagine."

"You mean the townspeople from Nathaniel Falls," I said.

She nodded. "From the moment she entered the world, Gabriela remained an extraordinary child. A glorious image of her father. Fearless, dark complexion, with his pale blue-grey eyes clear as a stream. The intelligence, the unquenchable curiosity, the way she grasped life. The two of them were inseparable. Carlos loved his son, Santo. But there was something about Gabriela that . . . well, he couldn't help but worship her. Everyone did."

She chugged the Makers Mark bottle with her head thrown back, seemingly oblivious that it was totally empty. She wiped her mouth with her sleeve.

"Carlos never knew how Gabriela came to follow him into the woods that night. Gabriela never told anyone. But I have a pretty good hunch who gave her the idea. You see, that priest, he was still lurking. He hadn't been with Esquivel at El Esplanade for some time. After Gwen's death, he took off, supposedly traveled throughout Africa doing missionary work, but then, rather suddenly, the old boy was back in town, having no place to stay and little money. Esquivel didn't object to his old pal shacking up at El Esplanade once again. I don't know for a fact, but I imagine the priest was quite jealous of Gabriela. He adored Esquivel. He must have hoped that Carlos and he would one day . . . I don't know. Live happily ever after? Like a couple of wild teenagers?"

Madelyn fell back in the chair. "However it happened, in the middle of the night in June, this was back in 1992; Gabriela was five, Carlos was at this Devil's bridge he'd constructed with these townspeople. When he was partaking in, whatever it was they did, a ritual of the utmost depravity, I'd imagine. Gabriela appeared from out of nowhere. She stepped right onto the bridge. You can imagine how disturbing such a scene would be for any child. But Gabriela wasn't afraid. Carlos, when he saw her, screamed at he to stop, go back. But in the chaos, when she saw her father, she did what any little girl who loved her father would do, she ran to him. Gabriela ran the entire length of the bridge, stopping only when she'd reached the other side. She was the first human soul to cross it."

Madelyn fell silent, sitting unsteadily forward. A white bony hand had emerged from the voluminous black satin sleeve, resting on her throat.

"Carlos was appalled. Everyone there immediately disbanded. Fires put out. Whoever and whatever these people were, they were ordered to leave the property. Carlos led Gabriela back to the house. To his relief, she seemed fine. She was herself. Wasn't even afraid of what she'd just seen.

He tucked her into bed and read aloud to her, a chapter from one of her favorite fairy tales, The Mysterious World of Bartho Lore. She fell asleep with a smile on her face, just as she always did. Carlos decided not to tell his wife. I don't know the extent of Delores's, Carlos's third wife, knowledge of what he'd been up to in the middle of the night, but there seemed to be an understanding that he was free to do what he liked, so long as he didn't involve the children. When Carlos went to bed that night, he prayed to God. An interesting choice, given how he'd been spending his free time. But it was to God. Even then, he didn't quite believe in the things he'd been doing. Now he hoped none of it was real. It couldn't be. The idea's really absurd. Is it not?"

She asked this with cynical delight, taking another swig from the empty Makers Mark bottle. Maybe she was guzzling the fumes.

"Within a week, Carlos began to notice a difference. Gabriela was always a watchful, gifted child, but now her gifts started having ferocious tendencies. He had some Chinese mobsters and an ambassador come to the house while they worked out some deal. Within two weeks, Gabriela was entirely fluent in the language. She also began staring, staring right into people, as if she could read their thoughts, see their fates unspooling before her lie a roll of thirty-five-millimeter. She still laughed, of course, was still so beautiful, but there was a gravity in her now that had never been there before. And then there was the piano."

Madelyn shuttered at the thought. "Delores was a trained pianist. Since Gabriela was four, she had a teacher from Juilliard travel up to the estate twice a week to give the girl private lessons. At five, Gabriela was good for her age but never had a real passion for the instrument. She preferred to be outdoors, riding horses and bikes, climbing trees. Now she sat down, shut herself inside for hours, and played until her fingers swelled with blisters. Within weeks, the girl could master any piece put before her, Beethoven, Bartok, in mere hours, the whole thing memorized. More and more, this shift in Gabriela was palpable. Carlos was too devastated to believe it. Yet he began to do research. Throughout history, alliances with the devil often manifest themselves in the virtuosic mastery of an instrument. In the eighteenth-century Italy, there was Paganini, still believed to be the finest violinist ever to have lived. The same true for Robert Johnson, the blues musician. He went to a crossroads in Tunica, Mississippi, and gave the devil his soul in exchange for total music mastery."

She paused, her breathing shallow, nervous.

"Delores was still ignorant of what had occurred. She thought her daughter was simply growing up with a rabid intelligence. But then she began noticing Gabriela was oddly cold to the touch, and when she took her temperature, rather than the normal ninety-eight-point-six. Gabriela was consistently ninety-seven, ninety-six. She took her to visit various hospitals. Doctors found nothing wrong. Delores worried especially when Gabriela began showing signs of behavioral problems. She'd stopped laughing. And when she became angry she had a temper that was frightening, very frightening. Carlos finally had to tell his poor wife. He showed Delores what he believed to be the devil's mark on Gabriela. Something called the toad's footprint. A sizable freckle in the iris near to the pupil. Gabriela had it in her left eye."

I stared at her. Madelyn had just described what Lupe, the housekeeper at the Warwick had talked about. Huella del mal. Evil's footprint. Elizabeth turned to me, clearly remembering how she'd pointed out the freckle in the medical examiner's photo.

"Delores naturally didn't want to believe it. But then there was a terrifying incident that changed her perspective. In the middle of the night, the whole house woke up to a man screaming in his bed. It was the priest. The pajamas the man was wearing, as well as the black clerical clothes in his closet, were on fire. He was on fire. The family managed to snuff out the flames, and Delores put the man, barely conscious, into the back of her car, so she could drive him to the hospital, because Esquivel, of course, could no longer drive.

He refused to leave the property. They didn't want to call an ambulance for fear of the terrible publicity. So, in Delores's frenzied state, driving like hell, she rounded a hairpin turn, lost control, and hit a tree, totaling her car. Santo rescued the man in a van, as this priest, drifting in and out of consciousness, moaning from the pain, inched toward death. He dropped him off at a rural hospital and took off. The priest was admitted under the name John Doe, third-degree burns covering his entire body. Gabriela had seemingly slept through the entire incident. But the next morning, Delores noticed Gabriela had a terrible burn mark on her left hand. Delores knew she was responsible. It was the moment she started to believe Carlos, that this devil's curse was real." Madelyn shook her head. "The priest survived, though I heard he vanished from the hospital a month after his admittance and was never seen again, not at El Esplanade, not anywhere, ever again."

I could hardly believe it. Madelyn had described in immaculate detail the incident I'd unearthed five years ago when I was investigating Esquivel. The motel desk clerk, Diane Hartman, had witnessed a car accident in the early hours of a late May morning. Delores Esquivel was behind the wheel. Delores claimed to be alone in the car, but Diane had sworn there was someone else, a man in the backseat dressed in black clothing, his face covered in bandages, a man she claimed was Esquivel.

It had been the priest, burned alive.

"How old was Gabriela at the time of the incident?" I asked.

Madelyn shrugged. Fifteen? Sixteen? Afterward, they sent her away."

"Where?"

"Some camp for unruly teens. It was a final, rather futile attempt to pretend the problem with Gabriela was ordinary."

I turned to Cooper. He was slumped down in the chair, ankle crossed on his knee, watching Madelyn intently.

"Delores was irate, demanded her husband fix it. He did have an idea. He believed it just might be possible to reverse this curse if they exchanged Gabriela's soul for another's. A swap with another child. This led to the rift between Gabriela and her family. Because when it was finally explained to her, Gabriela wanted to accept her fate. But Esquivel was always searching for a way out. He did until the very end. He became consumed with it as it cannibalized the family.

There would be times when Gabriela was perfectly normal when they'd hope that whatever darkness he was succumbing to was entirely in their heads. But then something would happen and they'd know it was happening. He'd be coming for her."

"He?" Cooper demanded suddenly. "Who?"

Madelyn turned to him. "Why, Satan, of course.

He chuckled. "Right."

She stared him down, her masklike face immobile.

"Iblis in Islam," she whispered. "Mara in Buddhism. Set in ancient Egypt. Satan in Western cavitations. It's surprising when you take the time to look at history how universally accepted he actually is."

Madelyn thoughtfully tilted her head, turning toward me.

"Carlos believed it would happen when she was twenty-four, twenty-five, some calculation of the full moons and all that. I don't know the nature of what went on, but at some point, the entire family became complicit in this design to transfer the promise onto some other child. Sadly, it wasn't that outlandish a concept. These cults prey on runaways, children who wouldn't be missed if they went missing. Many of these people get pregnant for the purpose of sacrificing the infant child on an altar. Occult crimes are very real in this country, only they're shoved under the rug by police because it's nearly impossible to convict in a court of law. Not because there isn't evidence. Oh no. These people can't help but leave evidence of their terrifying rituals It's hard to clean up after yourself if you spill blood weekly. No. It's because juries can never quite believe. It's a fantastic leap that they just can't make. Not real life."

She fell silent. In a mechanical reflex, she fastidiously unscrewed the bottle, put it to her lips, but at last noticed, stunned, that there was nothing left, not a drop.

"How do you know so much about all of it?" asked Elizabeth quietly.

Madelyn turned, seemingly about to berate her, but then lost steam, only gazed down at her hands, crumpled on her knees. She considered them as if they weren't part of her, but strange insects that crawled up her legs and she was too weary to brush them away.

"Carlos trusted me. He told me everything. He knew I'd understand the pain. Once I experienced such loss, it gutted me. It left me with just my skin. When you love like that and lose, you never recover. Carlos knew I'd know how it felt. I'd spent time with Gabriela, I certainly didn't believe any of it when he first told me. But then I took her with me on vacation when she was about eight. We were sitting on the beach near Cote Plongee in Antibes and I'd catch her staring at me. It was as if she saw my past and my future, even my soul where it was headed when I died, struggling forever in limbo. It was as if she saw it all and she pitied me."

This gutting loss had to be a reference to Madelyn's dashing fiancé, Knightly, dumping her for her sister, Olivia.

"This Priest," I said, after a moment. "Do you remember his name?"

"People just called him, priest, sort of playfully sarcastic. I remember him during the day fishing, I'd spot him from a distance standing on the shore by the lake all in black, like an accidental inkblot seeping into the bright landscape of sky and blue lakes and trees. I wouldn't know what he was doing until I was near him and noticed his long fishing rod and tackle box, that he was standing there so immobile, patiently waiting for a fish. He looked like he had the self-control to wait forever. Gwen gave him the nick-name Ragno. The Tarantula."

"What?" I asked. "**Tarantula.**"

"Tarantula." She slurred the word. "How he moved. So silent."

"Was his real name Steven Paulino?"

"I ... I don't really know."

Madelyn was slipping away again, growing feeble, hunched back in the chair so no light hit her and she was little more than a ghostly white face floating in the dark. I'd had little confidence that what she told us would be sentient, much less the honest truth. Yet, again and again, she'd surprised me, disclosing details that corroborated everything I'd uncovered.

And now: this revelation about the Tarantula.

"Did you ever meet Esquivel's assistant, Marissa Garcia?" I asked.

Madelyn shuddered with distaste. "Jaguar? But of course. Wherever Esquivel went, his little Jaguar followed. She loved him, of course. Did his every bidding, every menial chore, no matter how cruel. All she asked of him in return was to breathe his air. I think she actually wished he'd eat her alive, so, at last, she'd be the closest to him. Living out the rest of her days huddled in the darkest corners of his belly."

"Where is he now?" Elizabeth asked after a moment. "Esquivel, I mean."

"The jackpot question. No one has ever answered it right." She mumbled this distractedly and didn't speak again for such a long time, her chin lowered to her chest, that I wondered if she'd actually dozed off.

"I imagine he's still there," she croaked at last. "or he's sailed away on his pirate ship out into the sea, never to return. With Gabriela dead, I would think, whatever last bit of humanity he had, my Carlos, he's let go of it. Let it fly. There's nothing holding him back now. Not anymore."

Madelyn made an odd choking noise and, bending over, began to cough a violent hacking sound.

"My bed," she whispered. "Take me to my bed. I'm so . . . so very tired."

Elizabeth glanced at me. It was my cue to assist Madelyn, though I hesitated. It was the fear of seeing her ravaged face close up, the worry she became too fragile to touch. She'd retreated again, gone far away, folded up like an old deck chair, so weathered it seemed possible she'd come apart in raw splintered beams in my hands. Elizabeth gently took the Makers Mark bottle from her, Madelyn was reluctant to let it go. Like a child unwilling to part with a toy doll, and then, bending over her, she gave her a hug.

"Everything's going to be okay," Elizabeth said.

I stepped beside her, and as carefully as I could, gathered Madelyn into my arms. She clamped her elbows tightly around my neck as I carried her out and down the hall, her face hidden deep inside the hood. When I set her down in her bed, Elizabeth and Cooper stepping in behind me, instantly she buried herself under the covers like a beetle hiding in the sand.

"Don't leave me yet," Madelyn whispered hoarsely from under the sheet. "You must read to me so I can sleep. Oh. Swallow. That was it."

"Read to you?" Elizabeth asked.

"I have a boy who comes. Every night at eight he comes and reads me asleep. There's The Count. Read me just a little please..."

"What book?" said Elizabeth.

"In the drawer. There, there. The Count of Cristo. He's waiting."

Looking at me uncertainly, Elizabeth reached for the handle of the bedside table. And I found myself hoping that Madelyn was telling the truth. She seemed to be referring to the drug dealer both Harold and Olivia had mentioned. It was a fantastic misreading of the world, that someone mistaken for a drug dealer was simply coming up here to read books aloud to an old woman, lightness mistaken for dark, heaven mistaken for hell.

But when Elizabeth pulled open the drawer, there was nothing inside, no book, nothing but wads of Kleenex and old letters.

Cooper and I searched some of the other drawers, but we could find only magazines and rubber-banded stacks of old notes and letters.

Cooper asked if she wanted him to read something to her, but she didn't answer.

At last, she was asleep.

Ninety

"I can actually understand it," I said, drowning the rest of my scotch, pacing beside the living room couch. "Esquivel confined himself to a claustrophobic compound in the wilderness. He never left. He became the king of a three-hundred-acre kingdom. He surrounded himself with people who idolized him, those hangers-on, allies, people who doubtlessly reminded him every day he was a god.

He comes to buy into it, this so called power. He cavorts in the woods in the middle of the night with locals who worship the devil. It's only logical that eventually the entire family, including Gabriela, comes to believe in it. And that belief destroys them."

"What if it is real?" asked Elizabeth quietly from the couch. Cooper was at the other end, pensively smoking a cigarette.

"You mean the powers Esquivel harnessed on the property?"

"Yes."

"In the forty-three years I've been alive, I've never seen a ghost. Never had a cold chill pass through me. Never seen a miracle. Every time my mind wanted to jump to some mystical conclusion, I've always found that inclination was simply born of fear and there was a rational explanation behind it."

"For someone who investigates, you're blind," Elizabeth said.

I didn't know what had gotten into her. From the moment we'd left Madelyn's apartment and come back here, ordering Chinese takeout and hashing it out, she'd been utterly convinced that everything Madelyn told us, including the curse of the devil, was categorically true, and any suggestion otherwise, including simple skepticism, infuriated her.

"It all makes sense; don't you see?" Her face was turning red. "Gabriela came to the city to track down this Tarantula. We don't know why. But she knew it was finally happening. This transformation. She knew the devil was coming for her at last."

"Gabriela believed it was happening, but it was only in her head."

"Then how do you explain that maid at the Warwick seeing evil's footprint in her eye? How Gabriela magically made Stanley Dewitt break her out of Mission Hills? Caesar at Onofrio described the way she moved as otherworldly. Even Cooper's story about her with the rattlesnake fits in with this. And what about the couple who lived at El Esplanade before Esquivel arrived?"

"Countless British aristocrats are eccentric. They marry their cousins. They're inbred."

"How do you explain what happened to Olivia?"

"She had a stroke. People have them every day."

She sighed. "How much evidence do you need before you wonder if it just might be real?"

"There will never be hard evidence that people get sold to the devil."

"You don't know that."

"This is Chicago. If people found out worshipping the devil actually worked, every ambitious jerk-off in the financial district, every cook county inmate, everybody hood rat in the projects would be practicing it in their studio apartments."

She glared at me. You're an idiot."

"All of a sudden. I'm an idiot?"

"Not all of a sudden. You've been one for a while."

"Because I don't buy into the power of some ceremony performed by a couple of country bumpkins? Because I ask questions? Need proof?"

"You think you know everything. But you don't. Life and people are right in front of you and you act superior and make jokes but it's just a cover for the fact that you're scared. If you were a child in first grade and a teacher gave you a crayon and asked you to draw yourself? You'd draw yourself this big!" She indicated a millimeter with her thumb and forefinger.

"And you at nineteen, you know everything. Back in Minot near Belcourt, N. D. you figured it all out. Maybe I should shack up with Moe or old Grubby Bill and that crazy bird, which by the way, doesn't have magical powers unless you call shitting all day magic!"

"You wouldn't know magic if it bit you right in the ass."

"The answer's simple," Cooper said.

I turned to him. "What?"

"We have to break into El Esplanade."

He announced it calmly, inhaling his cigarette.

"What you guys are saying is irrelevant. We don't know where people's belief ends and what's factual begins. Is there even a difference? But we do know three things."

"What?" asked Elizabeth.

"One. Gabriela was tracking down this Tarantula, and that makes at least some of what Hughes told us sound right. Gabriela wouldn't let that guy off the hook, not if he was responsible for the devil's curse. So if one thing Hughes said is right, logically the other stuff should at least be considered. Two, if Esquivel was involved in that black magic, whether it's real or not. Gabriela got sucked into it because of him. And that makes me want to kill him. Three, if any of this is true, people want to know about it. That doesn't make any difference to me. I care about Gabriela and nothing else. She sent me that Parrot because I think she wanted me to find out the truth about her family. It was her way of confiding in me, the way she knew about Mondo."

Of course, he was right. In some ways, I'd known from the beginning where this was all heading: back to El Esplanade.

"We'll find a way to break in," Cooper went on. "And whatever evidence we find, whatever truth we uncover about the Esquivel's, however, screwed up or however innocent, afterward, all three of us will decide together what to do with the knowledge. We'll take a vote, and that'll be it."

He eyed me with obvious mistrust as he said this, exhaling cigarette smoke in a fast stream.

"But first we find the Tarantula," I said.

Ninety-One

The following day, we planned to be at Steven Paulino's antique shop The Broken Door when it opened at 4:00 P.M., but in the mayhem of the past week, I'd forgotten one crucial detail: Santa Barbara. I had Kim for the long weekend. Angela called me early, telling me that Kim's new nanny, a woman named Staci Dillon, was going to pick up Kim from school at three-fifteen and bring her straight to my apartment. Angela had given the woman a set of my keys, so this wasn't a problem; I figured she could let herself in and wait with Kim until we returned from the antique shop.

But the entire morning passed, the early afternoon, and there was no word from this new nanny. I called her every half-hour, wondering how in the hell my ex-wife decided to trust a woman who ended her name in an i. She might as well have hired someone named Ibiza or Tequila. Finally, at two-thirty, Staci called. She'd had an emergency; her seventeen-year-old son had been in a car accident on the Dan-Ryan Expressway. He was okay, but she was coming from a downtown hospital and running about an hour late. The earliest she could be at my apartment was five. I assured her it was not a problem for me to pick Kim up from school. This meant, however. I'd have to bring Kim with me to The Broken door, an unpleasant prospect.

"Call Angela," said Elizabeth. She might have a backup nanny."

"I can't do that. She's about to get on a plane."

"What about some 1-800 emergency nanny service?' asked Cooper, sitting on the armrest.

"I can't send a stranger to pick up Kim."

Cooper and I can go to the shop," said Elizabeth.

"And I sit this one out?"

She nodded. It wasn't a mystery where that suggestion was coming from; she was still stonewalling me after last night's heated discussion about what was real and what wasn't.

"Just take her with us," said Cooper. "If it's sketchy? Leave."

I said nothing, thinking it over. We were close to something. I could feel it. If I left such a critical confrontation in the hands of Cooper and Elizabeth, the lead could be blown entirely. Paulino could be tipped off, and he'd slip right through our fingers.

But to put Kim in any kind of danger was inconceivable.

"Better decide soon," said Cooper. "We need to go."

Ninety-Two

There was no obvious storefront and no sign, only a closed garage door with peeling red paint.

Dead vines clung to the brick façade in long coils, like coarse strands of hair left on tiles after a shower. The upper floors were derelict; the windows were broken or boarded up. The building had once been quite elegant, probably, detailed plaster Corinthian columns flanked the garage; there was a row of yellow and blue stained glass windows along the ground floor, but now it was all encrusted with dirt and washed out, as if the building had been buried for years and excavated only days ago.

I stepped up to one of the doors, checking to see if there were apartment buzzers, and was amazed to see the name right there, Paulino, written neatly by hand in black pen beside a buzzer on the second floor.

"He must live above the shop," Cooper said quietly, staring up at the building.

The second floor was the only one with windows that weren't blown out. They were tall and narrow, the glass filthy, though in one I could see long yellow curtains hanging there, and a terra-cotta pot with a small green plant.

"Shawn." Kim was yanking my hand. "Shawn."

"Yes, sweetheart."

"Who's that man?" Kim asked, pointing at Cooper.

"I told you. That's Cooper.

She squinted up at me. "He's your friend?"

"Yes."

She considered this seriously, scrunching her mouth to the side. She the frowned at Elizabeth, who'd moved toward the other door, trying the handle.

"It's locked," Elizabeth whispered, shading her eyes as she looked in the window.

Kim was wearing her Spence uniform, white blouse, green-and-blue plaid jumper, though Angela had naturally added her Merchant Ivory touches: a black coat with puffed sleeves, velvet barrette in her ringlets, black patent-leather shoes. From the moment we'd picked Kim up, she'd been shy and watchful, toward Cooper, in particular. She was also extremely squirmy, shuffling her feet, bouncing on my arm, putting her head way, way back to ask me something, all of which signaled she was coming down off some serious sugar and needed a snack.

"It's dark inside," said Elizabeth, still peering in the window.

"What time is it?" I asked.

Cooper checked his phone. "Ten after four."

"Let's give it fifteen minutes."

We left, heading west down the block headed to a corner café. I bought Kim a root beer float, again explaining that we were on a field trip and afterward we'd go to The Creamery for hot fudge sundaes. She barely paid attention and only pretended not to want the root beer float, transfixed, instead by Cooper. I didn't know what this intense fascination meant until he was standing in line to order another coffee.

"Do you want to watch me jump from here to right there?" Kim asked him, pointing at the floor.

Cooper glanced at me, uncertain. "Uh, sure."

Kim readied herself, feet together at the edge of one of the orange floor tiles, and then, making sure Cooper was watching attentively, she jumped the length of the café, stopping at the display of coffee mugs.

"That was awesome," Cooper said.

Kim swiped her curls from her eyes and took off hopping again.

If worse came to worse, I could wait with her outside. It was a bustling street with trees and sun, a constant stream of cars. Even if the Tarantula was a maniacal presence, there was nothing he could do now, not in the light of day.

Ten days later, we headed back to The Broken Door. Nothing appeared to have changed. The garage door was still closed, the windows dark.

Cooper tried the narrow wooden door, turning the handle, and this time, it opened. I stepped behind him.

It was a dim warehouse filled with antiques so densely heaped, chairs on top of tables on top of wagon wheels, that the way into the store wasn't obvious. The door didn't even open all the way, and the entrance was crowded with a birdbath encrusted with birdshit, a rusty sundial, banged-up steamer trunks, and piled on top if those, an Eisenhower-era radio, faded brass lamps with yellowed shades, stacks of old newspapers.

Cooper and Elizabeth crept through the narrow opening, disappearing inside. I bent down, scooping up Kim in my arms.

"No," Kim protested. "I'm too big."

"It's just for a minute, sweetheart." I put my finger to my lips and widened my eyes, going for the hard sell that this was an incredible game, and we stepped inside.

Overhead fluorescent lights sizzled with blued, noisy light. Cooper and Elizabeth were far ahead, quickly making their way single-file down what looked to be the only discernible pathway in a constricted gorge through piles of junk. The place was cavernous, an entire block deep, though the light gave up on reaching the outer reaches of the store, letting it wallow in dirty shadow. There were tables and wardrobes, a cracked suitcase labeled Asbestos Fire Suit, Sherlock Holmes pipes, a carafe with a coiled preserved cobra inside it, a red bottle reading Champion Embalming Fluid. Comic books rose in piles all around us like red rock formations in Arizona. I held my breath due to the overwhelming stench, something between mothballs and an old man's halitosis.

I had to proceed carefully because the store looked rigged as if it was hoping you accidentally elbowed something so the whole place came crashing down and you were charged a couple hundred thousand bucks for the damage.

As Kim and I went deeper inside, squeezing past a sewing machine. An antique train set, a wooden Quaker chair with what looked to be a mummified dog resting stiffly against the seat, we reached a section packed with barbaric-looking old medical equipment.

I moved Kim to my other side so she wouldn't see it: toddler-sized hospital beds with grayed mattresses blemished basins that had probably held leeches, rubber tourniquets, and crusty yellow vials, pumps and syringes, a wooden case featuring silver tongs, large and small. Dented tin lockers stood stiffly along the back wall. Hundreds of brown medicine bottles, everyone with a white label, too far away to read, were clustered on a stainless steel table, which had worn out leather restraints dangling off the sides. To restrain someone during their lobotomy. I glanced apprehensively at Kim. Thankfully, she was staring clear in the opposite direction, at Cooper.

He was wandering toward the back, where there appeared to be a long wooden table piled with papers and an antique cash register.

"Hello?" he called out loudly. "Anybody here?"

Elizabeth, wading through the store far on the other side, looked captivated. I wasn't surprised. The place was right up her alley, especially the vintage clothing hanging along the walls like scarecrows: old 40's dirt-brown dresses, fluffy pink strapless gowns worn to some 1950's prom. She stopped beside a hat tree, carefully plucked a purple felt hat off, a crispy black feather glued to the side, lifted her chin, and put it on, then set about climbing through the junk to get to the speckled mirror propped against a black wagon wheel.

"Hello?" Cooper shouted. Frowning, he picked up what looked to be a real bayonet, the end rusty and pointed.

"I don't want to be carried anymore." Kim was kicking like a colt.

"You have to. This place is enchanted."

She asked. "What's enchanted?"

"This place." I stepped around an African drum, it looked to be made out of human skin, cured and dried, heading after Cooper.

Suddenly, I accidentally kicked the leg of a wooden table and it collapsed at the center. It was piled with tarnished skeleton keys, chrome car hood ornaments, a dirty crystal chandelier, and it all started to spill off, a loud cascade of crystal drops, chains, hundreds of metal keys clattering stridently onto the floor. Clutching Kim, who mashed her face against my shoulder, I managed to catch the chandelier with one hand and right the table legs with my knee.

Cooper snapped his fingers.

He pointed at the back wall, where I saw a cruddy skylight and a narrow door with frosted glass. A human shadow had just moved directly behind it, though, as if sensing we were looking, it froze. It looked like a man, elongated head, broad shoulders.

"Anybody there?" Cooper called out again.

After a slight hesitation, the door opened and a man poked his head out. It was too dark to see his face, but he had a full head of orange-blond hair.

"I'm sorry. I didn't hear anyone come in."

The voice was husky yet delicate, oddly so. With a sharp intake of breath, the man stepped inside, closing the door behind him. And yet, facing us, he remained exactly where he was, his arm tucked behind him, his hand probably on the doorknob as if considering escaping back through there in a matter of seconds.

It had to be him. The Tarantula.

He was a massive presence, at least 6'6", with a hulking, muscular build. He wore all black, the only interruption in his black attire a priest's white collar.

"How may I help you?" His voice came out in a rush, followed by silence, almost as if the words accumulated in his mouth like pebbles in a drain, then suddenly burst out, giving him this strange, jarring cadence. "Are you looking for something in particular?"

"Yes," said Cooper, stepping slowly toward him. "Steven Paulino."

The man went absolutely still.

"I see."

He said nothing else, didn't move a muscle for at least half a minute. I could see, even from where I was standing a fair distance behind Cooper and Elizabeth, his shoulders rising and falling.

He was afraid.

"Don't bother making a run for it," Cooper said, stepping toward him. "We know who you are. We just want to talk."

The man lowered his head in submission, his hair, an unnatural bronze color, catching the light.

"You're the police, I take it?" he asked.

None of us responded. I was surprised by the assumption. I was, after all, holding a child in my arms. Perhaps he hadn't noticed me. He kept staring at the floor.

"I actually knew you'd come," He said. "Eventually. So you found it all up there, is that it? At long last, it's coming out." He whispered this with evident fear, again, in that low eerily female voice.

"How many were there?" he asked.

"How many what?" I demanded, stepping toward him.

He raised his head, noticing me for the first time. He then turned to stare pointedly at Elizabeth and then Cooper, slowly gathering that he'd misjudged the situation: We were not police. And though he did nothing specific, I was somehow aware that as this dawned on him, his shoulders relaxed, his head rose an inch, as if he no longer was deflating himself or tucking himself away.

When he finally looked back at me a chill of unease shivered through me. I was certain he was an even blacker form hovering there by the door as if extreme confidence were slowly returning to him and it made him swell slightly, come more darkly into being.

What was it Madelyn had said?

You see, that priest, he was still there, hanging on, silently waiting at the perimeter. An oily shadow always around. Though the man's face remained immobile, his eyes, what I could see of them, flicked curiously around Kim.

I needed to get Kim away from him. Now!

Ninety-Three

I moved with her back down the narrow pathway toward the front of the shop. I needed a safe enough distance but close enough where I could keep an eye on her. About ten yards away I found a large, plum-colored velvet armchair, the seat worn white. Beside it was a table with a stack of magazines and a yellow plastic horse, nothing of any danger.

"Nooooooo," Yelled Kim, in a whiny tone as I put her in the chair. I don't want to."

"Honey, I need you to wait right here."

"It's enchanted." She stared up at me, her face distraught and crumpled. She was on the verge of tears.

"Not anymore, honey. It's fun."

She shook her head and clamped her arms around my leg, burying her face against my knee. I picked up the horse.

"Holy moly! Do you know who this is?"

Keeping her forehead glued to my thigh, she craned her face back an inch to eye the toy sideways.

"It's Hi Ho Silver. Incredible. He's a thousand years old, and if you're nice to him he'll tell you all his horse secrets. Now, I'll be right over there. Do not touch anything. I'll be right back. And then you and I are going to have huge ice-cream sundaes, okay?"

There must have been something intriguing about the horse, he looked to date back to the forties, his saddle and reins painted on, because she took to him, sullenly turning him over in her tiny little hands.

Unfortunately, they'd all been listening to this interaction, Elizabeth, and Cooper apprehensively, Steven Paulino with what I took to be a faint smile on his face. But as I moved toward him he immediately lowered his head, as If he didn't like anyone staring directly at him.

I stepped between him and Kim so he wouldn't have a view of her.

Just a few more minutes and then I'll get her the hell out of here.

"Let's start with Gabriela Esquivel," Cooper said. How do you know her?"

He didn't answer.

"Looking for me?" the man repeated. "You mean hunting me." "Why?"

He took a few cautious steps away from the door, reaching down to grab a metal stool hidden beneath a table. He dragged it slowly toward him across the concrete floor, it made a loud grating, rasping sound, which he seemed to enjoy, then he slipped around it and perched on the very edge facing us. He hooked the heel of his shoe, a black cowboy boot with elaborate white stitching, on the top rung.

He sat there like that, staring at us like a muscular old swan, once majestic, now barely alive, so unnervingly graceful for such a towering presence. He was in more light now, and I could see a deeply wrinkled face, though on the right side, from his eye down into his neck, the skin was blistered and scarred.

Madelyn must have been telling the truth. Because that scarring had to be from the night she'd told us about when Gabriela had allegedly burned the Tarantula alive.

"What were you doing on the thirteenth floor of the Warwick?" I asked.

He looked surprised. "I, uh, well I was meeting someone," he said.

"Who?" demanded Cooper.

"Unreal Dreamer." He smiled. That's what he called himself. We met on the internet."

"Who was paying who? Cooper asked rudely.

Paulino lowered his head in meek acceptance. "I was paying him."

"What happened?" I asked.

"I followed his very specific directions. I obtained the room. Put it under my real name. I stripped down to nothing but a bathrobe. And when I heard the knock, three times, I opened the door. I expected a beautiful boy to be there." He paused, swallowing. "Certainly not that thing."

"You mean Gabriela?" I asked.

His eyes met mine. He seemed to find the simple mention of her name repellant.

"She set you up," I said.

He nodded. "I've never been so horrified. I shoved her aside. Ran screaming down the hall into the elevator, shaking, convulsing from the shock. I ran through the lobby out onto the street wearing nothing but a bathrobe. No keys. No wallet. I'd left thousands of dollars in the room. But I had to get out of there. My life depended on it."

From his raspy, saccharine voice you'd have thought he was a nervous fifteen-year-old girl sitting there, not a hulking man in his late sixties. I couldn't get used to this disconnect between his lilting voice and his physical self. In fact, the more he talked the more unnerving it became.

Something else about the man was off. For one thing, I hadn't expected him to pull up a chair, sitting down to chat without nay evident discomfort or resistance. Madelyn, I understood her desire to talk, an isolated and neglected woman, so eager to bathe in the attention of a captive audience. But this gnarled human bird? Why tell us the truth so easily? There had to be something he wanted from us.

Uneasily, I looked back at Kim. She'd put down the horse down on the table and was closely inspection him.

"Where did you see Gabriela again?" I asked, turning back. "Les Silencio?"

Paulino was visibly astonished by the mention of the club. He shifted on the stool, hunching his shoulders and back before going still.

"My, my. You have done your homework. That's right."

"How did she know you'd be there?" Cooper asked him.

"I assumed she found my members card in my wallet, which I 'd left back in the Warwick hotel room when I'd fled. On the back, there's a private number to call in order to arrange for your captivity. I found out later the Gabriela had called and made arrangements to come as my guest."

He paused heavily breathing in and out, a sensuous, nauseating sound.

I was with my subjugator in my cell when she stepped out of the dark. As if from the stone walls themselves. I screamed. I ran away, alerted security.

They went right after her, chasing her down along the beach by the cliffs, a whole fleet of guards. But they came back empty-handed. They said her footprints simply cut out as if she'd flown away like a bird. Or she'd walked right into the waves and drowned." He lowered his head, gazing at his lap. "The following day, there was no sign of her. But I knew it was just a matter of time. She'd be coming."

"And she did?" I asked.

"Oh, yes. Most definitely."

"Where?"

"Right here." He held out his arm, indicating his own shop. "I was doing inventory in the back, when suddenly I was aware that all light had retreated from the store, like the sun had fled, cowering behind a cloud. Alarmed, I glanced up. And she was right there."

He pointed toward the front of the store, where light from the street streamed in through the stained-glass windows and the cracked door.

"She hadn't seen me yet, so I crouched down, crawled across the floor on my hands and knees, trying to be as silent as I could. I reached the back corner and hid inside there."

He turned to his right, gesturing toward a huge double-door closet in the far corner.

"I heard every step she took, coming closer and closer toward my hiding place. As if she was the devil coming. There was a long stretch of silence. I heard her reach for the handle on the door. Very slowly it creaked open. And I knew that was it. That I'd come face-to-face with my own death."

He fell silent and shivered, hunching his shoulders. Trying to ignore the repulsion flooding through me, I turned again checking on Kim. Thankfully, she and the horse were now the best of friends. She was explaining something of great importance to him, whispering in his ear.

"Why'd she come after you?" asked Cooper suddenly.

Paulino said nothing, only guiltily lowered his head.

"You worked with the townspeople from Nathaniel Falls?" asked Elizabeth gently, taking a step toward Paulino. "You helped them access El Esplanade property?"

"I did," Paulino said, smiling wanly, grateful for her kindness.

"How did it work, exactly?" I asked. "You made a deal with them?"

"I did," he whispered meekly.

"With who?"

He shook his head. "I never knew. There were so many of them. I'd just moved to Nathaniel Falls. I met Carlos for the first time, quite by accident, at the General Store. His wife had sent him into town to buy her gardening gloves. He asked me what I thought of the selection. 'Which of these gloves are fit for a fairy queen?' It was the first thing he said to me. We had an instant attraction. When men desire each other, they crash together like wrecking balls, quenching their need right then and there, as if the world were about to end. We began to meet around town, and within the month he invited me to his estate. He gave me my own suite in the top tower, mahogany with red damask curtains, the most beautiful room I'd ever seen. Several weeks later, I didn't have any money at the time. I felt that if I built up some goodwill with the locals it would help me setting up my ministry."

"But you're not a priest," I said.

"I attended two years of seminary. But yes, I dropped out."

"Yet you wear the outfit. Isn't that sacrilegious?"

He only smiled weakly, slowly rubbing his palms together.

"Why'd you drop out?" asked Elizabeth.

"I didn't have what it takes to make it in the Catholic Church."

"Funny. I've noticed scum flourishes with surprising ease through the top dioceses," I said.

Paulino didn't answer, and I turned to check on Kim. She was dancing the plastic horse along the surface of the table.

"So, what was this mutually beneficial arrangement?" Cooper asked.

"I'd help get them onto the property," Paulino said. "It was simple. All I had to do was cut open a bit of the wire military fencing in the southern perimeter of the property, which would allow access to El Esplanade by canoe via a narrow rivulet which emptied into one of the lakes on the property. I was also asked to open up the tunnels."

"The tunnels?" I asked.

"A labyrinth of underground passageways exists beneath the entire Esplanade property. They've been there since the mansion's construction, so servants could move easily throughout the grounds, avoiding bad weather. Carlos didn't know they existed when he purchased the estate.

The British couple who lived at El Esplanade before Carlos had sealed them off and the realtor had no clue or their existence. I was asked by this bearded stranger to unseal them. It was fairly easy to do, took me no more than a few nights' work. They were crudely barricaded with random bits of wood and nails, snippets of poetry and odd verse scribbled backward on the brick, almost as if the person who'd done the job had been totally insane. The other thing I was asked to do was open the front gate. Then I'd simply go back to bed. The tunnels are vast, laid out lie a Tarantula's web. There is a central point where one can see the many different tunnels diverging to other secret parts of the property. I didn't know what they all were. I always stuck to the tunnel leading to the gatehouse. It was the only one I dared go down. And that was it. Certainly, what I did to Esquivel was a betrayal. But honestly, I really didn't see the harm. The property was immense. Why not let these poor locals, who had nothing, use the grounds for their pagan rituals if it made them happy?"

"Did you participate in the rituals?' asked Cooper.

Paulino seemed insulted. "Of course not."

"But Esquivel did," I suggested bluntly.

Paulino closed his eyes for a moment, as if in pain.

"The night he discovered the tunnels, he caught a lone woman running through them on her way to the site they used. Carlos followed her, the idea being he'd confront them all. Instead, he somehow became involved." He smiled feebly. "For every man, there exists bait he cannot resist swallowing."

"What did these rituals entail?" I asked.

"I don't know. Carlos refused to tell me."

"What exactly was the nature of your friendship with Carlos?"

The question made him shy. "We had a . . . a bond."

"According to you," muttered Cooper. "It's funny how one-sided those can be."

Paulino bristled. "I didn't do anything to Esquivel. He was the vampire. He made you feel like he loved you like you were the dearest person in the world to him: all the while he was sucking you dry, leeching the life out of you. You'd spend an hour with him.

Afterward, you were a carcass. You lost all sense of yourself, all dimension as if there were no difference between an hour and the chair you were sitting in. He'd be more alive, of course, invigorated for a week, He'd have constant women, thinking of more ways to make money. There was no end to his appetites."

He blurted all of this heatedly and was about to go on but caught himself, abruptly falling silent.

"How long did you live with Esquivel at El Esplanade?" I asked.

"Not long. Our friendship became strained after the death of his first wife. Gwen. She was so jealous of our bond. I thought it best to leave. I traveled abroad. But when you flee someone, no matter how far you roam, that person will follow you as doggedly as the stars in the sky. In fact, their hold on you grows even stronger. I was gone fifteen years. When I returned to Nathaniel Falls, I went to El Esplanade and asked Carlos if I might stay with him again. I hoped we could turn over a new leaf, go back to how things had been before the death of his first wife. But he had a new one now, Delores, and a beautiful child, Gabriela.

After a month he pulled me aside and said I should think about my future, where I was finally going to set up the church I'd always dreamed of. Surely it would be far away from him. 'Time to let the vines take over,' he was fond of saying, which meant there's no use keeping parts of the house manicured and well lit, not when he had no intention of ever entering those rooms again. He lived his life like that. He was the sprawling mansion of grown-over chambers, trees winding through the broken ceiling, plants twisting up through the floors. I understood what he meant. He'd done it so many times before me. He was dismissing me. Giving me my orders to dissolve. Fade too black, Carlos was always moving on, always warring, always loving, Grasping toward the next mysterious stranger, the next island, the next sea. And what he left behind was always in ruins. But he never turned around to see it. He never looked back.

Ninety-Four

I was deeply wounded. He became the kindest and the most barbaric man, at the same time. He shifted between these traits arbitrarily, when it suited him. With Esquivel you felt like you were following a beautiful twinkling light, luring you into the woods. As soon as you lost all sense of direction, were unable to find the way back, it turned on you viciously, exposed your nakedness, blinded you, burned you. I couldn't move on. I hadn't moved on from Carlos in fifteen years. I don't know why the hell he thought I would then."

He snarled this, spitting, unable to control himself, but then just as quickly silenced himself. He took a breath to regain his composure. I could only stare. Madelyn called him oily, such a strange description. But he was an insidious trickle of oil oozing out of a loosened pipe, dripping silently, relentlessly, to the floor. The stain it made barely visible at first, but then over time immense, repugnant. And yet for all his pathetic self-pity, I sensed a very real and very deep gash of pain inside him, which had never healed.

"Shortly after his dismissal of me," he went on, "I slipped into his little girl's room in the middle of the night, it was so absurdly easy. Ironic, really, that he'd done nothing to protect his most cherished creation, Esquivel, of all people, Esquivel who always warned us we should be afraid of our own shadow, that there was nothing scarier in the world." He smiled "She wasn't afraid when I shook her awake. She sat up, rubbed her eyes, and asked if I'd had a bad dream. Quite the understatement. I told her something had happened. I needed her help. I said her father had been kidnapped by trolls and we had to travel deep, deep down into the darkest wood to rescue him. I pulled her roughly out of bed, telling her that she had to be silent or they'd come for her mother and her brother and they'd kill them. She didn't say a word. I took her straight to the basement and down the steps, down into the tunnels. I didn't even bother to put her little shoes on or give her a coat. But Gabriela wasn't afraid. Oh, no. she was Esquivel's daughter, after all. Five years old and she was so certain, so devoid of all fear.

I can still remember the sound of her bare feet, how soft and clean they were, padding along the filthy ground next to mine.

How my flashlight touched the hem of her white nightgown, scalding it as we followed that passage. It was like a black vein that twisted on and on in front of us. When we reached the central area she told me she hurt her foot. It was bleeding. I think she'd stepped on a nail. But I pulled her on and down the narrow tunnel that would lead us to the clearing. And the crossroads. I'd never been there before. I'd never dared go."

He shook his head, clasping his hands, interlacing his fingers as if in prayer. I turned to check on Kim. She'd placed the horse atop the stack of magazines and was quietly chatting with him and stroking his mane. *Just a few minutes longer.*

"At last," Paulino whispered almost inaudibly. "Just when I started to imagine we'd reached the end. "There was only a dirt wall with a metal ladder. I climbed up first and unlatched the ladder. It opened up into a dense section of woods, and far to my right, beyond what appeared to a bridge over a rushing river, I could see them. A crowd. And a bonfire. Orange3 light like a strobe on their pitch-black robes. And yet the sound they were making, like nothing else I'd ever heard before. It was like animals, but no animal I ever heard. Like a goat, a pig, and a man, all in one beast. I was petrified. I could not go farther. I reached down and grabbed that little girl roughly by the arm, hauling her up the ladder. She cried out from the pain. I shoved her out of the hole. And I told her now was her only chance to save her father from burning in hell. I pointed toward the fire and I said her daddy was right there, at the end of that bridge. All she had to do was run to him, run as fast as her little legs could carry her, and she'd save him. She listened with the look of wisdom in her eyes, gray eyes that were really his eyes. It was like she knew what I was doing like she understood completely."

He paused to catch his breath. "I couldn't watch her do it. I didn't dare. I descended the ladder, pulled the hatch into place, locking it so she wouldn't be able to get back in. Then I sprinted back through the tunnel. I hadn't gone two minutes when I heard the most gutting screaming. I recognized the voice. It was his. My love's Esquivel. It sounded as if he were being mauled, as if his beloved dogs were ripping him apart, tearing off his arms and legs. It was his love destroying him. I didn't stop. I ran back through the tunnel to the house, all the way upstairs to my room. I hid under the covers all night, my heart pounding in horror over what I'd done. I was waiting for him to come for me. I knew he wouldn't hesitate to kill me for retribution. And yet. . . I was wrong. Dawn came. It was sunny. The sky was blue, the clouds like candy as if nothing had happened at all. Like it had all been a bad dream."

He took in another long, deep breath, moved his other foot to the top rung of the stool, tucking his arms into his lap, hunching over, collapsing into himself.

"The transformation that started taking place . . ."

His voice cut out in apparent incredulity.

"Before I never believed, you see. Of course not. But I couldn't help it now. There could be no other explanation. Carlos was devastated. He had no idea about my role in the whole thing. Gabriela, for some reason, did not tell him. And yet, if I found myself in the same room with her, I'd catch that little girl watching me. I knew she was thinking about that night and what I'd done to her. But Carlos, entirely ignorant, was desperate for me to stay on. He needed me because he wanted to cling to God now. God, the boring relative ignores, no one calls, no one writes until they need a serious favor."

He smiled.

"I made myself indispensable. For the next ten years, I lived with the family. I gave my life to him. I educated Carlos on Catholic theology. I helped him study and pray, pray for his own soul, but especially Gabriela's which was slowly, inveterately turning dark. I suggested an exorcist. But then, it wasn't possession, was it? No. It was a promise. A deal. After researching legendary pacts made with the devil throughout history, I came across a potential solution. If Carlos found another child to take Gabriela's end of the bargain. An even exchange. One pure soul for another. Gabriela might go free. And I'd read that if one were to try such a thing, a simple transfer of debt, one needed not harm the other child in the process. One needed only an article of clothing or object that had belonged exclusively to this new child. I told Esquivel about the idea quite arbitrarily, not thinking he'd actually try such a thing. Esquivel, for all his flaws, loved children. But he began to leave El Esplanade in the middle of the night. He had his chauffeur drive him to different schools in the area, where he'd wander the playgrounds and the athletic fields and the hallways, looking for some child's small lost belonging. When he returned to the house with his loot of little shirts and little shoes, plastic soldiers and teddy bears, he'd stick them in a bag and take them down to the crossroads. And there he tried to exchange her, night after night, week after week. I was the only one who knew. But it wouldn't work. Nothing did."

Ninety-Five

I felt too stunned to speak. It was, of course, exactly what the anonymous caller. John had described to me years ago.

It had been real, after all. I had not been set up. The man had been telling me the truth. I felt dizzying exhilaration at the realization that I had not been deceived. There's something he does to the children, John had claimed. And it was true. The reason Esquivel had visited those schools in the middle of the night was that he was hoping to use them, exchange them, save Gabriela's soul by condemning theirs.

"It was because he could find no equal to Gabriela," Paulino continued. The devil had been promised a child of such perfection, such intelligence, depth, and beauty, it was proving impossible to find her replacement. Like finding a stand in for an archangel. But Carlos wouldn't give up. He'd try and fail and try again. He'd do whatever it took to save her. No matter what amount of guilt and horror was left on his hands. He knew he was already beyond salvation. But she wasn't."

Paulino swallowing, his breath shallow, lowering his head. "A few months after I made this suggestion for a swap, I woke up in the middle of the night to the most unbearable pain. My bed was on fire. I was on fire. So were the clerical clothes in my closet, the curtains in my room. They were ablaze, withering as if alive. I screamed, bumbling around, trying to get out of the bathroom, to water, but Gabriela was blocking the doorway. Her left hand was on fire, it wasn't hurting her, a wild look in her eyes. Triumph. It was the last thing I remembered. When I regained consciousness, I was in a hospital and learned I'd been dropped off anonymously at an emergency room. I didn't know who had driven me or how, but I could save myself. I disappeared. And so it remained, for eight years, until a few weeks ago, when she found me."

So everything Madelyn said was true. Paulino was the burn victim in Delores's car, and Gabriela was sent to Gateway Wilderness Camp for what she'd done.

"When we arrived, why did you think we were the police?" Elizabeth asked.

Paulino glanced at her. "I thought you'd found evidence upon the property."

"Evidence of what?" I asked.

"What Esquivel did, trying to save her. When the clothing and the toys didn't work. I thought . . . no, I panicked that he'd grown so desperate, he'd moved on to using the children themselves. I think they might be up there somewhere. Buried. Unless they were all burned, incinerated in the mill ovens to nothing." He closed his eyes in anguish. "'I will show you fear in a handful of dust,'" he whispered.

The implication of what he was saying rendered me mute.

The entire shop and everything in it seemed to freeze from the revulsion of it, darkening, sinking deeper into shadow, holding its breath. I was stunned by his mention of a single word: burned. It triggered a memory of something I had in my old notes, what Doc Larsen, Esquivel's next door neighbor in Nathaniel Falls, had told me years ago. *Now they set fire to all their garbage,* he'd told me. *You can smell it when it's hot at night. Burning. And sometimes when the wind's blowing southeast I can even see the smoke.*

"What did she do to you?" asked Cooper suddenly.

Paulino glanced up at him, uneasy.

"When she opened up that closet and found you cowering in the corner, what did she do? You're still alive, aren't you? You're still wearing that sacrilegious getup. What did Gabriela do that you were so friggin afraid of?"

Paulino only lowered his head.

"You can't even say it, can you?"

Paulino opened his mouth, but no sound came out. Then he gasped a bizarre gagging sound that prompted disgust to flood through me. He was, without a doubt, one of the most wretched beings I'd ever laid eyes on.

"She pulled me to my feet," he said. "And she . . ."

"She what?" shouted Cooper.

"She . . ." Paulino was crying. "There's really nothing more terrifying"

"WHAT?"

"She told me she . . . forgave me."

The words were so fragile and unexpected, no one spoke.

Paulino remained frozen on the stool, his shoulders hunched as if waiting for divine retribution, for God or even the devil to strike him from the world. I was about to break the silence, but abruptly, the man jerked his head up and stared right at me.

It was such a penetrating look it stunned me.

His eyes were completely dry.

For seconds, all I could think was that I'd misjudged his despair and self-loathing because his aged, carved-up face was unmistakably thrilled now, excited, his eyes pricked with light.

It was too quiet.

There was no whispering, nothing behind me. I whipped around. The chair where Kim had been sitting was empty.

"Kim!"

I lurched down the narrow passageway, knocking over stacks of magazines a wooden walking stick clattering to the ground. I wheeled around, my heart pounding, staring into the hat racks and banker's lamps, rocking chairs and vintage radios, and none of it was Kim.

"Kim!" I shouted.

Suddenly, there was a rustling noise.

To my relief, Kim poked her head out of the junk. She'd been hiding under a dining room table laden with animal taxidermy, elk heads with antlers, bobcats, and lizards, monkey skulls. She was clutching the plastic horse tightly against her chest.

"Kim! I thought I told you not to move!"

She blinked in alarm and obediently started toward me. But then there was a loud scraping sound. An Art Deco lamp with a wide crystal shade standing beside her, shuddering, tipping forward.

"Kim, don't move!"

I scrambled over a steamer trunk, comic books, a bird skeleton under a glass dome smashing to the floor, but I knew I was too late.

Kim pitched forward, falling, and the lamp crashed right beside her, the shade exploding over her onto the floor seconds before her piercing screams. I climbed over a rolling stretcher, pushed aside globes and dolls to get to her, my Kim, my dearest Kim, barely aware of the chaos behind me, shouts and echoing footsteps of someone racing out of the shop.

Ninety-Five

The neon lights of the hospital washed out Angela's face, made it pale and soft as she stared back at me as if she were underwater.

"The doctor said she'll have bruising and swelling for a few weeks. Possibly a black eye."

"What about the stitches?"

"Four on her hand where they removed some glass. But it will heal."

I numbly stared down the hall to Kim's curtained cubicle, fighting the lump in my throat. Bruce was in there with her. Though he'd pulled the curtains, I could still see Kim through a crack between them. She was snug in bed under a mound of blue blankets, her face puffy and red, a square white piece of gauze taped to her chin. The hospital emergency room attending physician stood beside her, talking to Bruce.

The doctor was more comfortable speaking to him. I didn't blame her. When I'd come running in here, shouting for help, Kim crying in my arms, the nurses had doubtlessly thought the worst, that I had hurt her.

And I had. Even when I was reassured that she'd be all right, I was bringing Kim into that hideous shop. Even more, gutting was my growing certainty that Paulino had somehow orchestrated it. I didn't know how and I didn't understand it, but I sensed that he'd sat down and willingly talked to us only in order to put is under the black spell of his story, and all the while he was working on a way to hurt Kim. I wondered if he'd done it as a means to distract us, make his escape, because, in the chaos of her fall, Paulino had sprinted clear out of the shop, Cooper instantly took off after him, but when he reached the street, the man was gone.

The emergency room staff sensed from my agitation I hadn't told them the whole story and thus were understandably relieved when Angels and Bruce arrived. I'd called Angela from the cab, and their private jet, minutes from taking off from Ohare Airport. She showed up within an hour and I'd been ushered by a nurse into the hallway.

Or was I wrong? Had it been a simple I'd been sucked so deeply into Paulino's story, the horror of what he'd done to Gabriela, that I was no longer thinking clearly.

"She was just playing," I said to Angela. "She tripped on the electrical cord."

"It doesn't matter," she said in a monotone voice. I stared at her, bewildered, but there was nothing to see. Her face was so drained of feeling, it was startling to behold as if a room I'd lived in all my life was suddenly without furniture, barren; piece by tiny piece, it had been dismantled, carted away. Such a gradual progression into emptiness I hadn't noticed it until now.

She shook her head, her bloodshot eyes electric green. "The doctors said you ran in here, shouting about someone hurting her? A priest? Have you lost your mind?"

I didn't have a response.

"We're finished with visitation."

"I understand."

"No, I'm going to the judge so it's official. You're not going to see her anymore. Ever."

"But, Angela..."

"Stay away!" She shouted it angrily, causing a nurse who'd just walked past to turn and frown at me. Angela smoothed down the front of her blouse and started back toward the curtains, but then she turned back.

"Almost forgot." She fumbled in the pocket of her blazer. "The nurse found this in Kim's coat pocket."

She held out a small figurine. I took it. It was a black wood carving of a serpent. I realized, after a dazed moment, that I'd seen it before; it was the same figurine that had belonged to the deaf child back at Normal Street.

He'd dropped it down the stairwell. I'd found it, given it back. *And now Kim had it.*

"This is a toy that you consider fit for your five-year-old daughter? I can't wait to show this one to the judge."

The sounds in the hospital, the intercoms, the clicks and phones ringing, the squeaks of a gurney wheel, footsteps on the floor, they all grew deafeningly loud in my ears, then, almost as quickly, silent.

Again, I could feel the sucking back of that black tidal wave rising over me. It was still rising, growing stronger.

Bruce had pulled the curtain aside, and I could see Kim staring up at a doctor, her tiny bandaged hand lying atop the blankets like a lost mitten.

I turned and suddenly sprinted down the hall.

"Come back here!" Angela yelled after me. "I want to keep that!"

I raced past an old man lying on a gurney, blinking at the ceiling, a doctor in a white coat. I pushed open the doors to the waiting room. Cooper and Elizabeth, sitting on the seats under the TV, glancing up at me.

"Shawn?" shouted Elizabeth.

I didn't stop, racing through the revolving doors, emptying me back into the night.

Ninety-Six

I reached Fascinations five minutes after closing time. The door was locked, but a handful of customers were still browsing inside. I pounded loudly on the glass. A woman stepped out from behind the register.

"We're closed!"

"I need to see Cleopatra! It's an emergency!"

She shook her head and stepped to the door, unlocking

"Dude, I'm sorry, but. . ."

I barged right past her, racing by the few remaining customers to the counter in the back.

"Is she here?"

A punky blond kid on the stool only stared in confused alarm. I dashed past him, yanking aside the black velvet curtain.

"Hey! You can't go in there!"

I stepped inside, finding Cleo seated at the round table, conferring with a young couple.

"This is an emergency. I need your help."

"He barged right in," said the blond kid hurrying in behind me.

Cleo looked unruffled by the intrusion.

"It's all right," she said. "We're pretty much finished."

The couple scrambled to their feet, grabbing the plastic bag of herbs off the table, and nervously walked past, giving me a wide berth, stepping after the blond kid through the velvet curtains, leaving me alone with Cleo. I reached into my coat pocket and pulled out the figurine. It felt strangely heavy in my hand, heavier than before.

"My daughter had this in her pocket. What the hell is it?"

Cleo rose, stepping toward me. She was wearing a white embroidered peasant blouse, jeans, her red Doc Martins, her hands and wrists laden with the same silver bracelets and rings as before. She scrutinized the serpent without getting too close to it and then turned, stepping to the cluttered shelves in the back, returning with a pair of latex gloves.

She snapped them on, carefully took the figurine, as if it were a dangerous explosive, and took it over to the table.

"You just found this?"

"Yes." I pulled up a metal folding chair, sitting across from her. "But I've seen it once before. Another child I encountered recently had it."

She turned it over in her hands, shaking it, listening to the interior. I could see now, in the strong red light overhead, the wood was intricately carved, every scale, fin, and tooth polished and pointed. The beast's leering expression looked lecherous, lips curled back, tongue protruding.

"Could it be used to mark a person?" I asked. "Give then some type of, I don't know, devil's marking? Have you heard of something called *huella del mal*? Evil's footprint?"

Cleo didn't seem to hear me, setting the serpent down at the center of the table. Bending forward, with great concentration, she grabbed it by the tail, which coiled up and over the body, sliding the figurine in a slow counterclockwise circle. She did this three times, the only sound in the room the figurine's jarring rasping on the wood.

Suddenly she whipped her hand away as if she'd been scalded, the snake falling onto its side.

"What?" I asked quickly.

She looked disconcerted. "You didn't see that?"

"No. What?"

With a deep breath, Cleo reached out again, grabbing the tail.

"Watch the shadow," she whispered.

I was so flooded with adrenaline; I could hardly bring myself to focus on the deliberate movement. And then I saw what she meant.

The shadow, resolutely black on the table, did not naturally follow the object. Instead, it froze as if snagged on something invisible, quivering with tension, the shadow's tongue elongating, pulling far out behind the figurine before swiftly snapping back into place and moving normally. Amazed, I blinked, leaning in, certain my eyes were playing tricks on me, but within seconds, it happened again. And again.

She reversed the direction, moving the figurine clockwise, and the shadow behaved ordinarily.

"How is it possible?" I asked.

"I don't know." She set down the figurine. "I told you I'm not proficient in black magic. I've never seen anything like this."

"But you've read something about it. In your extensive witch education."

She looked at me. "I can't help you. You need to visit a real practitioner of black magic."

"I don't know a real practitioner of black magic. I only know you, so you're getting to the bottom of this, even if it means we sit here for weeks figuring it out."

I leaped to my feet, the folding chair falling backward with a crack as I raced to the back of the room. The counters were disordered, burnt candles and ashtrays, scraps of paper scribbled with recipes for spells, battered notebooks, plastic sachets of powders marked yes and no, jars of black ashes. The shelves were crammed to the ceiling with musty texts.

Book of the Sacred Magic of Bramba the Mage. 777 and Other mystical writings of Bagwan Chi-Rashnesch.

Cleo suddenly stood beside me. "Calm down."

The Evil Eye. Book of Tobit. The Essential Nostradamus. I yanked down Encyclopedia of Popular 19th Century Spells from the top shelf, black paperbacks showering the floor, a red pentagram on the cover.

"You'll make it worse," Cleo said. "Potent black magic around an unstable mind is like enriched uranium near a fuse."

I opened the encyclopedia, scanning the contents page.

"There might be another option," Cleo said. "But it's a long shot."

I looked at her. "Well, what are you waiting for?"

She looked grudgingly at her watch, sighed, and moved to the back corner, where there was a small sink, stacks of notebooks, and a bulletin board propped on the counter laden with papers. She lifted the pages, looking for something riffling through hand-drawn maps of Which Country, Pennsylvania, a pamphlet from the Crystal Science League, the timeline of John the Conqueror, photographs of Fascinations employees, the Magical Practitioner's code of Ethics. She inspected a small scrap tucked underneath a postcard of a demonic looking man and took it down, grabbing the cordless phone off the counter.

I stepped beside her.

It was a faded classified ad circled in red pen and torn from a newspaper. It read simply; **For The Grimmest Situation Only.** Followed by a phone number.

"That's your expert? Are you kidding?"

"I said it was a long shot," Cleo snapped, dialing the number.

I took the paper. On the reverse side there was a half-torn headline that read **Flooding Suspends,** and above that, **The Lafourche Gazette**, November 8, 1983.

"No answer," Cleo said.

"Try again."

Sighing, she dialed again. After another three tries, she shook her head.

"I'm sorry. I don't even know what the number is. The paper's been here forever. No one knows where it came from. Come back tomorrow and we'll try again.

I grabbed the phone, pressed redial, pacing, my heart pounding with every unanswered ring.

It can't end like this, not with my daughter vulnerable to some dark hell I'd unwittingly unleashed on her.

As I silently repeated this, I realized with a wave of sickened understanding that Esquivel must have chanted the very same thing when he'd learned Gabriela had run over the devil's bridge.

This truth I'd been chasing, slowly it was becoming my own. Suddenly, the ringing stopped. There was a click on the line. I thought for a moment it had gone dead, but then I heard faint wheezing.

"Hello?" The connection was full of static. "Anyone there?"

"Who's calling?"

The voice was a prehistoric gasp. If it was a man, woman, or creature, I had no idea.

Cleo, frowning, grabbed the phone.

"Hello?"

She cleared her throat, her eyes widening in surprise.

"Yes. This is Cleopatra at Fascinations in Chicago. I hope it's not too late to be calling. We have the grimmest situation."

She fell silent, seemingly being reprimanded, but then she smiled at me, relieved, and hurried back to the table.

"I understand. Yes, ma'am. Thank you. If you want to check the stove, I'll wait." Cleo paused, taking a deep breath, staring at the black figurine. After a minute, in a bland, clinical voice, she succinctly explained the situation.

"And the inverse shadow is totally misbehaving," she added.

She fell silent, listening, her face grave. After ten minutes or so, she put a hand over the receiver.

"Go to the bookshelf," she whispered. "See if you can find a book called Symbols of Black Alchemy Animal and Mineral. Should be on the top shelf." She listened for a moment, frowning. "Green cover."

I raced to the back. It took me just a minute to find it, a thick hardback by C.T. Jaybird Fellows. I yanked it down, carrying it back to the table.

"We need to identify the animal before she can help," Cleo whispered.

I flipped open the book, scanning the musty pages, the drawings of animals discolored, the type old-fashioned and faded.

Dragon. Heart. Liver. Deer.

"I understand." Cleo squinted at the figurine. "Fins, a tail with a small suction on the end. Like something between a snake and a fish."

Pig. Goat. Tiger. Worm.

"Look up leviathan," Cleo whispered heartedly.

Owl. Pillar. Pine Tree. Leviathan.

The colored picture on the page for leviathan was nearly identical to the figurine. It had the same leering face, the distended tongue.

"That's what it is," announced Cleo happily into the phone, sliding the book toward herself, gazing down at the entry. "Out loud?" she cleared her throat. "The leviathan is a primordial sea serpent and one of the Dukes of Hell," she said. "Dante designated the creature the incarnation of total evil. Saint Thomas Aquinas described him as one of the Seven Deadly Sins, envy, the monstrous craving for that which you don't have. In the Middle East, he represents chaos. In Satanism, he's a demon of the inferno, which can be harnessed by the witch or warlock and discharged into the natural world for destructive means."

She paused listening.

"Let me ask him." She eyed me. "How many children did you see with this?"

"Two."

"Did they have anything linking them? Did they go to the same school, have the same hobby, were they distantly related by blood? Anything like that?"

I couldn't answer. My mind spinning. Because I'd suddenly recalled Stanley Dewitt's house, when his daughter, wearing that cherry-covered nightgown, had tiptoed after me down the driveway. She'd been holding something in her fist, something small and black. It was this figurine.

"No," I said. "There were three. Three children."

"What did they have in common?"

I rubbed my eyes, trying to calm down, to think.

"They were between four and six years old. They all had contact with a certain woman. The one who laid down the killing curse on our shoes. Gabriela." I'd said this, really only considering Dewitt's daughter and the deaf child at Normal Street. But then the conclusion of my own words hit me: *That meant Kim had encountered Gabriela.*

But that was impossible.

Angela never allowed Kim to talk to strangers. Yet she'd found me at the Reservoir. It wasn't so vast a leap, then, that she'd found my child.

"How did they act?" Cleo asked. "Any strange behaviors? Whispering? Twitching or tics? Trancelike countenances? Any talk of death or violence?"

I couldn't answer her. The horror of what I'd unknowingly done made me feel as if the room were caving in on me.

I'd brought the Esquivels right to Kim. It's like a tapeworm that's eaten its own tail. There's no end to it. All it will do is wrap around your heart and squeeze all the blood out.

"Hello?" Cleo prompted.

Why in the hell didn't I turn away when I had the chance?

"Excuse me, but we have a real live black witch on the line," Cleo hissed, clamping her hand over the receiver. "We interrupted her while she was gutting a mild snake for a tranquility spell. And she sounds like she's three breaths from going tits up. If I were you, I'd focus. How did the children behave?"

"I didn't see my daughter with it. My ex-wife found it in her coat pocket. But she seemed normal."

"What about the others?"

"One child was deaf. He was upset when he dropped it. He nearly had a tantrum, but calmed down when I returned it to him."

"Irrepressible imprinting," Cleo whispered hastily into the phone, then glanced at me. "The third?"

Dewitt's daughter. "I wasn't around her," I said.

"You saw nothing out of the ordinary?"

I thought back to that night, the dark yard strewn with forgotten toys, shivering trees, the dog barking in the distance, baby screaming.

"Her favorite doll was found decomposing in a kiddie pool," I blurted. Cleo looked startled. "A baby doll?"

"I'd been missing for a few weeks. They'd looked for it everywhere."

"And?"

"Her father fished it out, gave it back to his daughter, even though the thing looked demonic, eyes missing, clumps of hair falling out."

Cleo waved me on impatiently. "What happened when he gave it back?"

"She was very upset. She cried. But later she chased me down the driveway, cradling the doll, and attempted to give me the figurine."

"Definitive evidence of doll magic," Cleo blurted excitedly into the receiver, relaying what I'd just explained. She listened for a minute.

"All right. I'll try it."

Ninety-Seven

She stood up, hurried to the back of the room, scribbling something on a yellow slip of paper. "I'll tell him. Thank you."

She hung up. Without a word, her face subdued with concentration, she crouched down, rummaging through the cabinets, pulling out books, candles, and balled-up newspaper. She returned carrying a pair of electrician's pliers, a red bowl, a black-and-white reversing candle, the same kind she'd given us during our last visit, and some tweezers.

She meticulously laid out the table like a doctor preparing a makeshift surgery.

"We're dealing with doll magic," she announced flatly, lighting the candle.

"What's that?"

"Poppets. Voodoo dolls stuck with pins. It's a doll connected by magic to a person to control their behavior. They're pretty common. This leviathan was bound by sympathetic magic to each child, which explains why the boy didn't want to let go of it. And we're about to find out why."

She sat down stiffly, closed her eyes, whispered something. She picked up the figurine and placed the head between the pliers. With one hand covering the serpent's body, she squeezed the handle, hard. It didn't budge. Cleo's face began to turn bright red, the bracelets and pendants clanging louder on her arms the harder she squeezed, her face wincing as if in pain, gnashing her teeth.

Suddenly, there was a loud sucking pop. Something flew past my face, hitting the wall, and fell to the floor with a sharp crack. Right beside my feet, there was now a small black rock wrapped in copper wire.

"Don't touch it," Cleo shouted.

A strong smell of sulfur filled the air. The figurine was not solid wood as I'd thought, but a thin shell. Using the tweezers, Cleo was cautiously emptying the contents, a gold-brown liquid, bits of dark hair and mud, into the bowl.

The sight of it, knowing this had been intended for Kim, made a wave of nausea rising in my throat. I'd been so arrogant believing Gabriela had been a viable way to get to Esquivel, to avenge myself, get my life back, when I hadn't realized that I had my own fragile corridor. Kim.

He'd reversed my own plan back on me. It was as if the man had known what I thought. Now there would be no end to it.

"Is my daughter cursed?" I asked.

Cleo blew out the candle.

"What do we do?" I pressed. "Tell me."

"Nothing," she answered flatly.

"Nothing?"

"This figurine contains a protection spell. It's not malignant. Quite the opposite." She smiled at my bewildered face, standing and moving to the back, returning with one of the volumes of Hoodoo Conjuration, Witchcraft, Rootwork. She sat down, flipping through the index.

"'Compelling oil,'" she read after paging to the entry. "'Commanding oil, calamus, a piece of obsidian rock,' which is volcanic glass wrapped in copper wire, that's what flew onto the floor." She glanced at me sternly. "It's a molten wall of protection." She grabbed the bowl, swirling the contents. "The leviathan was used to ward off any evil that tried to advance upon the child. The spell inside protected the carrier. Any child given this toy would play exclusively with it for the heyday of the spell. About a hundred and one days. Any other deeply loved toy would have to be confiscated and hidden, so as not to compromise the potency. To submerge it out of sight in a body of water is ideal. That was the first hint this was domination through doll magic. This person, Gabriela, must have stolen the doll, hiding it in the pool so as not to compromise the effect of the figurine on the child. But when the doll was returned to the little girl, she reclaimed her beloved toy and could no longer play with the leviathan. The protection was broken." She frowned. "There's one slightly weird detail that the witch mentioned."

"What's that?"

"In magic, you fight same with same, so using the form of the leviathan, the symbol of envy, thou shall not covet, Gabriela seemed to believe these three children would be envied and coveted. Any idea why?"

I could only stare at her, incredulous.

The exchange. A simple transfer of debt. Gabriela knew her father, Esquivel, and her brother, Santo, would come looking for her after she escaped from Mission Hills. Encountering the children in her path as she tracked down the Tarantula, she must have been concerned Esquivel might try to use them, one soul for another, in a final attempt to save her life.

This led to a rift between Gabriela and her family, Madelyn had said. Because when it was finally explained to her, Gabriela wanted to accept her fate. But Esquivel was always searching for a way out. He did until the very end.

"My daughter?" I managed to ask, my voice hoarse.

"She'll probably be fine."

"Probably? You're not sure?"

Cleo stared at me. "A tornado knocks a house down, killing the owner, and it's a tragedy. Then you learn a serial killer lived there and the act becomes a miracle. The truth about what happens to us in this world keeps changing. Always. It never stops. Sometimes not after death." She stood up, grabbing the yellow scrap of paper she'd scribbled on, handing it to me. "This is where you send payment to the witch. Any amount you think is fair. She prefers cash."

It was a P.O. box in Layette, Louisiana.

"What do I owe you?" I asked.

She shook her head. "Just go home."

I gazed down at the beheaded leviathan, capsized on the table. It actually looked as if it had faded to a slightly lighter shade of black as if it had started to wilt like a flower clipped from its life-sustaining branch, though perhaps it was just my imagination. I'd walked into this room with a belief that I could distinguish between what was factual and what was an invention of the mind. Now I wasn't sure I know the difference.

I stood up, the chair shrilly scraping the floor.

"Thank you," I said to Cleo.

She nodded, and I stepped back through the black curtain, leaving her staring after me.

All of the customers were gone, the lights switched off so the scarred wooden floors were doused in orange light spilling in from the street. Two workers waited behind the register, speaking in low, worried voices, though they fell silent as I walked past them and unlocked the door.

Ninety-Eight

"Where you guys from?" the woman asked me.

She was plump, with a round friendly face. She'd been behind the desk the night before when her husband had checked us in.

"Joliet," I answered.

"Not too bad a drive. You guys up her to do a little canoeing?"

She must have noticed the canoe strapped to the roof of my car.

"It's gonna be cold the next few days, so be sure to dress in layers?"

"About that extra key?" I asked.

"Right. You're in room number?"

"Nineteen."

She unhooked the keychain, handing it to me. "Need any maps or directions?"

"No, thanks," I said, grabbing the shopping bag at my feet.

"Our restaurant serves dinner until eleven. Everything's home-cooked. We got an apple pie. You should try some."

"Thanks for the recommendation."

I excited through the glass door. As I dinged closed behind me, I turned back and saw the woman's friendliness had been erased from her face and she was inspecting me carefully over her bifocals.

I waved and took off down the covered walkway.

Last night, after sizing up every roadside motel along the way from El Esplanade and Nathaniel Falls downtown center. I chose Valley View Motel, because of its anonymity. It was forty miles north of Nathaniel Falls and sat sulking right off the side of the road: twenty dreary rooms, each rationed one cruddy window and a black door.

The motel had a popular restaurant, the parking lot crowded with cars, people from all over the country. Across the street was a busy campground. I'd guessed Valley View saw enough traffic for the proprietor not to pay close attention to any particular guest.

I was way off on that one. The woman had stared at me as if she knew within a matter of days she'd be picking me out of a police lineup.

I made my way along the walkway, scanning the parking lot. It had cleared out after lunch, leaving only a handful of cars, nothing suspicious, no one watching. A bald man exited a white sedan, stretching and yawning as he made his way toward the motel office.

I stopped outside #19, second to last on the end, and knocked once. Cooper opened it. I slipped inside.

"How'd you make out?" He locked the door behind me.

"Fine. I had to go all the way to Crystal Lake." I handed him the shopping bag, and pulled out the new camera battery, this morning he'd discovered his wouldn't charge, so I'd gone out for a replacement. "She only has one extra room key. Who wants it?"

"Give it to Elizabeth."

I walked over to the double bed where Elizabeth was sitting, eating a protein bar, and handed it to her. She smiled wanly, her eyes lingering a moment too long on my face. I knew what she was thinking, what we all were thinking: What if this plan we'd methodically prepared over the past twelve days was a mistake?

We had weighed the possibilities. There was no other option. If I called Katie Horrigan and told her that I suspected occult crimes had been taking place at El Esplanade, she'd tell me what I already knew: Police would need hard evidence for a warrant, the evidence I did not have.

The one thing I did have was knowledge of a covert way to access the property. The Tarantula had claimed he'd cut open the fence for the townspeople along a narrow stream. Madelyn had mentioned it originated from Fox Lake.

Inspecting detailed maps of the area. I could find no such river. It was only after finding a geological map that dated back to 1953 that we uncovered where it just might be, a frail, nameless rivulet that twisted off the lake's north shore, meandering through dense forest, right onto El Esplanade grounds.

If we managed to locate this stream and covertly enter that way after nightfall, we could see what was at El Esplanade, once and for all. If there was evidence not just of occult practices but what the Tarantula had suggested, actual child killings. We'd gather what proof we could, exit the way we'd come before dawn, then get it into the hands of authorities.

The plan was a blind risk, not to mention illegal, immoral, crossing the line of even the slackest ethics of police investigations, totally outrageous. It could very well get one of us arrested, or injured. For me, it could mean a new low of professional disgrace. I could only imagine the headlines. *Back for More: Fallen Detective Caught Breaking into Esquivel Estate. Judge Orders Comprehensive Psychiatric Evaluation.*

I'd explained all of this to Elizabeth and Cooper, emphasizing that it was my decision, one that was personal, not professional, and they'd be better off remaining behind. But Cooper was as resolute as I was. He said grimly. "I'm in," as if it were something he'd resolved long ago. Elizabeth was also adamant.

"I'm coming," she announced.

And so it was decided.

Over the course of the past week, however, as we'd memorized the plan, assembled supplies, even as we'd driven the seven hours north of the city, a bleak landscape of gray sky, roads smothered with trees, the reality of what we were doing seemed to swell exponentially in magnitude. It was a mountain we'd started climbing, which grew beneath us into a rambling skyscraping ridge, holding us back.

Every word Elizabeth chirped in her singsong voice, mind if we stop at that gas station? I'll have the French toast with maple syrup, thinking we're doomed, I regretted that I'd even allowed her to come along.

I was concerned that as much as we'd uncovered about Gabriela and her father, I still didn't have the complete picture. Cleo had warned me of this: the truth about what happens to us in this world keeps changing . . . it never stops.

It was possible El Esplanade, and Esquivel himself was like that locked hexagonal Chinese box of Anderson's I tried to pry open years ago: something that should remain forever sealed, its contents hidden from the light of day for good reason.

Though Cleo had assured me the spell inside the leviathan was not malevolent, there was little solace in this. Even if Gabriela had meant to protect Kim, even if Cooper had loved Gabriela, she was still a shifting cipher, her movements that night at the Reservoir impossible to fathom. The mystery of how Kim came to have the figurine in her coat pocket, the idea that Gabriela had once approached her, shook me awake in the middle of the night, filled me with anxiety made it all the more critical by the knowledge that it was my fault.

I'd put her in harm's way. I couldn't help but wonder if it had shown me my true nature, a raw view as infinite and irrefutable as two facing mirrors, the selfish blind man I was and always would be. My countless phone calls to Angela to check on Kim went ignored. And there was the question of the Tarantula and The Broken Door.

I went back to the antique shop after leaving Fascinations, the same day of Kim's fall. I found the store locked, windows black. Elizabeth and Cooper returned with me the next day, and two days after that, every day after. We monitored the building from the shadows of the porch across the street, waiting for a light in an upstairs window, a curtain gently pulled aside.

Yet the building remained inscrutable and silent.

The Tarantula had obviously come back, packed a suitcase, and banished onto the night, perhaps forever. It wasn't hard to imagine; his past had caught up with him, after all, first with Gabriela, then the three of us. Yet The Broken Door's red crumbling façade, the mystery of his absence, and even more chilling, what exactly had happened to Kim in his shop, all left questions that ate away at me, exhausting me, like a fever that wouldn't break.

I wasn't even confident I was thinking lucidly. Kim was a line that had been crossed. Staying so nimbly out of sight, letting us view only the twisted shadows he made on the wall.

Esquivel still existed primarily in my mind, the most powerful place for any enemy to hide. His very lifestyle told you that. The suspected but unseen threat, fueled by the imagination, was punishing and all-powerful. It would devastate you before you even left your room, your bed before you even opened your eyes and took a breath.

That leviathan figurine with its quivering shadow, sliding along the table with a mind of its own, it was proof of a hidden world beyond the one I'd taken for granted all my life, the reality that science and logic assured me were ever constant and changing only within a fixed set of laws. That misbehaving shadow was the edge of the unknown. The world's certainty and truth had revealed a fault line. It was a minute tear in the wallpaper, which could be ignored, chalked up to me mind playing tricks on me. Or it could be torn back, farther and farther, into an ever larger and grotesque piece, eventually tearing off completely, exposing what type of wall? And if that wall were knocked down, what lay beyond it?

The only way to handle these uncertainties was to shove them aside and concentrate on a concrete plan.

Cooper had finished lacing up his boots. He stood up, zipping his jacket. Elizabeth was in front of the mirror, applying, for mysterious reasons, red lipstick fit for a Parisian jazz club. Smacking her lips, she crouched down, pulling up her army fatigues and thermos-underwear to rearrange the hunting knife strapped to her ankle, which I'd bought her yesterday at a nearby Walmart.

The least I could do was make sure she could defend herself.

"Okay, troops. Let's go over this one last time."

I unzipped the backpack, removed the map. Our carefully hatched plan, it was the rope for us to hold on to. And yet I couldn't help but wonder if, fumbling along that cord in the dark, we'd find out that the end was tied to nothing.

Ninety-Nine

We drove to Fox Lake, the long way, keeping away from the center of Nathaniel Falls. It was a tangle of meandering roads, everyone deserted. We were in a rental, a black jeep, but there was no way of knowing who in town was involved in what took place on El Esplanade property, and I didn't want to risk drawing any attention. We'd monitored Normal Street, not to mention every car behind us during the drive upstate, and we didn't appear to be followed.

I'd forgotten in the five years since I'd been here how impenetrable the wilderness can be, how suffocating. Evergreen trees, maples, and oak trees swarmed the hills, massive branches reaching out over the road as if to smother us, soaking up what little daylight there was. Log cabins, groceries, out-of-business video stores stood forlornly in one crumbling lot after the next.

"It's the next left," said Elizabeth. Within a few yards, I saw the sign: **WELLER'S LANDING**. I slowed, made the left into the parking lot. There were two other cars, a blue pickup and a black sedan, probably other paddlers already out on the lake. I inched into a distant spot in the farthest corner, half hidden by a large hemlock, and shut the engine off.

"We're clear," said Cooper, looking out the back windshield.

"Any last minute concerns?" I asked. I looked at Cooper in the rearview mirror. His pointed stare told me everything. *Nothing would stop him now.*

"Bernstein?" I asked.

Elizabeth was yanking a black knit cap onto her head, tucking in the loose strands of hair.

"Oh, shoot. Can't believe I almost forgot." She reached into her vest pocket, pulling out two small plastic packets. She opened one, removed a thin gold necklace. Beckoning me to lean forward, she unclasped the chain and fastened t around my neck.

"This is Saint Benedict."

It was a piece of jewelry, the pendant emblazoned with a gaunt, robed Jesus type.

"He's the napalm of Catholic saints," Elizabeth said, reaching back to put Cooper's around his neck. "You drop Benedict into a situation, you don't need anything else. He'll protect us from what's up there."

"Thanks," said Cooper.

"You have one, too?" I asked her.

"Of course."

"Then let's move."

We unloaded the car quickly, to minimize the risk of a witness noticing us. But also I knew that to hesitate now in any way would only let serious doubt flood in, like water in a rowboat full of holes.

Cooper carried the paddles to the launch area, I unhitched the canoe from the roof. Elizabeth grabbed the life jackets, the backpacks. I hid the car key under a rock by the hemlock, in the Jeep, we took off across the parking lot.

We lowered the canoe into the water, and Cooper stepped in, heading to the bow, shoving his backpack behind his seat. Elizabeth clambered in after him, binoculars swinging from her neck. I grabbed my paddle, threw in my backpack, was just about to climb in when I noticed my cell phone vibrating in my jacket.

I thought of ignoring it, but then realized it could be Angela. I pulled off my glove, unzipped the pocket. It was a blocked number.

"Hello?"

"McCarthy."

I recognized the voice. It was Katie Horrigan.

"Shit, this connection's crap. Sounds like you're halfway around the world. Let me call you back."

"No, no," I blurted, flooded with an ominous feeling that something was wrong. "What's the Matter?"

"Nothing. Just wanted to get back to you on that tip you gave us."

"Tip?"

"For child services."

The landlord and her deaf nephew back at Normal Street.

I'd forgotten that I'd called Katie about them.

"Sure you gave me the right address? Seventy-five Normal?"

"That's right."

"They checked it out. There's no certificate of occupancy for the building."

"What?"

"There was no one living there. No tenants in . . ."

Abruptly, her voice cuts out. Loud metallic echoing filled the line.

"Hello?"

". . . illegal . . . a couple times last week . . ."

"Katie."

". . . knee deep in major . . ."

Her voice cuts out onto wild static.

"Hello?"

". . . thing was okay. McCarthy, you still there?"

"Yes. Hello?"

A clanging screeched across the line and it went dead. I tried calling her back, but it wouldn't connect. I waited another minute, in the off chance she'd manage to get through again, but the phone had no service. I zipped it back into my jacket pocket, explaining to Cooper and Elizabeth what she'd just told me.

"What do you mean empty?" asked Elizabeth.

"There were no tenants."

"But that's impossible."

"Is it?"

"No, said Cooper. "Maybe they were illegal's. When we showed up, it was too much attention."

"But Gabriela's neighbor," interjected Elizabeth. "Heidi. She wasn't illegal. She had an American accent, and she told us she'd lived there for a year. Why would she take off?"

"To avoid arrest for prostitution."

Elizabeth was unconvinced. "It doesn't seem right."

They fell silent, waiting for me to weigh in. I recognized the moment for what it was, the chance not to go ahead, to reconsider everything, and go back.

The sky had faded from white to gray, the surrounding forest hushed and still. I climbed in and grabbed the paddle.

"We'll look into it when we get back," I said.

100

There wasn't a stream, only a swamp. We'd spent the last hour crossing Fox Lake, Cooper and I paddling in silent tandem. Battered by shifting currents and a cold, unrelenting wind, we sailed past deserted islands crowded with pines and a ghost tree growing straight out of the water, its gaunt trunk and scrawny branches raised heavenward like an outcast pleading for his like. Now, having reached the north shore, we were doggedly searching for the hidden rivulet that would take us into El Esplanade. We were trapped in muddy water barbed with grasses and covered with thick green algae, which broke apart in clumps, then, after we'd edged through, resealed, erasing all signs of our passing.

The wind had dissipated, strange, as it had been so turbulent minutes ago out on the lake. Dense trees surrounded us, packed like hordes of stranded prisoners. There wasn't a single bird, not a scuttle through the branches, not a cry, like everything alive had fled.

"This can't be right," said Elizabeth, turning around.

I hadn't realized, sitting behind her, how worried she'd become.

"Let me see the map."

She handed it to me along with the compass.

"We should go back," she said, staring into the reeds.

"What?" asked Cooper irritably, turning.

"We can't get stuck in this in the dark. We can't sleep here."

"Who said anything about sleeping here?"

"We're supposed to be following a stream. Where's the stream?"

"We'll give it a little longer," I said.

Within minutes, we were stuck on a submerged log. Cooper, without hesitation, got out, standing thigh-deep in the muck, shoved us loose.

Climbing back in, his jeans were coated with mud and strange neon algae, though he didn't seem to notice or care. He stated resolutely ahead as if in a trance, beating the grasses with his oar.

I couldn't help but imagine he was thinking about Gabriela because out here, the stark emptiness of the wilderness seemed to naturally summon regrets and fear.

Our progress remained slow. The swamp reeked of decay, a smell that seemed to be coming off the algae, which only grew thicker the deeper into this bog we drifted. We had to shove the paddles straight down to wrestle the canoe even an inch past the sludge and yellow reeds rising around us, forming a suffocating corridor.

I checked my watch. It was already after five. It'd be nightfall in less than an hour. Our plan had been to be on El Esplanade property now.

Suddenly Elizabeth gasped, clamping a hand over her mouth and pointing at something to her left. A faded piece of red string had been knotted to one of the reeds, the end dangling in the water. I recognized it immediately. Madelyn had claimed Esquivel discovered such strings when he'd first moved to El Esplanade. They'd led him to the clearing where the townspeople performed their rituals.

"We're going the right way," Cooper said.

We pushed on, the swamp suddenly deepening, the mud diminishing. A frail but discernible current appeared, seemingly out of nowhere. The only sounds were the laps of the water, the grasses bending around us, whispering against the sides of the boat.

"I can see the fence," said Cooper.

Sure enough, for ahead, I could make out the dark silhouette of Esquivel's military fence cutting across the stream, marking the southern edge of his property. When we were twelve feet away, we extended the paddles to the bank. The fence looked like something surrounding a defunct federal prison, the chain links rusted, the top looped with razor wire. Where the water passed underneath, the ends gnarled and twisted back, leaving a triangular hole about a foot wide.

"See any cameras?" I asked.

Elizabeth, looking through the binoculars, shook her head.

I unzipped my backpack, removed the fluorescent bulb, and climbed out, heading to the fence. Immediately I spotted three wires running horizontally across the distorted chain links. They hung loosely, and on the closest metal fencepost, they'd twisted free of the casings.

I tapped the metal end of the bulb against the wires. It remained dim touching the first two. But on the third, the one closest to the ground, the bulb glowed orange and blew out.

After all these years, it was still a live wire. I stepped closer to the stream, following the cable's path as it hung slackly between the severed links, dangling across the top, continuing on the other side.

"There's an electric current in the wire," I said, stepping back to them. "It just blew out the bulb."

"Killer security system," Cooper said. "No pun intended."

"It's not funny," said Elizabeth, looking at me uncertainly.

"There's enough room to pass," I said. "We each lie-down. Go through one at a time."

The other option was to swim through, without the boat, it'd be easy to get by unscathed, but for us all to be soaked from the neck down in temperatures about to fall below twenty degrees would be a major handicap, making a systematic search of the property difficult. Passing under the wire inside the canoe was our best bet, so long as we each stayed lower than the goat's rim. The canoe was fiberglass, but there was aluminum detailing along the outer edges. I wasn't an electrician, but You didn't have to be a brain surgeon to realize that if the wire touched the aluminum we were toast, no pun intended.

"Cooper," I said, "you're first."

He shoved his backpack into the center of the canoe and, lying down in the hull, crossed his arms. Pulling away we took a moment to reposition ourselves, angling the bow toward the mangled opening. It was probably just my eyes adjusting to the fading light, but as we glided forward, I swore the fence's wires seemed to constrict, squirm like plants sensitive to movement.

When we were two feet away, suddenly we slipped into a strong current and were whipped sideways, crashing against the opening, the wire lowering from the impact.

"It's about to touch," whispered Elizabeth.

"Keep your arms off the metal," I ordered.

She raised her paddle as I shoved mine in, forcing the bow through, the chain links scraping the boat. We eased in another few inches, and I realized the wire was lowering again as if it were a rigged trap. Before I could react, it struck the rim of the canoe. I waited for a white blast of electricity.

Nothing.

I thrust the paddle into the water, keeping the canoe steady in the undercurrent. I propelled us forward another foot or so. Cooper was on the opposite side, the wire in front of Elizabeth, the chain links rasping.

"You're clear," I said.

Cooper sat up. Elizabeth slid the oar to him, and she inched forward, curling up into a fetal position in the hull.

"If I get zapped and it's my time to go, I just want to say I love you both and these times have been the best times of my life."

"It's not your time yet, Bernstein," I said.

We jostled forward. There was no sound but the water, the screech of the wires as they curved, protesting against the boat. Suddenly, we hit something submerged and the wire dipped, tapping the sides. I swore I heard a faint sizzle of voltage charging around us, though as soon as I did, the wire raised, we slid through, and it was my turn. I lay down in the hull, the water rumbling around me.

"Any last words?" Cooper asked.

"Try not to kill me."

The canoe lurched, that thin wire striking the sides inches from my nose. It slipped over my head and was gone.

"We're in," Cooper said quietly.

I sat up, checking behind us, surprised to see the fence was already quickly retreating. The current had increased, the water pooling, as if excited by the prospect of delivering us to, what?

But that fence wasn't actually a fence. It was a booby trap. Maybe Madelyn hadn't mentioned this secret entrance so innocuously, but to plant a seed in our heads, so we'd try to enter exactly this way. Why? To annihilate us on that wire? Or was it to get us securely inside Esquivel's property, trapping us in here?

101

As we paddled on, the night descended around us like a black tide coming in before the forest had been blanketed with an unsettling stillness. Now noises echoed from every direction. Branches snapped. Leaves rustled. Trees shuddered, like all the wild animals that hid during h day were rousing now, crawling out of their holes.

My eyes gave up trying to discern anything beyond Cooper's silhouette at the bow and Elizabeth's hunched shoulders in front of me. I recalled, with a twinge of anxiety, the feeling of suffocation Olivia Wainscott had described when visiting El Esplanade. I wondered if I was experiencing it, a vague sense of disorientation, detachment, drowning. I assumed it was just adrenaline and nerves, but then I felt, very clearly, a marked heaviness, as if after inhaling all of this moist air, it was now suffused inside me, slowing my limbs, suppressing my thoughts.

Cooper motioned ahead. Visible at the end of this black tunnel of trees was a shimmering surface.

Graves Pond, where Gwen, Esquivel's first wife, had drowned. We reached the mouth in less than a minute, pulling over to the bank, listening, Elizabeth pulled the binoculars away, nodding, and we silently eased the canoe out, veering right, keeping tight to the perimeter under the cover of overhanging branches.

Far to our left on the opposite side, a wooden dock became visible. It looked abandoned, a crude wooden ladder hanging over the side and into the water. Steps led onto a stone path that twisted up a steep hill gradually coming into view.

Suddenly, Elizabeth and Cooper jolted upright.

And then I saw what was coming, what was slowly rising over the crest of the hill like a dark sun. El Esplanade. It sat in the moonlight, night gray. Its grandeur looked straight, out of the Spanish countryside, a lost world of horse-drawn carriages and candlelight. Spiked gabled roofs pitched upward, piercing the sky. I could make out an ornate entrance pavilion, a colonnade across the front drive, three stories of windows, every one of them unlit, all of it fortified with shadow, as if shadows were the very mortar that kept it standing.

In fact, the house seemed to challenge the laws of the physical world, the inevitable slide of man's grandest constructions into decay and ruin, boasting instead that it would be rising over that hill for centuries to come.

A wild overgrown lawn raced breathlessly up to it from Graves Pond. There was no sign of life, no movement. My feeling was the mansion had been abandoned for some time.

We extended the paddles ashore, the canoe beached in the mud, and the three of us climbed out, pulling on our backpacks, Cooper and I carried the canoe up the bank and into the trees, set it down behind a fallen log, covering it with leaves and branches. Elizabeth shoved a stick into the mud to use as a marker, so later we'd know where to find the boat. Then we took a moment to survey one another. Cooper hooked invigorated, his face toughened by the dark. Elizabeth looked disconcertingly blank. I squeezed her shoulder for reassurance, but she only fumbled with her jacket zipper so it was zipped all the way to her chin

"Remember the emergency plan," I said softly. "Anything happens; we meet back here."

With a nod of mutual agreement, we took off. The plan was to check the house first, see if we could get in, and from there find the clearing in the woods where they performed the rituals. We walked due north, keeping to the perimeter if the pond, and then proceeded single-file up a steep knoll through the woods, heading in the general direction of the house. We reached the summit, staying hidden along the tree line, overlooking the eastern wing of El Esplanade.

Up close, the mansion was palatial, yet I could see how weathered the façade was, the limestone streaked and discolored. I could make out elaborate detailing on pediments and corners, black ironwork and carved stones along the roof. Perched on window ledges and above doorways, what at first glance looked like real birds roosting there were gargoyles in the form of crows. There was a domed glass solarium on the ground floor that led out onto a columned loggia, so soaked in darkness it was as if a black vapor had leaked out of the house and fermented.

A stone pathway led from the terrace steps, winding through tall grass to an enormous wall of neglected privet at the rear of the house, banishing somewhere beyond it. I knew from aerial photographs it led into the estate's sprawling gardens, which had featured prominently in Esquivel's snapshots. A check of Google Earth had bled pathways and sculpture, though most of it was shrouded under wild greenery.

"I'll see if anyone's home," Cooper said.

"What? No. We're waiting here."

But before I could stop him, he stepped right out onto the lawn, jogging nonchalantly down the hill. Reaching the steps to the terrace, he ducked and slipped right up them, out of sight.

My shock over what he'd just done quickly turned to outrage. I should have known he'd be reckless, follow his own private agenda. I had every intention of going after him, dragging him back, when I froze.

A dog was barking. It sounded close.

Elizabeth turned to me, horrified. I held up my hand. We'd considered the possibility of dogs and had bought clothing with scent elimination, which supposedly masked our smell from animals.

The dog barked again, angry and insistent.

And then a single faint light appeared in a gabled window along the roof. It was shrouded with a heavy curtain but unmistakable.

Someone was home.

The dog went silent as a sudden gust of wind whipped through the trees. There was no sign of Cooper. Presumably, he was hiding somewhere on the terrace, waiting for the chance to make his way back. But then I heard the unmistakable thud of a heavy door heaving open, followed by staccato thumping and the jingling of a dog collar.

I unzipped Elizabeth's backpack, groping through the clothing, finding the pepper spray. I shoved it into her hands just as a massive hound dog, barking furiously, came bounding across the mansion's front entrance.

It looked like something between a Russian wolfhound and a Jaguar, its mangy coat splotched gray and white, a long curled tail.

The dog froze and howled another warning bark as it gazed down the grassy hill toward Graves Pond, ears pricked. A second dog appeared, this one bigger and all black. It loped around the house exactly in our direction, stopping some twenty yards from the terrace where Cooper was hiding. It growled ominously. Then, nose to the ground, the dog loped up the hill toward us, zigzagging through the grass.

"Get back to the canoe and wait for me there," I whispered.

Elizabeth hesitated.

"Do it now!"

Petrified, she took off, barking exploding around us as if I ran in the other direction out onto the lawn. I headed straight down the incline, racing past the terrace and along the stone path, making a beeline for the hedges. When I looked over my shoulder and saw the two dogs that were chasing me, plowing through the tall grass, I ran as fast as I could along the hedgerow, finding an opening, and barreled blindly through, careening down a white-pebbled path overrun with weeds.

The dogs sounded close behind me, paws ricocheting across the stones. I appeared to be running through a garden maze, tall walls of hedge growing high around me, birdbaths scarred with lichen, plants clinging to trellises. I could make out crumbling statuary, a headless girl, a man's naked torso entwined with a snake. Colossal shrubs, probably once topiaries, rose around me, their animal shapes long melted away.

I tripped down some steps and raced into a narrow alcove with a dried up fountain, a wrought-iron gate. I stopped, listening. The dogs sounded like they'd multiplied, coming from every direction.

I crept over to the wrought-iron gate. Suddenly a dog leaped up on the opposite side, snarling. I lurched away, expecting, at any moment, its jaws to sink onto my arm, but only frustrated yowls exploded behind me. I swung back out, instantly spotted another dog bounding toward me at the opposite end of the corridor.

I Bent down, finding a hole in the hedge, and scrambled through, running out into an open yard, a large swimming pool at the center covered with a plastic tarp. I sprinted to the farthest corner and bent down, yanking off my gloves, groping at the nylon strings.

I could hear the dogs whimpering, searching for the way in. I managed to undo a few knots, pulled back the tarp, and almost gagged when I saw what was inside.

102

It was putrid black water. I yanked off my backpack, plunged my boots in first, and then, gritting my teeth, slipped inside, the icy water seeping into my clothes, swallowing me up to my neck. I pulled my backpack in, doing my best to keep it dry, though here was only about a foot of space between the tarp and water. I removed the camera from the front pocket, yanked the corner of the tarp back into place, and blinking in the sudden darkness, floated away from the opening.

Instantly, I heard that insidious jingling. The dogs had found me, barking, racing around the perimeter, whining, their paws clicking rhythmically across the flagstones.

I fumbled my way along the perimeter as quietly as I could, groping at the broken tiles covered in slime, the coldness starting to eat away at me.

I kept my eyes on the ribbon of light cutting between the tarp and the side of the pool, my left foot striking something underneath me. A drowned deer? I'd reached the next corner, kicking my way around it, a ripple of water splashing a little too loudly. I froze.

I could hear footsteps, heavy set. Someone was coming, striding along a paved path and entering the yard.

"What is it boys?" It was a man's low voice.

The dogs whimpered as they continued to race around to pool, the man coming closer. Then he stopped.

Esquivel?

Suddenly the powerful beam of a flashlight danced across the tarp, sending a spasm of panic through me, the gold circle gliding to the corner where I'd crawled in. I pressed my back against the tiles, trying to remain motionless. I heard faster footsteps, the whisk of the tarp being flung back. The flashlight sliced across the water, illuminating blackened leaves and branches, disembodied shapes, frogs, maybe squirrels, floating deep inside the pool.

The beam hovered a few feet from my backpack, slipping closer. I tucked the camera under the tarp on the ledge, took a deep breath, and carefully sank all the way underwater, pulling my backpack in behind me. I fell a few feet and then opened my eyes, trying to ignore the searing sting, watching the beam of light slip over my head.

I waited, my lungs feeling like they were going to explode, trying to remain calm. We'd been fine, the three of us, just a few minutes ago. How had it all unraveled so quickly?

The beam hovered over me for a few more seconds, then, at last, slipped away to inspect another corner. I floated back to the surface, gasping for air.

Suddenly a sharp scream pierced the night. It sounded like a woman.

Elizabeth?

The dogs erupted into vicious barking, their paws thumping, flashlight streaking away. I heard fumbling, then footsteps striding across the stones. Soon there was only silence around me. They were gone.

I grabbed the camera, then kicked back toward the opening, but when I reached the corner, I saw the tarp had been pulled back into place. I reached out, my fingers grouping underneath the plastic. The strings had been reattached.

I set the camera on the ledge, pulled my backpack over, fumbling inside the front pocket, found the pocket knife, yanked it open with my teeth, and gripping the knife awkwardly in my frozen fingers, began to saw at the ties.

I managed to sever a few, I shoved the backpack out first, then blindly heaved myself onto the pool's edge, freezing wind instantly pummeling me. I lifted my head and saw with relief, I was alone.

I crawled to my feet, dragging my backpack up over my shoulder. I grabbed the camera and staggered across the yard, heading toward the arched opening in the hedge, rancid water squelching from my boots with every step.

I stepped outside the enclosure, finding myself on another stone path, what had to be the garden's western boundary. To my right, beyond a stretch of overgrown lawn, loomed a forest of dense pines, vast and black, and to my left, sitting high on the hill, beyond tangled greenery, the mansion.

It remained in darkness.

I took off across the grass and into the cover of the forest, following the tree line southward, back around the hill toward Graves Pond. A dank cold was shuddering through me, but I ignored it, trying to break into a jog. My legs wouldn't respond. I stumbled over branches and tree trunks, going east, I could see a clearing to my left, shimmering water through the trunks. Within minutes, I reached the same mouth of the stream by which we'd entered the pond and lurched across it, thigh-deep in the water and mud, moving as fast as I could up onto the bank.

I reached the western side, traipsing along the shoreline, and saw with relief, and amazement, the small branch Elizabeth had stuck in the mud.

"Elizabeth. Hey," I whispered, walking straight into the woods. When I found the fallen log, I stopped dead. The branches and dirt had been thrown aside.

The canoe looked around the trees seemingly locking me in an infinite prison. I stepped back to the lake's edge, staring out at the moonlit water. It was deserted.

Cooper and Elizabeth must have been caught. Or they took off, leaving me stranded. Or they'd been chased, escaped, and planned to make their way back when the coast was clear. Or someone else had found the boat and confiscated it, someone waiting for me, watching.

I listened intently for footsteps but heard nothing. I couldn't stay here. And I couldn't use a flashlight for fear someone in the distance would notice it. I took off around the perimeter of the lake, following the general direction the three of us had originally taken.

A dog barked. It sounded miles away. But I picked up my pace and headed directly up the hill, feeling the last bit of warmth somewhere in my gut flickering as if seconds from going out. I stopped, starting far off to my right. There was some type of structure standing beyond the trees, glowing faintly blue in the dark. I took off toward it.

It was a gigantic warehouse, a flat roof, no evident windows. I rounded the first corner, finding a set of steel doors, a rusted chain looped through the handles, secured with a padlock. I quickly searched the ground, found a suitable rock, carried it back, and smashed the lock a few times until it twisted off. At this point, I didn't care if the world heard me.

I slung the chain to the ground, pulled the door open, and stumbled inside. The moonlight flooding in behind me illuminated a crude beamed wall, a concrete floor, the back of a brown couch farther ahead, a blanket folded neatly over the back, all of it retreating into pitch darkness as the metal door closed behind me with a resounding thud.

I took off my backpack, untied my boots, stripped down to my boxers, nearly tripping over a raised step, collapsed on a couch. I felt around for something to warm me up. Thankfully found an old blanket. I huddled there, shivering uncontrollably, willing my mind to thaw. I realized after a dazed moment that all I really wanted to do was sleep, which led me to believe I had mild hypothermia. I resisted that thought as soon as it came. Sleeping will kill you. It's the drug your body gives you before closing up shop.

Minutes passed, I didn't know how long I'd sat there. I couldn't move my arm to check my watch. My thoughts kept slipping out of reach, like tiny deflating buoys I was trying to grab a hold of.

After a while, I realized my eyes had adjusted to the dark. I sat staring at an open newspaper laying on a coffee table in front of me.

The Crystal Lake Sentinel.

POLICE PROBE BOY DEATHS.

104

I blinked. I was sitting in a modestly furnished living room. There was a white shag carpet on a wooden floor, and modern chairs, curtained windows, a brick fireplace.

I've seen this room before.

Hanging on the wall opposite were three framed pictures beside a tiny kitchenette. A floor lamp with a cream shade hung over the couch I reached up and tried the switch.

Instantly, the pale light illuminated the room.

A wicker chair stood beside the front door, a man's herringbone overcoat slung over the back. To my right, atop an end table, there was an Art Deco bronze statue of a woman balancing a crystal ball on her head. Emily, weeping in terror, grabs the statue to use as a weapon before dashing down the hall, hiding in a bedroom closet. This couch I was sitting on, Emily sat right here in the opening scene, reading the newspaper about the latest child murder, as Brad entered, slinging his coat and briefcase on that chair beside the door.

I looked up. There was no ceiling, only scaffolding some forty feet overhead. Lights had been rigged up there, a few pointing down at me.

It was a movie set. This had to be the infamous horror film set Esquivel was rumored to have built.

I was in Brad and Emily Jackson's living room from *Panic Attack,* an ominous tale of suspicion, paranoia, marriage, and the inscrutability of the human psyche.

Brad a handsome professor of medieval studies at a small liberal arts college in rural Vermont, is newly married to Emily, a young woman with a lurid imagination. She becomes preoccupied with a string of local unsolved murders of young boys, every one eight years old, and begins to suspect her husband is the killer. *Panic Attack* ends without a definitive ending as to whether or not Brad is guilty. I felt he was, though the internet and almost certainly the Blackboards were rife with arguments for both sides. I remember Brad's beaten up briefcase which Brad fastidiously stows away in a safe along with his thumbscrews, a medieval torture device, every night when he returns home from teaching at the college.

Brad's briefcase dominates the movie so entirely; Emily becomes obsessed with it, desperate to steal it, break the locks, see what her husband was keeping inside. Neither Emily nor the audience is ever allowed to see what's inside, a feeling similar to the scene in Pulp Fiction.

At the end a confrontation between Emily and Brad, when they are fighting each other, Emily convinced she must fend off a psychopath; Brad convinced his wife has gone crazy, the briefcase inadvertently slips down onto that floor between the bed and wall. It remains there, unnoticed, tucked inside this tiny Vermont cottage, which, with Emily, an orphan, taken away to a mental hospital and Brad *dead*, will remain deserted for an unknown period of time.

The final shot of Panic Attack is the briefcase, a slow tracking shot pulling out from under the bed, winding down the hall, out the front door past the police cars, into the woods, fading too black.

I rolled off the couch, some feeling had returned to my legs, and stepped across the room to the fireplace.

I walked over to the bookshelves. Panic Attack had been made in 1978, and the worn-out paperbacks were from that time; *Looking for Mr. Goodbar, Salem's Lot, The Gemini Contenders*. So was the brown and mustard yellow wallpaper, the lacquered furniture, the orange swag lamp hanging by the front door, the orange-tiled kitchenette, an old GE waffle maker on the counter. The place had been frozen in time feel as if life had stopped here mid conversation. No one seemed to have set foot here in decades.

I stepped through the doorway, heading down the narrow corridor. It was dim. I fumbled my way, opening two false doors, they opened back onto the warehouse, though the one at led to another room.

The Jackson's master bedroom. I moved to the closet and slid aside the door. Emily's clothing hung along the racks, housedresses, a pair of bell bottom jeans, pairs of platform shoes and go-go boots. I stepped to the other end, which had Brad's clothes, wool slacks, tweed jackets.

I grabbed a pair of the brown corduroy pants from the top shelf, and a yellow polyester button-down. And I put them on rapidly because I didn't want to even attempt to get my mind around the fact that I was donning Brad Jackson's seventies-era clothes, that I was literally rummaging through Panic Attack.

The pants were a few inches short in the leg, but they fit well enough. I pulled on a red sweater really tight in the sleeves, found a pair of argyle socks in the chest of drawers, an orange portable RCA record player on top, James Brown's, *I Feel Good,* on the turntable. After putting them on, I stopped in the doorway.

Remembering the briefcase, a sudden chill went up my spine, I crouched down, squinting under the bed. It was too dark to see anything, so I stood back up, stepped to the bedside table, switched on the lamp, and yanked the bed away from the wall to get a better view.

Immediately there was a clattering thump. It was there.

I stared at in in disbelief.

The infamous Samsonite fawn-colored briefcase.

It had been wedged against the wall and the other bedside table in the corner. I was shocked, and yet, what did Emily say in the movie? **Wherever the briefcase goes, Brad follows.**

I found myself looking over my shoulder to the empty doorway, half wondering if I was going to see Brad's warped shadow projected on the wall.

I grabbed the case by the handle, it was surprisingly heavy and set it down on the bed.

I tried the latches. Locked. I realized then I knew the combination. Emily goes to great lengths to figure it out. It was the date that marked the sacking of Rome, the final low in the decline of the Roman Empire, marking the onset of the Dark Ages.

410

I spun the numbers into place. The locks popped open.

I lifted the lid.

It was piled with papers. I went through them, pulling out an issue of Time dated July 31, 1978, "The Test Tube Baby" on the cover. Under that was a stack of handwritten papers, graded with handwritten comments. Marcie, you make a very nice argument that the Dark Ages were a natural rotation of history, but you need to go deeper.

When I saw what was underneath that, I froze.

Neatly folded in the corner was a boy's plaid button-down shirt. I picked it up, feeling a wave of revulsion as the shriveled rigid sleeves unfolded in front of me as if they had a fragile will of their own.

The front of the shirt was stiff, covered in deep brown stains. It looked harrowingly real, a real souvenir from a real murder. The fabric itself seemed beaten, as if the residue of unimaginable violence had soaked and dried into the fabric.

It was a hell of a lot of effort to go through for a prop that never appears in the film. I recalled the ravaged white suits I'd found in Madelyn's closet. I accessed the deepest, most tormented parts of myself, she'd said. Parts I was petrified of opening because I doubted I'd ever get them closed again.

Maybe Esquivel created real terror, terror in this warehouse, real murders. Was it possible?

105

It would explain why none of the people who knew Esquivel well ever spoke of the experience of staying at El Esplanade. Perhaps they were complicit to the horrors that occurred during their visits to the estate. I recalled a remark that Olivia Wainscott said that struck me rather strange, Esquivel's interrogation of her when she visited him. I believe his questioning was to find out how isolated of a person she was, who would notice if she went missing or changed in some kind of way.

Undoubtedly, Esquivel looked for people he could manipulate. He had an obsession with capturing what was factual; he'd forced his son, Santo, to perform in these horror reenactments and sent him to the hospital so they could reattach his fingers. I also knew that Esquivel sometimes used illegal immigrants, a complicit squad of men and women who would never speak of what they'd seen.

I suddenly felt wild exhilaration over the thought. How easily it fit in with everything I'd learned about the man, following in his daughter's final footsteps.

Esquivel obviously took great care in assembling his players, all from different backgrounds, some with no acting experience at all. He brought them here to live in his remote world, locking them inside it, allowing them no contact with the outside. Who would willingly agree to such a thing, signing away their life to one man?

Cooper had asked Madelyn this. Yet did he need to? Millions of people walked through their lives numb, dying to feel something, to feel alive. To be chosen by Esquivel for a film was an opportunity to just that, not simply for fame and fortune, but to leave their old selves behind like discarded clothes.

What exactly did Esquivel make them endure? Everything his characters did? Then his night films were documentaries, live horror, not fiction. He was even more depraved than I'd realized. A madman. Satan himself. Maybe he hadn't always been, but it was what he'd become living here. But if his films were real, how easy it would be for the man to slip into harming real children, in order to save Gabriela.

I rummaged through the remaining papers in the briefcase. There were only lectures and notes, a typewritten letter from Simon & Schuster, dated January 13, 1978. Dear Mr. Jackson: I regret to inform you that your novel, Murder in a Dark Alley, will not fit within our current list of fiction titles.

I remembered Brad had a wall safe he was always unlocking, but it was in his home office, which didn't appear to be attached to this set. There was a door off the bedroom, which in the film opened into a bathroom, but when I opened it, there was only the black wall of the soundstage.

I locked the briefcase, returning it to its infamous spot under the bed, and then rolled up the child's blood-soaked shirt, tucked it in my pants pocket; I didn't want to lose it, so it was safest to keep it on me. I switched off the lamp and headed back down the hall.

I rooted through my sodden clothes scattered beside the couch, finding my camera in the jacket. Thankfully I'd had the forethought to keep it dry, because it still worked, unlike my cell phone and flashlight. Both were dead. I took a few shots of the living room and kitchenette, fully stocked with seventies-era food: Velveeta cheese (still edible after thirty years), Dr. Pepper,

Swift Sizzlean Pork Strips, then stepped to the edge of the living room, staring out.

From the lamp, I could see the soundstage extended far in front of me. Beyond the couch, a wall of steel pipe scaffolding was supporting something, probably another set, constructed on the opposite side. I realized, after a dazed moment, that I was still shivering. My jacket was still soaked, so after lacing up my boots, I strode to the front door, grabbed Brad Jackson's herringbone overcoat off the chair, and put the thing on, again, not letting my mind consider the absurdity of it, that I was donning the coat of a probable psychopath.

Hopefully, it wasn't contagious.

I checked my watch but saw it had stopped after being submerged in the pool. It read 7:55, which couldn't be right. It had to be later.

And then, heaving my backpack over my shoulder, I stepped out of Panic Attack, following along the scaffolding to see what else was in this massive warehouse, what other creations plucked from Esquivel's treacherous mind I could sift through like an archaeologist searching for bones.

106

When it became too dark to see anything, I took a picture, looking at it on the camera's screen.

An enormous red bird had been crudely spray-painted across the concrete wall to my left. I'd seen it before. It was a symbol used to signify Esquivel's territory. This same symbol was used to mark all his packages of illegal drugs he had coming into the country. A way to let people know what to expect if they do anything to interrupt the flow of his empire's interests. I moved on, stepping around the end of the scaffolding, entering what appeared to be a vast room. I could dimly make out a massive mountain in front of me strewn with boulders. I took another photo and realized the mountain was garbage, the boulders corroded gasoline barrels, sprouting like giant mushrooms across the expanse.

I took off across it, knocking right into a wooden sign.

CRESCENT CITY LANDFILL
DO NOT ENTER
HAZARDOUS

I was in *House of Pain*.

The film's meek and mousy heroine, Leigh, a receptionist at a car dealership by day, community college student by night, agrees to spy on her best friend's husband and not only becomes smitten with him, a native German named Axel, but gets dangerously entangled in his gangland dealings.

The first night, she follows his maroon Mercury Grand Marquis all over town, eventually ending up here sometime around dawn, the Crescent City Landfill. Leigh watches Axel park his car and take off on foot across the junkyard, flocks of seagulls wafting off the trash like a screeching exhaust.

He carries a small bag, its color the unmistakable robin's-egg blue of Tiffany, the jewelry store. Spellbound, Leigh tiptoes after him, her hair going frizzy, her frumpy blouse untucking from her skirt. She climbs inside an old funeral hearse to spy on the man as he scales the hill to an overturned school bus.

After removing a paper bag from behind the front wheel, Axel sticks the Tiffany bag in its place. Leigh waits for him to drive away then makes her own way to the school bus, skidding and sliding through the debris.

She pulls out the Tiffany bag, and inside finds a small blue Tiffany ring box, a box commonly used for engagement rings. Leigh is about to open it, when, noticing a black car pulling into the junkyard parking lot, she loses her balance and slips, the blue Tiffany box clattering through an open window into the derelict bus. Leigh goes after it. Within minutes, the thug known simply as Z shows up to collect the Tiffany bag. It doesn't take him long to discover the bag empty, Leigh, cowering inside the bus. And that's the moment House of Pain morphs from voyeuristic suspense into a spellbinding wrong man nightmare.

The landfill didn't smell hazardous. There was a musty dampness in the air as if this were a subterranean basement sealed for years, and faintly within it, a smell of gasoline. I stopped to check behind me and saw with surprise that it looked as if I were actually outside. Colossal screens mounted along the scaffolding gave the impression of the wide open sky. I could discern ghostly clouds painted there, though at least twenty feet above, the screens cut out to the empty black soundstage. The effect was dizzying, seemed to suggest some truth about the inherently inflexible nature of human perception. If only you looked a little further, McCarthy, you'd see it all gave way to . . . nothing.

I hadn't noticed it before, but down along the section where I'd entered was a small gravel parking lot fringed with bushes, there sat one car. I realized it was Leigh's boxy blue Chevy Citation, straight from the 1980's. It looked as if it were waiting for her to come back.

Maybe she never had. Maybe Leigh had never left this warehouse or El Esplanade. I couldn't recall if I'd heard the name ever appearing in another film.

I turned, squinting far ahead at the indistinct smudge on the hill, realizing as I stumbled that way, it was the overturned school bus, the very one Leigh gets trapped inside. In the final minutes in the House of Pain, she's forced in there by thugs, blindfolded and bound. Though she struggles courageously, determined to untie her hands using a metal spike jutting out of a derelict seat, the question of her fate is left unanswered. As she whimpers and flails, the movie fades to black, though her cries can be heard throughout the end credits, barely drowned by the Beastie Boys song "Posse in Effect."

The incline was surprisingly steep, and I began to trip and slide in the plastic bags, blown-out tires, mattresses and cracked TV's. I'd gone a few yards when I realized not just that the incline was growing even more vertical, but that my movement was dislodging the trash beneath me. I could feel it shifting, and within minutes the entire mountain was surrounding me.

I froze but found myself falling backward, nearly submerged in an avalanche of rusted cans and garbage bags. I scrambled upright, untangling myself from a biohazard suit, surfing toward the perimeter of the set as the entire hill continued to loosen, including that bus. It was impossible to get up there. I groped my way to the edge of the sky, lifted the fabric, and scrambled through the scaffolding as the landfill continued to crash behind me. I'd had enough of House of Pain.

I'll be damned if I was going to die buried alive in Esquivel's trash. I lurched to my feet and took off down the dark corridor. Far ahead, at the very end, what looked to be a mile away, was an opening with a pale red light. I hoped it was the way out.

107

Every now and then I stopped to listen, hearing only the wind howling across the roof high overhead. I had to get out of here. The longer I walked, the more a distant red light remained, persistently far-off. I couldn't help but wonder if I was hallucinating, or if this warehouse's concrete floor was somehow a treadmill and I was running in place. At one point I smelled, rather bizarrely, lake water. It was strong, intermixed with the scents of seaweed and sand. It had to be another film set, built behind the scaffolding rising up to my left, but it was too high to see anything.

I could see the red light getting closer and felt a nerve racking curiosity about what it was.

I stepped around the corner.

It was the greenhouse from Silence Waits for Me.

What was it Anderson had said? "If there was one setting perfectly evoked the treacherous mind of a psychopath, it isn't the Bates Motel, but rather the Esquivel family greenhouse, with its domes of moldy glass and corroded iron, tropical plants growing inside like insidious thoughts run amok. The frail sand pathway snaking through the foliage like the last vestige of humanity shrinking out of sight."

The greenhouse was a dome roof, rectangular structure, built out of glass panes and pale green oxidized iron, the architecture mimicking the Royal Greenhouses in Brussels. It sat in serene seclusion in a dense medieval forest of Douglas firs. The intense red light was emanating from inside the greenhouse. Then I remembered, of course, from the movie.

It was the crimson plant lights.

I waited to be sure I was alone and stepped out onto the lawn, the silvered grass crunching under my boots. I stared down at it, unsettled because it looked so real, bathed in a morning dew. I bent down to touch it. It was plastic, the dew actually showed the shiny iridescent paint sprayed across every blade.

I reached the stone path, following it to the greenhouse's single steel door, the back door, if I remembered correctly. The glass had become pressed against the panes like the hands and faces of a trapped crowd, frantic to get out. I grabbed the iron doorknob, noticing it was in the form of a sinister looking letter *E* for Esquivel, and heaved it opened.

108

A boiling blast of humidity hit my face. It had to be at least ninety-eight degrees inside.

A pathway of immaculate white sand led away from the door, though, within a few feet, the dark knots of plants mushrooming from every direction buried it from view. Suspended overhead were green iron barrels lit upon with row upon row of cherry-red and blue lights, giving the greenhouse the look of a gigantic oven set on broil.

In Silence Waits for Me, the greenhouse had a longtime deaf-mute gardener, Elmer, the prime suspect in the Red Forest killings, later found to be innocent, lovingly tended these plants.

I looked around and realized that someone had come here regularly to tend these plants. They looked exactly like they did in the film. I grabbed a giant black leaf beside my shoulder, rubbing the surface to make sure it was real. It was.

Silence Waits for Me, I recalled had been shot in 1992. The bulbs of these plant lights wouldn't have lasted twenty years.

Someone must come here regularly to tend these plants.

A chill inched down my spine, but I stepped resolutely inside here, either, roasted alive by these lights. But even when I wedged the rubber door stopper found buried in the sand just inside, the heavy iron door kept thudding determinedly closed right behind me, so I gave up, letting it slam. I checked to make sure it would still open, then headed down the path, shoving aside the foliage.

It was like the amazon. Root stalks as solid and twisted as water pipes laden with white tubular flowers, trees at least eight feet tall, limbs barbed with thistle, black star-shaped blooms, buds with tiny red berries, all of it clutched to my face and arms like swarming orphans desperate for a handout, for human contact. Their aromas were overpowering and pungent, sweet as honeysuckle, though as soon as I inhaled them they seemed to turn earthen and foul. Given that I was wearing three layers of Brad Jackson's wool clothing suitable for a brutal winter in Vermont, I was already sweating profusely. But I did my best to ignore the heat, jostling past a cluster of verdant trees laden with drooling yellow blossoms as big as my hands.

They collided with my face, getting into my nose and mouth, the pollen tart and acidic. I spit, left with an acrid aftertaste. Within a few yards, I saw with relief something I recognized; the koi pond.

The pond was a perfect circle made of stones, filled to the brim with black water. In Silence Waits for Me, giant Amazonian lily pads floated across the surface. And when Special Agent Fox nearly drowned in there, held underwater by the killer, he clawed at then for dear life, but they only dissolved delicately in his hands.

Now the pool was devoid of plants, the black water so slick and smooth it looked to be made of plastic, though as I shoved my way past the foliage to reach the stone perimeter, I saw perfectly well it was real. I dipped my finger in to make sure. Lazy circular ripples marred the reflection of the red lights and the hulking glass and iron dome overhead.

I assumed there'd be no koi left, not twenty years after the film was shot. But no, in the murky water, I glimpsed a white and orange streak through the murk. As quickly as it appeared, it vanished.

Someone must come here regularly to feed the fish.

In the film, Elmer notoriously fed them Cracker Jacks from a box he kept in the front pocket of his filthy dirt-streaked Levi's overalls.

Maybe he still did.

Maybe the poor man worked in here, lived in here.

The thought made me turn, my eyes scanning the twisted leaves for some sign of the old gardener, his black face wrinkled and glistening, the bright gold tooth in his smile. The greenhouse his holy sanctuary, the one place in the world he doesn't have to be afraid.

I took a moment to recalibrate my mind, to assure myself that I was alone and whatever I found in here was a narrative plucked from Esquivel's mind. I was not and never had been in Silence Waits for Me. Although as I noted this, I realized the very fact that I needed to reassure myself of such a thing was horrifying in itself.

I wiped the sweat off my face and headed around the pond's perimeter, staring into the red-soaked greenery.

Within minutes, I found what I was looking for Elmer's tool shed. An old wooden door was ajar, the same crooked sign nailed to the outside, **Keep Out**. I gently pushed it open.

Elmer wasn't home.

It was no bigger than a walk-in closet, filled with meticulously organized shelving, cubbyholes housing envelopes of seeds, plastic trays, terra-cotta pots, bags of mulch and fertilizer. Directly in front of me, facing the greenhouse's glass walls, too dirty to see through, sat a desk and tall stool, where Elmer could always be found smiling his cigars, reading his comic books, and listening to the Temptations.

Atop the desk beside a faded magazine, was an ashtray with a half smoked cigar in it. I stepped inside to pick it up. It smelled recent.

Next to the desk on the wall was an old bulletin board, jumbled with poorly written directions for tending the soil and plants, a tattered postcard of colored shacks standing on stilts along the edge of a dark bay. I tugged it free and checked the reverse side. There was no address, only four scribbled words on the back.

Someday soon you'll come.

I put it back, turning. Various gardening tools had been mounted along the walls using old spikes, hand sickles, Austrian scythes, pruning saws, axes of all different sizes. I moved over to inspect them, the same way Special Agent Fox had inspected them.

In Silence Waits for Me, the eleven teenage bodies of the Red forest killings had been mutilated in ways mimicking accidents that occurred at an old paper mill, chemical burns, boiler explosions, industrial roller entrapment. But there was another constant: Each victim was a high-school student killed by a stab through the left ventricle of the heart. Using a pair of hedge shears, the pointed blades exactly nine and a half inches long.

Special Agent Fox sneaks in here in the dead of night to examine Elmer's gardening tools, every saw, snips, and clippers trying to find a blade with that exact measurement. He comes up empty-handed. Because the hedge shears weren't hidden in the work shed, as he'd suspected.

Now where the hell are they?

My eyes were stinging, and I was drenched in sweat, getting steamed alive in here like a lobster. The heat was so overpowering I could hardly think, hardly remember that pivotal scene at the end, when Elmer accidentally finds the shears buried somewhere in here, in one of his beloved flower beds.

I remembered they were encrusted in blood and the look on the poor man's face when he came across them planting a new set of seeds, seeds with a bizarre name. His look was of such horror.

Real horror?

Was it my imagination or was it actually getting hotter in here?

I shrugged off my backpack, yanked off my coat and sweater, leaving them on the desk. I wrenched a garden hoe off the wall and exited the shed, slipping around the Koi pond.

Elmer was the only person in the movie to know the truth about the murders.

I really needed to get my hands on those shears.

I stepped into the flower bed, traipsing through plants growing so thickly I couldn't see the ground.

I bent down noticing a white handwritten sign stuck into the dirt.

EYE-PRICKLES, it read.

I stepped forward a few feet, spotting another sign.

DEATH-CHERRIES.

There was countless similar sigh arranged under the leaves.

BLUE ROCKET. TONGUE TACKS. SCORCER'S VIOLET. PSYCHO PLANT EXTRACT.

That one sounded familiar. Pushing up my sleeves, I raked the garden hoe through the dirt and immediately felt something hard in the loose soil. I bent down, seeing something shiny.

It was a brass compass, the glass face cracked.

It had belonged to Elmer. The compass was a source of ridicule throughout the movie. The whole town mocked the way he constantly pulled it out of his overalls, closely inspection it as if to make sure he was still on the course of his very important journey around the world, the joke being that the poor man had been born in Red Forest and had never set foot outside the tiny town.

I pocketed the compass and shoved the Garden hoe deeper into the dirt, the blade catching on something else.

I crouched down to inspect it. It was a half-decomposed cardboard box, sodden and limp, though I could make out the letters on the front.

Cracker-Jack.

I threw it aside, ignoring the unease flooding through me, doggedly digging into the soil again. And I felt something else there, something bulky. I bent down to see it.

Something buried deep in the dirt.

Fighting a wave of nausea, it had to be the oppressive heat, the red lights making every plant and flower, even my own hands, look blood-soaked, I stabbed the hoe directly downward. It caught in some roots. Crouching, I brutally tore out some of the plants, leaves, and limbs shuddering in my face in protest.

I could feel it in my hands, something is hidden here, something hard.

Something human sized. *Elmer?*

It made no sense. At the end of the movie, Elmer was in the clear, safe. He was keeping the killer's secret, and if anyone could keep a secret it was a mute man. Then what the hell was buried here? Why were his compass and box of Cracker Jack, the two items the gardener was famously never without, hidden here? Had the killer decided to finish him off? Had Esquivel?

Had Esquivel been murdering innocent people here for sacrifice? Offerings?

As my mind spun suddenly I was aware of, somewhere far away. A dull thud. It sounded like a door banging closed. I scrambled to my feet. I could hear faint footsteps of more than one person, two, maybe three. The echoed through the warehouse, moving quickly.

I was no longer alone. I tried to ignore this reality for a few seconds, frantically digging through the flower bed with my bare hands.

I just needed one glimpse of what was here. I uprooted plants, throwing them aside, tunneling through the soil, my fingers feeling something.

It felt like denim. Elmer's overalls.

I fumbled to get the camera out of my pocket but realized I'd left back in my coat on the desk. To excavate whatever, it was buried here would require clearing away the entire flower bed.

I paused listening.

Those footsteps were getting louder. They had to know I was here. I'd have to come back.

I stepped out of the foliage, racing back around the pond to the work shed. I grabbed my coat, pulled it on, throwing the backpack over my shoulder. I fought my way through the plants to reach the back door.

109

I opened it a crack, staring out at the deserted lawn. I darted out, breathing in the freezing air, relieved to be out of the gory crimson light, the tropical heat, barreling into the crisp darkness of the fresh night breeze.

I froze. The entire building was echoing with footsteps, seemingly coming down the same passage where I'd entered Silence Waits for Me.

I took off in the opposite direction, moving down a stone path out of the grounds straight into a vast desolate beach of white sand dunes and bristling sea grass. In the distance, an angular beach house rose high in the sky on stilts.

It was the house from, A Small Evil.

I headed across the sand toward the house and beyond it, the moonlit lake. My sense was this set would take me back to the Jackson's, and hopefully the exit out of here.

Suddenly, far ahead, a dark figure with a flashlight streaked over the dunes, heading straight for me.

I whipped around, stumbling back out, careening through the next opening I could find, racing down the middle of a deserted street.

It was the Main Street of a small town, a ghost town, that I didn't recognize, though I could see fairly well, due to the blinking red and green Christmas lights that were strewn up over the road.

Dark storefronts slipped past.

SILVER DOLLAR SALOON.

SUNSHINE GROCERY.

PASTIME GENTLEMAN'S CLUB, MEMBERS ONLY.

Sprinting footsteps ricocheted behind me. I leaped up onto the sidewalk to the dream-a-lot movie house, heaved the door open, and sprinted past candy and soda counters and down a narrow hall, theaters advertising Distortion at eleven-thirty, Chasing the Red at twelve.

I yanked open the first door and it dumped me, thank Christ, back into the warehouse and smacks onto something hard, a concrete wall. I ran along it, looking behind, and saw the flashlight, there were bars of scaffolding and I began to climb. I'd gone ten, twelve feet when I reached a wooden platform. I scrambled up onto it.

"See anything?" I heard a male say below.

"He headed the other way."

I waited several minutes, and, when the lights were farther off, cautiously stood up. The platform was sturdy, the rigging supporting tungsten lights pointing downward onto some kind of stone interior. A pillar stood about four feet across from me with a banner reading, I could barely make out the words, stir the waters. It was Father John's church from Black Stained Windows. Just beneath me along the wall were black stained windows, a three-inch ledge. I bent down, sliding down onto it, and with a silent Hail Mary, leaped across the divide, intending to grab the pillar and slide down.

I missed. I reached out, seizing some sort of mounted wood plaque to break my fall. It wrenched loose, tiles clattering around me as I crashed to the floor, the plaque skidding across the stones.

Shit! I scrambled to my feet, seeing a flashlight slipping down the arched passageway in front of me, illuminating a vaulted ceiling, alcoves with statues. I hurried away from it down the rows of pews, heading to the back portal, spotting the confessional in the back corner. The simple sight of it made my stomach plunge, but I unlatched the ornate door, it emitted a faint moan and climbed inside.

It was tight with my backpack on, pitch black.

I crouched down to the floor, waiting.

Within seconds, I heard someone enter the church and stop, no doubt inspecting the smashed hymn board I'd pried off the wall.

I waited, my heart pounding, noticing a stench. Vomit? Urine? The footsteps resumed, the flashlight edging closer, illuminating the confessional door, which I could see was a carved wood screen of vines and flowers. I recognized the pattern and could hardly believe now I was staring out of it with dread, exactly as Father John had gazed out, albeit for somewhat different reasons.

The movie's opening scene took place right in here when John was conducting his first confessional duties. He was fresh out of seminary and believed, with the arrogant optimism of the young and inexperienced, that he would lead the depraved to the righteous path. After waiting for more than an hour without a single penitent sinner showing up, a mysterious figure at last enters the other side in a rush, sitting down on the seat with an ominous thud.

The memory made me inadvertently crane my neck to inspect that confessional window only a few inches above my head, the dark latticed smoke screen ensuring total anonymity.

This enigmatic stranger, as the priest soon realizes, knows John's dark secret, that he put his three-year-old daughter on a south side rooftop, allowing her to teeter on the edge while chasing the roosting pigeons, and then, losing her balance, and fall to her death on a sidewalk below, all the while, John watched from a crack in the window and did nothing. John had his reasons, of course, he believed his little girl to be the devil incarnate. But as for who was watching him that afternoon, who this mysterious person was poised behind the screen, someone who vows in a knowing whisper to tear him apart and make him renounce God, it takes John the whole film to figure it out, the identity of the person even more terrifying than his secret.

I realized the footsteps sounded as if they were retreating down some other passage, the faint light now gone. I rose a few inches, sitting on the wooden seat just behind me, listening. I appeared to be alone. Had it been this side of the box Father John had been sitting on or the other? Was I on the good guy's side or the side of evil? Where was that damn smell coming from? I leaned forward, staring through the screen, the latticed openings in the form of minute crosses.

I froze in horror. Someone was there.

There was a person sitting on the other side.

I hardly believed my eyes, yet hearing the breathing, the shifting of heavy fabric, and then, as if aware that he was now being observed, he slowly turned to face me.

I barely could make out a face shadowed by a dark hood. The next few moments happened so fast, I was hardly aware of what I did: I blasted out of the box, passing the entrance to John's office and through a door, which if I remember correctly led into an underground crypt.

It was too dark to see. I reached out, waiting for the feel of cold stones, then realized I'd been emptied back into the soundstage.

I heard pounding, a chorus of neon lights moaning above. The lights were coming on. Suddenly I was drenched in bright light, half blinded. I stumbled forward, feeling a door handle, pulled it, wheeling out into another freezing room.

But it wasn't a room.

Real leaves crunched under my feet. The real wind rushed my face, and looking up, I swore that was a real moon over my head.

110

I didn't let myself believe it, that I'd actually escaped that soundstage. But after running a few yards, I looked back and saw the warehouse sitting quietly in the woods behind me. It looked innocuous, so pale and blank-faced, no hint of the levels of hell that lay inside.

I was back in the cold, hard reality, thank Christ. I ran back down the hill, heading toward the pond. The men must not have realized I'd escaped because no one was running after me anymore. Who the hell were they? And what had I seen on the other side of that confessional?

I checked my watch, forgetting it was broken: 7:55.

I fumbled in my pockets, taking a quick inventory of what I had. The child's blood-soaked shirt and Elmer's compass. They were there; so was my pocket knife, but my camera was gone. It had been deep inside the pocket but must have fallen out when I'd yanked my coat back on. Berating myself for such sloppiness, fighting the urge to go back for it, I broke into a sprint, the wind hissing punitively in my ears, the moon lighting the way.

A dog barked. It sounded like one of the hounds that had chased me but frustrated now, tied up, though it was probably just a matter of time until the animal was set loose again.

I'd come up to the pond. I crept to the water's edge, staring through the foliage to its shimmering surface. There was still no sign of Cooper, Elizabeth, or the canoe. Cooper and Elizabeth, I realized with amazement those names seemed to come at me from far away, deep in my past. How long had I been in that soundstage? Years? Was it some sort of wormhole, a dimension away from time? I hadn't thought about them, not their well-being or the mystery of where they'd gone. I hadn't been aware of anything except Esquivel. Those sets were narcotics, dominating my head so entirely there'd been no space for any other thought.

They must have gone for help. They were paddling back the way we'd come, safe. I needed to believe this so I wouldn't give up on Gabriela so easily. Neither would Elizabeth. They must both be here somewhere, then, wandering, running in desperate circles.

Squinting out at the opposite shoreline, I spotted another one of the flashlights moving over the crest. The person seemed to be hurrying down the path to the wooden dock. Something was running through the grass. It had to be one of the dogs.

I stepped away from the lake's perimeter, breaking into a jog, heading east. I could gage my direction from what I knew of the lake's position. East was the shortest distance to the property's perimeter and the closest public road, County Road 12. It was my best bet for help. My priorities had changed. Lives might be at stake now, if Elizabeth and Cooper were trapped somewhere inside here, possibly hurt, or worse.

Considering this as I ran, I'd unconsciously taken Elmer's compass from my pocket, clasping it as if it were a prized possession, the last hope. I saw in surprise that though the glass face was cracked, the needle was shakily pointing due north.

I turned in a circle to check its bearings. They were spot-on. *The thing actually worked.*

I raced on, every now and then checking the compass to make sure I was on course, *just as old Elmer had checked it*, much to the entertainment of the entire town.

When in the hell was I going to have the chance to go back to that greenhouse? I'd given up too soon. Elmer, if he was actually buried there, would remain an entombed secret. My mind spinning, I forced myself to keep moving. The forest seemed to parade past in a cruel loop, like the synthetic backdrop in an old movie where the character's chat and drive but never look at the road. Were these real trees? Every trunk of every spruce was elongated and bare, identical to the others.

And then, staring off to my left, I saw it again, the warehouse.

I froze, horrified.

I'd run in a complete circle.

Elmer's compass had been playing tricks on me, deliberately leading me astray. But no, taking a few steps toward the hulking structure, I realized this one was cylindrical, a silo, the exterior painted yellow. I turned my back to it, breaking into a sprint.

Within fifteen minutes, I'd reached a paved road. It had to be the lower section of El Esplanade's driveway, which meant I was going in the right direction. Reassured, I veered away from it, keeping under the cover of forest but following its general direction. Within minutes, I could discern for ahead the dark blur of the military fence.

I sprinted towards it, flooded with relief. There were no discernible electrical wires. I took a chance, running my hands along the rusted links, waiting for a shock.

I felt nothing.

I grabbed the chain link and began to climb. I was six feet off the ground when I noticed, far off to my right, two roofs protruding through the foliage, each with a blackened spike.

El Esplanade gatehouses.

I recognized them because I'd driven up here years ago. I'd climbed out of my car and took a snapshot of the entrance, so desperate to get inside here. Now so desperate to get out. I recalled what the Tarantula had told us, how he'd taken that underground tunnel, which linked the mansion to a gatehouse, in order to help the Nathaniel Hills townspeople, enter the property.

It meant, if the Tarantula had been telling the truth, access to that maze of tunnels underneath the property was right there, yards away, so close. I could see it with my own eyes.

After a split second's hesitation, I was clambering back down the fence and back into El Esplanade, my mind screaming in protest. I leaped into the overgrown grass, moving along the fence, heading straight for those two cottages flanking the wrought-iron gate.

The first one had no entrance. The second had a narrow black door, a window at the top. There was no discernible light inside, no evident camera, the paint was flaking, the glass too filthy to see through. I needed one quick look at the entrance to those tunnels, to substantiate Paulino's story, *and then I'd get the hell out of here.*

It was locked, so I smashed the window with a rock, unlocked it, and slipped inside. It was a minuscule room, with a window overlooking the approach to the gate, a desk with an old computer, an office chair covered with dust. The floor was bare, except for a small black carpet in the corner.

I walked over to it and pulled back the rug.

There it was; a small wooden hatch. I slid aside the metal bars, grabbed the rings, and heaved it open, staring into the raw black hole. Concrete stairs, barely a foot wide, led sharply downward. I moved down a few, crouching to take a look.

The tunnel extending in front of me was pitch black. Only a few feet of brick walls were visible before cutting out onto a darkness so absolute it looked as if this part of the world had been left unfinished, a raw edge of the earth, which gave way not just to simple darkness, but to outer space.

Staring into it, my head urged me to get the hell out now, close the hatch, climb back over that fence while I still had the chance.

But what did I have on Esquivel? What did I actually know?

I tried to mentally grab hold of a few hard facts to stay afloat. I had in my pocket a few items, which might incriminate the man, but could very well amount to nothing as far as the law was concerned. I had stories, eyewitness accounts, testimonies, the truth that Gabriela was dead. But was it enough to bury him? I'd hardly pierced Esquivel, my great white whale. He could go on with his black magic, his love horrors. Gabriela was dead, so there was no need for an exchange, but had he stopped? What had I seen with my own eyes?

As I considered this, the decaying brick walls of the tunnel seemed to constrict imperceptibly around me. Just what, exactly, was I escaping unscathed from? Going back to?

An empty apartment. No one would be waiting for me when I made it back home. Life would go on as before. I'd go on as before. Just to think of it was suddenly unbearable.

What in the hell was I waiting for? When the truth of your life is right in front of you? It's here, right now, beyond the pitch darkness. Even if I couldn't see it now, it was somewhere in front of me.

Do I dare? I took three more steps down. The air was frigid, a frigid cold that ate at my bones. I yanked off my backpack, rummaged in the pocket for my flashlight, tried turning it on, but it still didn't work. I removed a Ziploc bag containing a box of matches, heaved my backpack on, and lit a match. The tiny orange flame trembled as I held it out in front of me.

I almost laughed out loud. The dark was shoved back just a few inches. The redbrick walls were crumbling, the ceiling low, thick with mold. It looked like a shriveled artery to hell. I checked my watch 7:58. I was making incredible time.

I moved back up, grabbing the hatch. I pulled it closed over my head with an irrevocable thud. *Had I just sealed myself inside my own coffin?*

111

The match abruptly blew out. I lit another and began to walk. When that one extinguished, I slipped on through the darkness as quickly as I could. There were a hundred matches in the box. I had to ration them. I remembered the Tarantula mentioning the distance between the gatehouse and the mansion was two miles. If I walked four miles an hour, within fifteen minutes I'd be halfway there. I waited for my eyes to adjust, but after a time I realized the swirling black liquid I was staring into were my eyes adjusting.

My footsteps became a metronome for my breathing. Beyond that, my hiking boots crunching down the grimy floor. There were no other sounds, just a marked pressure of being sealed in, as if this passage were cutting under a body of water.

When I couldn't stand the dark any longer, when I actually began to feel confused as to whether or not I was actually moving, I stopped and lit another match.

The constricted corridor had shrunken around me, and was now less than four feet wide, extending identically in both directions. I realized that seeing the fragile light was infinitely more disturbing than just plunging forward in the total darkness. I might as well put my head all the way under. Just don't stop swimming. When that light burned out, I dropped the match and kept on going, my right hand running along the crumbling bricks as a guide. It kept me tethered to the world, to reality, because this darkness was so total it became physical, a thick black curtain. It turned me upside down, made me wonder if I was actually submerged in black water and I'd forgotten which was the way to air and light. Gravity seemed to be feeble down here.

I tripped on something bulky, instantly gripped with an irrational fear. Was it a body, a severed limb? I kicked a second time. It sounded like a bed sheet.

A red piece of silk lay on the ground, covered in dust.

I picked it up. It was a woman's dress, cranberry red, old-fashioned with long sleeves and a black plastic belt. Nearly all of the front buttons were missing. I studied the neck and glimpsed the pale purple label of Esquivel's longtime female tailor, Carmona, seconds before the match went out.

I unzipped my backpack, stuffed the dress inside, zipped it back up, and kept going. After a time, I worried that I'd accidentally turned around and was blindly heading back to the gatehouse, but I didn't stop.

It was just disorientation, the dark victimization of the mind. How flimsy was a single person's authority, his confidence about his place in the world? Give him fifteen minutes of this, even Einstein would start to doubt the laws of the physical world, who he was, where he was if he were alive or dead.

To my horror, I kicked something else. It scuttled noisily across the floor, something hard. It sounded like a piece of wood.

No. It was a bone. I lit another match.

It was a woman's black leather pump with a square scuffed heel, covered in dust. I checked my watch without thinking: 7:58.

I stood up again, holding the match out in front of me.

The view was a carbon copy of the one from before, a widened brick corridor disappearing infinitely in both directions.

It looked like I hadn't moved.

I continued on, trying to remain calm. *Why was the dress down here? Had a woman tried to escape?* Very much like the boy's blood-soaked plaid shirt in my pocket, the dress looked like the vestiges of violence. To die here, alone and cold, to never be found, never be loved again. Kim would think I'd abandoned her. I tried to wrench my mind away from these thoughts, turn my attention to something cheerful, but this place, so black and cold, extinguished levity within seconds.

I stepped on something.

Pebbles.

I stopped, so many of them, hard round, rolling underneath my boots. *Children's teeth? Molars? Sprinkled here like crumbs?*

I fumbled with another match, lighting it.

They weren't teeth, but the red round plastic buttons of the dress. I bent down to inspect them. A few feet away, lying along the wall, was the other black shoe. I grabbed a handful of the buttons, shoved them into Brad's overcoat pocket, and stood up again.

It was exactly the same view, a black tunnel extending in front of me and behind me, eternal. I was on a treadmill, running in place. I was trapped in a fourth dimension, purgatory, where there was no time or progression, only inert floating.

The match, I realized, was burning my fingers.

I let go of it, lurched forward, faster now. I could feel my mind faltering as if on a tightrope, threatening to lose its balance.

I lit another match and saw with relief only a few yards ahead, a break in the tunnel. In my haste to get there, the match blew out. I hurried. When I felt the wall open up to my right, I lit another match.

I was in a small circular alcove, gaping mouths of more tunnels fanning out, seemingly in all directions. I slipped past them, seeing faint words scrawled above each opening in the crude white paint.

GATEHOUSE. MANSION. LAKE. STABLES. WORKSHOP. LOOKOUT. TROPHY. PINCOYA NEGRO. CEMETERY. MRS. PEABODY'S. LABORATORY. THE Z. CROSSROADS.

I remembered the Tarantula had mentioned there existed, at this central point, other secret passageways, which led to other hidden parts of the estate. I lit another match, holding it up to the word painted on the wood right in front of me. *Crossroads.*

It's what the Tarantula had called the clearing where he'd taken Gabriela.

Crudely nailed planks, once blocking the passage, had been hacked away with an ax. It was what Paulino had done for the townspeople. Only bits of splintered wood and twisted nails had been left, some strewn on the ground.

This corridor was cruder than the others, barely three feet wide, and liked as if it cut straight through granite, the walls slick from water seeping in from somewhere. Taking a step down it, I could see more words had been scrawled in the rocks in the same white paint. Further down, there were drawings of stick figures with protruding noses and screaming mouths.

I stepped forward to read some of it. ***If ye go further leave all your love here on the floor. Warning: ye will leave this path neither animal, vegetable, or mineral. Say goodbye to ye lamb. May the Lord help y***

The match flickered out.

I lit another and forced myself to take one more step inside, holding the flame out. It swiftly extinguished, a subzero wind blasting my face, swelled and quickly dispersed. Then, I heard sizzling in my ears, so deafening and close, I lurched backward, stumbled on the uneven floor back into the alcove, dropping the box of matches.

Shit. My heart pounding, I knelt down, groping for it along the floor. It had disappeared.

Something was with me here, standing behind me, toying with me. Trying not to panic, I wheeled around unsteadily, getting down on my hands and knees, fumbling got the matches in the dirt.

Calm down, McCarthy. The matches have to be here somewhere.

The side of my left hand hit something. *Matches*. I grabbed them. But somehow, impossibly, the box had been tossed far behind me, wedges against the opposite wall between two passageways. *It was like the leviathan's shadow. It had a mind of its own*.

I got to my feet, ignoring that thought, lit a match, and stepped back to the opening.

Crossroads. The tunnel twisted sharply left and out of sight. I took another step down the passage, the flame burning calmly now. Just for the hell of it, I reached into my pocket and removed the compass, curious to see what direction I'd be heading.

I could only stare down at it, incredulous.

The red needle wouldn't stop spinning, around and around. It was too much for my mind to calculate, so I dropped it back into my coat pocket and, trying to forget I'd ever looked at the thing, I took off down the corridor.

112

I didn't know how long I walked.

I had a distinct feeling I wasn't alone.

It was a bone-chilling understanding that I was in close proximity to something alive and only seconds from running headlong into it. Yet when I held the flickering flame in front of me, expecting to see a face, animal eyes, there was only darkness in every direction.

The Tarantula's insidious voice began to worm its way into my head, growing louder with every step, like that day at The Broken Door, he'd been narrating not his own secret, but his future, this walk, *my walk. I can still remember the sound of her bare feet, how soft and slender they were, paddling along the filthy ground next to mine.*

Was that what I was hearing, what I sensed beside me? Gabriela?

I kept walking, listening, but there were only my own boots, trudging on. After a time, the Tarantula's voice faded and my mind became blank, a chalkboard, smeared with half-erased thoughts.

Gabriela had come this way.

And Esquivel. He walked this, every time he had a new child to try and barter with Satan. Anything to save his daughter.

I could discern a strong smell of metal mixed with the heavy moisture and mud. At one point, I heard a distant rumbling, as if, overhead, animals were thundering in a stampede across the property, fleeing in terror.

I touched the slippery rocks, warm water trickling through my fingers. The walls felt as if they were vibrating. Pebbles came loose from the ceiling, rattling to the ground. But then the noise was gone, the tunnel as silent as before, and I was left wondering if my anxiety, needing some type of outlet, had I conjured the whole thing up.

I kept going, noticing that my brain felt loose inside my skull as if it were melting. I noted with a stab of horror that I was sweating like I was back inside that greenhouse, as if I'd never escaped, never gotten out from under the blood-splattered lights. Yet I shivered riddled with chills, the feeble flame I was holding revealing what I already knew: The black tunnel unspooled in front of me, on and on.

The moment I accepted it, understood I could be in grave danger wandering down here, I'd reached the end. A few feet ahead, a bent and rusted metal ladder extended to the ceiling.

I paused, listening, hearing nothing but the howls of powerful wind. I grabbed the rungs and climbed up, my arms and legs oddly weakened feeling like they were filled with sand. When I reached the top, I could feel another wooden hatch above me, seemingly identical to the one I'd entered at the gatehouse. I slipped back the rails, shoved my shoulder against it, and opened the hatch.

I was in a dense forest of birch trees, the entire world in razor focus. I could make out every leaf and branch, rock and weed bathed in the green underground in blackness, like my eyes, ecstatic to be granted one last chance to see, they're doing their best.

I climbed out.

113

I took off down a rutted dirt path, noticing, tied to an overhanging branch, a red string dancing in the wind. A few yards ahead, I saw a bridge. *The Devil's bridge.*

Just thinking about it sucked the breath from my lungs.

There was no one here. I was all alone. The wind was howling furiously, shoving the coattails of my coat so far out, it felt like a crowd of groupies were grasping at it.

The bridge was arched, made of dark gray stone. The construction looked meticulous as if every piece had been laid by a master's hand, a delicate cured structure up and over a deep ravine, where I saw, as I stepped closer, a river was raging, icy and black. I noticed the water didn't flow freely but dammed around the rocks, then rolled over them in lumps like tar. Yet the sound of an ordinary river surged in my ears.

Or was that the wind?

The bridge was long, ending in another grove of trees.

Gabriela ran the entire length of this bridge.

She was the first human to cross it.

I stepped onto the first laid stones. I had nothing to fear. The curse was finished. The devil had what he wanted. Gabriela. Yet I found myself whipping around to stare back into those skeletal trees to make sure no one was there, that Kim hadn't somehow followed me, believing I'd been kidnapped by trolls.

When I was halfway across. I was hit by a rush of vertigo. It was as if the bridge had been rising imperceptibly under my feet, because I could see great distances, high over the branches of an immense forest, stretching out for miles, churning in the wind like a mad sea. A roof with black spikes protruded from the treetops, so far away.

A nauseating dizziness suddenly overtook me, and I had to turn away, staring ahead to the bridge's end.

Something was there.

I felt myself go numb. It was only half human. What the other half was, I didn't know. It was tall, seven or eight feet, with gaunt arms and a round, wide face so coarse it looked like bark. I could see its eyes, round red eyes, like two fire holes in the dirt, a mouth of thorns.

I had to be hallucinating. Or I was asleep, in a coma. *Dead.*

What in the hell was happening to me? How flimsy sanity was.

I waited for my eyes to tell me it was an illusion, a hoax of the birch trees and the shadow falling in dark piles across the bridge as if they'd been severed from the objects that head created them. I reached for my pocket knife, realizing I was holding Elmer's compass.

How had it snuck into my hand again? The red needle had stopped spinning and was now pointing straight ahead.

The wind launched into another shrieking rage. I blinked, staring back to the end of the bridge and saw in disbelief that, *that thing* wasn't a trick of my eyes. It was still there, yet beginning to slink away, its bony limbs gyrating as if caught in some invisible eddy before vanishing into the trees.

Get off this bridge, a voice screamed in my head. I tore down the incline, slipping on the leaves plastering the stones, stumbling blindly off, barreling down a dirt path, which led me to a circular clearing.

It was deserted.

That strange vision, whatever it was, had to be hiding somewhere. *It was here they performed the rituals, where Esquivel became one of them.* I stepped forward, the movement making me so off balance I fell to the ground, staring up at the night sky, a sky so smooth it looked like black liquid had been poured between the trees. *What was happening to me?* My limbs were melting.

I willed myself to sit up straight. I wasn't sitting in the ordinary dirt, but fine black powder glittering with minerals, a few feet away, a charred log. I reached for it, astounded that even though it looked like the ordinary remnants of a bonfire, it was as heavy as iron, I couldn't lift it.

A ripped piece of white fabric caught underneath it. *It looked like it'd been torn off a child's blouse.*

I pulled it free, but a blast of wind whipped it out of my hand, sending it tripping like a stray white leaf across the clearing, vanishing into the trees. I stumbled running after it. When I saw where it had escaped to, what had just sucked it down, I could only stare in horror.

It was a trench filled with children's belongings.

I could make out every item lying there, some fifteen feet below tiny slippers and T-shirts, baby dolls and trains, undershirts and sneakers, all of it decomposed and sodden, some blackened as if burned.

It was here where Esquivel had thrown it all, the stolen objects, his attempts at an exchange. I could see it so vividly, a clarity that seared my eyes, his mania, his desperation, his willingness to let every corner of his soul go black so that his daughter might live.

I realized in shock that I was lying face down in the dirt.

How long have I been lying here? Hours? Days?

I lifted my head, which was throbbing, the dark ground and spindly trees swinging drunkenly away from me.

I wasn't alone.

Black robed figures were standing farther off, all around me, silent, hidden by the dark, as if they'd grown off of the shadows themselves. One suddenly streaked between the trees, wearing ha hooded black cloak, and then another beside him. And then another.

They were moving toward me. I scrambled to my feet.

"Stay where you are," I said. "Don't come any closer."

Was that me shouting? The voice sounded miles away. I fumbled for my pocket knife. It was gone.

It wasn't normal, how fast they moved, faces missing inside those black hoods, and them I felt hands gripping me as I was pulled backward.

There was the night sky and then suddenly a bag thrown over my head, smells of dirt and sweat and my herringbone coat.

No, no, it was my backpack, wrenching off of me, my arms pulled like they were trying to tear them off. I heard one man's terrible screaming. When the cries didn't stop and I could feel being hoisted into the air, I realized the screams were my own.

114

When I opened my eyes I was aware of nothing but a moth. It was small, pale white in the dim light. It appeared to be injured. One of its wings would fold over its back. Just a few inches from my nose, it was trying to climb a dark wall. It walked up the wood and kept falling off, trying again, falling. Ruffling its wings, it moved straight toward me. It had a furry head and brown legs, antennae working in apparent consternation. Sensing I was alive and large, it shifted directions, away from me and back to the wall.

It was cold. The air was subzero. My hands were numb.

Where in the hell was I? I was flying. The draft on my face was the wind pummeling me as I swerved to avoid a cluster of black clouds, atmospheric particles, ice and dust and sharp snowflakes spraying my face. A shrill note was ringing in my ears, a painful sound like a long needle stitching my brain.

I tried to sit up, but my head hit something.

I reached out. It was a smooth wooden wall.

I was inside something, a capsule spinning upside down, vibrating with velocity. But it was only a dream. I let go of my fear. I stretched out my legs, I was still wearing boots, and they encountered another wall on both sides. This enclosure I was inside, this spaceship, tight, yet a good foot or two larger than I was.

I opened my eyes, blinking but there was nothing to see, just like being suspended high above the Earth, between layers of atmosphere and outer space. The ringing in my ears went silent.

I had nothing to worry about because eventually, I'd wake up. That's what dreams were for, the waking, the floods of relief, shock that the mind could be so easily deceived, tangled sheets, sunlight streaming through a window. But then, *what was the hurry*? If the dream was born of my subconscious fears and desires, why not remain inside here a little while longer, soaring through space, to explore the dream, ransack it, find out its laws and parameters and what I'd been so afraid of.

My arms reached out around me, groping at the sides.

Aha, same as below and above. The coffin. I am in my coffin.

I opened my eyes. This wasn't a dream, I realized with sudden horror.

I couldn't wake up. I am awake.

The pale white moth, somehow it had made it onto the ceiling and it was crawling in circles, like it, too, were realizing it was trapped, that there is absolutely nowhere to go.

I began to shout, banging on the walls with my fists, hitting and kicking. It sounded like I was only calling into an empty hole in the earth. *Oh, God, no. This couldn't be right. This couldn't be real.*

Suddenly, I understood. I was meant to know where I was. To understand the fresh air in here would keep me alive for days, even weeks, as I struggled and fought the inevitable, so I could lucidly consider everything I was about to be ripped away from.

My mind froze as I tried to remember where I'd been only moments ago. I had the feeling I'd traveled for miles.

My arms felt as if they'd rowed across an ocean. Maybe I was dreaming, then, because dreams had so many layers, so many slippery departures and ends of ends I couldn't find footing or the slightest edge for my fingers to grasp hold of.

I reached out feeling the space around me.

Odd. The coffin appeared to have more than four sides. I maneuvered myself around on my back, using the heels of my boots to propel myself in a circle, counting the walls. But I had no endpoint, and when I'd counted twelve, I was certain I'd done more than one rotation.

I leaned down to my right foot, untied the laces around the metal hooks of my boot, and wrenched it off. I turned onto my stomach, shuffled myself close to a wall, feeling for a corner, leaving the shoe there as a marker, and the I slipped along the floor counterclockwise, my hands counting. One. Two. I spun around like a captive animal inspecting the boundaries of his cage. Three. Four. Five. Six.

I touched the boot again. Six sides, a hexagon.

Horror gripped me once again. It actually had a face and legs, a massive beast with the skin of black rubber, a bony spine, and it was perched right beside me, waiting for me to give up hope so it could feast upon me. I struggled and kicked, banging my head multiple times, screaming for help, *someone, anyone*, though after a while, when there was no answer, when that shrill noise had returned, ricocheting inside my skull like a lazy bullet without the strength to make its way out, I could only lie back down, wheezing, in my six-sided coffin.

I closed my eyes, letting my fear wash over me. I had to bathe in it, accept it, drink it down, let it cover me like sludge.

Then it became not so extraordinary, not so fearsome, *and so I could think.*

Images wafted through my head. I thought of Kim playing hopscotch across a checkered floor. El Esplanade came into view, dark and colossal, rising up on its overgrown hill, then I saw myself in an overcoat, running across a bridge, figures like a black fog overtaking me, blotting my out.

They must have dumped me here. Why couldn't I remember? My memories, they'd been hacked into, tinkered with, cut away, because there was nothing in my immediate past, nothing at all.

But if there was a way in, there was a way out.

I opened my eyes, realizing, in my wild flailing, I must have accidently brushed the moth off the ceiling. It seemed to have sought refuge in a corner, and once again, fluttering its wings, it was trying to climb the wall.

Taking care not to squash the thing, I managed to put my boot back on, then spun on my back like the rotating minute hand of a clock. Each foot that I moved, I pounded downward on the walls with my feet. On and on I went, the beating noises oddly muffled, so much despair flooding through me it felt as if it were splashing off my elbows and feet.

When I heard the fifth-panel crack, I struck it a second time. The wood buckled right in half, splintering, falling through. I looked down at my feet, my heart pounding.

A gray rectangular hole stared back at me.

I immediately twisted around, staring out the opening, my euphoria quickly sliding back into horror.

There was nowhere to go, only another wooden panel just two feet away.

It appeared to be another box.

I pulled myself through. There was incrementally more light and more space, though my old coffin took up most of it, sitting in the center. I couldn't sit up in here, either, the ceiling just a few inches higher. I crawled on my stomach along the outside perimeter and when I scrambled past the hole I'd just crawled out of, I knew I was right, I was inside yet another hexagonal box.

What the hell was this? A hell of coffins built like Russian Matryoshka dolls, one inside the next, on and on, toward infinity? Or was it a mind game built from an M. C. Escher print? A scene from a horror movie? I tried to think back, but I knew I had never seen anything like this.

If I broke out of the first, I could break out of the second. Wedging my back against the first hexagon, positioning my feet on the outer walls, I bashed each panel as I had before, making my way around the perimeter.

I did it once, twice, three times. Not one wall gave way.

I inspected the first coffin and could make out in the faint light smooth wood, the side panels painted black. The sight suddenly triggered a memory deep in the storm-flooded cellars of my head.

And then it hit me, exactly where I'd seen this before.

The realization was such a shock, I could feel myself falling away from whatever flimsy reality I'd just been grasping, and I dropped backward, spinning through cold black space.

"There it is," Anderson had said. "The mysterious threshold between reality and make-believe . . . Because every one of us has our box, a dark chamber stowing the thing that pierced our heart. It contains what you do everything for, struggle for, wound everything around you. And if it were opened, would anything be set free? No. For the impenetrable prison with the impossible lock is your own mind.

115

Right now, a box like this was sitting on top of Anderson's coffee table in the living room, beside a pile of faded newspapers and a tray of tea. It was the infamously locked box that belonged to the killer in Death Waits for Me, his prized possession containing the thing that had destroyed him as a child, a box that had never been opened. Anderson had caught me trying to pick the lock. And just a few weeks ago when I'd visited him, I'd held it in my hands, shaking it, amused to hear the same old mysterious thumps inside, wondering what in the hell they could be.

They were me. Those rattles were my bones. *What I'd wanted to see inside, I was now locked in.*

I heard myself gasp out loud at the irony of it. I could feel tears welling in my eyes, sliding off my face. It was too cruel an ending to fathom, a punishment that was pure Esquivel. The man was showing me that some mysteries were best left untouched, that the truth of them was the unknown. To try and wrestle them open, letting their contents come too light, was only to destroy oneself.

Suddenly filled with such rage, I began to pound very wall around me, over and over again, like a reptile trying to hatch. I shoved my back against the ceiling, heard it crack, and thrusting my shoulder against it again, felt it give way. I climbed up, emerging onto a floor, blinking in the increased light at a third black hexagon boxing me in. *How long would it go on? How many cages were there*? I pounded every panel until another gave way and another. I kept escaping, crawling through walls that broke down, one box giving way to another, clambering forward and backward, up and down, so disoriented at times, I had to sit, letting my legs and arms settle on the ground, feel which direction gravity was coming from, so I'd know which way was up and which was down.

I didn't know how many boxes I'd crawled through, it felt like dozens, the light increasing with each one, inching ever closer, when, pressing against a ceiling, abruptly the floor gave way.

Bright light, and I was plummeting, falling straight down.

I reached out, grabbed the edge of the box seconds before it flew by, desperately hanging on as the panel I'd just smashed struck the ground.

I looked down, blinking.

Maybe it was just my faltering vision, my eyes unable any longer to register great depths or space because it appeared as if I were hanging from the top of a skyscraper, the concrete ground about a mile below.

A bright light was pouring in from somewhere, through a window out of sight. Craning my neck upward. I could see that I was inside a vast metal tower, dangling like a bit of snagged thread out of a hole in the bottom of a large wooden structure, which appeared to be suspended from the ceiling.

There was nothing else here except a single metal ladder, which extended from the ground, up the steel wall, disappearing from view over the top of this box.

I had to get up there. I couldn't go around the outside. *The only way to climb out was to climb back in*. I swung myself up onto my elbows, the entire structure swaying dangerously from the movement. The cables or ropes, which were keeping this thing suspended in the air, emitted weird sounding creaks, like the whole thing, were literally hanging by a thread as if I were hanging by a thread.

I managed to pull myself back into the box, and then, trying to keep my movements easy so as not to dislodge the entire structure, I crawled back through every hole in every hexagon that I'd made. It felt nauseating to do this, to be breaking back inside the boxes from which I'd just liberated myself, my mind protesting as the light around me fell away as if with it went my every hope for escape. For my life.

I spent the next few hours searching for another way out, pounding the other panels in the other hexagons, trying to find the walls that would take me up to the top, to that ladder.

But no matter how hard I pounded, nothing gave way. I couldn't help but suspect in my brutish demolition, my fury, I'd inadvertently destroyed the correct way out of here, the only way, and all I could do now was wait for the inevitable.

Time became a milky liquid I let myself float on, drifting away from this box on its lazy current, back and forth. Then I realized I was lying on my right side, gazing through the hole I'd made in that very first coffin. A sudden sound of fluttering caught my attention, waking me from a dream.

The moth.

I'd forgotten about it. I was overwhelmed with relief at the simple sight, the understanding that I wasn't alone. It was crawling on the ceiling, but fell off, and then calmly righting itself, took off again for one of the walls. I leaned in, gently brushed it into my hand.

Working its antennae, it began walking around, exploring the boundaries of its new cage, which was, of course, the palm of my hand.

So I would die in here. *I'd leave my little life.* I'd barely worn it out. Life had been a suit I'd only put on for special occasions. Most of the time I kept it in the back of my closet, forgetting it was there. We were meant to die when it was barely stitched anymore, when the elbows and knees were stained with grass and mud, shoulder pads uneven from people hugging you all the time, downpours and blistering sun, the fabric faded, buttons gone.

Kim came into my thoughts. She came the way she always did, cuddling over to me with her brown bare feet and her smiling face, staring down at me, wrinkling her nose. What would she think when Angela told her I'd disappeared? I'd become a mystery she'd have to give life to. I'd become a hero, a world explorer who'd gone missing searching for buried treasure on the high seas, more courageous than I'd ever been in real life. Or no, I'd be a cavern in her heart she'd brick up and wallpaper over, hang the painting in front of and potted plants, so no one would ever know that dark and hollow passage was even there.

I could hear Anderson, just like if he were suddenly here, staring dubiously at the walls enclosing me before downing the vodka with a shot glass in hand. *Did I not warn you, McCarthy, that to capture Esquivel was to try and trap shadows in a jar? You wanted the truth, here it is. It's boxes inside of boxes. What made you so certain you could ever figure him out? That his questions even had answers?*

But what had Anderson shouted, when he'd caught me drunkenly trying to pick the lock on that hexagon box? "Traitor!"

"Philistine!" and yet, before he'd slammed the door in my face, he'd said something else. "You couldn't even see where it opened." It was a hint that I wasn't seeing all of it, not the full picture, that I was blind to something, that the way out wasn't the way out.

I had it wrong.

I noticed the moth had managed to fly even with its injured wing. It was crawling again across the ceiling of that first box. I stuck my head inside, watching it move in circles, and then, working its antennae and legs, it paused, then slipped through a hole in the wood, vanishing from sight.

I reached out, running my hands across the ceiling, feeling where the moth had disappeared, an opening the size of a grain of rice. Tracing my fingers along it, I could feel something else, an indentation. I fumbled through my own clothing, which felt strangely foreign and detached from me, as if I were riffling through the pockets, of another man, a man who was passed out or dead. I groped, hoping to find some type of tool to use, yet the only hard object I could find was some type of pendant around my neck.

It was the Saint Benedict necklace Elizabeth had given me. I yanked it from my neck and, wedging the metal into the crack, inched it along the trench. After I'd gone all the way around it, I could see it was some type of circular door. I managed to lift up the wood a few centimeters, enough to wedge my fingers underneath. The door, a circular panel, came loose in my hands, falling away.

I was staring into a black pipe entirely devoid of light, nothing visible at the end.

I reached out, running my hands along the smooth metal sides, accidentally grazing that moth. It fell out onto my cheek.

I rolled over, collecting the insect onto my hand, and then, making sure it was all right, tucked it in the inside pocket of my coat, where I hoped it'd remain safe and alive. Then I wedged myself up inside the pipe. It was tight, horrifyingly, like being trapped in an old air vent. There were no rungs to climb, nothing to grab hold of. All I could do was inch blindly up into the pipe by pressing against the sides as hard as I could, bracing myself with the soles of my boots. Within a few yards, I encountered a wall.

I pressed against it. It opened easily and I shoved it back, blinking in the bright light.

The metal ladder was directly over my head, bolted to the ceiling. I pulled myself out onto the top of the wooden hexagon, staring around me. This box I was standing on was a perfect replica of the box back at Anderson's. the light was flooding in through narrow windows in the ceiling, though there were no trees visible and no sky, only white light. I couldn't tell if it was artificial light or from the sun.

I took another step. Suddenly there was a jolt and a sharp snap. I reached up, tightening my grip on the ladder's rung just as the entire hexagon box swung out from under my feet, dangling for a moment by a piece of thread before breaking loose. And then the entire box was plunging, a spinning black box tumbling out of the sky. There was a sucking noise and then an explosion as the boxes shattered on the ground below.

I didn't wait, and I didn't look down. I swung from rung to rung. Heading toward that wall in front of me where the ladder twisted downward. As I moved, I noticed with amazement that the tiny white moth had managed to escape my coat pocket. It was now crawling down my arm, over the cuff of my sleeve, slipping over my watch.

It was still only 7:58.

Reaching the tower wall. I started my descent, the metal bars slipping eagerly into my hands and under my boots. But then, I began to realize in horror, the ground with its piles of demolished wood, it wasn't getting any close, no matter how long I traveled. I was never going to reach the ground, never feel it hard under my feet, never wake up.

Suddenly I was no longer on a metal ladder.

I was tripping frantically down another black corridor. It looked exactly like the one leading to the crossroads. *Had I been walking it for days and, reaching no end, simply lay down on the ground and fallen asleep?*

Or was I passed out on the living-room couch back in Panic Attack?

Abruptly I reached a wall with a ladder, at the top, another wooden hatch. I climbed up, sliding aside the rails, and opened it.

I was in an abandoned factory surrounded by hulking machinery with rested blades, piles of stripped logs and rubble. I scrambled out, racing across a floor strewn with wood chips and sawdust, heading for the small door.

What in the hell was happening? I was outside, racing through a field of grasses up to my waist, across old railroad tracks. I was sprinting past a derelict caboose on which someone had spray-painted another red bird when I realized in shock I'd been running the entire time with my eyes closed.

I opened them as blinding sun crashed into my eyes.

"I think he's dead."

Something sharp poked my shoulder.

"Oh, my God. Don't touch him. He's covered in maggots."

"That's not a maggot. That's a moth."

I opened my mouth to speak, but I couldn't. My throat felt like it's been burned. Sight slowly came back into my eyes. I was lying on my side in a muddy ditch. Two teenagers, a boy, and a girl, were staring down at me. The boy appeared to have been prodding me with a long branch. Behind them, a blue station wagon was parked on the shoulder of the road.

"Want us to call you an ambulance?" the girl asked. I rolled upright, my head throbbing. I stared down at myself, dimly taking an inventory. I was wearing a heavy overcoat, corduroy slacks, hiking boots, argyle socks, all of which were caked in black mud. My right hand, covered with dirt, was clasping something. My fingers felt dead as if the bones had been broken, the flesh had swollen stiff around them, because they refused to loosen their grip on what they clutched so resolutely, what I realized was a brass compass with a shattered face.

And I was alive.

116

"You were gone for three days," Elizabeth said.

I could only stare back at her, unable to speak.

I'd been lost inside El Esplanade for three days. How was it possible?

And the fact that all three of us were together now, alive, unhurt, huddled in an isolated booth in the back of a country restaurant called Dixie's Diner, is also bizarre. The last four hours had transpired in such a haze, I wondered if there was a time delay between what was happening in the world and my brain perceiving it.

Struggling to my feet in that ditch. I'd managed to convince the two teenagers not to call the police but to give me a ride back to the Valley View Motel. They seemed rather enthusiastic to oblige, probably due to their suspicion I could very well be the top developing story in the local news themselves star witnesses. As we drove, they cheerfully informed me they'd been partaking in a cleanup project for their high school, picking up trash along the side of the road, when they'd found me.

"We thought you were dead," said the boy.

"What day is it?" I managed to ask.

"Saturday," the girl answered with a shocked glance at the boy.

Saturday, holy shit. We'd broken into El Esplanade on a Wednesday night.

They found me along Mount Sheridan Road, close to route 90 and lake Michigan, which I knew from poring over so many maps of the area was about fourteen driving miles to Fox Lake, some twenty miles from El Esplanade. *Had I been running through the wilderness and passed out? Or had someone driven me there, left me like a sack of garbage on the side of the road?*

I had no idea. My memories seemed to have been trashed, ripped and crumpled, strewn haphazardly around my head.

When the teenagers asked me what had happened, I managed to put together an excuse for drinking too much the night before, my confusion over where I'd just woken up and what in the hell had happened to me quickly slid onto paranoia over my present, including these two kids who'd randomly found me. There was something about them that was a little too vivid, from the peace sign scribbled in blue ink on his arm, her bare feet propped up on the glove compartment, toenails painted yellow, the way he turned the radio way up, playing Dylan's "Like a Rolling Stone." This suspicion made my heart begin to pound in alarm as I sat in the backseat, watching the marijuana leaf ornament swinging from the rearview mirror.

I didn't fully believe that I just might be free of el Esplanade until we barreled into the Valley View parking lot. I thanked the kids and climbed out, waiting for them to swing back onto the main road, accelerating away, before I walked up to the room. #9.

I did nothing but stare at the door for a moment, wondering what was going to find on the other side. *An empty room, untouched since we'd left it?* Or was a stranger staying there now, someone who'd claim he'd been there for weeks, no sign of Cooper or Elizabeth? Or would my knock be answered by one of those figures in a black cloak, the nightmare beginning again?

I knocked. There was a long pause.

And then the door, which was chained from the inside, opened just a crack, someone peering out. It closed again, the chain slid back, and suddenly Elizabeth was flinging her arms around my neck. Cooper appeared right behind her, silently hastening us inside, taking a suspicious look at the parking lot before closing and locking the door.

The first thing we decided to do was check out of the motel, get into the car, get the hell out of here. Elizabeth was agitated and had, I noticed, terrible scratches down her cheeks. She kept saying, "What happened to you? We thought they got you. We thought . . ." But Cooper only snapped that we should get out of here now and we could talk when we were away from this place, his terse explanation being that he'd noticed a banged-up maroon Pontiac loitering around the parking lot.

"It had to be them," he said, zipping up his gray hoodie, grabbing his canteen off the bed. "The windows are tinted black. It looks like it's from the seventies. And it's missing a headlight."

As I watched the two of them darting around the room, hastily stuffing clothing and toiletries and snacks into their backpacks, I remembered that I no longer had my own.

Where had I left the bag? Those figures had pulled it off of me.

I stepped dazedly in front of the mirror beside one of the beds and saw I was still wearing Brad Jackson's herringbone coat.

Its extreme heaviness was due to not just the dampness and mud but the pockets, they were stuffed with objects, one of which I noticed, as I pulled it out with a wave of revulsion, I didn't even recall seeing, much less taking it with me.

And then I saw my face. I understood the teenager's shock, even Elizabeth and Cooper's worried sideways glances. I looked crazy. There was no other word to describe it.

I rinsed the smeared mud off in the bathroom, watching the thick sludge spinning down the drain.

We left the motel quickly, Cooper climbing behind the wheel. *They had the jeep but not the canoe.* I meant to ask them about it but I felt so tired I couldn't muster the strength. Cooper drove like we were being tailed, careening down deserted roads, pines and maples and empty fields spinning past, all the time eyeing the rearview mirror. Elizabeth, in the passenger seat beside him, was subdued, her hands clasped in her lap.

"You see the Pontiac?" she whispered.

Cooper shook his head.

We'd been driving for about three hours when Elisabeth pointed out a white farmhouse perched on the side of the road, *Dixie's Diner, Homemade Food That's Doggone Good*! The parking lot packed. Only then did I feel I just might return to normal. My right arm was showing signs of life, tingling as if filled with needles. My fingers were moving again, though the palm of my hand, where I'd been holding that compass, was swollen. The horror of El Esplanade seemed to be drying on me, as if it were black water I'd been swimming through and now it was evaporating from my skin, leaving the faintest film.

The three of us filed into the restaurant and Cooper asked the hostess for the booth in the back. I didn't know what she meant. I'd taken off the coat, rolled up my sleeves, and saw now that my arms were covered with a horrific-looking rash.

As we slipped into the booth, Elizabeth said, "We've been waiting for you three days."

"Hey," said Cooper. "Let him eat."

We ordered food, and I was able to piece together from their disjointed and strung-out commentary that in the three days I'd been missing, apart from a few searches along the roads around El Esplanade, they'd been too paranoid and worried about me to leave the motel. They hadn't left El Esplanade together. Elizabeth had been the first to make it back, arriving at the room at five in the morning the same night we'd broken in. It wasn't until after six that evening, Thursday, that Cooper showed up, driving the Jeep.

"I thought I was going to have to go to the police," said Elizabeth. "I didn't know what I'd say. 'We broke illegally into this estate and now my accomplices are being held, hostage.' I got the number of your police friend, Katie Horrigan. She didn't pick up."

"Can I interest you in any dessert?" the waitress asked, suddenly beside our table.

"I'll have a slice of apple pie," I said hoarsely.

"Anyone else?"

Elizabeth and Cooper stared at me in surprise. I was surprised myself. It was the first time I'd managed to speak with a normal voice.

They ordered pie and coffee, and then, after the waitress brought the food, Elizabeth, who'd been so jittery and talkative as she ate, fell silent, touching the scrapes on her cheek as if to check that they were still there. Cooper seemed lost in thought. It was obvious then, the two of them weren't simply upset over my three-day disappearance. They'd each had their own strange experiences up there.

I also noticed uneasily, looking around, that Dixie's Diner, so cheery and bustling only minutes ago, had unexpectedly cleared out.

It was just the three of us now and, hunched over the counter, an elderly man in a green-and-black checked flannel shirt, who looked as gnarled and spindly as the walking stick propped beside him. It was as if whispers of what we were about to tell one another, about El Esplanade, were already suffused in the air here, already drifting out of our mouths, darkening the placed, and any innocent soul or carefree person couldn't help but subconsciously sense that the time had come to leave.

"Let's start with the canoe," I said.

117

"We don't know what happened to it," Elizabeth answered. "We think they took it."

"They?"

"Those people living there."

She glanced uncertainly at Cooper. He added nothing, only hooked his index finger through the handle of his coffee mug, frowning.

"I told you to wait for me at the pond," I said to her.

"I meant to. But when I ran down the hill, I got mixed up and went too far north. When I backtracked, I was heading toward the canoe, when someone grabbed my shoulder from behind. I screamed, sprayed him with the pepper spray, and then I just ran."

"Did you see the man's face?" *That scream I heard, it had been Elizabeth.*

She shook her head. "He had a flashlight. Blinded me with it. I kept running until I realized there was no one behind me. After an hour I came to this dirt road winding through the woods. I took off down it, hoping it'd lead me off the property and I'd be able to go for help."

Abruptly she fell silent, looking apprehensively at Cooper. "Did it lead you off the property?" I asked.

She shook her head.

"Where did it lead you?" I prompted when she didn't go on.

"To this concrete lot. An old-fashioned truck was parked there. At the center were these gigantic metal boxes. Five in a row. At first, I thought it had to be an electrical plant used for powering the estate. Or maybe they were traps for wild animals. They looked cruel. But then I smelled smoke. I got closer and, shining my flashlight on them, I saw each one had a rusty door and a chimney sticking up into the air. Strewn all over the ground was a pale gray powder. I didn't realize until I'd walked through it that it was ashes. The boxes were incinerators. And they'd been used recently because I could still feel the heat coming off them."

Incinerators.

The word made me suddenly recall those tunnels originating from the underground alcove, those blackened entryways and the rudimentary words scrawled above the openings in white paint. I couldn't believe it and I didn't know how, but I remembered everyone like they were the refrain of a nursery rhyme I'd sung as a child, the lyrics lodged in my mind forever.

Gatehouse, Mansion, Lake, Stables, Workshop, Lookout, Pincoya Negro, Laboratory, Crossroads.

Elizabeth frowned. "I remembered the next-door neighbor in the trailer that you'd interviewed. Doc Larsen, how he told you that Esquivel set fire to all their garbage. I went up to one and unlatched the door. There was nothing but black walls, piles and piles of ashes. The smell was awful. Synthetic, but sweet. I opened the other doors, raked a tree branch through the ashes to see if there was anything left. There was nothing, not one hair. I started combing the ground, trying to find some piece of evidence of why they were going through so much trouble to destroy. It wasn't until I inspected the truck that I found something."

"What?"

"A glass vial used for drawing blood at a doctor's office. It was wedged along the side in the rear bed. It looked empty, but there was a tiny pink label on the side with a biohazard symbol. They must use the truck to transport medical waste or toxic garbage from somewhere at El Esplanade to burn in those ovens. The vial must have accidentally fallen out."

She took a breath. "It made me wonder if the whole area was contaminated. I began to feel sick, so I ran." She stared at the table in front of her. "I had a feeling someone was following me, but every time I looked around, there was no one. When I reached the fence, I didn't even think about it, I went right over it. I didn't care if I died or got electrocuted or cut up. I climbed right through the razor wire, didn't feel a thing. I just wanted to get out, and nothing would stop me."

"How did you get back to the motel?"

"I reached this paved road, this had to be around four in the morning, and a red station wagon pulled up, a tiny old lady behind the wheel. She offered me a ride. I was petrified. I thought for sure she was one of the townspeople. She even looked like a witch with a green blouse and all these rings on her fingers. But I was so tired and she looked so fragile, I got in. she drove me straight aback to the motel and said, 'Take care of yourself, girl.'

And that was it. Nothing happened. I staggered into the room and slept for thirteen hours."

I stared at her. I could feel the outskirts of another headache coming on, but I tried to focus, to think. *A glass vial used for drawing blood? Medical waste*? Why would Esquivel have such things?

Her mention of Doc Larsen made me remember the other incident he'd told me about, the UPS delivery of medical equipment intended for El Esplanade, but accidentally arriving at his own trailer. Nothing we'd learned over the course of the investigation, no one we'd interviewed had mentioned a detail that validated this story or Larsen's suspicion, that there was someone injured or ill up at El Esplanade, except perhaps now, Elizabeth and these incinerators she'd just described.

Cooper had been listening to her with annoyed detachment, occasionally glaring at her over some specific detail she mentioned, the word incinerators, the glass vial labeled biohazard.

"What about you?" I asked him. "What happened?"

"Cooper got inside the mansion," blurted Elizabeth excitedly. "He found Gabriela's room."

"I don't know if it was her room for sure," Cooper countered.

"But, of course, you do." Clearly surprised by his sudden reticence, she turned to me, leaning in. "He found letters that he's written Gabriela, ones she'd never answered. They were kept safe, in order, right beside her bed. It looked like she'd read through them a million times. And there were pictures of them together on top of her desk. Then he found her practice room."

"I don't know if it was her practice room."

"But you found a piece on the piano she'd written, called Tiger Foot."

"Tiger Foot?" I asked, puzzled.

"Cooper's tribe name from the Wilderness Gateway Camp."

Cooper looked livid. "I don't know what I found up there, okay. I don't know.

"How did you get inside the house?" I asked him.

"Climbed up onto the roof. Found a window unlatched."

"What was it like inside the house? Abandoned?"

"No. It was nice." He brushed his hair out of his eyes and seemed unwilling to elaborate, but, as I was waiting expectantly, he sighed. "It was a castle. Gigantic. Gloomy as shit. Mahogany walls. Tapestries with unicorns. Snarling bear heads. Painting depicting storms and mayhem, with people in pain. Wooden chairs, big as thrones. Knights swords hanging on the wall, and an iron chandelier with burned white candles covered in wax. Not that I had much time to browse. Someone let the dogs back in. I found that was unlocked. I hid in there for hours."

"It was filled with thousands of filing cabinets," added Elizabeth.

"Filing cabinets?" I asked. "Containing what?"

"People looking to work for Esquivel, pictures, resumes, with weird notes written on the back." She waited for Cooper to explain it to me, but, again, he looked infuriated by her candor.

"What kind of notes?" I pressed when neither of them spoke.

"Personal details," said Cooper.

"Such as?"

"Background, Phobias Secrets."

"It reminded me of the audition Olivia Wainscott described. Remember how he asked her those weird personal questions?" she glanced at Cooper. "What was the one you told me about? That woman named Shell Baker?"

"Her picture looked like it dated back to the seventies," he said. "Someone had written on the back of it, 'No family except a brother in the Army, hates cats, diabetic, doesn't like to be alone, sexually inexperienced.' Another was, like. 'Raised in Texas, car accident as a five-year-old child, left her in a back brace for a year, painfully shy.'"

"Did you take anything with you?" I asked.

He seemed irritated by the question. "Why?"

"For evidence?"

"No. I put it aback and got the hell out of there."

"Then Cooper found a torture chamber," Elizabeth blurted.

"It wasn't a torture chamber," he countered angrily. He looked at me.

"Another room in the basement just had a bunch of wooden stretchers and planks, metal straps, antiques, I didn't know what half the shit was. I slipped out, snuck upstairs to the third floor. I found what I think was Gabriela's room, was looking around when I accidentally knocked over a lamp. Someone must have heard me because I could hear someone coming up the stairs. I darted into a closet while this person, it sounded like a woman, wandered around. She righted the lamp and them she left. Only she locked me in. I couldn't unlock the door from the inside. I was going to unscrew the doorknob, but then I heard one of the dogs outside the door. He had to have known I was in there. But he didn't bark. There were giant bay windows in the room overlooking the hill and pond, but when I climbed out, there was a sheer drop. I stayed in the room all night, silent, waiting for the dog to leave. About five in the morning, someone whistled and it ran downstairs. I unscrewed the doorknob, managed to get out of the house without encountering anyone. I made a beeline for the canoe, but naturally, it was gone. So I just followed the same stream that we'd come in on. I got lost. I wandered deep into a swamp, ended up in mud chest-high. I came upon a group of campers who looked at me like they thought I was the Lock Ness Monster. They told me I was in a section called the Pilchers Pond Primitive Area, which is all the way east of Fox Lake. It was about six at night when I make it back to the Jeep."

Any sign of one of the Esquivel's living at the house?" I asked.

"No. The top floor was where the family had their bedrooms. No one slept there all night. I think the other people with the dogs were caretakers. Not that I saw any of them up close."

"You didn't enter any other room in the basement?"

"No. they were all locked."

"What about upstairs? Anything unusual?"

He nodded, his face somber. "I found a closed-off wing toward the back of the house. Up a flight of spiral stairs into this tower was a bedroom suite. Half of it was brand-new. Brand new hardwood on the floors. You could see where the old meet the new. I wondered if it'd been remodeled after a fire. And maybe that had been the Tarantula's room. There was nothing there, though. Not a photograph, not a clerical collar. Nothing."

"What about this Pontiac you saw in the Valley View Motel parking lot?"

"I think it's one of the caretakers. I had to leave Gabriela's doorknob unbolted, so they know someone entered her room."

"Any sign she'd been there in the days before her death?"

"Yeah," he admitted quietly. "I don't know how, but . . ." A smile flickered across his face, went out. "She was still in the air."

Expressly avoiding eye contact, he took a sip of coffee.

"Now it's your turn," Elizabeth whispered eagerly, leaning in.

118

What happened to me? *Did I even know*?

I told them everything I remembered, beginning with the dogs chasing me all the way to my return to the Valley View Motel. I didn't consciously choose to tell them in such detail, Elizabeth looked stricken, Cooper slightly infuriated, which made me wonder if it was wise to be so uncensored, but each word I uttered seemed to wrench loose the next until all the confusion and horror came tumbling out in a landslide.

When I'd finished, they said nothing for a moment, speechless. And I was relieved. I don't think in all of my days on the force, I'd ever needed to tell someone exactly what had happened, as if to do so was to finally walk out of there, pull myself out of those tunnels and shadows, once and for all.

"What do you mean you found something you didn't remember taking in Brad's coat pockets?" Elizabeth whispered.

Before answering, I looked around to make sure our waitress was still back inside the kitchen. We were the only ones left in the restaurant. Even the elderly man who'd been seated at the counter was now shuffling out the door, leaning heavily on his cane, his every step an effort.

Brad Jackson's mud-soaked coat sat folded on the seat beside me. I pulled it over and, object by object, emptied the pockets, placing each item on the table in front of us. Elmer's compass. The child's blood-soaked shirt. They looked odd here in the neon lights, out of place, souvenirs from a nightmare.

"These I remember taking," I said. "But not this."

I fumbled in the pocket and pulled out the final object lying at the bottom. It was a three-jointed set of bones, weathered and dirty, about five inches long.

"What is that?" asked Elizabeth.

"It looks to me like a portion of a child's foot. But I don't know."

"Where did it come from?"

"I'm guessing I came across it somewhere and took it, thinking it could be evidence. But I really don't remember."

Elizabeth's alarmed gaze left the bones on the table and moved toward me.

"You don't remember if those people did anything to you, or . . ."

"No."

"What about how you got into that hexagon?"

I shook my head.

"It's obvious you were drugged," said Cooper.

Elizabeth anxiously bit her lip. "Now what do we do?"

"We'll have some of this analyzed," I said. "Find out if it's human blood on the shirt or human bones. If it is, we need to find out whom they belong to. Was the Tarantula correct in his suspicions? Is there a mother rout there, waiting for news of her missing child? I can't prove what I saw up there was real, but I can prove Esquivel believed in the curse. How far did he go in his work and in his hope to save Gabriela? The man blurred fiction and fact. His art and his life were the same."

"That's not what we decided," Cooper muttered. "We made a deal before we broke into El Esplanade all three of us would decide what to do with the information. Not just you."

"But we don't know what we have yet."

"What do you want to gain from all of this?" He stared at me accusingly. "Your name in friggin lights? The glory of stripping the great Esquivel naked so you can parade him on a leash in front of the world for everyone to look at? So you can gloat that this is really what he is? And he wasn't so great? You think that's what Gabriela would've wanted?"

"I don't know what she wanted."

"This isn't your lottery ticket. This is her life. I'm not going to let you turn it into some cheap tabloid story."

"We know what she went through," he went on angrily. "We know the kind of madhouse she grew up in, what sort of family she had. How she lived her life. We know why she climbed to the top of that elevator shaft by herself in the middle of the night and jumped.

It was to put an end to it. We know. You even saw that ditch filled with the shoes and suck down until you're full?" He furiously shoved back his plate, fork clattering to the floor, and stalked out of the restaurant, the door slamming behind him.

"He saw something up there," whispered Elizabeth. "Don't know what. He'll probably never tell anyone."

It had started to rain, and Cooper, zipping up his jacket, gazing at the ground, ducked away from the window, out of sight.

"Whatever he was looking for," she said, "whatever he wanted from her, he found it.

119

The drive back to the city was tense and mostly silent. I stopped at River Rentals Inc. in Pine lake to pay for the missing Souris River canoe, explaining to the kid with dreadlocks behind the counter that it had been destroyed.

"Seriously? What happened, man?"

I could only hand him a credit card. He definitely didn't want to know.

We pulled onto the highway and immediately Elizabeth fell sound asleep in the seat beside me. I thought Cooper had too, but every time I glanced in the rearview mirror, he was only staring out the window his face unreadable, his thoughts probably somewhere back at El Esplanade.

Elizabeth was absolutely right. Cooper had admitted he's spent the night in Gabriela's room, and I couldn't help but suspect something he'd seen there or encountered had changed his view of what had happened between them. It had somehow set him free. And he'd let it fly, that gorgeous blackbird of a love he'd been keeping in a cage. What was it like for him, every day standing outside in the wind and rain to stare at the Lake, yearning for some sign of her, never giving up hope? At El Esplanade perhaps she'd finally come into view, a ship coming neither toward him nor away, only riding that perfect line between heaven and earth, long enough for him to know that she had loved him, that what they had was real before slipping out of sight, probably forever.

I certainly understood his anger toward me and his desire to protect Gabriela. I'd even anticipated it, that the deeper we got into the investigation, the more disturbing the truth about the Esquivel family, Cooper and I would inevitably clash over what to do with the information. But for me to let it end here, not to go all the way, was not an option.

Hours later, at dusk, we were back in Chicago, driving down its battered blocks of pedestrians and potholes. Cooper asked me to drop him off at his apartment. The only words he said during the entire ride.

He climbed out of the jeep, pulling his backpack over his shoulder.

"I'll see you guys," he said curtly and slammed the door.

"Wait," said Elizabeth.

She hastily scrambled out and threw her arms around his neck, hugging him right on the sidewalk. He chucked her affectionately on the chin and moved up the steps to his building. When she climbed back in, I was surprised to see that she was crying.

"Bernstein. Hey. What's the matter?"

"You don't get it." She wiped her eyes. "We're never going to see him again."

"What? Don't be silly."

She shook her head in disagreement, watching him disappear inside. I was surprised by the pronouncement, to say the least, certain it couldn't be true. It couldn't end like this, not here when so much was still unanswered, but then I remembered his apartment, the bare walls, and the bag from South Dakota, the lyrics from "On The Road Again."

Had he found all the answers he needed and was he finished with us, is it as simple as that?

I didn't know what to say because abruptly Elizabeth was heartbroken. She silently wept all the way out of the lower South side, up to the Near North. I tried comforting her but ultimately was too drained to do more than concentrate on the simple task of getting the rental Jeep back to Budget.

A hot Saturday night in Mag Mile was detonating around us. As we walked back to my place, negotiating the dense crowds and honking cars, Elizabeth didn't say a word. When I let us back into the apartment, she ignored my question about whether or not she wanted any dinner, scurrying upstairs to Kim's room.

I headed to my office. It looked solemn, untouched. Gazing at the windows, the night, I actually wished Octavius was there on the windowsill to greet me. I could've used the company; he might be a silly bird, but he was reasonable. We'd taken him to a kennel to be looked after. There was nothing and no one here.

I tried calling Angela, I had an overwhelming desire to hear Kim's voice, to hear that she was all right, but she didn't pick up. I left a message. I went upstairs and took a shower, locked everything I'd taken out of El Esplanade in my safe, and climbed into bed. I'd stuck Brad Jackson's coat on a hanger, hanging it on the back of my closet door. It looked oddly limp there, oddly lifeless. *Had I gone far enough up there? Seen enough at El Esplanade to get to the bottom of it?*

120

I woke up gasping and lurched upright, expecting to hit my head on the ceiling of yet another hexagon, only to realize I really was at home. Elizabeth was perched on the edge of my bed.

"Holy shit. You scared me."

"Everything all right?" I sat up, propping myself up on the pillows. I was relieved to see she was no longer crying. "Are you upset about what happened? I'm sure you're wrong about Cooper."

"No. yes. It's just . . ."

"What?"

"When we were tracking Gabriela before, she was alive. Now I can feel she's gone. And when Cooper said goodbye it reminded me of Willow Falls. There the endings hit you hard because they're sudden. Like one day Amelia who loves flowers is there in the dining hall with her oxygen tank ordering the fruit plate, and the next? She's nowhere to be found. All they leave out is this memorial and what it is depends on what hallway you lived on. Like if you lived on the first floor they put up an easel with a laminated picture of you smiling and knitting with your glasses around your neck. But if you lived on the fourth floor, they put this guestbook out to sign with flowers and a poem about loss printed off the Internet. And that's it. After two weeks they take it down, the poster and the guestbook, and it's like you were never there. I hate it so much."

"I just hate it so much."

"It's not fair."

"It's not, but then, that's the game. It makes life great. The fact that it ends when we don't want it to. The ending gives it meaning. But now that you mention it, will you promise to off me when I'm ninety and never leave home without an oxygen tank? Make a day of it. Just roll me and my wheelchair off the Dearborn Street Bridge and call it a life. Deal?"

"They should really tack that on to the marriage ceremony. "Do you promise to love, honor, obey me, and also to kill me when I can no longer stand in a shower?"

"I really love you, Shawn. "She blurted the words. They took me so off guard, I wasn't certain I'd heard her correctly, but then she slid forward in the dark, kissed me on the mouth, then sat back, studying me intently, as if she'd just added a key ingredient to a new science experiment.

"What'd you do that for?"

"I told you. I love you. And not as a friend or a boss, but real love. I've known it for twenty-four hours."

"Sounds like a stomach bug that will pass."

"I'm serious." She scrambled on top of me, sitting Indian-style on my shims, and before I could stop her, the girl leaned in and planted another kiss on me, her hands clasping the sides of my head. I was almost too tired to do anything about it but managed to grab her shoulders and pull her away.

"You need to go back to bed."

"You don't think I'm pretty?"

"You're gorgeous." She was inches from my face, really squinting, as if it were a section of a globe she'd never closely inspected before, an ocean filled with strings of unnamed islands.

"So what's the matter?"

"To my knowledge, Woodward and Bernstein never took it this far. I'd prefer we didn't, either."

"You're making a joke?"

"You have your life in front of you. You're young, and I'm . . . an old guitar." I had no idea where that unfortunate metaphor came from, maybe I was half asleep, but I suddenly had a very unpleasant vision of myself as a worn out old rock and roll guitar that has been played out.

"You're not. You're amazing."

"You're amazing."

"Well, two people who feel that way should be together right now this second and not think." She scrambled eagerly right alongside me as if we were together in a compact camping tent. She felt scrawny and light, and as she rolled over me, her hair and smell of soap fell around my head like a waterfall.

"Elizabeth. Please go to bed." I shoved her back, a little more forcefully this time. "I love you, too," I went on. "You know I do, but, not like that."

I was aware of how shoddily stitched together the words were, suddenly I was a kid in the hall standing outside my locker about to head to math. But that was how it went sometimes, the English language, when you really needed the right words, they crumbled to clay in your mouth. That's when all the real things were said.

"Why are you treating me like I don't know my own feelings?"

"Experience. I'm forty-three. Maybe even forty-four."

"In olden days' people only lived to thirty, so I'd be ancient."

"And I'd be dead."

"Why do you have to joke? Why can't you just be?"

I didn't answer, only held out my hand, waiting for her to take it. "You know I'll always be on the sidelines," I said, "cheering you on. You're a powerful woman. And you're going to go on being powerful, for miles and miles, for years. I'd only slow you down."

"Maybe I want to be slow. Why do people have to keep moving away from each other all the time?" She was on the verge of tears again. She wrenched her hand away. "Cooper's right. You're not attached to anyone. You only love yourself."

She waited for me to disagree, but I didn't. Maybe it was the effect of the last three days. I was spent, had no more will to exert anything on my own.

"You're going to ruin everything. Like Cooper said. You don't care about me. Or Gabriela. She means nothing to you. Even now. All you care about is the hunt."

She struggled off the bed, left like a white comet shooting through the room.

"Elizabeth," I called out. But she was gone.

121

    My alarm went off at seven. By seven-thirty, I was out the door.

    I took the Blue Line out to the north side of town, to BeBe's Deli, an old school Jewish deli, I got there when it opened, and then with bags of bagels and fresh lox in hand, I rode the L-Train to its very last stop, at Ohare. If I was going to pay an unannounced visit to Katie Horrigan on a Sunday morning, I could only come bearing gifts, and Katie had a weak spot for poppy-seed bagels, Nova Scotia salmon, and Yiddish delicacy called Schmaltz Herring, a cured white fish that to me tasted like leather encrusted in salt. To Katie, it was heaven. She lived in a mug shot of a house: red brick, sobered, bleary-eyed, square. More than a decade ago, I'd once dropped her off at home when we were working late on the same case, her father had just died, leaving her the house and I'd quietly made note of her address, on the off chance I ever needed to find her.

    There was no answer when I rang the bell, so I sat down on the leaf-strewn steps to wait, wondering if she's already headed into the city to the station or if she'd moved. But then I noticed the empty dog's water bowl and the bald tennis ball in the yard under the single bush, and within fifteen minutes I spotted Katie speed-walking down the sidewalk. She was wearing her maroon North Face jacket and carrying two large deli coffees. In true Horrigan fashion, she wasn't surprised to see me.

    "If you're selling Bibles, I got twelve of them already," she said, skipping past me up the stairs.

"I'm peddling another powerful religion. BeBe's Deli goodies."

Thankfully her gaze couldn't help but dart curiously down to the plastic bag in my hands. But she said nothing and then, nimbly balancing one coffee atop the other, opened the screen, unlocked her door, and fast as a burrowing mole, she darted inside. She was furious I'd shown up, that was clear, but she also didn't slam the door and bolt it.

"Some girl left me a voicemail the other day, claiming you were in mortal danger." She was shrugging off her jacket, hanging it on a hook.

"That'd be my assistant, Elizabeth. She can be convincingly dramatic."

"I don't know why she thought that'd be anything other than wonderful news to me."

"I'm sorry," I said through the screen, Katie quickly disappearing down a hallway. "I'm sorry I'm here. But I need your advice, and if I didn't think that you would absolutely care, I wouldn't bother you. Just hear me out. Then throw me out. And as far as we're concerned, we never met."

This must have had its satisfying prospects, since not a minute later, she was escorting me into her dining room, or perhaps her living room. Whatever it was, it was empty, apart from a yellow carpet, a wobbly folding table, two chairs, and a pillow bed in the corner covered in dog hair.

I unzipped my pockets and pulled out two plastic bags, one containing the child's blood-soaked shirt, the other the bones. Obviously, I didn't volunteer where I'd stumbled upon them, though based on Katie's silently fuming face, she had her suspicions. But the moment she saw the shirt on the table, her demeanor changed. And I knew then that I wasn't off-base or crazy, because if that shirt could take Katie Horrigan by surprise, even if it was simply a prop, it was a realistic one. Without taking her eyes off it, she set aside her two coffees, it was clear now both were hers, examining the shirt through the plastic. She zeroed in on it like a microscope, squarely considering it, going very still.

"Is it blood?" I asked.

"Hard to say. If it is, it's an old stain. Ten years at least. Must have been kept somewhere dry or the cotton fibers would have degraded. Or there's an inorganic blend in the shirt. It acts like blood, though, because of the stiffness. Another substance wouldn't cause such rigidity."

"What about the bones?"

She removed them from the plastic bag, testing the weight in her hands.

"No idea. I'd have to have an anthropologist take a look."

"Could it be part of a child's foot?"

"The human foot is long and narrow; weight largely is borne on the heel. A nonhuman foot is broader, weight borne on the toes. But it gets more confusing the younger the bones, as they're not fully developed. Infant ribs can look like a small creature even at a macrostructural level. Cranial bones of children often resemble turtle shells."

Saying nothing more, she set aside the bag and, grabbing one of her coffees, took a sip, watching me closely.

"By the way, some heads are rolling over that suicide you're so interested in."

She meant Gabriela. "Whose head?"

"You remember a lawyer that lobbied against an autopsy, the Jewish faith against desecration of the body and so on. Only her body disappeared in the middle of the night. It's also why those pictures were missing. Someone was paid off."

"Pictures?" I repeated, not following her.

"I told you. Some of the body shots were missing from her file. They never appeared on record. There's a departmental witch hunt going on, trying to get to the bottom of the whole thing. It's a mess. And I'm sure they'll come up empty-handed. Those types of tracks tend to dissolve before they're even laid. The girl's family's got power."

I remembered, then, Katie mentioning the missing pictures in the file, Gabriela's front and back torso."

"Our phone call, the other day," I said, after a moment, "about the child services case. It wasn't the best connection."

"There was no certificate of occupancy for the building. No sign of anyone living there."

"Any idea who owns the building?"

"It's registered to an LLC. Something Chinese. I have it in my notes. I'll call you with it. And I will quietly look into this." She picked up the plastic bags off the table, shooting me a penetrating look, "even though I should have you booked for being a royal pain in my ass. It'll take a month to process, at least. Lab's backed up. Don't ever show up here again. You look like shit, by the way."

She slipped out of the room with the bags.

"Thank you," I called out to her.

"You need to get that right hand checked out," she shouted from the depths of her house. "You got something stuck in there, and it's about to turn into staph."

I had no idea what she was talking about until I stared down at my hand. She was absolutely right. The swelling and redness had gotten worse.

What I'd thought to be encrusted dirt in the palm appeared to be a splinter embedded deep in the skin under my thumb. Seeing it gave me a sudden stab of paranoia. *Had those people in black cloaks marked me? Put another curse on me? Was it a dart steeped in poison? A rusted, tetanus-yielding nail?*

I had to get home. "How can I repay you?" I called out after a minute when I realized Katie, preoccupied with something else now, wasn't ever returning to the living room. "Can I get you another German Shepherd, a yacht, an island in the South Pacific?"

"You can get out of my house," she called from somewhere.

122

Back in Chicago, I stopped at the emergency care clinic on Thirteenth Street. The waiting room was crowded and it took nearly three hours for a doctor to see me. I explained I'd just come back from a camping trip.

"I can see that," he stated cheerfully, pulling the curtain closed. He was a chipper, quick-talking young man with over-caffeinated energy and Scotch tape accidentally stuck to the back of his white coat. "You have contact dermatitis. Did you by chance do a fair amount of hiking through heavy foliage? Looks like you came into contact with something you're allergic to."

I was about to clarify that I'd been in the upper Illinois woodlands when I realized that I also had been in the swimming pool. And I was in the greenhouse. I could have got bitten by any number of insects in there.

"What type of plants in the greenhouse?" The doctor asked after I sketchily explained some of this.

"One was called Psycho Plant Extract. I can't remember the others."

"Psycho Plant Extract," the doctor repeated, tilting his head. *And that didn't make you want to run screaming out of there?* He seemed to be thinking.

"I've also gotten stuck with something, a bed splinter."

I showed him. Within minutes, a nurse was cleaning my hand with water and a topical antiseptic and the doctor, wielding a scalpel and a long pair of tweezers, was slicing into the palm, whitened pus oozing out she took hold of something embedded inside and pulled it out.

When I saw what it was, I was too stricken to speak, though the doctor threw it on the stainless-steel table beside us.

"Looks like you had quite a camping trip," he said, smiling. "Maybe next time try the beach."

It was a blackthorn off some type of plant, though my first thought was that it was a sharp twisted fingernail, crooked and two inches long.

123

By the time I made it back home, it was after four. I was looking forward to seeing Elizabeth, filling her in about Katie, showing her the blackened spike I'd just had extracted from my hand. And we could get back to work. But the moment I entered my apartment, I heard an odd banging upstairs.

Racing into Kim's room, it looked as if Moe Gulazar's closet, maybe Moe himself, had exploded all over the carpet. Sequined gold leggings, a mink stole (suffering from mange), silk blouses, and striped neckties were draped everywhere. Elizabeth, in a pair of black Lululemon yoga pants and a tuxedo shirt, sleeves rolled up, was packing up the clothes. I noticed Jesus and Judy Garland were no longer taped to the wall.

"What's going on?" I asked.

She glanced at me over her shoulder and then turned away, folding a pair of purple hot pants and shoving them into one of those Nordstrom's bags.

"I'm moving out."

"What?" Just like that, I am finished with this case."

"Okay. First of all, you don't find amazing sublets just like that in Chicago. It takes months. Years, sometimes."

"Not for me."

"And where did this amazing sublet come from? Michael the Archangel?"

"Craigslist."

"Okay. Let me explain something. People who use Craigslist tend to be hookers, homicidal maniacs and massage therapists who give happy endings."

"I already checked it out."

"When?"

"This morning. It's a huge room on the side of a townhouse in the Logan Square neighborhood. It has a big bay window, lots of light. All I have to pay is five hundred a month and share a bathroom with this really cool old hippie."

I took a deep breath. "Let me tell you about cool old hippies in Old Town. They're nuts. They study tarot cards and eat soy. Sometimes they eat tarot cards and study soy. Most haven't left this their neighborhoods since Nixon was president and have unidentifiable plant life growing under their toenails. Trust me on this one."

"We just had lunch. She's super nice."

"Super-nice?"

She nodded. "She grows organic tomatoes."

"Fertilized with the carcasses of her thirty cats."

"She was a photographer's assistant for G Q for years."

"That's what they all say."

"She had an affair with Axel Rose. He wrote a song about her."

"It would probably be 'Welcome to the Jungle,'," I said.

"I don't know why you're freaking out. It'll be cool."

It'll be cool. I felt as if a rug were being yanked out from under me when I'd been standing on hardwood floors in bare feet.

"This is because of last night," I said.

She only raised her chin, grabbing her High School yearbook, frowning dramatically as she thumbed through it.

"Your angry because I was a gentleman? Respected the boundaries of our working relationship?"

She snapped the book shut, sticking it inside the bag. "No."

"No?"

"No, it's because of Hamlette auditions at Steppenwolf."

"Hamlette auditions at Steppenwolf."

She nodded triumphantly. "They're reversing the genders of all the roles, so there are finally good parts for females. I'm going to try for Hamlette, so I have to practice my monologs night and day. It'd drive you crazy because you hate my acting."

"That's not true. I've grown quite fond of your acting."

She was folding an old gray cardigan with a sequin flying bird pin on the shoulder and a massive gaping hole in the right elbow that resembled a silently screaming mouth.

"You yourself said last night that I have to go hurtling forward into space and you'll by my cheerleader on the sidelines. So that's what I'm doing."

"Why would you take my advice?"

"I said it was temporary. That it was until we found out about Gabriela. And we did. And I have money now."

I'd paid Elizabeth before we'd gone to El Esplanade, including a very sizable bonus that I was now sort of regretting.

"Plus, you're going to be hung-up with Gabriela's father nothing else matters to you."

I let that remark sail past me like a grenade blowing up inches from my face. She wouldn't stop zipping around the room like some insect with ten thousand hands and arms, folding, packing it all away.

"The investigation isn't over yet," I said. You're quitting in the end zone, the fourth quarter, ten seconds left, three downs to go."

She stared at me. "You still don't get it."

"What don't I get? I'd be fascinated to find out."

"You don't see that if Esquivel had ever done something that hurt anyone, Gabriela wouldn't have allowed it. I trust her and so does Cooper. You obviously don't trust anyone. Here's your coat back." She'd brutally yanked Angela's black coat off a closet hanger and threw it over the bed. It sagged onto the floor. I'd given it to her weeks ago, so she'd have something without feathers to wear to Olivia Wainscott's. She'd loved it, saying with unabashed joy that it made her feel like a French person, whatever that meant.

"I gave it to you," I said.

She put on the coat, stepping in front of Kim's Big Bird mirror, and took a very long time fixing a bright green scarf around her neck.

She then grabbed a black fedora off the bedpost, setting it delicately atop her head like a lost queen crowning herself. I followed her downstairs in a sort of daze. She set down her bags, heading into my office. She picked up Octavius from the kennel. She crouched beside the cage. "When Grandma Bernice gave me Octavius, she gave me the directions that went with him," she said. "You have to give him away to someone who needs him. That's part of his magic. You're supposed to know the right time to give him away, and it's when it hurts the most. I want you to have him."

"I don't want a bird."

"But you need a bird."

She unlatched the door, and the bird fluttered into her palm. She whispered something into his invisible ear, returned him to his swing, and then she was moving again, slipping past me down the hall. She didn't stop until we were outside on my stoop.

"I'll go with you. Interview the hippie. Make sure this person wasn't part of the Symbionese Liberation Army."

"No, I'm handling it."

"So that's it? I'll never see you again?"

She wrinkled her nose as if I'd said something crazy. "Of course, you're going to see me again." She reached up on her tiptoes and hugged me. The girl gave the greatest hugs, skinny arms clamped around your neck like zip ties, bony knees bumping yours. It was like she was trying to get an indelible impression of you to take away with her forever.

She grabbed her bags and took off down the steps.

I waited until she rounded the corner, then took off after her. I knew she'd kill me if she saw me, but thankfully the sidewalks were mobbed with shoppers, so I was able to stay out of sight. Tailing her all the way into the subway, where she hopped on the Red Line. She got off at LaSalle Street.

Emerging from the packed station, I lost sight of her. I looked everywhere, even began to panic, worried that was it. I'd never know what happened to her, if she was safe, Bernstein, the precious gold coin slipping out of my fumbling hands, disappearing into Chicago's millions.

But then I spotted her. She was walking with her usual corkscrew gait past Gino's Pizza. I kept following her until she stopped in front of a shabby brownstone. I held back, slipping into a doorway.

I watched her skip up the stairs and ring the bell.

As I tailed her I mapped out the various rescue scenarios, barging in the front door, kicking aside the nine cats, the raccoon, four decades' worth of old newspapers, racing past the stoners making out on the couch, and the psychedelic poster for saving the planet, all the way upstairs to Elizabeth's room: bug friendly, stench of musty old clothes. Elizabeth, perched on the edge of a futon, would spring to her feet, throwing her arms around my neck.

Woodward? I made a huge mistake.

And yet. Through the building was certainly dodgy, rusty air conditioners, window boxes with dead plants, I noticed on the first and second floors there was not one but two bay windows, and they did appear to get a lot of light.

No one had answered the door. Elizabeth rang the buzzer a second time.

Let no one be home. Let the super nice hippie have had a family emergency back in Woodstock, or if someone answered, let it be a half-naked singer-songwriter with a tattoo on his chest the read **welcome to the rainbow**. *Please, Lord, let me just rescue her one more time.*

The door opened, and a plump woman with frizzy gray hair appeared, wearing a striped apron streaked with dirt from a flower bed or clay from a potter's wheel. She was unquestionably into tarot cards and soy, though I might have been wrong about everything else. Elizabeth said something, and the woman smiled, taking a Nordstroms bag as they disappeared inside the door closing.

I waited for something, music turning on, a light. But there was nothing, nothing for me, not anymore, only a soft breeze coursing down the block, pushing the stray yellow leaves and the bits of trash caught along the curb.

I walked home.

124

    I'd decided it'd be wise to take a few days to recover from El Esplanade, clear my head before organizing my thoughts and wrapping up the investigation. I had that persistent sense of having swum through leagues of blackened water, my insides still aching, my mind still streaked with mud.

    Yet real life was calling. I had unpaid bills, voicemails, month-old emails I hadn't bothered to open, quite a few from friends who'd written *I'm worried* and *You OK* and *WTF*??? In the subject lines. I wrote them all back, I'd bought a replacement HP laptop a week before we left for El Esplanade, but to do even this simple task seemed pointless and irritating.

    I began to realize, with a sort of morbid fascination, that I hadn't actually left El Esplanade, not entirely. Because the moment I was in bed, lights off, I needed only to close my eyes and I was back there. That property, maybe it was an unrequited time I'd always be returning to, the way others returned in their dreams to golden childhood dances, or battlefields, weekends at a lake house with some girl in a red bikini. Half awake, half dreaming, I plunged back inside that estate, wandering its dark gardens and statues hacked to pieces, past the dogs, the blinding flashlights manned by shadows. I backtracked through the tunnels, no longer searching for evidence to incriminate Esquivel, but some crucial part of myself I'd accidentally lost up there, like an arm, or my soul.

    That fear I'd felt, the disembodying confusion, seemed to be a drug I was now addicted to, because moving through the ordinary world watching CNN, reading the Sun-Times, walking to Intelligentsia Monadnock Coffeebar to have a coffee, made me feel exhausted, even depressed. Perhaps I was suffering from the same problem as the man who'd sailed around the world and now on land, facing his farmhouse, his wife, and kids, understood that the constancy of home stretching out before him like a dry flat field was infinitely more terrifying than any violent squall with thirty-foot swells.

Why did I assume that I'd be fine, be able to process El Esplanade as if it were a trip to Egypt or the time in Mexico I'd been held for eleven days in a jail cell, a harrowing experience to digest and get over? Not this thing. No, El Esplanade and the truth about what the man had done were still turning in my stomach, very much alive, pulsing and drooling and intact, making me increasingly sick, maybe even killing me.

This restlessness was made all the made worse by the fact that I was alone. Everyone was gone. Elizabeth was right. Cooper was as finished as was she. I called him twice, heard nothing. I didn't understand it, how they could both be done with the case and me, just as simple as that. Could they so ignorantly conclude that it all ended here. Didn't they want to know if those were real human bones I'd found up there, that there were no other children hurt in Esquivel's mad attempts to save Gabriela's life? Weren't they curious about the obvious remaining question, where was Esquivel now?

I drew all sorts of scathing conclusions, that they'd finally shown me their true colors, they were young and shallow. It was a larger indicator of the problems of today's youth. Raised by the Internet, they flitted from one fixation to the next with all the gravity of a mouse-click, but the truth was, I missed them. And I was furious that I cared.

It made me remember Cleo's pronouncement all those weeks ago when she'd found the killing curse on the soles of our shoes.

It pulls apart the closest friends, isolates you, pits you against the world so you're driven to the margins, the periphery of life. It'll drive you mad, which in some ways is worse than death.

I hadn't taken it seriously. Now I couldn't help but note how accurate it was turning out to be, the isolation and fractured friendships, the sense of being pushed to the outer margins of life.

Unless that was just Esquivel. Maybe he was a virus contagious, destructive, mutating constantly so you never quite grasped what you were dealing with, silently sewing himself onto your DNA. Those with even the barest exposure contracted a fascination and a fear that replicated to the point it overtook your entire life.

There was no cure. You could only learn to live with it.

After three days of wandering in my apartment, avoiding the box of the remaining Esquivel research, taking antibiotics and steroids for my hand and rash, I realized that to try and relax was making me so uncomfortable, I had little choice but to let it remain murky.

At eleven o'clock on Wednesday night, I hailed a taxi and told the driver to take me to Normal Street. Horrigan, unsurprisingly was right. When I stepped across the street staring at the shabby walk-up nestled by a viaduct, it appeared that every tenant, for whatever reason, had vacated.

Now every window was dark, though I could make out the ruffled pink gauzy curtains on the fifth floor. I tried the front entrance. It was locked, of course yet, staring through the small window, I noticed that the names had been removed from the mailboxes.

I took off toward Market Street, and within two blocks, past Mai Loo's Hair Salon, where I'd taped up Gabriela's flier in the window all those weeks ago. I was surprised to see that it was still there, only faded by the sun.

Gabriela was little more than a ghostly face, the words **HAVE YOU SEEN THIS GIRL?** Barely legible. Seeing it gave me a nagging feeling that time was running out, or maybe it was simply moving on.

Cooper and Elizabeth were gone, and now, so was Gabriela.

125

I'd tried Angela countless times, hoping for an update on Kim, but I'd still heard nothing. As much as her stonewalling drove me crazy, I did sense it meant the Kim was okay. If anything was seriously wrong, she'd phone me. At least, this was what I told myself.

As Katie Horrigan had explained, it was going to take at least a month until I knew if those were human bones I'd found up the El Esplanade So in the meantime, there were a few critical leads to follow up on.

I logged on to the blackboards, checking out rumors about the real world fate of Rudy Rodriguez, the actor that played Elmer. It seems that Rudy was a charismatic elderly man who had been spotted by three different individuals on three different occasions around Nathaniel Falls between October 1994 and August 1999. When I'd been inside the greenhouse, I'd had a distinct feeling that Elmer was somehow still there, tending his plants and fish, and these three sightings seemed to suggest that I was right.

Had Rudy never left? Had he loved his time at el Esplanade so much, or been so brainwashed, that he'd chosen to stay on as Elmer, preferring his character to real life? Was he dead now, externally buried in his fictitious gardens? I couldn't find any records of Rudy's family or where he'd come from. However, I was even more startled by the posting that detailed his disappearance inside Mag Trophy Appliance's, a store on the outskirts of Nathaniel Falls.

I'd come across the word Trophy back at El Esplanade. It had been scrawled above one of the entrances to the underground tunnels.

Had that particular corridor led to Mag Trophy Appliance, clandestinely linking Nathaniel Falls to El Esplanade? It was too specific a word to be a coincidence. And it explained how Elmer could have evaporated into thin air. He'd disappeared through a hidden hatch inside the store and headed home along this passage. I checked on the Blackboards for any other people that may have resided at El Esplanade, that I thought were most likely to be interviewed by Esquivel's assistant Marissa Garcia.

These people had scattered into the wind like ashes tossed in the air. I couldn't tell if they were fleeing something by disappearing into new lives. Or had they uncovered the truth about Esquivel, seen the man up close, and that horror was what made them run?

Or was it the opposite, had they been set free? Had they slaughtered the lamb, as they called it on the Blackboards, no longer restrained by anything; after working for Esquivel, were they able to design the wildest life they could fathom for themselves and set about fiercely living it?

From my vantage point, it was impossible to know if it was freedom or fear that drove them, or perhaps it was neither of these things and they'd been unleashed by Esquivel onto the world, his devoted disciples, sent out to do his bidding, his work, which was only God knows what.

Whatever their motivations, I wondered if they felt anything similar to what I was feeling, the exhaustion, the nightmares, the sense of dislocation, as if somehow I'd went beyond ordinary life and could no longer fit back down into it.

I was searching into this, looking on the Blackboards, not so facetiously for "aftereffects of Esquivel" and "known symptoms," when I was abruptly ejected from the site.

No matter how many times I unplugged my laptop, restarted the settings, got a new IP address, tried a new username, it resulted in the same exit page. Had I been banned, shut out, or found out?

126

    I turned my attention to investigating those plants that I'd hacked inside the greenhouse. The emergency room doctor's last words had been that I'd encountered a potent irritant and it'd be helpful to know what it was, in case the rash didn't improve. It was improving, had practically banished within twenty-four hours of my taking the steroid medication. Yet one search for Psycho Plant Extract was enough to set off alarm bells.

    Psycho Plant Extract was one of many nicknames for Datura Stramonioun or Jimsonweed, a plant so poisonous one cup of the tea could kill a grown man. According to Wikipedia, side effects of either sucking the juice or eating the seeds produced and inability to differentiate reality from fantasy, delirium, and hallucinations, bizarre and possibly violent behavior, severe mydriasis, dilation of the pupils, resulting in painful photophobia, intolerance to light, that can last several days. It gave men a sense of their upcoming deaths, turning ordinary people to natural fools.

    It's possible that, under the heat of those oppressive lights, sweating like a pig, I'd gotten drenched with the pollen and had unwittingly ingested it.

    I looked up every other name that I remembered, Tongue Tacks, Death Cherries, Blue Rocket, Eye-Prickles. I couldn't find Tongue Tacks or Eye Prickles anywhere, but the Blue Rocket was aconitum, one of the deadliest plants on Earth. It could be absorbed through the skin, resulting in convulsions, and within an hour, a prolonged and excruciating death similar to strychnine poisoning. Death cherries equaled belladonna, also lethal and known for its fantastic hallucinatory properties, a man of which came from one's hopes and mental wishes, turn them into a wild reality.

I hadn't realized it, but when I'd unwittingly wandered into that greenhouse, it was akin to stepping inside a nuclear waste plant with a slight leak in one of the reactors or walking through hell with a gasoline soaked suit on. It was a wonder that I wasn't dead, hadn't passed out somewhere on the property, fallen down a gorge, even jumped off the devil's bridge, imagining I could fly. Beyond the obvious horror of my safety, it now called into question everything I'd seen and experienced up there. I could no longer trust a single recollection after I'd entered that greenhouse.

Had I actually seen that stick man or been trapped inside those hexagons? Had I seen that deep ditch, or had my own overpowering hope to find tangible evidence up there conjure it up right before my eyes? Those people in black cloaks who'd swarmed me, one of them waiting inside that church confessional, had they been real? Or a drug-induced incarnation of my fear?

Now I couldn't prove it either way. I might as well have smoked a friggin crack pipe. It was an infuriating development, to say the least. Disgusted, vaguely enraged at myself for not being more careful, I decided to turn my attention instead to something concrete, something categorically real, researching missing persons in the Northern Illinois woodland.

Within a few hours, using the database from the National Center for Missing & Exploited Children, I'd compiled a list of individuals who'd gone missing within a three-hundred-mile radius of El Esplanade between 1976, the year Esquivel had moved into the estate, and the present day.

There was a markedly higher incidence of missing persons after 1992, the year of Gabriela traversing the bridge and the devil's curse.

There was also a young boy who went missing in Antioch, Illinois 144 miles from El Esplanade in May 1978. The four children reported killed in were between the ages of six and nine, it was a flimsy lead, but if Horrigan got back to me with confirmation that it was human blood, it was a worthwhile place to start. One of the children, Joey Hamilton, was six years old when his mother, a waitress, parked illegally on the curb and popped inside the restaurant to pick up a check, leaving her son alone in the backseat. She'd locked the car but left the back windows cracked. When she returned less than ten minutes later, the car was unlocked and her son was gone. He has never been seen again.

The other incidents were similarly haunting, so many last seen and symbolic detail's: Sophie Dickenson's necklace. Jessica Carter's crayon drawing of a black fish discovered in her bed when she was found missing by her parents. Unfortunately given that Esquivel would probably know how to obscure his tracks, no detail I read overtly linked any of these cases to Esquivel. No sighting of a mysterious man wearing black lenses that blocked out his eyes.

Nothing, but the one tenuous clue. Laura Helmsley's locker had been ransacked a week before she ran away from home, and she'd reported her journal stolen to the school office. This detail was vaguely reminiscent of the incidents John, the anonymous caller, had described.

Had Esquivel stolen the girl's journal, hoping she might serve as an equal exchange for Gabriela? Police believed Laura had simply run off with her older boyfriend. They'd been caught on camera at a White Castle drive-thru two days after she disappeared.

But there'd been no word from her in more than ten years. Before I'd read about the hallucinogenic plants. I might have believed in an alternate possibility, that the world had simply opened up and swallowed these people whole. It actually seemed the only logical explanation in the case of Kurt Sullivan, who disappeared across thirty yards of an easy hiking trail in the Moose River Plains Wild Forest (Ninety-four-miles from El Esplanade). He left his family, skipping around the bend back to the campsite to put on longer socks, and was never seen again. A six-hundred-man search, which included help from the U.S. Air Force, elicited not one clue as to what had happened to the boy.

Shadows with wills of their own, killing curses and devil's curses, rivers that ran black and beasts with bark for skin, the world with invisible fissures that anyone could accidentally fall down into at any time. I could have actually considered it after what had happened to me at El Esplanade. Hadn't this investigation of Esquivel been hinting at the outskirts of such a reality, a world that was infinitely mysterious, shrouded with the questions that were impossible to explain? Esquivel might very well be a madman, have fatally erased all boundaries between fantasy and reality in his life and work, but hadn't he been legitimately able to harness some kind of power up there, whatever it was? Hadn't it been true? Hadn't I witnessed it with my own eyes?

Now I didn't know what I believed. It was logical I'd simply been exposed to too many Psycho Plant Extract.

Anyway, what was Esquivel, or Elmer doing keeping that greenhouse thriving with enough toxic plants to wipe out an army?

The more missing person's cases I read, the more those mysteries seemed to fray into a million threads. Still, I jotted down the various details, vague developments mentioned by local newspapers and missing-person blogs. Then my mind overloaded, I tore myself away from the computer, deciding to head uptown to Onofrio.

If Gabriela had frequented to shop as a child, as Cooper had told us, I wanted to talk to someone who knew her from those early days. The manager we'd spoken to, Caesar DePasquale might be helpful finding such a person.

When I arrived, however, I was shocked to learn something odd had happened, or else it wasn't odd at all, given what I'd been researching the past three days.

Ceasar DePasquale was gone.

127

"What do you mean?" I asked.

"He quit," said the young man behind the Onofrio counter.

"When?"

"Two weeks ago."

"Where did he go?"

"No clue. It was pretty sudden. Mr. Froehlich, the owner, was pissed because we're short staffed now. I'm just an intern. But Caesar had been having some problems, so."

"Do you have his phone number?"

The kid looked it up and I dialed it, heading out of the shop, the Fazioli piano that Gabriela had played still sat in the window.

I stopped on the sidewalk in disbelief. A recording announced that the number had been disconnected.

I didn't know what it meant, only that something was wrong. I hailed a cab and ten minutes later was striding into the lobby of Madelyn's building. I recognized the chubby faced doorman as the second one who'd been on duty the day I'd approached Harold.

"I'm looking for Harold," I said, stepping toward him.

"He doesn't work here anymore. Got a brand new gig on the Mag-Mile. Some swanky white-glove building."

"Which one? I need the address."

"He didn't say."

"I need to go upstairs to see Madelyn." I handed him my business card. "I'm a friend of Olivia Wainscott's."

"Madelyn?"

"Madelyn Hughes, apartment 1421."

He looked uncomfortable. "Yeah, Miss Hughes isn't exactly . . . home."

"Where is she?"

"I can't discuss the particulars."

Alarm flooding through me, I handed the man a hundred bucks, which he cheerfully pocketed.

"They packed her off to rehab," he said quietly. "She had an incident. But she's all right."

"Could you still let me into her apartment?"

He shook his head. "Sorry, no. No one's been up there since."

"I know Olivia's out of the country, but call her assistant she'll authorize it."

He looked doubtful but waited patiently while I found the number. "Yeah, hi," he said into the phone after I dialed for him. "This is The Dearborn Plaza. I got a gentleman here." He squinted down at my business card. "Shawn McCarthy." He went on to explain the situation, falling silent.

And then, abruptly, his face so amiable before sobered. He looked at me, visibly startled, then hung up without a word.

He stood up, coming around the side of the desk, his arm out to escort me toward the door.

"You're gonna have to be on your way, mister."

"Just tell me what she said."

"If you harass any of the people here again, I'm gonna call security. You don't have any connection to Olivia Wainscott."

Outside, I turned back, speechless, but he was standing staunchly at the door, staring at me.

I headed swiftly down the sidewalk. When I reached the corner, I dialed Olivia's assistant's number myself. She picked up immediately.

"This is Shawn McCarthy. What the hell just happened?"

"I beg your pardon, sir? I don't know what you're talking about."

"Cut the bullshit. What'd you tell the doorman?"

She said nothing, seemingly deciding whether or not to feign ignorance. Then in a cold, curt voice. "Mrs. Pierre would prefer it if you did not contact her or any member of her family."

"Mrs. Pierre and I are working together."

"Not anymore. She wants no further connection to your activities."

I hung up, seething, and phoned The Dearborn Plaza management company to get Harold's home phone number.

I was disconnected.

128

I went back home and systematically tried contacting every witness we'd encountered during the investigation.

Lexi, the bachelor party entertainer who'd tipped us off to Gabriela heading to Les Silencio. I called the number on her business card and was informed by the automated recording that her voicemail box was full.

This didn't change, not even after five days.

I dialed Stanley Dewitt. I no longer had the page torn out of the phone book that had been stolen when my office was broken into but found it after calling directory assistance.

There was only a busy signal. I tried the number every hour for the next seven hours. It remained busy.

After learning from the assistant director of housekeeping at the Warwick that Lupe was no longer an employee at the hotel, I decided to track down the red haired young nurse who'd run out in front of our car at Mission Hills. I remembered her name, Christina Granger, Stanley Dewitt had mentioned it.

"Christina Granger was a student nurse in our central administration for three months," a man in the nursing department explained.

"Can I speak to her?"

"Her last day was November third."

That was more than three weeks ago.

"Is there a number where I can reach her? A home address?"

"That's not available."

Was this somehow my doing? Had I lost my mind? The primary symptom of madness was near-constant amazement at the world and a suspicion of all people from strangers to family and friends.

I had both symptoms in spades. Why wouldn't I? Every witness, every stranger, and a bystander who'd encountered Gabriela were extinct now. They'd silently receded like a fog I hadn't noticed was lifting until it was gone. It was what had actually happened to my anonymous caller, John, years ago.

Or did I have it all wrong? Had these people run for their lives, going missing, absconding to the outer reaches of the world, like the countless people that were interviewed at El Esplanade. What were they afraid of, him because they talked to me about his daughter? With my notes stolen, there was no record of what they'd told me about Gabriela. Their testimony now existed solely in my head, and Cooper's and Elizabeth's

But even they were gone now.

Then, it existed solely in my head.

Filled with sudden worry that Elizabeth and Cooper might have vanished in the same way as the others, I called both of them, leaving messages to call me back. I then phoned Angela, suddenly wanting to hear Kim's voice, irrationally worried she, too, was gone. It went to voicemail. I left a terse message, threw on my coat, and left the apartment.

129

In the fading daylight, Stanley Dewitt's driveway looked so different from the night the three of us drove up here, I hardly recognized it. I pulled over to the shoulder, cut the engine, and climbed out.

Immediately I was hit by a smell: *smoke*.

I started up the drive. Some overgrown branches had been split backward and broken in half as if a large truck had driven up here. The charred smell grew stronger, and when I crested the top I stopped, staring out at the lawn in front of me.

Stanley Dewitt's ramshackle house had burned to the ground.

I headed toward it, light headed with shock. Both cars were gone. All that remained was a charred air conditioner and half a splintered swing.

My guess was the fire had happened a week ago, maybe longer, and it wasn't an accident. I climbed through it looking for evidence, but the only identifiable objects I found were a blackened ceramic bathtub, the burnt base of a La-Z-Boy, and a plastic doll's arm reaching out from the rubble. Seeing it made me wonder if it belonged to the baby, the doll Stanley had fished out of the kiddie pool. Immediately I made my way across the overgrown grass toward the far corner of the yard.

I spotted it exactly where it had been before, still partially inflated yet turned upside down. I flung it upright and saw, apart from the encrusted leaves, a sizable black splotch stained the bottom.

It had to be where Gabriela had hidden the doll, so her spell inside the leviathan figurine would work. It was oddly overwhelming to see as if that black mark was the last confirmation that what we'd learned about her life and death had been real.

Who had torched the house? Had Stanley and his family been inside when it happened or long gone, like every other witness Gabriela had met?

I spent a half hour roaming the debris trying to find answers, once disbelieving and angered by the finality of it. I felt as if this scorched devastation wasn't simply Dewitt's house, but the entire investigation.

Because all of it was gone, wasted and me, the last man too late, trawling through it, digging for an underlying truth now gone.

Starting back to my car, I spotted lying in the tall grass, something small and white.

It was a cigarette butt.

There were four. I picked up one and saw the strange, minuscule brand printed by the filter. I hastily collected all four butts and then, my head spinning, sprinted down the driveway.

Davidoff.

130

Anderson, dressed in black corduroys and a blue plaid flannel shirt, was speaking in front of a packed lecture hall. There were at least three hundred students, everyone hanging on his every word.

If anyone could give me answers about all the people associated with Esquivel mysteriously disappeared, it was Anderson. A criminal historian and expert on the empire of Esquivel.

Rather dramatically, Anderson turned on his heel, raising the remote, like a sorcerer pointing a magic wand, and a film clip appeared on the gigantic screen behind him. It was the final minutes of *Se7en,* which featured Morgan Freeman and Brad Pitt as Somerset and Mills, and Kevin Spacey as John Doe in the back of the police car.

I knocked a second time on the window, and this time, Anderson heard me, jolted in evident surprise, glanced back at his students, and scurried over.

"McCarthy, what the hell," he hissed, opening the door a crack.

"I need to talk to you."

"Can't you see I'm in the middle of something?"

"This is an emergency."

His dark eyes blinked at me behind his glasses. He glanced over his shoulder. His students remained transfixed watching the clip, so he quickly darted out onto the hall, silently closing the door.

"What in the world . . . you know I don't like to be interrupted while I'm teaching. There's a little something called creative flow."

"I need the names of your cats."

"Excuse me?"

"Your cats, your friggin cats. What are their names?"

A female student walking past turned, looking at me warily.

"My friggin cats?' Anderson repeated, staring at me. "This is why I've never liked you, McCarthy. Not only are you rude and demanding, but cats you've been introduced to fifteen, sixteen times you don't have any recollection of as if they're somehow beneath you." He opened his mouth, on the verge of rebuking me further, but must have noticed I was frantic because he pushed his glasses farther onto the bridge of his nose.

"Their full names or their nicknames?"

"Full birth names. Start with the one you told me about the other day. Something about Davidoff Turkish cigarettes."

Anderson cleared his throat. "Davidoff cigarettes. Bernardo the Burglar's son. One-Eyed Pontiac. The Peeping Tom shot. The Know Not What. Steak Tartare." He kneaded his eyebrows. "How many is that?"

"Six." I was writing them down.

"Evil King. Phil Lumen. And last but not least, the shadow. There you have it. Enjoy." With a matador's Ole, he started for the door.

"These are what, Esquivel's trademarks?"

He sighed. "McCarthy, I've explained it countless times."

"How do they work, exactly? Where do they appear?"

He closed his eyes. "In every detail of nefarious business Esquivel constructs, rain or shine, at least one or two, sometimes up to five of these trademarks, signatures, if you will, show up unannounced, like a long lost family member on Christmas Eve. Naturally, they cause a great deal of drama." He squinted at me, observing my scribbling. "What's this about, anyway?"

I reached into my pocket, holding out the cigarette butts. Anderson, frowning, picked up one, scrutinizing it, and then, probably reading the brand printed by the filter, stared at me in alarm.

"Where in God's name did you find this."

"In the country. At the scene of a house fire."

"But they don't exist except in Esquivel's dream world.

"I'm in one."

"Excuse me?"

"I think I'm inside an Esquivel make believe world. One of his narratives. And it's not over."

"What are you talking about?"

"He set me up. Esquivel. Maybe Gabriela, too. I don't know why or how. All I know is that I tried to uncover the circumstances around Gabriela's death and every person I spoke to, everyone who met her, has disappeared. The man had a penchant for working with reality, manipulating his employee's, pushing them to the brink. Now he's done it with me."

Anderson's mouth was open, his eyes wide with disbelief. He appeared to have entered some kind of unresponsive fugue state.

"Just tell me about the cigarettes," I said.

He took a breath. "McCarthy, this is really not good."

"Can you be a little more specific?"

"Didn't I tell you to leave him alone?" his voice trailing off while putting his head in his hands.

"The cigarettes!"

He tried to collect himself. "If you find the cigarette's after they have been smoked, it means you're marked, McCarthy. Your fate is sealed. You're doomed."

"But there's some way out, right?"

"No." He arched an eyebrow. "There is a very slim chance if you manage to make a huge and improbable leap of faith you will survive, but it's like jumping from the top of one skyscraper to the next. It almost always ends with you splat on the sidewalk, either dead or caught forever in a sticky hell, struggling in your cocoon.

I jotted it down. "What about Bernardo the Burglar's son?"

"Esquivel's longtime hitman. His full name is Christopher Heath. He's a brawny Eastern European. His father was a notorious gangster known back in the motherland simply as the Black Eye.

The man successfully managed to escape every gulag they ever locked him in and he taught his only son, Christopher, all of his techniques.

Esquivel used Christopher in every situation that required special attention. He did all the dirty work, the cons, the beat downs, the breaking and entering, the car wrecks, the disappearances. He is fast as the wind and can escape anything at any time."

It took only a second for me to know where I'd encountered him.

"I chased him," I said. "I spoke to him."

"You spoke to Bernardo the Burglar's Son, and lived?"

Quickly I explained how he'd broken into my apartment, hightailed it across Erie Street going toward Navy Pier, posing as a cruising gay man and then vanishing in the blink of an eye.

"McCarthy, how could you miss it? He used the Horny Geezer on you, one of his most legendary cons."

"What about One-Eyed Pontiac?"

Anderson thoughtfully interlaced his fingers. "There's always a dark-colored Pontiac, black, blue, or deep maroon, with a single headlight. Whatever object of person it illuminates in its single glaring light will be annihilated."

I remembered it immediately: Cooper had claimed to see such a car in the parking lot of the Valley View Motel when they'd been waiting for me to return from El Esplanade. I hastily made a note of it, Anderson eyeing my scribblings.

"You saw the One-Eyed Pontiac?" He gasped, putting his hand over his mouth. "Don't tell me you were in its headlights."

"I wasn't. someone else saw it. The Peeping Tom Shot?"

He blinked in flustered exasperation. "It's Esquivel's trademark shot. The peeping tom is a single shot into the back of another person's head. And that person doesn't know he is being watched, while he is watching someone else. I thought it over, but it didn't seem to shed any light on what I'd encountered over the course of the investigation.

"The Know Not What?" I went on.

Anderson shrugged. "He's the henchman, the right-hand man, the face-man, the flunky. He appears when his boss will not passively carry out his orders with no judgment, thereby releasing a dark, malevolent force upon the world. The phrase comes from the Bible, of course. Luke, chapter twenty-three: 'Father, forgive them, for they know not what they do.'"

It took me a moment of racking my brain, and then the answer hit me. It was so obvious I nearly laughed out loud. I scribbled down his name.

"Santo Esquivel?" said Anderson, reading over my shoulder. "What do you want with Santo Esquivel?"

"He's been following me."

"Esquivel's son? But how did you know it was he?"

"He's missing three fingers on his left hand."

Anderson looked startled. "That's right. Santo was always a strange silent young man. Badgered by his father, lovesick for the same older woman for yours."

I hastily made a note of it. "Steak Tartare?"

Anderson eagerly licked his lips. "In every instance of inner circle betrayal from a defector, a turncoat, a whore, a deserter, someone that cannot be trusted. Esquivel reminds us of our omnipresent inner cannibal, a reminder that we all are, in the end, ravenous beasts who will satisfy our ugliest desires when the timing is right. They say it's his favorite meal.

"Evil King?"

"Evil king," Anderson announced officially, clearing his throat. "He's the villain. A universally terrifying character of both myth and the real world. He can look outwardly disgusting or totally innocuous. Usually, it's someone in a position of great power. The smarter and more conniving the Evil King, the more turbulent and satisfying the tempest he creates."

That one was easy. Esquivel.

"Phil Lumen?"

Anderson nodded. "A small detail. The Phil Lumen Company is the manufacturing import-export business that Esquivel uses to expand his empire.

Everything Esquivel gets from overseas comes from Phil Lumen Company, which is Latin for Love of Light. Occasionally the name is called out in airport intercoms. 'paging Mr. Phil lumen', please report to United Airlines Terminal B.'"

I didn't recall hearing anything of the kind, not that I would have noticed.

"The Shadow?"

Anderson paused, smiling sadly. "My favorite. The Shadow is what people are hunting throughout life. It's a potent force that bewitches as much as it torments. It can lead to hell or heaven. It's the hollow forever inside you, never filled. It's everything in life you can't touch nor hold on to, so ephemeral and painful it makes you gasp. You might even glimpse it for a few seconds before it's gone. Yet the image will live with you. You'll never forget it as long as you live. It's what you're terrified of and paradoxically what you're looking for. We are nothing without our shadows. They give our otherwise pale, blinding world definition. They allow us to see what's right in front of us. yet they'll haunt us until we're dead."

It was Gabriela. Anderson had seamlessly described my encounter with her at the Reservoir. As he watched me write down her name, his black beady eyes moved from the word to my face.

"What else?" I asked.

"What else about what?"

"Esquivel's mind. His stories."

After a moment, Anderson shrugged, a wistful expression on his face. "Those constants festering inside Esquivel's brain are all I've ever been able to come up with. The rest, as they say, is history, I've never liked that phrase, but revolution. Constant upheaval. Conversion. Rotation. Oh, dear." He jolted upright, struck by an idea. "One thing, McCarthy."

"What?"

"Often, at some point in Esquivel's world you will be faced with a choice, a fork in the road, sitting there either your life will be starting new, to meld into his world, or your life will end completely.

I made a note of it, feeling an insidious wave of dread as I did, folding a scrap of paper into my pocket.

"Thank you," I said to Anderson, abruptly he appeared to be in too ruminating a mood to speak. "I'll explain when I have more time," I added, starting down the hall.

"McCarthy."

I stopped, turning. He was staring at me.

"I need to give you the last bit of advice in the off chance this rather extraordinary and enviable situation in which you find yourself is actually true, that somehow you've fallen deep down into an Esquivel experience."

I stared back at him.

"Be the good guy," he said.

"How do I know I'm the good guy?"

He pointed at me, nodding. "A very wise question. You don't. Most bad guys think they're good. But there are a few signifiers. You'll be miserable. You'll be hated. You'll fumble around in the dark, alone and confused. You'll have little insight as to the true nature of things, not until the very last minute, and only if you have the stamina and the madness to go to the very, very end. But most importantly, and critically, you will act without regard for yourself. You'll be motivated by something that has nothing to do with the ego. You'll do it for justice, for grace, for love. Those large rather heroic qualities only the good have the strength to carry on their shoulders. And you'll listen."

He licked his lips again, frowning.

"If you're the good guy, you just might survive, McCarthy. But of course, there are no guarantees with Esquivel."

"I understand."

"Good luck to you," he said, then spun quickly on his heel and, without looking at me again, vanished back inside his classroom.

131

I cased the townhouse, the one Cooper had broken into, for the next eleven days. I returned home to unrestful sleep, of course, leaving a small thread clandestinely strung across the base of the front door, secured with a microscopic piece of attaching putty, so I'd know if anyone entered while I was away.

But the thread remained intact.

At this point, all that I accepted as the truth was that somehow I'd been artfully set up, beginning, I sensed, with Gabriela appearing that night at the Reservoir. But why or how it had been planned and executed, whether or not the witnesses we'd tracked down had even been telling the truth about Gabriela's behavior, what was real, what wasn't. I didn't know anymore. Could something be real when all evidence of it was gone? Was something categorically true if it lived on only in your head, same as your dreams?

Esquivel, in his life of work and play, had blended fantasy and reality, and so he seemed to be flagrantly showing off to me, much to my chagrin, such an intermingling of truth and fiction. Perhaps it was his way of underscoring for me, not just his superiority, that he was beyond unmasking, that I'd never catch him, but that, in some cases, the biggest truth about a family, about a person's life, was the fantasy and it was only a simple man's mind that craved one being tidily distinguished from the other.

Cooper and Elizabeth, shortly after I'd interrupted Anderson's lecture, had both called me back within a few hours of each, worriedly asking if I was all right. It seemed, then, that the two of them had not disappeared like all the others. They were only preoccupied with getting on with their lives. Elizabeth was in the midst of practicing Al Pacino's opening monolog from Glengarry Glen Ross, which she was planning to do for her Hamlette audition at the Goodman Theater. My conversation with Cooper, though civil, was stilted, part of which was because we were constantly interrupted by his incoming calls and he hadn't exactly forgiven me for my choice to keep stripping away the truth about Gabriela. They both asked me if I was still working on the investigation, but didn't seem to want to hear the answer. I sensed that Gabriela was something in their pasts now, a dusky beautiful day they wanted to remember in a certain moody light, with a certain haunting theme song, and they didn't want to hear another experience that would tarnish this image.

I hung up with both of them, mentioning nothing about the disappearances of every one of our witnesses or anything about the Davidoff cigarettes, the Esquivel trademarks that seemed to have peppered the real-life investigation.

There was one crucial person, however, who remained exactly where I'd found her. I went back to Fascinations, stepping unannounced through the black curtain into the back room, expecting to see someone new sitting at the round table who'd duly inform me Cleo had moved to the Louisiana bayou.

But to my surprise, and relief, Cleo was there. She was surprised to see me, and after a few awkward, pleasantries, which involved me asking her is she knew Esquivel, the drug lord, public enemy number one.

"No," she answered, viably confused. She gazed, at checking the red bulb in the light overhanging the table to see if by chance it was manufactured by Phil Lumen, it was GE.

I thanked her and swiftly left, my mind obsessively replaying the last time I'd seen her when she'd showed me how the leviathan's tail moved with a mind of its own.

That had been real.

It couldn't be explained away by my having ingested Psycho Plant Extract. It was a hint of the reality of black magic, of dark and invisible fractures cutting through our ordinary world.

Wasn't it? Thinking all of this over for days, finally, I received the phone call I'd been waiting for.

"McCarthy. Katie Horrigan."

I felt uneasy hearing her voice. Something told me I was not going to like what she said about the strained shirt I'd given her and the bones.

"We were able to take a look at what you gave me."

"And?"

"There's nothing there."

She paused as if sensing I'd be distressed by the news.

"There's no blood, animal or otherwise, in the Kimple. What they found was trace glucose, maltose, some oligosaccharides."

"What's that?"

"Corn syrup. It might have been soda, some canned or bottled beverage that spilled on the shirt. How it was stored over the years must have created the stiffness. But it's such a degraded Kimple, it's hard to say."

"There's absolutely no chance it's human blood?"

"No chance."

I closed my eyes. *Corn syrup.*

"And the bones?" I asked.

"They were traced to family Ursidae, probably Ursus Americanus."

"What's that?"

"A black bear. It's probably the foot of a bear cub."

A black bear.

"You need a vacation," Katie said. "Leave town for a couple weeks. The city can screw with tour head. Like all toxic love affairs, you need to take a break before you go back in for more pain and heartbreak."

I had nothing to say because it couldn't be right. I'd been so certain, of the movie sets, that they had contained real human suffering. It couldn't end like this.

"You still there?" Katie asked.

"I'm sorry to have bothered you with this," I managed to say.

She cleared her throat. "You need to move on. I understand, believe me, how this stuff gets to you, that there's nothing more important than finding that hidden door which will lead to the underground bunker where the truth is sitting there behind bars. But sometimes the truth just isn't there. Even if you can smell it and hear it. Or there just isn't a way in anymore. It's grown over. Rocks have shifted. Shafts caved in. there's no human way to get to it, not even with all the dynamite in the world. So you leave it at that. And you move on."

As she said this, a phone began to bleat on her end, though she ignored it.

"The dark side of life has a way of finding us all anyway, so stop chasing it."

"Thank you, Katie, for everything."

"Forget it. Now, would you go to the beach, get a girlfriend, a tan, something?"

"Sure."

"Take care."

"You, too."

The line went dead. A black bear's foot.

I went about the rest of my day, trying to get my mind off the sheer disappointment, telling myself to accept it, that Cooper and Elizabeth were right. I'd come to the end of the road. And found an undeniable dead end. There was no evidence of any crime.

But then, I realized, there was one last stone to turn over. There was one person left who might shed light on the situation, who could explain from an insider's point of view what it all meant, and that person was Esquivel's longtime assistant, Marissa Garcia.

I needed only to wait for her to return to the townhouse. I'd wait as long as it took. And when that woman finally appeared, whether it was tomorrow or three years from now, I'd be ready.

132

It happened the twelfth day I'd been watching. Just after five o'clock in the evening, I was returning from a deli when I noticed a petite woman in a black coat walking swiftly down the sidewalk, half a block in front of me.

It was Marissa Garcia. I recognized her immediately, the hastily cropped gray hair, hunched, stalwart bearing like a tiny bull poised to charge. As if she didn't want to be seen, she hurried up to the steps, disappearing inside.

I waited for a few minutes, and when the street remained deserted, I grabbed the wrought-iron gate spanning the townhouse's first-floor window and began to climb. I needed Garcia off her guard, and I remembered how Cooper had done it, wedging his feet between the bars, bracing his right foot on the old-fashioned lamp over the front door. Seizing the latticed railing along the second floor high over my head, I headed to the window on the right, the one that Gabriela had disabled from the house alarm.

Garcia had turned on quite a few lights in the entrance hall below, because the light was shining through the doorway opposite, allowing me to see. It was an ornate wood-paneled library, every piece of furniture covered in white sheets. It was empty.

I took out a credit care, wedged it under the window's sash, lifting it just enough to get my fingers underneath, slid it open, and climbed inside.

Cooper had said the night he'd broken in, that the townhouse looked frozen in time. He found every object to be sitting precisely where it's been seven years before, the day Gabriela and he were due to leave for Brazil and she'd stood him up. same exact sheets tossed randomly over the furniture, he'd said, the same Chopin music on Gabriela's piano. Now everything was meticulously covered and put away when I lifted the sheet over the massive Steinway, positioned in the far corner by the bookshelves, there was no music. It seemed to me someone, Marissa Garcia, perhaps, had packed up the house more carefully now, maybe as a result of Cooper breaking in. Or else the family had asked her to do it after Gabriela's body had been found.

There was an armchair facing the library's entrance, which overlooked the lit up landing and spiral staircase. I say down, waiting, and within minutes I could hear footsteps rapidly coming up the steps.

Suddenly, there she was, Marissa Garcia, in baggy gray wool slacks and a white blouse, hurrying across the landing, headed for the next flight.

"Miss Garcia."

She froze, stunned, and whipped around, staring in at me, though probably couldn't see much beyond my silhouette.

"Or do you prefer to be called Jaguar?"

She lurched furiously to the doorway, sliding her hand over a light switch, and suddenly the library was bathed in dim gold light from the overhead lamp.

When she saw me, she sized me up with enough scorn for me to know she knew precisely who I was.

"Sorry to drop in like this."

"You people just can't take a hint. I hope you like sleeping in jail." It was a deep, throaty voice, which sounded better suited for a truck driver or a six-foot bouncer, not such a hefty yet diminutive woman. She was barely five feet but shaped like a cinder block. She strode into the library and snatched a cordless phone off the counter, started to dial.

"I wouldn't do that."

"No?'

"Jaguar is an intriguing nickname. Personally, I'd have wanted my term of endearment to be a little less incriminating. Human trafficking for forced labor? My friend at ICE, Immigrations and Custom's Enforcement, tells me there used to be quite a racket originating from your hometown. Puebla, isn't it? Apparently, a mysterious woman arrived in an empty minivan once a year and left with it chock-full of people, stacked in the back like firewood. I've spoken to a few. The punishment per offense is a minimum of three to seven years. How many films did the work up there? Ten? That's thirty to seventy years. After El Esplanade, I expect federal prison will be quite a culture shock."

As I spoke, I'd been watching Garcia's face. The second I'd said human trafficking; I knew I'd hit the bulls-eye.

And thank God, because I was bluffing. I had no friend at the ICE and not a single witness. For the last few days, I'd pored over my hastily rewritten notes, trying to nail down something, anything to use against Garcia. I kept returning to her nickname, mentioned by both Julie Froehlich and Madelyn Hughes: Jaguar. A Jaguar was a wild predator, but it was also slang for anyone who escorts illegal aliens over the Mexican-U.S. border.

They could range from makeshift mom-and-pop organizations to those sponsored by billion-dollar drug cartels.

Julie Froehlich had specifically mentioned the crew had used the nickname, and thus I wondered if it was because Garcia had been their actual Jaguar. That, combined with her birthday in Mexico and Madelyn's assertion that Garcia did Esquivel's dirty work, I made the theoretical leap that it just might be Garcia who had transported all of the illegal aliens to El Esplanade. The arrangement probably was that they worked on premises for three months, witnessing any number of appalling acts, and then, after being sufficiently threatened so they'd never spill the beans, were free to go. It was unquestionably a long shot, and I hadn't expected it to work, until now, when I'd watched the color drain out of Garcia's face.

She'd transformed considerably in the years since her bright-eyed teenager wedding photo. It was as if all those decades serving the director, standing in such close proximity to him, had petrified her, made her gray hair grow coarser and wirier, her low brow heavier, her lips tighten as pulled string. There seemed nothing left in her that was light or carefree. Perhaps that is what happened when one decided to forever be a fixture in the dark side of life.00

She hadn't moved a muscle, only watched me intently. She put down the phone.

"What do you want, Mr. McCarthy?"

"To have a heart-to-heart."

"We've nothing to discuss."

"I disagree. We can start with Gabriela Esquivel being dead at twenty-four, then I have another problem, the fact that everyone I've talked to about Gabriela has gone missing, including a man's house, burned to the ground. If you talk to me, maybe my friend at ICE will let your slave-labor operation slide."

She looked furious but bit her tongue, striding deliberately to the bar in the corner and pouring herself a drink.

"If that was slave labor, then millions would die to be slaves," she muttered. "They lived like kings."

"They couldn't leave. So technically they were slave prisoners."

"It's how they paid for their crossing, all agreed to ahead of time. There was no coercion and no lies. At the end of their time agreement, we could hardly get them to go. They wanted to stay forever."

"Like kids not wanting to leave Disneyland. Touching."

She narrowed her eyes. "What do you hope to gain out of all this?"

"The truth."

"The truth." She smirked, quick as a spark off a defunct lighter, then looked serious. I could see she was genuinely shocked by my showing up here, of that I was certain, and seemed now to be deciding how best to handle the situation, the quickest way to be rid of me. She must have decided to play along, at least for now, because she cocked her head to the side and smiled stiffly.

"Can I get you a drink?"

"So long as it's not poured over arsenic."

She fixed me a glass of Jameson from the same bottle she'd served herself, and hurried over, thrust the glass at me.

I noticed as she sat down on the couch adjacent, she actually had a small wheel tattoo on the back of her left hand, exactly as I'd read weeks ago on the Blackboards. The anonymous poster had claimed it was evidence Garcia and Esquivel could be the same person. Staring at her rigid profile now, I considered the possibility that this was Esquivel. But there was something about the woman, in her stocky lieutenant's bearing, in her flitting eyes, so subservient and unfulfilled, as if the eternal object if her attention was not present, but standing somewhere in the wings.

No, she was most certainly not Esquivel. I was positive. And she was stalling.

"Before you demand to see the scaffolding, Mr. McCarthy," she said, staring me down, "make sure it is what you actually want to see. The cranks and the ropes and the metal supports. The rust and the heavy chains. Lights painstakingly positioned overhead. It's a different reality than what you may think."

She tilted her head as if struck by a new thought, closely scrutinizing my face and smiling thinly.

"It's funny. I'd have thought you of all people would have been onto her. You really never saw it?"

"Saw what?"

"Surely you must have noticed hints. Here and there, clues."

"Hints of what?" Suddenly I sensed I no longer had the upper hand in this situation, that Marissa Garcia had recovered, or I'd never had her in a corner in the first place.

She raised an eyebrow. "You really never figured it out?"

"Figured out what?"

"Gabriela was sick."

"From the devil's curse."

She chuckled. "I can assure you, and so can an army of doctors and specialists around the world, Gabriela never suffered from a devil's curse. Or any other type of curse. She had cancer. Acute lymphoblastic leukemia. She had it off and on all her life."

I stared at her, stunned.

First infuriated inclination was to tell her I knew what she was doing, force-feeding me another lie so I'd trust her. It was a preposterous assertion and I knew it wasn't true.

It couldn't be.

But then, almost as quickly, I wondered if I'd missed something, if Cooper had, if this real-life illness, had been there all the time, written in the sand, and we'd been straining our eyes, staring for out to sea, never once looking at our feet.

"Call Northwestern if you don't believe me," Garcia added petulantly. "Find someone to bribe in the records department, and they'll tell you. Gabriela was treated there three times, the first time when she was five, the second when she was fourteen, and finally when she was seventeen, also at Loyola."

She looked at me with triumph. "You'll see I'm right."

I said nothing, going through the dates in my head. Gabriela had been only five years old when she'd crossed the devil's bridge, condemning her to the curse. At fourteen she'd abruptly abandoned her classical music career, I felt a rush of disbelief: At seventeen Gabriela had called Cooper, crying. She was desperate, he'd told us. She couldn't live with her parents anymore. She wanted to go where they couldn't find her. Had she wanted to escape her illness?

"It isn't your fault," Garcia said as if reading my mind.

"Whatever wild nonsense you've come to believe in, curses and Satan, the bogeyman, though honestly, I'd have expected a grown man, a veteran detective, to be a little more skeptical. But give yourself a break. Gabriela was a charismatic girl. You'd be surprised what she's convinced people of over the years. She was quite proficient in making people believe the impossible. Like her father. They had a knack the both of them for taking you by the hand, looking deep into your eyes, so you'd follow them down into the passageways of the absurd and unbelievable and live there forever a total convert. I know I did it for forty-six years. Gave up everything, my husband, my kids. But now that it's over I can see. Probably because I'm not one of them. I live in the real world, and so do you."

She said it insistently, even angrily, crossing her arms.

"Her sickness tore the family apart. For young children the prognosis for all is good. After the first round of treatment, most have remissions that last a lifetime. It wasn't the case with Gabriela. Every time we thought she was out of the woods, that she would at last be granted the gift of a life without round after round of shots and steroids, spinal taps, and stem-cell transplants. A few years had passed, she'd was tested, and the doctors would give us the terrible news. Ruby had returned."

"Ruby?" I repeated.

She nodded, eyeing me. "It was Gabriela's name for her illness. She nicknamed it, the way other children nickname imaginary friends, which will give you a good sense of the way her mind worked. When she was five, one morning she came into the kitchen, and as she ate her bowl of cereal she cheerfully announced to her mother that she had a new friend. Who? Delores asked her. Ruby, she answered. It was a strange name. No one knew where she'd heard it. Ruby is going to kill me, Gabriela said. Everyone was startled, but then, she was her father's daughter. Dramatic, blessed, or you might even say cursed, with the most graphic of imaginations.

The very next day, Gabriela became sick with a high fever. Tiny red spots covered her arms and her back. Delores took her to the hospital, and the doctors gave us the terrible news."

Carlos didn't want anything to do with his business anymore. It's excruciating for a parent to lose a child. But it's even worse to watch your child suffer, day in, day out, teetering interminably between life and death, living a life of death. But you go through with it, continue to fight because you hope one day it won't be like this. Life can be so cruel. It doles out just enough hope to keep you going, like a small cup of water and one slice of bread to someone on the verge of starvation."

She paused to sip her drink. "Gabriela made the decision not to tell anyone outside of the family," Garcia continued. "Against her doctor's advice. But she was adamant. She didn't want to be pitied. She said she was only sick at the time, it would hurt much more to be tiptoed around, treated as if she were a fragile butterfly with a ripped-off wing than to suffer at the hands of Ruby. We all made a pact with her, swearing never to tell anyone. And if Gabriela wasn't well enough to go out into the world to experience life, her father arranged for the most fascinating and outrageous of lives to come to her. In between her hospital visits to the city several times a week, she was home schooled at El Esplanade, and the estate became a backdrop, a hostel, a secret hidden lodging, populated around the clock with philosophers and actors and artists and scientists, all of them teaching Gabriela how to live and think and dream, teaching all of us, really."

I was immediately reminded of the afternoon picnic Julie Froehlich had described. Gabriela had been six years old. It would have been around the time she was finishing treatment if Garcia was telling the truth. *Gabriela took my hand and brought me down to a deserted part of the lake where there stood a willow tree and tall grass, the water emerald green. She asked me if I could see the trolls.*

"Delores had a concert pianist from Juilliard come to the house three times a week to give Gabriela lessons. Doctors had warned us, some of the very potent drugs used in treatment could have long term effects on her nervous system, weakening her motor skills and dexterity, making something like playing the piano difficult, if not impossible. Her hands and fingers might go numb, have increased sensitivity. She might experience dizzy spells. In Gabriela, however, the drugs had the opposite effect. She was able to play with astounding speed. Her memory, her ability to master even the most complicated of pieces went into overdrive, became superhuman. It was at the piano she began to live again, escape death, sailing over continents and mountain ranges and seas.

Gabriela was strong, but when Ruby returned it would be logistically impossible for her to travel to her concerts and undergo another round of treatment. She had to give it all up. And she did."

Garcia fell silent.

My mind was spinning from the symmetry of the equation I suddenly faced magical on one side, scientific on the other, a dark pulsing myth and an acceptable reality. Esquivel was desperate to save his daughter, as any father would be, but from a devil's curse or terminal cancer? Gabriela sudden musical genius at the piano caused by her traversing the devil's bridge or a side effect from the chemotherapy drugs she'd taken as a child?

I thought back to what Anderson had told me, describing Gabriela in concert. *She had knowledge of darkness in the most extreme form.* But what had given her this knowledge, staring the devil in the face, knowing he'd take her soul, or turning corner after corner of an endless illness, wondering if death was waiting for her on the other side?

The explanations were like two sides of the same coin, and the side that I favored revealed something essential about the person I was. Prior to the investigation when it comes to Gabriela I'd have believed the side most others would, the side that was logical, rational, exact. But now, much to my own shock, like a man who suddenly realized he was no longer the person he recognized, that other impossible, illogical, mad sides still had a very firm grip on him.

I didn't want to believe it, didn't want to accept that Gabriela, such a fierce presence in every story I'd ever heard about her, that she could be singlehandedly struck down by real life. I wanted a wilder explanation for her death, something darker, bloodier, more insane, a devil's curse.

"Things became difficult when Gabriela underwent treatment that second time," Garcia continued sternly. "She'd always had a strong personality. As strong as her father's. The two of them began to fight constantly. Doctors warned us that the steroids Gabriela was taking could produce volatility, explosions of temper, even violence. No one could control either of them. Not Delores, not me. It was like living with two dragons and the rest of us were bluebirds, taking cover in closets and under stairs, hoping not to be incinerated by the crossfire."

"What did they fight about?" I asked.

She arched an eyebrow. "I don't know if you know much about the temperament of men in Mr. Esquivel's type of work, but they have a hunger unknown to ordinary men.

If you're going to commit to such a person, you have to accept it or there'll be no end to your suffering. To survive such a person you must bend and twist all the time like a thin piece of wire, making allowances. It's always changing, the shape you're in. there were always other women. Other men. Other everything. Delores accepted it. But Gabriela, when she was old enough to understand, thought it unconscionable, a sort of gluttony on his part, a lack of integrity, a total betrayal of the family. One of his longtime lovers came to town and moved back into El Esplanade, a man Gabriela did not like. One night, she set his bed on fire. Delores, not wanting the negative publicity, drove the man, screaming in pain, from the property in the dead of night. Along the way, she was in an accident. Santo rescued the man before an ambulance arrived and managed to get him to an emergency room without being noticed by anyone. But Gabriela got her wish. The man disappeared."

She shot me a look. "I suspect you know most of this already."

I nodded. "The man was Steven Paulino. The Tarantula. A phony priest."

"It was my suggestion to send Gabriela to that camp," she said.

"Gateway Wilderness Therapy," I stated.

"The place came well recommended. When we were notified an accidental death had occurred there, some young boy drowning during a rainstorm, you can imagine how we felt. Yet when I picked up Gabriela she was . . . different." She shrugged, a faintly cynical expression on her face. "She'd met a boy. The loneliest boy in the world, she called him. She described him as a beautiful red maple leaf that had detached prematurely from its tree. And it floated through wind and rain, scuttled down drains and across fields, absolutely alone, connected to nothing. Yet there was something fundamentally good about him, she believed. Shortly afterward she tracked him down and they began whatever, a correspondence. I don't know what they wrote or said to each other, only that she was vital and alive again. Her father was relieved. We all were. Gabriela wanted to leave El Esplanade, be around ordinary people, an ordinary life. He bought this place for Gabriela."

She paused to glance tiredly around the room as if recalling how warm and bustling it had been buried like a lost civilization under the white sheets.

"It felt like the beginning of something. We enrolled her in school here. I prayed he'd return to his former self."

Garcia, draining the rest of her drink.

"The prognosis for cancer gets worse after more relapses. The window for long-term survival begins to close. Toxicities have been building in the body, which is being demolished from the inside out. Early that May, Gabriela was due for a checkup. She didn't want to go. Because she knew the truth, of course. She always did. Her doctors recommended a treatment involving clinical trials, an experimental program in Houston. Shortly after that, Delores discovered, hidden inside Gabriela's bedroom, a packed suitcase. And two one-way tickets to Brazil. When Delores confronted Gabriela, she said she was running away with Cooper and there was nothing anyone could do to stop her. She didn't want treatment. But, of course, her life was at stake. She was just a teenager. This boy she claimed was the love of her life, some juvenile delinquent, none of us took it seriously. Who really loves at the age?"

Romeo and Juliet," I said.

"And Cooper and Gabriela. Gabriela and her father fought horribly over it. He threw her into the car, locked the doors, and told her she was going to Houston whether she liked it or not. She could tell the boy the truth or not. But Gabriela decided not to. She said to love someone who is dying is torture. She'd rather the boy hate her because within that hate is the motivation to move on, to forget, to vanquish, better that than be gutted by loss, to long for something that can never be.

And for that deep love to turn into something else, like pity or revulsion, Gabriela couldn't bear it. She cut all ties with the boy. And went to Houston. She almost died there, but it was more from a broken heart than the disease."

Garcia fell silent, her hardened profile softened, ever so slightly.

"Gabriela got better?" I asked, after a moment.

"Yes. She went to college. She had to leave early spring semester due to dizzy spells and fatigue, but after she rested at El Esplanade she was able to return her sophomore year. And she was all right. She graduated and then six months ago, it began again."

"Ruby?"

Garcia nodded thoughtfully, staring at the coffee table. My mind was spinning because two things she'd said struck me. First, the detail about Gabriela leaving early her freshman year. It had actually been mentioned in the magazine article. Reading it, I'd wondered about the reason behind her mysterious departure, and now here it was, explained.

Second, there was a question of timing.

"How long was Gabriela treated at the University of Texas?" I asked

"Eight months? Why?"

She nodded slowly, puzzled. "She did the maintenance therapy back in Chicago. Why?"

"Did the family order medical equipment for her? A wheelchair? Or something from a company called Century Scientific?"

"I ordered everything for her. El Esplanade was outfitted like the Mayo Clinic. Everything to keep Gabriela comfortable, so she wouldn't be needlessly disturbed. She had round-the-clock nurses monitoring her."

"And the garbage at El Esplanade is burned at night?"

"Nathaniel Falls is always swarming with people trying to see the infamous Carlos Esquivel. It's their Mecca. They migrate there from around the world, hoping for a chance to work for empire. The last thing he wanted was someone trawling through his trash, discovering a prescription revealing that Gabriela was sick and jabbering about it on the Internet. We had to protect her. Though in the end, protection is just another cage."

It had all come together. The incinerators Elizabeth had seen up at El Esplanade, the glass vial marked biohazard, Doc Larsen's accidental UPS delivery back in December 2004, it all made sense now, in light of Gabriela's sickness. But the rush of solving these last few mysteries was almost immediately replaced with something else, a sense of hollowness, even grief.

I felt let down. I always did, slightly, when I'd come to the end of an investigation when looking around, I realized I was void of dark corners to investigate.

And yet, this was different. The desolation came from the realization that all of the Orichi were dead. They'd never existed in the first place. Because however much I might not want to face it, wanting something larger than life for Gabriela, some other tempestuous reality that defied reason, alive with trolls and devils, shadows that had minds of their own, black magic as powerful as Nuclear bombs, I knew Marissa Garcia was telling me the truth.

And her truth razed everything, clear-cut that magical and dark jungle I'd wandered into following Gabriela's footprints, revealing that I was actually standing on flat dry land, which was blindingly lit, but barren.

133

"The business with you started because she was sick again," Garcia blurted with evident contempt.

I drained my drink, feeling the scalding whiskey course down my throat.

"How's that?" I said, a little unsteadily.

She turned to me, exasperated. "I told you, Gabriela was a charismatic girl. Thanks to her inventive upbringing, her solitary life at El Esplanade, her sickness, she had trouble distinguishing made-up stories from real life. When Gabriela was ten, Delores made the mistake of inviting a witch doctor from Haiti to reside for four months at the house for fun. She didn't realize it would permanently uproot Gabriela's imagination, like running along a coastline filled with quietly roosting flamingos, displacing them. Suddenly, everything in Gabriela's head became riotous and squawking and in motion, all pink feathers and screeching and flapping wings everywhere. She came to believe in it all, voodoo, witchcraft." She shook her head. "I found spells she'd laid for me in my own room, protection from evil, or so she claimed. She was certain she'd been marked by something evil, that the devil was causing her illness. It was heartbreaking, and delusional. Gabriela was terrified to be in close physical proximity to people she cared about because she believed she'd harm them. She claimed this darkness growing inside her overtaken by the devil, that it made her dangerous, lethal. The idea was, of course, absurd."

Garcia sighed, "six months ago, when we learned she was sick again, her mental state became especially precarious. She had periods of not knowing where she was, or who she was. Not that it was her fault, after what she'd withstood as a child, having to look at death's door, over and over again. She made it clear she did not want to be in a hospital bed anymore, plugged into tubes and monitors, weak with morphine. Delores refused to accept it. She took Gabriela, against her will, to a clinic hoping it'd bring her to her senses, that she'd agree to another round of treatment."

"And that clinic was Mission Hills."

Garcia nodded. "She escaped as you know, thanks to some horny half-wit working in security. Gabriela was a master at manipulation, especially with men. They melted and sweated and went weak in front of her like a bunch of idiot's. She vanished into thin air.

It was horrifying for all of us. We'd no clue where she'd gone. Santo and Bernardo searched everywhere for her, but she was clever. She knew how to remain invisible. We found out later she'd shacked up in a tenement slum on the south side."

"On Normal Street."

"Delores went out of her mind with worry. By then Gabriela had grown quite sick. Delores wanted her to die at home with her family around her. Still, we had a few inklings as to where she'd go. There wasn't a day that went by that she didn't think about that boy. Cooper, she'd kept track of him over the years, knew he'd gotten in trouble with the law, was making a mess of his life. We sensed she'd seek him out in some way. The other option, of course, was you."

"Me?"

"She'd been interested in you ever since her father dealt with you snooping into his life the only way he knew how. Fighting fire with fire."

"Dealt with me? Is that what Esquivel called it?"

A challenging look flickered across her face, but she remained silent. "Was it a setup? Who the hell was the man who contacted me, then? John."

She shrugged. "Someone paid to lead you astray."

"But what he told me, Esquivel visiting all of those schools in the middle of the night."

"A juicy fabrication. And one just salacious enough for you to blurt it out and hang yourself by your own hubris. I'm sure it was a painful lesson for you to learn, Mr. McCarthy, but a man like Esquivel needs only one fundamental thing in order to thrive. And he'll do anything to keep it."

"And what is that?"

"Darkness. I know it's hard to fathom today, but a man such as Esquivel needs darkness to create fear, and that fear gives him power. His invisibility. The less the world knows about him, the more strength he has. The more inanities about him the world believes, the smaller and dried his lifestyle shrinks and shrivels into a sugary treat waiting to be consumed. Did you ever think he'd ever let that happen?"

As she said this, in her still, very much alive reverence for Esquivel took over in her voice, tossed it high into the air, made it swoop in figure eights, trailing wild red ribbons, a voice otherwise lying in a dull heap on the ground. I'd also noticed that during the entire conversation Marissa Garcia hadn't actually said the words Carlos Esquivel, not a single time, mostly referring to him as he or Gabriela's father.

It had to be her private superstition or she didn't like cavalierly intoning the word as if it were akin to God.

As she stood up, stalking over to the bar and returning with the whiskey bottle, hastily splashing it into our glasses, I considered what she said. If there was no devil's curse, there could be no reason for Esquivel to obsess over an exchange, no reason to visit those schools at night, no pit filled with children's belongings. Had I been hallucinating, after all, thanks to the Psycho Plant Extract?

"To comprehend the force that was Gabriela," Garcia said, sitting back against the couch, clutching her drink, "you must understand, she was her father's daughter. The family's favorite fairy tale was Alice in Wonderland. That's what they were, fantastical creatures spinning the ordinary days and turning them into a dream land. And so Gabriela reconceived her illness to be a devil's curse."

"But it wasn't just Gabriela who believed it. Madelyn and Steven Paulino were also pretty convinced."

She scoffed, "Madelyn is a drug addict. She'd believe the sky was yellow and full of lemons if you told it to her. Especially if you wrote it in a fan letter. She spent time with Gabriela. Became swept up in her tales. And Paulino, after what Gabriela did to him? The man went out of his mind. He believed her to be the devil's queen, trembling at the sight of a flea."

I suddenly recalled how Paulino had described, without shame, crawling on his hands and knees across his shop to hide from Gabriela, cowering in a wardrobe like a terrified child.

"What about Esquivel? How he ran the drug trade empire? Did he bring his work home?"

She looked at me, her stare challenging. Everyone who worked for him knew what they were getting into. They were dying to work for him. But if you're asking me if he ever crossed the line into pure insanity, he didn't he knew the limits he could take."

"What are they, exactly?"

She narrowed his eyes. "He was never a murderer. He loves life. But believe what you want. You'll never find any evidence."

You'll never find any evidence. That was an odd thing to say. It sounded almost like an admission, almost. I thought back to the boy's tiny shriveled shirt, caked not in blood but corn syrup, according to Horrigan. What Garcia was saying certainly backed up the results Katie Horrigan had given me, whether I wanted to accept it or not.

"Why has everyone I've talked to about Gabriela disappeared?"

"I took care of them," Marissa said with a hint of pride.

"What does that mean? They're all lying in an unmarked grave?"

She ignored this, sitting up stiffly. "I also took care of the coroner's photos of Gabriela's body, and then the body itself, before she was cut open in front of strangers like a lab rat. I've paid everyone off handsomely and sent them on their merry way."

"How did you know who I talked to?"

She looked surprised. "Why your own notes, Mr. McCarthy. Surely you remember the break-in at your apartment. They were very helpful for tying up loose ends."

Of course: the break-in.

"We were disparate," she went on. "We didn't know where Gabriela had gone, what had happened to her in the time she'd vanished from Mission Hills and ended up in that warehouse dead. The only thing we did know was that she came here one night, broke in and took money from a safe. I suspected you'd know more. Mission Hills, after all, informed us that you'd showed up there, snooping. We broke in to find out what you knew."

"Any chance I can get my laptop back?"

"It's been a costly enterprise, in the wake of her death, getting rid of each witness. But it's all in keeping our promise to her, never letting anyone know the truth. It's what he wanted. Gabriela's history will now forever remain where she wished it, where she believed in her heart where it always was, beyond reason, between heaven and earth, land and sky, suspended much closer to legend than ordinary life, ordinary life where the rest of us, including you, Mr. McCarthy, must remain."

"Where the mermaids sing," I added quietly, reminded of the Prufrock poem. As Cooper had explained it, the mermaids were the one thing the family was always seeking out, always fighting for, life's most stunning and precarious razor edge. Where there exist danger and beauty and light. Only in the now. Gabriela said it was the only way to live.

Marissa Garcia, I noticed, was staring at me, her mouth open, in shock, seemingly surprised I knew such an intimate detail about the family. She decided not to delve further into it, however, taking a long sip of her drink.

"Madelyn suffered an overdose," I said. "Did you have anything to do with that?"

"I asked her drug dealer to scare her a little. I didn't expect him to nearly bump her off."

"Your compassion is very moving."

She glanced at me. "It's the best thing that could happen. It got her out of that apartment. Right now she's sitting in an ocean view suite at Promises in Malibu, climbing up onto that first, very high, very worn out step of all twelve-step recovery programs."

"And what did you say to Olivia Wainscott?"

She shrugged. "Nothing. She's out of the country. But I did speak to her secretary. I paid the girl a small fortune to avoid you like the plague and not to pass along any of your messages to her employer."

"And Stanley Dewitt? Why did his house burn down?"

"He needed the insurance money. He was in dire financial straits, two kids, no job. When I explained who I was, that I was there to offer a helping hand, he was quite receptive. If you ever approach him again, he'll swear he's never seen you or Gabriela before in his life." She lifted her chin, satisfied. "Everyone in this world had a price, Mr. McCarthy. Even you."

"You're wrong. Some of us aren't for sale. Who set the house on fire?"

"Santo and Bernardo. Bernardo is a longtime friend of the family."

"Who smokes Davidoff cigarettes?"

She was visibly irritated by the question. "Santo. It was his father's favorite brand."

Again, she deliberately said his father, rather than simply Esquivel. She was taking the long way to avoid a certain hazardous stretch of road.

"Years ago," she went on, "he cleaned out the world's supply. Davidoff. The brand's been discontinued since the mid-thirties. It's very rare. But he bought up every last pack from every obscure tobacco collector across the globe. He liked the caramel smell, the gorgeous packaging, and the fact that it was the only detail he remembered about his natural born father, a Spaniard, whom he'd last seen when he was three. But he especially liked the way they burned. It's like nothing else. The smoke spirals through the air like it's alive. 'Like a swarm of white snakes were struggling to be free,' he once said to me."

She'd gone on with strange, unchecked fervor, her eyes bright and raised to the ceiling, her mouth twitching in excitement. But then, remembering me, she stopped herself.

"I don't see why it's so important to your, these details," she muttered in annoyance.

"It's where the devil is. Haven't you heard?"

She eyed me disdainfully. "You've done a lifetime's worth of mining, Mr. McCarthy. Maybe it's time to come back to the surface and go home with whatever lumps of coal you've managed to dig loose."

"And be on my merry way. Like all the others."

She shrugged, unperturbed. "Do whatever you like with the information. Of course, now there's no one in the word to back up your story. You're all alone again with your wild claims."

Staring at the woman, I couldn't help but marvel at her smug meticulousness, the way she'd managed to get rid of each and every witness, one by one.

"What happened to Gabriela's mother? Delores?"

"Gone. Somewhere in Europe. With her precious child now dead, there's nothing keeping her here. Too many dark memories."

"But you don't mind them."

She smiled. "My memories are all have left. And when I'm gone? They're gone."

I frowned, suddenly doubtful again of what she'd been telling me, suddenly struck by something. Maybe it was the last dying whisper of magic, the Orichi's and devils, the supernatural powers of one startling woman before it was all laid to rest.

"But I went up to El Esplanade," I said, "I broke in."

"Did you?" Garcia interrupted excitedly. "What did you find?"

Her reaction was puzzling, to say the least. She actually looked thrilled by my admission.

"A perfect circular clearing in which nothing grows," I went on. "A maze of underground tunnels. Soundstages. The film sets entirely intact. Everything is overgrown and black. I walked over the devil's bridge. And I saw . . ."

Garcia was hanging on my every word so excitedly, waiting for me to continue, I fell silent, bewildered.

"Who lives there?" I went on. "Who are the watchmen with the dogs?"

She shook her head. "I have no idea."

"What, you . . . you no longer work for the family?" I asked.

"You really don't understand. El Esplanade's been donated to the City of Chicago, for the betterment of the unfortunate of the City. It belongs to them now. They've overtaken it. Quite a few squat there year-round. It's a dangerous theme park, left, free of charge, to his most dedicated addicts. It's become a secret rite of passage, a cult expedition to be there, wander the grounds or get swallowed inside it. They can fight over it, tend it, destroy it, rule it as they see fit. He hasn't set foot there in years. It's finished for him. His reign is over."

I wondered if it could actually be true, the men who'd chased me, the mongrels. I'd been terrorized by street punks? I'd hardly managed to get my mind around this when I had no choice but to reach for the other question she'd just left dangling in front of me.

"Where is he?" I asked.

"I was wondering when you might ask me that." She turned away, staring somewhere in front of us, her expression like a truck driver looking out at a lonely road twisting interminably in front of her.

I suddenly had a vision of that old desk sergeant years ago, cautioning me that some investigations are infected, that they're like tapeworms. A tapeworm that's eaten its own tail. No use going on with it. Because there is no end. All it will do is wrap around your heart and squeeze all the blood out.

For the first time since I'd met her, Marissa Garcia smiled warmly at me. And I knew then I had it wrong. Because here it was. The end. The tail. I'd found it, after all.

134

I felt shocked there was no security.

I expected something miserable. How could it not be? A place where men and women were tucked out of sight so they could bumble around the end of their lives, a place like Willow Falls. I thought about phoning Elizabeth for this very reason, asking her to come, but then, sensing she'd say no, left it alone. But once I'd turned off the highway and pulled into the place, following the neatly paved driveway to the series of cream-colored signs and stucco buildings with red tile roofs, I saw Enderlin Estates Retirement Community was trying its best to bring to mind a Spanish hacienda taking a very long siesta. There were plantings and courtyards and chirping birds, a twisting stone path that led promisingly toward the main entrance nestled behind a wrought-iron gate.

I checked the paper where I'd written the address Garcia had given me. *Enderlin Estates. Apartment 210.*

I walked into the deserted lobby, took an elevator to the second floor, encountering a redheaded nurse behind a front desk.

"I'm looking for Apartment Two-ten."

I headed down the carpeted hallway, passing a young nurse helping an elderly woman with a walker. The door marked 210 was closed, and the name, the beautiful generic Bill smith, was mounted on a tiny blue plaque beside the door.

I knocked and, when there was no answer, turned the knob. It opened into a large sitting room, sparsely furnished, awash with sunlight. There was a bedroom on the left with a single bed, a dresser, a Virgin Mary, her hands together in prayer. No photos, no personal items of any kind, but Garcia had doubtlessly seen to this, so there would be total anonymity or, as she put it, nothing to bring back dark memories. "What he needs now is peace," she'd said with a look of warning.

"You looking for Bill?" a cheerful voice asked behind me.

I turned. A nurse stood in the open doorway.

"I just took him to the morning room."

She explained how to find it. I made my way back down the elevator and along the main hall, passing activity calendars, an advertisement for Movie Night, *The Road to Rio*! stepping through the double wooden doors into an old-fashioned glass-walled solarium. The room was bright and cheerful, filled with potted palms and flowers, white wicker chairs, a gray stone floor. Classical piano music played feebly from somewhere, an old stereo beside a bookshelf packed with paperbacks.

It was crowded. Elderly men and women, moving as if they were underwater, hair that looked like a few wisps of a cloud, sat at tables with jigsaw puzzles and checkerboards. A few nurses sat among them, quietly reading aloud, one pinning a pink carnation to an old man's lapel.

Yet my eyes were pulled away from the activity to one man. He sat alone on the farthest side of the room in the corner, his back to me. He was in front of the windows, staring out. And even though he was in a wheelchair, wearing an old gray sweater and old-man shoes, there was something sturdy about him, something oddly immobile.

I stepped toward him.

He gave no indication he was aware of my approach. In fact, he seemed unaware of anything at all in the room. His gaze stripped of those ink-black circular lenses he'd allegedly worn all his life, remained fixed out the window, where a vast lawn ringed by woods stretched out like an empty lake, it's surface gold-green and hard in the afternoon sun. He had a dense head of silver-white hair, which showed no sign of relenting, a sizable stomach, which seemed more imperial, even threatening, rather than fat, as if like some Greek God with explosive moods and appetites. He had swallowed a boulder and it hadn't killed him, just kept him brutally secured to the ground. He was sitting back easily in the chair, his hands, massive workman's hands, loosely hanging off the armrests, the war an exhausted king might relax on his throne. His face was different from how I'd pictured it, less certain somehow, slightly more drooping and crude.

Yet I was certain it was him.

Esquivel.

I could even see the faded wheel tattoo on his left hand, exactly where Garcia's had been. His gaze remained somewhere out on the lawn like an anchor that's been thrown there. It was as if he was picturing something, a final look back at his life.

Perhaps he was thinking about Gabriela, when she was young and impressionable, becoming daddy's little girl. Thinking about family times.

Garcia had warned me he'd be aware of nothing.

"A day or two after Gabriela learned she was sick again, this last time, he went to bed early," Garcia had told me. "He was always up at four A.M. working, living. But he didn't come down. Alarmed, I went upstairs.

I found him in his bed, propped upright on his pillows as if a ghost had come in the middle of the night to talk something over. His eyes were wide open, staring out at nothing. He was catatonic, a television turned on, but one single channel only static." To my shock, Garcia had gone on to explain it all in great detail. His doctors, certain he'd suffered a stroke, transferred him to a nursing facility for the elderly in Westchester, Enderlin Estates, outside of Dobbs Ferry, the decision to use the alias Bill Smith, so he wouldn't be hounded or hunted, but left to live out his final days in peace.

I told Garcia it was a wild coincidence, this prevalence of death, two vibrant lives drawing to an abrupt close, first Gabriela, now Esquivel. Granted, he wasn't technically dead, but given the kind of life he'd lived, he was unresponsive, his spirit locked forever inside him, or else, it had already fled.

"It's not a coincidence," Garcia snapped like she found the word insulting. "He was finished don't you see? Men and women who have fulfilled what they meant to those who have found answers to a few grave questions about life. Not all the answers, but a few they end their lives when they choose. They're ready, and he was. He'd lived exactly like he wanted, wildly insanely, and now he's ready for the next. He'd wrung every drop of life out of himself, leaving only dried -up piles of nerves and bones. I know as sure as I know my own name he'll be dead within a matter of months."

I'd found Garcia's demeanor startlingly efficient and brisk for a woman who'd just lost the focus of her life, the sun that had ordered her days. But then she lifted her head and I saw there were tears in her eyes, waiting for me to leave, so they could slide freely down her sunken cheeks. Silently she led me downstairs to the front door, extended her hand with a brusque

"*I'll see you*", a statement we both knew was a lie. And though I didn't especially like Marissa Garcia and she hadn't exactly warmed to me. We had come to a sort of unspoken understanding. Found on a surprising patch of common ground both of us spectators swept up in the rogue tidal wave that was Esquivel.

And now here he was, less than two feet away.

And he became a fragile old man.

I'd been fighting no one. The crimes, the horrors I'd tried and found Esquivel guilty of, seemed laughable now, considering the fact that, all those moments I'd been so certain he was outmaneuvering me, he'd been right here, probably sitting peacefully like this in front of this very window.

I couldn't help but be awed by the shock of it.

Even like this, he was having the last word.

Strange emotion abruptly swelled in my throat. It might have been a laugh or just as easily a sob. Because I realized, staring at this man, that I was actually just staring at myself. At what I'd become much sooner and more suddenly than I'd ever expected. Life was a freight train barreling toward just one stop. Our loved ones streaking past our windows in blurs of color and light. There was no holding onto any of it, and no slowing it down.

It was so calm standing next to him, so lonely. I swore I could hear his breathing, every breath he borrowed from the world then set free. It wasn't the simple lungs of an ordinary man, but the faint howl of a gust of wind as it snagged the rocks of some far-off bluff by the sea. I wondered, another unchecked wave of feeling rising in my chest, what in the hell I was going to say to him after all this, all I'd done and come to see if I had the nerve to say anything at all.

Or maybe, like a child encountering the reassembled bones of a dangerous species of dinosaur he'd dreamed about, read with a flashlight under a comforter for nights and days, maybe I was going to simply reach out and touch his shoulder Wondering if in that touch I could get a sense of what he must have been like when he was alive, in his prime, roaming the Earth, a force of nature, when he wasn't silent grayed bones on display, but something splendid to behold.

In the end, all I did was pull up a chair and sit down beside him. And together, for what seemed like hours. We did nothing but stare out at that empty lawn, which seemed to hold in its strict boundaries and flawless green. The empty space in which we could pile our memories and questions. What I became aware of the music again, piano music, a pale, listless approximation of what Gabriela would have played, I realized then that all I was going to say to the man was *"thank you."*

I did. Then I rose and left, not looking back.

135

What can I say about the ensuing weeks?

Madelyn said it best, "When you finally returned to your real life after working for Esquivel, it was as if all of the colors had been turned way up in your eyes. The reds were redder. Blacks blacker. You felt things profoundly like your very heart had grown giant and tender and swollen. You dreamed, and wow, what dreams they would be."

I drove home from Enderlin Estates, pulled the curtains, and slept for twenty hours, asleep as blacked-out and resolute as death. I woke up around nightfall the following day, shadows streaked across the ceiling the dying light outside making the street blush with the elegance of a memory.

My old life took me back, the old faithful dog that it was.

I was somewhat shocked to learn it was December. I spent a few evenings at dinners with friends, most of whom assumed I'd been away, traveling. I let them believe it. In a way it was true.

"You look good," quite a few of them remarked, though certain lingering stares seemed to suggest this wasn't exactly true, there was something else different about me, something they sensed best left alone. I wondered, half-seriously if it was residue from the devil's curse. Even though it had turned out not to be true, perhaps one never recovered from having once believed. Maybe certain far-flung attic rooms in the brain had been violently broken into, doors bashed in, lamps were broken, desks flipped upside down, curtains left dancing strangely by open windows, rooms that would never be reached again or ever reordered.

But I was thankful for the company, for friends, for light conversation forgotten as soon as it began. I joined in wholeheartedly, I laughed, I ordered wine and duck and dessert, and people slapped me on the back and said they were happy to see me, that I'd been away too long. But occasionally I slipped, unseen, outside all the talk and gawked in at it, wondering if I'd stumbled back to the wrong table, the wrong life. I felt at once rested and relieved that investigation was over, but also vague regret, even a dulled longing to go back, to return to something I couldn't pinpoint. A woman I hadn't realized had bewitched me until she was gone.

Lines of laughter on a face, rude waitresses with bony arms, dark figures hurrying along sidewalks eager to get somewhere. Nearby voices filled with dusk, cabs and panhandlers and one drunken girl screeching like a wounded bird, all of it flushed with a warmth and sad beauty I'd never seen before.

Maybe it was a consequence of reaching the end of the lifelong passion, finding out the dark, crazy, gleaming tale had concluded the only way it could in the real world, with mortal people doing mortal things, a father, and daughter, facing their deaths.

Because there could be no doubt about what Garcia told me. I'd phone the hospital posing as a health insurance agent from a disorganized HR department. After telling a few half-truths to three different assistant department heads, and giving Gabriela's social Security number taken from the missing person's report, one of the few documents left behind, three different people confirmed it on two different days. Gabriela had been treated in the pediatric oncology department in 1992 and 1993, 2001 and 2002, and finally in 2004 in conjunction with the University of Northwestern, exactly as Garcia had said.

At night I strolled home on the crooked sidewalks, past silent apartments with lit-up windows filled with lives. Glasses clinking, the street gasping with laughter as the door of a bar was shoved open, these sounds seemed to follow me longer than they ever had before.

I hadn't returned to the Reservoir after seeing Gabriela there, but in the aftermath of learning about her sickness, I went back.

There was no hint of her, not in the water or the green lamplight or the biting wind, the shadows that threw themselves at my feet. I ran, lap after lap, and could think only of how she'd gone to the warehouse and what a lonely walk it must have been. Up the steps in the edge of the elevator, which was the edge of her life, staring down.

She'd been dying when she'd appeared here. It made sense, given the way she'd walked. She'd been weak, in an especially precarious mental state, according to Garcia.

Even accepting this, still, something gnawed at me. I'd come to believe Gabriela had sought me out because she wanted to tell me something, something crucial and real, her circumstances preventing a direct approach. Now even this had an explanation.

Garcia had mentioned Gabriela's fear, that she might cause physical harm to anyone she came in close proximity to, a fear that could very well have begun when she learned what had happened to Olivia Wainscott or the tattoo artist when they'd been in her presence.

It had to have been why she stayed away from me.

In all the stories I'd heard, Gabriela stood for the truth. She was the antithesis of weak. Even hunting the Tarantula, she'd sought him only to forgive him. To accept now that it had been delusions that brought Gabriela out here, spinning her straw into gold, a master of manipulation, as Garcia put it, felt off.

What did Gabriela want me to know?

I took so many laps around the track I lost count, and then, lungs burning, exhausted, I left, jogging down Lake Shore Drive. Just like I had the night I'd seen her.

Staring across the platform, the neon light flat and bright. I wondered if I could manifest through sheer will, her boots, her red-and-black jacket, that she might come one last time. So I could get a clear glimpse of her face. Once and for all know the truth behind her.

But there was no one.

Even the sci-fi movie poster that had been there before, the sprinting man with his eyes scribbled out, even he was gone. Replaced with an ad for a romantic comedy starring Bill Murray.

He just doesn't get it, read the tagline.

Perhaps I should take the hint.

136

Days later, I packed away the Esquivel research, what was left of it, anyway, shoved it back inside the cardboard box and the box inside the closet, Octavius quietly looking on.

I took a mountain of dirty clothes to the dry cleaner, including Brad Jackson's herringbone coat. But then, eyeing the sad thing slumped over the counter, under piles of my button-downs. I had the sudden paranoid thought that it was the last shred of evidence, my last tie to the insanity of El Esplanade, and if Brad's coat were cleaned and steam pressed, encased in plastic with a paper draped over the shoulders reading McCarthy's House of Horrors! If all this was gone, would my recollections be lost also? So I awkwardly pulled the filthy thing back out of the pile, and returning home, shoved it in the closet behind Gabriela's red jacket and shut the door.

I wanted to see Kim. I wanted to hear her voice, have her hang heavily on my arm and squint up at me. But Angela never returned my calls, not one. I wondered if her silence meant she was working with her lawyers to petition for a new custody arrangement, like she'd threatened to do in the emergency room. Finally my old divorce attorney called with this very news.

"They set a court date. She wants to restrict visitation."

"Whatever she wants." This appeared to jolt him, as simple acts of kindness did to attorneys.

"But you might never see your daughter again."

"I want Kim to be safe and happy. We'll leave it at that."

I did secretly go uptown to check on her, one late December afternoon. The day was graying from the cold, giant snowflakes drifting bewildered, through the air, forgetting to fall. I didn't want Kim to see me. So I remained behind a few parked cars and a delivery truck watching the gleaming black doors of her school opening. The bundled up children in coats spilling out onto the sidewalks. To my surprise, Angela was there waiting, and after she tucked Kim's hands into black mittens, they took off.

Kim was wearing a new blue coat. Her hair was longer than I remembered, secured in a ponytail under a black velvet hat. She looked more mature too, quite seriously informing Angela of something about her day. I was overcome. Because I saw suddenly, how it would always be for me. Kim's life unfolding like slides in an old projector I'd always be clicking through in the dark, stunning leaps forward in time, but never the uncut reel.

But she was happy. I could see that. She was perfect.

When they crossed the street, I could make out only their blue and black coats. A surge of yellow cabs and buses flooded Michigan Avenue and then I couldn't see them anymore.

137

It arrived on January fourth, an e-mail from Elizabeth inviting me to her Chicago theatrical debut at the Briar Street theater. In that way off-off-Broadway production of Hamlette. She'd done well in her audition and had won the lottery for all Chicago actors, an actual paying part. Granted, she was only Bernarda, one of two Elsinore castle guards, renamed from Bernardo, who appeared solely in act one, scene one, and she received just $50 per performance, but still.

"I'm a real actress now," she wrote.

I went opening night, in a small theater. As soon as the lights went down and the heavy black curtain was noisily hauled aside. There was Elizabeth in blue light, her blond hair in two long braids, climbing up to a rickety castle lookout tower made out of plywood. She was surprisingly good, infusing all of her lines with the comical, wide-eyed naturalness I'd heard so many times. When she encountered Hamlette's mom's ghost, who in a strange costume was wearing a garter belt and white teddy and thus came off as a strung-out spirit who'd sauntered in from not purgatory, but the Crazy Horse in Vegas. Elizabeth tripped and stumbled backward naively announcing, "It's here!" and "It was about to speak, when the cock crew!" the audience erupted with delighted laughter.

The play ran without intermission. When it was finally over, after Ophelia offed himself by throwing back too many Xanax, Hamlette finally had the nerve to off her bitchy stepmom, and at long last, Fortinbrassa and her army of gal pals arrived fashionably late at Elsinore wearing nylon miniskirts straight from the Ice Capades. I remained in my seat.

When the theater emptied, I was surprised to see someone else had remained behind, too.

Cooper. Of-course.

He was sitting in the last row in the very back. He must have snuck in after the lights went down.

"McCarthy."

Like me, he'd brought Elizabeth a bouquet of flowers, red roses. He'd gotten a haircut. Though he was still wearing his gray will coat and Converse sneakers, he had on a white button-down shirt, which looked as if he hadn't found it on the floor of his apartment, the circles no longer carved so deeply under his eyes.

"How have you been?" I asked.

He smiled, "pretty good."

"You look good. Have you quit smoking?"

"Not yet." He was about to add something, but his gaze moved behind me, and I turned to see Elizabeth stepping out from the curtain. I was relieved to see she was still sporting the old transvestite's wardrobe, black leggings, one of Moe's purple tuxedo shirts, that she hadn't changed. Because Chicago could do that to you in no time, streamlining and sanding, polishing and buffing you into something that looked good, but like everyone else.

Elizabeth gave us the tightest of hugs and waved goodbye to her cast friends.

"Bye, Rachel! You were amazing tonight!" Rachel, a pretty bleached blonde, had played Hamlette and delivered "To

Be or Not to Be" with all the somberness of speculating, "To text or Not to Text." "Ronnie, you left your hat on the prop table."

Elizabeth, beaming, amped up on theater energy, pulled on her coat and suggested we all go grab a bite. As we exited the theater, she linked her arms through ours, striding down the sidewalk. Dorothy reunited with Scarecrow and the Tin Man.

"Woodward, how have you been? I missed you. Oh, wait. How's Octavius?"

"Immortal, as always."

"You both brought flowers? You guys got chivalrous all of a sudden?"

We went to a breakfast place on North Broadway near Clark and Fullerton. We piled into a booth. Elizabeth staring at our faces like they were foreign newspapers she'd finally got her hands on, filled with the latest news from home.

"You both look good. Oh." She yanked off a glove to display the inside of her left wrist, across it a small tattoo, three words.

Just Do It

"It's so I never forget Gabriela." She bit her bottom lip, glancing nervously at Cooper. "You don't mind, do you?"

He shook his head. "Gabriela would have loved it."

I went to Dragon Master for the tattoo. But that guy we talked to, 'Tommy? He moved back to Vancouver. So this other guy did it. Hurt like oh hell. But it was worth it."

I'd completely forgotten Tommy, the tattoo artist. Then Garcia had sent him on his merry way, too.

Elizabeth took my startled look for disapproval. "I knew you wouldn't like it. But it's tiny. And I can cover it up with makeup. And before my wedding, I can always get it removed."

"What wedding?" I asked, in a loud and concerning voice.

"One day. If I have one. But Woodward, will you give me away? I was thinking that I didn't have anyone to do it."

"Yes. Provided it's twenty years from now."

We ended up staying out until five in the morning, getting drunk and loud, leaving the dinner for some unmarked speakeasy in a Chinatown Laundromat where Cooper was a regular. Leaving that for an after-hours club where Elizabeth's friend Maxine was a hostess. Or leaving that for some dive bar on Lake Street to play pool and take over the jukebox, playing Joy Division's, *Love Will Tear Us Apart*. "This is our anthem," said Elizabeth. Cooper displaying remarkable dancing skills, spun her around the room. They told me what had happened in their lives since those two months we'd spent holed up together, chasing the truth about Gabriela, and Esquivel.

Esquivel was fully committed to conquering off-off Broadway, fitting in auditions posted in Backstage with a full-time job at Healthy Eats. Healthy Eats, the brainchild of Josephine, Elizabeth's hippie landlord, was a highly appetizing vegan, sugar, and gluten free, macrobiotic cupcake shop on the north side. Elizabeth showed us her new head shots, which featured her eyeing us over her shoulder, her hair straightened and cascading. Elizabeth Edge Halliday, the picture announced in elaborate cursive. If the headshot had a voice, it would be a husky English whisper on Masterpiece Theatre.

"Do you really need the Edge?" I asked her. "Elizabeth Halliday is more than enough."

"The Edge gives it an edge," said Cooper.

Elizabeth lifted her chin. "You're outnumbered, Woodward. As usual."

She leaned over the pool table and, squinting with concentration, shot the cue ball. Three solids ricocheted into opposite pockets. Apparently, there was a billiards room at Willow Falls she'd never told me about.

"I figure I'll give it a good ten years to try and make it big," she went on, moving around the table to line up her next shot. "Then I'm getting out while I still can. I'm going to buy a farm with hills and horses. Have some kids. You'll both come visit. We could have reunions. No matter where we are in the world, we'll come together for one amazing day.

"I like it," said Cooper.

"I have a boyfriend named Jasper," she added.

"Jasper? I said. "He sounds like he highlights his hair."

"He's a first-class person. You'd like him."

"How old?"

"Twenty-three."

"But an old twenty-three?"

She nodded and looked away, suddenly shy, and stepped around the table so I couldn't see her face.

Cooper, as it turned out, had been about to leave Chicago altogether when he'd received Elizabeth's e-mail, so he delayed his departure by a week to have this last chance to see the two of us. He'd given up his apartment. He was heading to South America.

"South America?" asked Elizabeth, as if he'd said he was going to the moon.

"Yeah. I'm going to find my mom."

In typical Cooper fashion, he chose not to elaborate further on this tantalizing premise, though I remembered something he'd said about his mom, that she was involved in some strange missionary work, the afternoon I'd first talked to him in his apartment.

Elizabeth nibbled her thumbnail, perched on the corner of the pool table.

"And after that what are you going to do?" she asked.

"After that . . ." He smiled. "Something really good."

We ordered shots of Patron and danced and reloaded the jukebox, my old man vintage music, as Elizabeth called it, The Doors, Harry Nilsson's "Everybody's talking'," and some Mick Jagger interspersed with Cooper's hip selections like House of Pain's "Jump Around" and Creed's "One last Breath."

At every moment, I felt Gabriela was with us, the invisible fourth member of our little party. I sensed we were all acutely aware of her, though we didn't need to mention her by name. It was obvious Elizabeth and Cooper had resolved her life and death in their heads. They believed in her without question, without a doubt. She'd made the world all right for them, even better. They still believed the myth, I reasoned, the myth of the devil's curse. They were still living in an enchanted world. Gabriela, not struck with cancer, but a wild avenging angel, and Esquivel, not catatonic in a nursing home, but an evil king who'd fled to the unknown. For the rest of their lives, they'd have this magical reality to turn to when their car keys inexplicably moved across the room, when they read stories about children who went missing without a trace when someone broke their heart for no good reason.

But of course, they'd think. It's the magic.

It felt as if we'd been to war together. Deep I a jungle, alone, I had relied on them, these strangers. They'd held me up in ways only people could. When it was over, an ending that never felt like an ending, only forever by the history of it, the simple fact they'd seen the raw side of me and me of them, a side no one, not even closest friends or family had ever seen before, or probably ever would.

And in between the laughter and the jokes, the music, a long stretch of silence fell over us. We were sitting side by side on a wooden bench underneath a dartboard and a neon sign. I saw the moment for what it was, the chance to tell them the truth.

I gazed at Cooper's profile, his head tipped way back against the wall, the gold strands of Elizabeth's hair stuck to her flushed cheek, the words shouting in my head.

You can't imagine what Gabriela hid from us. It was the ultimate triumph of life over death, never to give in to her illness, never to stop living. It suddenly occurred to me that perhaps Gabriela had not been so delusional in the last days of her life, a truth Marissa Garcia had been so keen that I accept.

Maybe she, displaying that searing intuition for people and a heart not even Garcia could take away from her, maybe she'd somehow intended this moment.

Perhaps she'd planned with her death, the three of us would find each other. It was why she chose the warehouse. She knew I'd go there looking for clues, and encounter Cooper who'd be wondering about the return address on the envelope. And why else would she leave Elizabeth her coat?

I realized the moment had drifted away. Cooper rolled off the bench, shuffling across the bar to put another song on the jukebox, which had gone silent, and Elizabeth went off to the bathroom.

I remained where I was. *That had to be it. I'd tell them both the truth one day. But now, tonight, they could keep their myth.*

Hours later, the bar was closing, turning up the lights, erasing the mirage of forever. It was time to go. I was smashed. Outside, on the sidewalk, I embraced the two of them, announcing to the empty streets of Chicago, they were two of the best people I'd ever met.

"We're family!" I shouted at the walk-ups, my voice half swallowed by the deserted street.

"We heard you, Aretha," said Cooper.

"But we are," Elizabeth said. "We always will be."

"With you two in it?" I went on. "This world has nothing to worry about! You hear me?" Elizabeth giggling, put her arm around me, trying to pry me off the telephone pole I was hugging like Gene Kelly in Singin' in the Rain.

"You're wasted," she said.

"Of course, I'm wasted."

"It's time to go home."

"Woodward never goes home."

Filing down the sidewalk, we fell silent, knowing it was coming within minutes, our farewell, knowing we might not see each other for a very long time.

We hailed a cab. That's what you did in Chicago at the close of a night, cramming together into your filthy yellow stagecoach with the faceless chauffeur, who delivered you, one by one, relatively unscathed, to your quiet street. The night would be filed away somewhere, one day brought out and dusted off, remembered as one of the best moments.

Life is made up of millions of moments, and this time spent with these two became so special to me. I love them both.

We piled in, Elizabeth in the middle. She, now exhausted with roses slung over her knees. Cooper was crashing on a friend's couch on Lake Street.

"Right here," he said to the driver, tapping the glass.

The cab pulled over, and he turned to me, extending his hand.

"Keep looking for the mermaids," he told me in a hoarse voice. He lowered his head so I wouldn't see the tears in his eyes. "Keep fighting for them."

I nodded and hugged him as hard as I could. He then kissed Elizabeth gently on her forehead and climbed out. He didn't immediately go inside but stood on the sidewalk watching us drive away, a dark figure drenched in orange streetlight. Elizabeth and I watched out the back window, the moving picture we had to dip our eyes on, reluctant to blink or breathe, as it'd become only a memory in seconds.

He held up his left hand to us, a wave and a salute. And the taxi rounded the corner.

"Now we're heading to St Mathew's on the near south side," I told the driver.

Elizabeth turned to me, eyes wide.

"You told me where you live," I said.

"I did not. I purposefully didn't."

"But you did, Bernstein. You're getting absent-minded in your old age."

She huffed, crossing her arms. "You spied on me."

"Nope."

"You did. I can tell."

"Please. I have better things to do with my time than worry about Bernstein's."

She scowled, but when the taxi pulled over in front of the brownstone she didn't move, only stared ahead.

"You won't forget me?" she whispered.

"It'd be physically impossible."

"You promise?"

"You should really think about coming with a warning, Do-Not-Remove-This-Tag. You'll fall in love with her against your will, like it or not."

"You'll be all right?"

She turned to me, really asking it, worried.

"Of course. And so will you."

She nodded as if trying to convince herself, and then suddenly she smiled as if thinking of an old joke I'd make, one she was finding funny only now. She keened forward and kissed my cheek. And then, as if some spell were about to break, she streaked out of the cab, door slamming, up the stoop with her leaden purse and arms full of roses.

She unlocked the door and stepped inside. But then, she slowly turned back, her hair gilded by some hidden light behind her. She smiled one last time. The door closed and the street went still.

"That's it," I whispered, more to myself than to the cab driver. I turned around sitting back against the seat, pale yellow light washing over me as we pulled away.

138

A few days after my night out with Cooper and Elizabeth, I'd just started recovering from my hangover. I was cleaning my office. I let Octavius out of his cage, so he might fly around for a little exercise. I yanked the leather couch away from the wall and noticed, wedged along the floor, the three black-and-white reversing candles Cleo had given us.

I'd forgotten them. They must have fallen there, unseen, when the room was ransacked.

We'd barely burned them, preoccupied with everything else. *But why not finish the job?* I set on a plate and lit all three. Hours later, when I was on the couch with a scotch and The Wall Street Journal, I glanced up and saw they'd burned down to nothing, just a sliver of white wax. The first and then the second extinguished as if waiting for my full attention, the wicks flaring orange for a moment before going out. The third held on, the flame twisting as if refusing to let go, to die, but then it went dark, too.

I realized my cell was ringing.

"Hello?" I answered, not bothering to check the caller ID. My accountant was due to call back to inform me my life savings was on its last leg and it was time to either apply for a new security position or consider another investigation, one that actually paid money.

"Shawn? It's Angela."

Fear instantly gripped me. "Is Kim all right?"

"Yes. She's great. Well, no actually, that's not true." She took a deep breath. "Is this a good time to talk?"

"What's the matter?"

She sounded upset. "I'm sorry for not returning your calls. I thought it was the right thing to do. But she's inconsolable. Shawn this, Shawn that. Crying, I can't take it." Angela herself seemed on the verge of tears.

"Does this Saturday work for you to spend some time with her?"

"Saturday works."

She sniffled. "Maybe she can spend the night."

"I'd love that."

"Good. How are you, by the way?"

"I'm great now. How are you?"

"Good." She laughed gently. "So, Saturday, then? Jeannie's back. She's recovered from mono."

"Saturday."

We hung up. I was unable to take my eyes off those candles.

They were smoking rather innocently, three long gray threads embroidering the air.

139

It was with the acute sense that a miracle had been at work, when on Saturday, Kim arrived on my doorstep with Jeannie in tow.

It was a clear winter day with all the bounce and bright-eyed resilience of a teenager, sky blue, blinding sun, the tow-day-old snow crunching like cake icing under our boots. I pulled out all the stops. Lemon and ricotta pancakes at Snuffy's on 47th and 1st Avenue. An expedition through FAO Schwarz where Kim was quite taken with a twelve-hundred-dollar life-sized Lioness from the Safari collection. We lost Jeannie after ice cream at Alfonso's Italian Ice, crashing from a sugar high, she opted to skip the day's crown jewel, ice-skating at Skate on State, next to Marshall Fields, meeting us back at my place.

"Please be careful," Jeannie said, giving me a hard, knowing look before collapsing into a taxi. But it was smooth sailing, with just one rough patch, fitting Kim's left foot into her skate. It seemed to get chewed up somewhere around the ankle and she screwed up her face, which prompted me to whisk it off and wrestle the skate wide open, doing a bit of phony strain like I was a prime contender for Mr. Universe, Kim giggled quite a bit and then we hit the ice, father, and daughter, hand and hand. It was packed with tourists they were too giddy to be native Chicagoans, but once we were swallowed by the mob, it was as if we were inside a sea of joy. Everywhere, it was colored parkas and laughter, sizzling woosh noises as Grant Park and Lake Shore Drive towered over us.

It was when we walked down the cobblestone sidewalk along Walton Street that good stuff happened. Kim disclosed the name of her best friend, Delphine. The girl sounded beyond chic at six, born in Paris. "Delphine comes to school in a limousine," Kim noted.

"Good for Delphine. How do you get to school?"

"Mommy walks me."

Thank God. Bruce was keeping his Bentley under wraps. I made a mental note to keep an eye on old Delphine. It sounded like she'd be climbing out of bedroom windows in no time.

Kim wanted to show me her new shin guards and soccer shoes also her knowledge of the difference between Fahrenheit and Celsius. She also very much liked her new PE teacher, a young woman named Lucy who was happily married to Mr. Lucas, who taught earth science.

Kim spoke quietly and categorically on each of these subjects, explaining them with senior official authority, me the cheerful ignorant underling. She also mentioned quite a few proper names, Clara, a dog named Maestro, Mr. Frank, something called The Tall Tale Circle, as if I knew precisely who and what each of these things was. And I was moved by this because it meant Kim sensed there'd never been a moment I wasn't with her, that I was always seeing what she saw.

After we greeted two passing dachshunds, Kim announced she was ready to go home. In the taxi, I asked if she'd had a good day. She nodded.

"And Honey?"

She was yawning.

"Remember the toy Mom found in your coat pocket?

It was an intriguing enough question for Kim to stare at me.

"The black snake?" I clarified, as casually as I could.

"The dragon Mommy got mad about?" asked Kim.

"Yes, the dragon Mommy got mad about. Where'd you get it?'

"Gabriela."

I did my best to look nonchalant. "And where did you meet Gabriela?"

"With Jeannie in the playground."

With Jeannie in the playground. "When was this, sweetheart?"

"A long time ago," Kim yawned again, her eyes comically heavy.

"Did you speak to her?"

She shook her head. "She was too far away."

"How far away?"

"She was by cars and I was on the swing."

"But how did she give you the dragon?"

"She left it." She said it with a teacher's exasperation as if already been explained many times.

"When? The next day?"

She nodded half-heartedly.

"Okay. You're the most astute judge of character I've ever met, and I greatly value your opinion. What'd you think of her? Gabriela."

She smiled faintly at the mention of the name. But her eyes were closing.

"She was magical . . ." she whispered.

"What? Kim?"

But she was out, head rolling against my arm, hands on her lap as if holding an invisible clump of flowers. When we got home I carried her upstairs so she could sleep, though Jeannie woke her up at seven to put her in her cloud pajamas. We watched Frozen. I make popcorn. When Jeannie went upstairs to take out her contacts, which seemed to be code for calling a boyfriend, Kim sat eating quietly on the couch.

It was the chance to ask her more about Gabriela, to fathom how on earth it had happened, but then, taking the seat beside her, she looked at me, chewing slowly with her mouth tightly closed, as if she knew very well, what I was about to ask and she found it ad that I still did not understand. Swallowing, she took my right hand, patting it like it was a lonely rabbit in a pet store, before reaching for her glass of soda.

And I realized, of course, Kim had told me everything.

140

She was magical.

When I said goodbye to Kim the following day, I have her the tightest hug and kissed her cheek, and then her hot head.

"I love you more than, how much again?" I asked her.

"The heavens and all the stars."

I embraced Angela. She wasn't expecting it.

"You're glorious," I whispered into her hair. "And you always were. I'm sorry I never said it."

She stared at me in shock as I made my way out of the lobby, smiling at the two doormen, blatantly eavesdropping.

"Did you get that? This woman is glorious."

The moment I got home, I pulled out the old sagging cardboard box again, spreading the few papers out on the floor.

What had I learned when I'd been trapped inside that hexagon box, about myself? You couldn't even see where it opened. It was a hint that I wasn't seeing all of it, not the full picture.

Maybe I still had it all wrong. Maybe I still wasn't seeing something that even Kim had seen. And Elizabeth. And Cooper.

All three of them believed in Gabriela. And I didn't.

But what if I did believe as blindly as Cooper, Elizabeth, and Kim? Was it blindness, or did they all see in a way that I didn't? What if I tossed reason and common sense into the air, let them soar dumbly out of sight, and believed in witchcraft, in black magic, in Gabriela? Burning the reversing candles had brought Kim back into my life. Yes, one could argue it was simply a coincidence that the moment they'd extinguished, Angela within a matter of seconds had called, but what if it wasn't? Maybe it was the black magic again rearing its head, insisting it was real.

What it I took a leap of faith and simply accepted that the truth behind this entire investigation resided not with Marissa Garcia, but with Gabriela? What it she hadn't been in an especially precarious mental state? The truth about her illness meant nothing. Why couldn't cancer be yet another symptom of the devil's curse, as Gabriela herself had believed? I might not have collected sufficient evidence up at El Esplanade. The stained boy's shirt and those animal bones, but that did not vindicate Esquivel from what I'd suspected, that he practiced black magic with the townspeople, that his night time activities weren't fictions, but real live horrors, that he'd used children to try and free his daughter from the curse, even crossing the line into hurting one of them, as the Tarantula had hinted.

There's nothing Garcia won't do to protect him. I'd read it on the Blackboards. Yet, oddly enough, she'd chosen not to protect him from me. She'd directed me straight toward him.

Or had she?

Anderson had warned me that I might encounter a figure stationed at the intersection between life and death. It will be a decoy. A substitute to grant freedom to the real thing. He's Esquivel's favorite illusion. He's always there when Esquivel's mind is at work, no matter what.

That figure could very well have been that man back at the nursing home, the stranger I'd sat down beside.

Bill Smith.

He could have been anyone, anyone with a hefty enough frame and muscular, just senile and soundless enough not to be aware he was passing for Esquivel. That wheel tattoo wasn't definitive proof. It could have been drawn there, even tattooed by Garcia into the man's hand in the middle of the night, when no nurse was watching. There was no security at Enderlin Estates, nothing stopping Garcia from doing what she wanted to whatever elderly stranger she chose, so he might serve as a feasible stand-in for her lord and master, thereby granting freedom to the real thing.

She'd wanted him to go free.

Perhaps Garcia was Esquivel's paid executioner, waiting for anyone who got too close to his whereabouts, who knew too much. Maybe she'd been waiting for me to come clamoring up onto that final wooden platform, and it was her job to tuck the burlap bag over my head and then the noose, ruthlessly leaving the ground out from under me, sending me flying, kicking, gasping back to reality, where she was so certain I'd stay.

"I live in the real world." She'd announced flatly. "And so do you."

She'd meant it as an order, a directive. She was giving me instructions, certain I'd follow then on my own accord because I was a realist, a skeptic, a practical man. And yet I'd noticed, too, there was something faintly scathing about the way she'd said the real world as if it were the most miserable of life sentences.

Gabriela's history will now forever remain where she wished it, where she believed in her heart it always was, beyond reason, between heaven and earth, land and sky, suspended much closer to legend than ordinary life, where the rest of us, including you, Mr. McCarthy, must remain.

Where the mermaids sing, I'd muttered.

Mermaids. There was something about that word that had bothered Garcia. And if it unnerved her, it could only mean one thing: It was too close for her comfort to the real Esquivel.

It took me all night, all day, and one more night after that to find the connection. I didn't sleep. I didn't need to. I retyped the notes that had been stolen, detailing every witness we'd tracked down who'd encountered Gabriela, everything I'd encountered at El Esplanade, every word I'd heard whispered about Esquivel.

When I did see it, I realized, it had been right in front of me, all along.

Gatehouse, Mansion, Lake, stables, Workshop, Lookout, trophy, Pincoya Negro, Cemetery, Mrs. Peabody's, laboratory, The Z, Crossroads.

The words had been scribbled above one of the thirteen blackened doorways down in the underground tunnels at El Esplanade.

Pincoya. It was a kind of mermaid.

"Long blond hair, incomparable beauty, luscious and sensual, she rises from the depths of the sea," read the entry on Wikipedia. "She bestows riches or choking scarcity, and all of the mortals on land live in answer to her whims." The creature had been spotted in one remote place on earth and only one, an isolated island off the coast of South America called Chiloe.

La Pincoya was just one of a throng of mythical creatures that haunted the island's shore, which remained shrouded in heavy mist and rain eleven months of the year. It was a bleak and inhospitable place, one of the remotest islands on Earth, an island with a legendary history of witchcraft.

I suddenly remembered, a detail Cleo had mentioned back at Fascinations the first time we'd gone to see her when she was inspecting the materials we'd given her of Gabriela's Black Bone killing curse.

I see some dark brown sand in here, some seaweed, too, she's told us.

She must have picked this up someplace exotic.

There wasn't much information about this island, Chiloe, but when I was reading a Spanish backpacker's blog, I came across another connection.

Puerto Montt.

It was the last city on Chile's mainland before the country breaks up like a cookie into hundreds of crumbled islands. The backpacker had traveled from Puerto Montt to another town, Pargua, and from Pargua took the ferry to Chiloe. The only way to access the island was by boat, apart from a few rudimentary airfields.

I knew I'd recently read about the city and after an hour of searching, I found where: in the Natural Huntsman, the article posted on the Blackboards about Rachel Dempsey's banishing from Nepal, Rachel Dempsey, who'd worked for Esquivel. Although there'd been no sign of her after she'd disappeared from her hunting expedition, nine days after she was reported missing, her satellite phone had been turned on in Santiago

Chile, and she'd made a brief phone call to a number that was traced to Puerto Montt.

I'd retyped the interview with Julie Mergener in Washington Square and recalled Mergener had mentioned the Santo Esquivel had been carrying on an affair with a woman ten years older than he, women named Rachel who had appeared on one of Esquivel's employee lists.

Checking the dates, I saw Rachel Dempsey would have been twenty-seven in the spring of 1993, the year Mergener attended the picnic. Santo would have been only sixteen, an eleven-year age difference.

It was close enough. So Rachel and Santo had seemingly been together. But what, exactly, had Rachel Dempsey planned to her hunting expedition in Nepal, to vanish off the face of the Earth? Disappear without a trace so she might resurface somewhere on that island on order to. . . What? Reunite in paradise with her lover, Santo? What was on that island?

The houses there had a singular style of architecture. Called palafitos. They were modest cottages built atop rickety stilts and painted vibrant pinks, blues, and reds, so they resembled long-legged water bugs swarming the coastline, which was not a tropical paradise, but thorny and gray, with sharp rocks and dark water that seeped across the beach.

I'd seen those stilt houses before.

It was when I'd been inside the greenhouse, in Popcorn's work shed. I'd noticed a postcard tacked to a bulletin board, those very same stilt houses pictured on the front of it. Thankfully I had the prescience to take it down and read the back, where someone had scribbled four words.

Someday soon you'll come.

There was more. The churches on Chiloe looked like no others in the world, a combination of European Jesuit culture and the native traditions of the indigenous people on the island. They were austere, covered in wooden tiles like flaking dragon scales and jutting steeples topped with a spindly cross. Like the palafitos, they, too, were painted wild colors, though their brightness evoked not jubilation, but the sinister cheer of a clown's face.

I'd seen one somewhere before. I raced back over to the floor, trawling the papers until I found it. In the Vanity Fair article, Gabriela's freshman-year roommate had mentioned, when Gabriela abruptly moved out with no word, all she'd left were three Polaroids, which had slipped, forgotten, behind her dresser. The snapshots had been included in the article, artifacts of Gabriela's lost existence, portholes into her world. I'd barely glanced at them.

Now, staring down at the first one, I felt light-headed with shock.

It featured a small, morose-looking church. It wasn't an exact match, but it had the same architecture as all the others on the island.

The second Polaroid featured a massive black boulder on a beach, seagulls circling overhead. The boulder had a mystical hole through the center as if God had punched his thumb through it, making an impish void in the world. I didn't recognize it. But the third featured a flock of black-necked swans, one of them carrying a cygnet on its back. Black-necked swans, I read on Wikipedia, were prevalent in South America. Yet they bred and hatched their young only in a few specific areas, one of which was Chile's Zona Sur, which included Chiloe.

Gabriela could very well have been on the island. It seemed to have been where she'd taken the Polaroids.

I opened up Google Earth, staring at a satellite view. Parts of the main island, Isla Grande, and almost all of the smaller islands around it freckling the blue sea were concealed by silvered clouds.

Had all this evidence been silently leading me there?

Garcia had been so adamant about keeping me down in the real world, ordinary life, making sure that I didn't keep chasing Esquivel. . . into what?

Warning voices echoed resoundingly through my head, one of the loudest of which was that old grizzled alcoholic detective back at the bar in Nairobi. Slumped over his drink, wearing his stained khaki jacket and fatigues, he'd warned me about the fates of the tree cops who'd worked the cursed case, the case without an end, the tapeworm.

One had gone insane. Another quit the investigation and a week later, hanged himself in a Mombasa hotel room. The third simply disappeared into thin air, leaving his family and a sweet pension.

"It's infected," the man had mumbled. "The case. Some are, you know."

I sat back thoughtfully in my desk chair. Octavius, I saw with disbelief, had chosen to fly as I'd never seen him do before. He was crashing drunkenly into the ceiling and windows, the Le Kimurais poster, his wings fluttering against the glass in excitement, or was it alarm at what I was about to do, where I was about to go?

Because I noticed now, the fates of those three detectives were not unlike the employee's who'd worked for Esquivel, those who, once they left El Esplanade, never returned to ordinary lives. They scattered to outer reaches of the world, most never heard from again, becoming unfathomable and unseen, beyond reach.

It began happening to me now.

Wasn't it? I was following in their footsteps, sending myself to the outer reaches of the world. Was I feeling something or had I been set free?

I wouldn't know until I saw what was there, if anything at all.

141

Four days later, I took a flight to Santiago, Chile, and another to Puerto Montt.

I strode through El Tepual airport to the baggage claim, brimming with children, families embracing, signs for informacion and Eurocar. I found my army duffel sitting alone on the revolving carousel as if it'd been awaiting me for months.

I took a taxi to the bus station and boarded the first one to Pargua. It was packed, half the seats occupied by rowdy boys in white knee socks, some madrigal singing group manned by a sweaty-faced director who looked ready to quit. An old woman took the seat beside me, giving me a wary look, but once she dozed off, her head bobbed gently against my shoulder like a buoy in the choppy water. Our bus, an old yellowed beast with filthy rainbows emblazoned up and down the sides, bumped its way through the streets, past Bavarian A-frame chalets out into the countryside.

The ferry to Chiloe Island left every twenty minutes. It cost a dollar. As we took off across the wind-chopped sea, I was surrounded by a large and boisterous group of tourists crowding the top deck. An Italian woman was trying to keep her thrashing hair out of her face as her boyfriend took a picture. He noticed me and motioned with a grin if I'd take one of them together. As I obliged, I couldn't help but wonder if someday someone might track them down and show them my photo as I'd showed Gabriela's.

Do you recognize him? Did he speak to you? What was he wearing? What was his demeanor? Did he strike you as strange?

Standing along the railing, staring out, I could see the island far ahead. It was revealing itself like a woman stepping out from behind a curtain, unhurried and deliberate, deep green rolling hills, white mist streaking the shoreline, soft lights twinkling through the vegetation, telephone poles with tangled wires, a homely beach. For a minute, a large black and white bird, some type of stormy petrel, flew alongside the ferry, very close to where I stood, diving up and down, calling out in one shattering screech before veering away on a new gust of wind, swallowed up by the sky.

We unloaded in Chacao, a frazzled village with the neglected countenance of a place people were constantly leaving. There, with many of the same people from the ferry, I boarded another bus to Castro, the largest town on the island. I checked into the hotel, the Caballio Roho. It was hard to miss bright red building on a wet gray street.

I'd read it was lively, popular with locals and tourists traveling cheap, known for good food and English conversation. My room had faded blue wallpaper, a cot only slightly larger than the massive Santiago telephone book provided on the bedside table. I took a shower standing beside the toilet, clean shaven, went downstairs to find the dining room. I ordered a funny named cocktail, what the waitress explained was the local drink, and when she lingered, asking if I was Australian, I took out the Vanity Fair article and inquired if, by some small chance, she recognized the landmarks in the pictures.

My question caused a great deal of intrigue.

It wasn't a minute before two fellow diners, as well as the Dutch bartender, were crowded around my table, hashing over the Polaroid's and probably me, in Spanish. The consensus was that, though no one recognized the tiny church, one on the locals, a petulant dark little man who, at the waitress's urging, waddled awkwardly over to us, hinting he did better on water, claimed to have seen the black boulder with the hole somewhere along the coast south of Quicavi when he was a little boy. That must have been seventy years ago.

"Quicavi? How do I get there?" I asked.

But the man only jutted out his chin, grimacing as if I'd just insulted him, and shuffled back over to his table.

The waitress leaned in with an apologetic look. "The *Chilote*, locals, we're very superstitious about Quicavi. It's north. About an hour's drive."

"Why are they superstitious about Quicavi?"

"That's where the man arrives."

"What man?"

She widened her eyes, as if unsure how to begin to answer, and swiftly moved off. "Just don't go at night," she said looking over her shoulder.

The Dutch bartender suggested I rent a car from his friend down the road to reach Quicavi before nightfall before nightfall seemed the most crucial part of the directions. Which was why, not an hour later, I was behind the wheel of a green four-wheel drive Jeep. Dating back to the eighties, heading down a twisting road with no shoulder and a width that barely fit two cars. I had my passport on me, all of my money, both dollars and Chilean pesos, my cell, a switchblade, and Popcorn's compass.

As I drove, checking the map and the compass, indicating I was driving northeast, the island seemed to shake loose around me. Undulating hills, horses grazing alone in fields, I passed an unmanned goat procession and two young boys escorting a sheep. I kept picturing my abandoned room back at the hotel, as if it were a newly minted crime scene photo imprinted in my head. My army duffel unzipped on the bed, clothes hastily were thrown inside, the itinerary from Expedia in the inside pocket, red toothbrush on the edge of the sink, tube of Colgate Total indented from my hand, and finally, the cruddy mirror that had held the last known sighting of my face. I wondered, suddenly if I should have left a note, something for Kim, a small clue, just in case. I'd left Octavius with her, assuring Angela I'd be traveling only for a few weeks, so Kim would know I was coming back.

And I was.

The Jeep began to gripe about some of the hills, and when we faced a particularly steep one, the road's pavement had given out long ago, now it was dirt and rocks. I switched on the four-wheel drive, flooring it. This killed the engine. I pushed it to the shoulder of the road and began to walk.

As if by black magic, a boy in a truck passed me, backed up, and offered me a ride. He spoke no English, the radio playing the Rolling Stones. Nearing the apparent edge of Quicavi, a thin sloping road splintering with dark houses, all of them leaning downhill as if desperate to reach the ocean, visible at the end, the boy dropped me off and continued on.

It was beginning to get dark, spitting light rain. I made a right onto another road, which led me into the heart of Quicavi. There was nothing overly sinister about the town, Cafes advertised free Internet and Pepsi, a large pig grazed in front of a grocery store. And yet every shop at ten minutes after six had dark windows, signs on the doors reading **Cerrado.** All that appeared to be open was a restaurant called Café Romeo, a few people hunched over the tables inside. When I reached the beach, a shack at the very end, what looked to be some sort of cantina, with its sharply pitched roof lit with lights. I headed toward it across the sand, which was rocky and black, the water sluggishly lapping the shore. I realized with surprise that I was alone out here. I ran through the last forty hours in my head, noting that starting with Ohare airport at five A.M. two days ago, until now, the number of people around me had been gradually dwindling. Like I'd walked into a roaring party and now, looking around, I saw I was the last guest there.

I reached the shack, and when I looked up, reading the weathered sign over the dark door, I stopped dead, stunned.

La Pincoya Negro. Black mermaid. That exact phrase had been scribbled above one of the doorways in the underground tunnels at El Esplanade. If I'd walked through it, would it have led me here?

"*Quiere barquito?*"

I turned. A scrawny old man was standing far behind me, close to the water beside a stake in the sand, a trio of weathered boats tied to it. He was the only person out here. He started toward me and I could see he had a kind smile, missing a few teeth, oil splattered slacks rolled to his shins, and wisps of gray hair strung across his tanned head, like a bit of sea mist still clung there.

I unfolded the Vanity Fair article, showing him the Polaroids.

The man nodded with obvious recognition at the church, saying something I couldn't understand, which sounded like,

"Buta Chauques. Isla Buta Chauques." When he saw the boulder with the hole, he grinned.

"Si, si, si. La trampa de sirena."

He repeated the phrase, his parched lips twitching in excitement. I did the rudimentary translation in my head. *The trap for the mermaids?*

The trap of the mermaids? I nodded in my confusion. And him taking it for some kind of agreement, grinned and lurched back over to his boats. He untied the largest and began to drag it toward the water.

"No!" I called out to him. "You misunderstood."

But he was jerking it with surprising strength by the bow, the boat's propeller digging into the sand as if trying to resist.

"Hey, forget it*! Manana!*"

The man made no sign of having heard me. Knee-deep in the water now, he was stooped over, yanking the starter cord.

I fell silent, watching him, and then found myself turning, staring back at the way I'd come.

There were a few lights, back at the end of that road. They looked lovely and soft, and suddenly I was filled with longing as if around the corners of those dark houses I might find a home and my old life. And everything that was known and familiar to me, all that I loved, if only I had the inclination to walk back there.

Yet as close as they appeared, they seemed also to be receding, warm rooms I'd already passed through, the doorways missing.

The man had managed to turn over the motor, thick smoke streaming out, a deep rumble tearing through the wind clattering across the rooftops of the shops behind me.

I walked to the boat and climbed in. an inch of seawater slurped in the hull, but the old man was unconcerned. Taking his position beside the engine, he unfolded a blue cap from his shirt pocket, pulled it low over his eyes, and with a single nod of evident pride, he began to steer us away from the shore.

We hadn't gone two minutes when I spotted deep green, seemingly uninhabited islands surfacing like giant whales to my left. I assumed we'd stop at one, but the man kept driving us past, one after the other. I saw there was absolutely nothing left in front of us, not a single landmass, nothing, only black churning ocean and a sky, equally empty.

"How much longer?" I shouted, turning around.

But the old man only held up a grizzled hand, muttering something voided by the wind, which seemed to charge his dirty gray shirt with bolts of current, revealing a frame as withered as an old shoe.

Maybe he was Charon, ferryman of the River Styx, transporting all newly dead souls into the underworld.

I turned back, staring ahead, trapped in the feeling that something was about to appear and the horror that nothing ever would. We continued on, I didn't know how long. I couldn't release my grip on the sides of the boat to check my watch or the compass. The waves growing violent, ocean spray soaking me as they turned upon themselves, beating the boat. Slowly I began to surrender to the possibility that we'd go on and on like this until the gas ran out, and when it did the boat's motor would clear its throat like an exhausted opera singer leaving the stage, and I'd turn to find that even the old man was gone.

But when I did turn, he was still hunched there, squinting far off to our left, steering us toward another massive green-black island growing out of the horizon, this one with a narrow beach fringed with foliage and beyond that, immense cliffs rising like muscular shoulders out of the sea.

The man grinned as if recognizing an old friend and when w4e were some twenty yards offshore, abruptly he cut the engine, staring at me expectantly as the boat pitched and jerked.

I realized, as he extended one oil-blackened index finger toward the water, still smiling, it was my cue to jump. I shook my head. "What?"

He only jabbed that dirty finger toward the water, and when I waved my arm, trying to tell him to forget it, a heavy swell blasted the boat. Before I could brace myself, I was abruptly tossed forward.

I was spinning upside down in the freezing water. I broke the surface, gasping, seawater filling my mouth, but as the ground found my feet I realized it was shallow. I kicked my way to shore, struggling to stand, bending over, coughing. But then I whipped around, horrified. I'd neither paid the man nor made any arrangements to get back.

He'd already restarted the motor and began circling the boat around.

"Hey!" I shouted, but again, the wind erased my voice. "Wait! Come back!"

He didn't react or didn't hear me. Shoulders hunched, bracing himself against the wind. He took off speeding across the water, motor screeching, and within minutes he looked like nothing but a speck of black on the ocean.

I looked around. There was just enough light left to see, farther down the beach, where the sand narrowed as if brutally shoved aside by the cliffs, a giant boulder. It had a hole through it.

The trap of the mermaids.

Stunned, I stumbled toward it, then quickly realized that an immense flock of seagulls, their cries extinguished by the roar of the ocean, were swarming not only around the boulder but most of the shoreline, feasting on something scattered across the rocks. The rain began to fall harder, so I took off, taking refuge under the foliage fringing the beach.

I noticed, just a few yards away, a plank jutting across the sand.

A series of boards had been flung over a muddy path leading straight back into the forest. I checked the compass, the needle resolutely pointing east, and then stepped onto the wood, the mud underneath belching from my weight.

I followed it, instantly hit with stagnant air, humid and thick, but also something else, a rush, a sensation that I was sliding toward something, being funneled into a hole I couldn't' climb out of and shouldn't try. Twisted branches wound around one another growing so dense all that existed was the sound of rain, like a crowd whispering overhead.

I began to walk faster, and the walk became a run, the run a sprint, the uneven planks hitting my feet, some snapping in half, sending me knee-deep in mud. I didn't stop, streaking past Tarantula ferns and bobbing flowers, waist-thick tree roots climbing out on either side of the path as if trying to escape. My only company appeared to be a single bird, which dogged me like a final warning, fluttering, chirping in the overgrowth until it flew right at me, black wings grazing my cheek, emitting a sharp cry before diving again into the dark. The pathway became an incline, growing steeper as if trying to shake me off, but I didn't stop, ascending so rapidly. After a while I couldn't feel the ground under my feet.

I spotted a house ahead. Nestled in the trees, it looked like so many others I'd seen on the main island, battered, covered in wooden shingles, a splintered shutter angling from a window. Grasping to catch my breath, I swung myself up onto the porch, grabbed the rusted knob, and opened the door.

It was a deserted room, stark wooden furniture, dim light, an old ceiling fan whirling overhead.

A large oil painting hung directly across from me on the wall. I saw a man's portrait, his distorted and chalky face retreating into a black background as if melting. I stepped inside, then froze, my eyes drawn to movement in the far corner. The, by the wall of dark shadows, sat two leather and wood mission chairs like waiting thrones. On a small table beside one, a cigarette burning, Davidoff, no doubt, white ribbons of smoke uncoiling in the air.

I moved toward it and spotted a pair of folded wire glasses, the lenses oval and pitch black. Beside them a bottle of Maker's Mark bourbon, *my bourbon,* I noted with astonishment and two empty glasses.

I turned, sensing someone watching me.

He was there, a hulking dark silhouette in the doorway.

Esquivel.

A hundred things went through my mind in that moment. Hunters glare their prey in the eyes and what do they see? I hadn't known I'd ever find him and, if I did whether I'd have the impulse to kill him, condemn him, or weep. Perhaps I'd pity him, brought to my knees by the vulnerable child inside every man. But I had a feeling he'd been expecting me, that we were going to do nothing more than sit down in those empty chairs, one father to another, and as the rain fell and the smoke coiled around us, weaving another hypnotic spell, he'd tell me.

There would be unimaginable darkness and streaks of blood inside it, this tale he told, which would probably last for days. Lots of screams and bright red birds, and astounding hints of hope, as the sun, in an instant, can christen the blackest ocean. I'd learn more about the lengths people went to feel something more than I ever thought possible and I'd hear Kim's laughter inside of Gabriela's.

I didn't know in the end what I'd find when it was over. Would I stare at the rubble and recognize his story as one of evil or fallen grace, or if I'd see myself in all he'd done, trying to save his daughter, in his insatiable need to stretch life as far as it would go, risking losing it.

Somehow, I sensed as soon as he told me, he'd find a way to be gone, faster than the wind across a field. I'd wake up somewhere far away, wondering if I'd imagined it, if he'd been here at all, inside this quiet house poised at the edge of the world.

It felt like the end of an era that had been my whole life. The one thing I did know, as I stepped toward him, that he was going to sit down beside me and tell me his truth.

THE END

ACKNOWLEDGEMENTS

There are so many people to thank I hardly know where to start. I would like to thank my girl Julie Mergener for being there to bounce ideas off of, and her input became a source of great strength. Julie became a great help in times of confusion.

I would also like to thank the girls at Truth Restaurant in Joliet Il.,. They were always so kind and attentive to me while writing this story, When I had trouble naming the characters their names always came into focus. Hence they are all mentioned in this book.

A very special thanks to Elizabeth Michener Apostolou. She read the story right along with me as I wrote it. Her advice and feedback were invaluable to me. As she is quite the accomplished writer herself.

Elizabeth worked with me through every step of this book. She is so very special. I am eternally grateful.

Thank You Liz!!!

Also a thank you to my writer's group. They are a constant source of information and advice in writing and publishing.

My friend and proof-reader, Karl Mackovic.

www.ingramcontent.com/pod-product-compliance
Lightning Source LLC
Chambersburg PA
CBHW050246170426
43202CB00011B/1577